FROM BAZOOKA TO BOSNIA

DICK VERKIJK

From Bazooka to Bosnia

Sixty years (non)journalistic experiences

Dedicated to Cor Gerritsen from Haarlem, Anatoli Marchenko from Moscow, four unknown Croats from Tovarnik and the tens of millions of others who were killed because of race-rage, religion-lunacy and party-psychopathism, thus just because of nothing at all.

A left-wing guy is called by the left a rightist if he establishes the realities of the "real-existing socialism" five years earlier than the left-fashion-of-the-day prescribes.

(An occasional note, from approx. 1980, found during the sorting out of my archives)

Woodenshoes Publishing House
2006

ISBN 0-9619226-8-0

Original title:
Van pantservuist tot pantservest – zestig jaar (on)journalistieke ervaringen.
Publishing House *Aspekt*, Soesterberg, Netherlands (1997)

Czech title:
Od pancéřové pěsti k pancéřové vestě – šedesát let (ne)žurnalistických vzpomínek.
Publishing House *Doplněk*, Brno, Czech Republic (2002)

Cover picture:
Jon Magnus. It shows the writer at the front near Dubrovnik, October 1991.
In the middle behind him Radovan Milosavljević, the information official of
the *JNA* who (extremely helpfully) accompanied him on his visits to the front
in Southern Croatia

Front and back cover design:
Brian Stuy/Dick Verkijk
Interior book design:
Van Swieten & Partner. Nieuwegein, Netherlands

Woodenshoes Publishing House, Sandy/Utah
DVerkijk@juno.com
www.woodenshoespublishing.com

EXCERPTS OF REVIEWS IN THE DUTCH MEDIA

Caspar Cillekens in the daily **Dagblad de Limburger** of December 18, 1997:
"His memoirs [..] are written with speed, in a way which sometimes gets across kind of casual. The anecdotes about the tricks he has played to get rid of his pursuers and to get his materials across the border turn his memoirs into a thrilling boys' book."

...

Dr. Jac. Schaeffer, historian, in the daily **Nederlands Dagblad** of November 1, 1997:
"The memoirs of Eastern-Europe-journalist Dick Verkijk are terrific: witty, honest, rich in content, involved but nowhere fashionable. Nobody knows Eastern Europe better than he, yet nobody has his feet so firmly on the ground. [...] Those are the stories, which turn the autobiography into a pure enjoyment. [...] He experienced the war [in Yugoslavia], drove himself with his truck on the mined small roads of Bosnia and went on – never reckless but yet with the toughness of a stubborn traveler – where others make a U-turn. [...] Verkijk submits, knows the language, knows about all the tricks. "

...

Paul Arnoldussen in the media supplement of the daily **Het Parool** of November 1, 1997:
"He made famous documentaries as "Operation Barbarossa" [1966], wrote "Radio Hilversum 1940-1945" [1974], a standard work on the broadcasting system during the war, reported from Eastern Europe far before it became customary and was a passionate follower of the East-European opposition in the communist era. Verkijk was – for a short time but still – in prison in Prague because of his work in Prague, defied rains of bullets in Yugoslavia and at the same time never flexibly adapted his opinions to his "bread-bosses." Verkijk is not the most wavering figure in journalism."

...

Peter Michielsen in the media supplement of the daily **NRC/Handelsblad** of January 2, 1998:
"Dick Verkijk was never to be intimidated in his striving to report on what the opposition in Eastern Europe had to say – the Andrzej Gwiazdas in Poland, the Václav Havels in Czechoslovakia, the Brašoveanus in Romania. [...] Nobody could stop him to allow the

critics to speak out. Concerning this, few in this profession have been so courageous, so persevering and so unyielding as Dick Verkijk. "From bazooka to Bosnia" reads as a picaresque novel of which you know that there is not one word of fiction in it. It reads like a bomb; [he was] an adventurer – but not one who looked for the adventure: it looked for him, and found in him a man, who was not easily put aside."

...

Sasha Malko in the literary supplement of the weekly **Vrij Nederland** of December 13, 1997:
"Dick Verkijk was one of the few Dutchmen who did understand what it was about behind the Iron Curtain. He knew it, and he acted accordingly. [...] Undeniable brave. Un-Dutch highly spirited. Very un-Dutch straight.
[He was] always in the center of the events, and at the right people. That demands a with knowledge confirmed intuition, persistence and of course the affection of the people in question. Many thousands of journalists have been in Eastern Europe, but still, after all those years, present ministers, parliamentarians and professors ask about Dick Verkijk – and warm greetings are transferred. Respect from former political prisoners is a scarce item, you don't gain that just like that.
Quite often he mentions his fear. Not an existential feeling, but a stinking fear of secret police, fear of a staged accident somewhere on a Romanian road. The perils at the borders in those days were no perils but small dramas with un unknown ending. Only an idiot without imagination is not afraid. Controlled fear makes a human being alert. He had already been picked up many times, pursued, put across the border, eventually shot at – yet he went on. He describes it sober and ironic, but a thing like that gets to everybody. The moving last chapter deals with dreams. A war dream about the liberation, a dream of being killed by a soldier, and a dream about Karadžić who in 1943 suddenly is in hiding at his neighbor's, and therefore cannot be drawn to the International Court in The Hague. It is only two pages; and it is the only fiction in the whole book."

...

Dr. Sipke de Hoop, historian, teaching at the History Faculty of the University of Groningen, in the **Internationale Spectator**, a scientific monthly on Foreign Affairs, in the March 1998 issue:
"Although putting his life in service of truth and justice, he was crossed in his journalistic career not only in Eastern Europe, but also in his own country. [...] Verkijk comes out in his memoirs as a reliable, upright journalist, who has to compete against narrow-mindedness and falsehood in his own circle. [...] The author is fearless, it appears. In Croatia he tries (in vain) to prevent a murder of four Croats by shouting in Serbian just before the execution, "Do not shoot, do not shoot." [...] His passion has turned him, despite all opposition of secret

services and difficult editorial staffs, into may be the best postwar Eastern-Europe-journalist of the Netherlands. [...] It is beyond dispute that he has an excellent journalistic instinct. The man, who lived in the past ten years in Montenegro, speaks Serbo-Croatian and who can be considered concerning knowledge and experience as one of the most prominent Dutch reporters on Eastern Europe, sometimes comes over (rightfully) as a bitter journalist. Not understood, left alone, yet so often being right. [...] The different angles turn his memoirs in an attractive book for a broad audience. [...] The descriptions of this involved insider give a moving and upright image of the difficult circumstances within an Eastern-European society. [...] The Netherlands is losing in the in the meantime retired Verkijk – nowadays living in the United States – a courageous, experienced and passionate journalist. Someone who has devoted his whole journalistic life for critics of dictatorial regimes. An unyielding idealist, who was not to be intimidated and ceaselessly and indefatigable searched for truth and justice. His memoirs are proving that he is also an excellent chronicler."

...

Bart Tromp (columnist and professor at the University of Leiden) in his column in **Het Parool** in November, 1997:
"It is a unique book, because I don't know anybody else, who so long and so persistently and so passionately has followed the developments in the former Eastern bloc. On top of that [he] writes with speed."

...

Philippe Remarque in the daily **De Volkskrant** of November 7, 1997:
"Verkijk went consistently and bravely on to draw attention to the suppression in Eastern Europe, also when this was not fashionable."

...

Dr. J.A.E. Vermaat in the daily **Reformatorisch Dagblad** of January 26, 1998:
"A fascinating story of a man, who was always one of the first ones on the spot at critical moments in Eastern Europe."

...

Finally a remarkable review of Arie Kleijwegt in the **Broadcast Magazine** *of October 1998. Remarkable, because he was the TV director of the company the author worked for from 1965-1970 and where he resigned because he did not agree with their fashionable leftish policies. Although sharing his opinions at the time, Kleijwegt felt overpowered by those fashionable leftishers within the company, who were suffering of the decease "Hollanditis," as they* *named it in the United States at the time. Now he strongly regrets that he did not support him and he apologized for it. He writes:*

"The homage, which Dick Verkijk now so late in his career obtains, is in my view a matter of great justice. Too long he is belittled, underestimated, made ridiculous. In this self-satisfied country one is, as known, more familiar with sweating it out than with dead straight opinions and convictions. And it was by no means marginal nonsense [what he did]. No, it was the unmasking of the Great Communist Salvation's Teaching itself with which he wanted to occupy himself, if necessary life long. Already shortly after the war, just grown out of the boys' keel, he recognized infallibly the communist fraud. What surprised him in the so-called progressive intellectuals, was their impotency (or was it unwillingness) to see, which was as clear as day to anybody with open eyes. [...] And shouldn't we consider in the meantime [to declare him] the Broadcaster of the Year? Because you know: too late is always better than never."

9

CONTENTS

INTRODUCTION FOR THE DUTCH EDITION

I drag my little cart through the mud, the type with which you always see flight attendants speeding by at airports. Yet mine has somewhat bigger and wider wheels. Nevertheless, it sinks far beyond its axles into the mud. All my belongings are on it: a big suitcase with my regular stuff, a smaller one with my video camera and cassette recorder plus accessories and my bullet proof vest and blue helmet. What am I doing here? It is March 1995. I had flown by plane from my assignment place Ljubljana, the Slovenian capital, to Split in southern Croatia, and from there by UN plane to Sarajevo. Without (the tons-weighting) vest and (the super light) helmet you are not allowed to fly with them.

I went there for the meeting "The thousand-day-siege of Sarajevo," organized by the mayor and meant for all other mayors from all the corners of the world. There is a cease-fire, the Serbs have withdrawn their heavy weaponry due to a UN ultimatum, but the siege, and thus the isolation of the city, continues.

A few days after me, Nicole Lucas of the Dutch daily *Trouw* arrived in Sarajevo. We have traveled around together in the war zones of (ex)Yugoslavia quite a few times in the past years and we decided that after the meeting we would go to Zenica. In normal times Sarajevo-Zenica was a car ride of at the very most half an hour. Now it was a Bosnian bulwark where almost nobody ever came – it was for years even more isolated than isolated, caused by the quadruple war of Serbs against Moslems, Croats against Moslems, Serbs against Croats and Moslems against both of them. After the Moslem-Croatian federation was forced upon the Croats by the Americans, the isolation had somewhat diminished, but Sarajevo-Zenica was still a world tour.

The most important thing was: how do we get from Sarajevo to Hadžići, the first Moslem town at the foot of Mount Igman on the other side of the Serbian belt around the city? Supposedly, there was a bus going from Hadžići to the other side of the mountain – and then we still had to find out how we could cross from the one Moslem area through Kiseljak in the Croatian part and wind up again in the other Moslem territory in which Zenica was situated.

We had good luck. A nice Dutch officer of the UN Information Service would bring us with his jeep to Hadžići along the road around the airport, especially constructed by the UN. It seemed to work out well. On the short side of the airport the well-known image of that relief plane, which had slipped of the runway, sagged through its left landing gear as a result and was laying there for years now degenerating. Just after that: a Moslem check point. There was once again a new rule: even a UN jeep was not allowed to go on without a special permit. There was nothing else for us left to do than to walk the next three miles. Walk? It was more sopping. The soft mud layer of the improvised path was about four inches thick. The subsoil was extremely uneven, because of which my much too heavy luggage, not suitable for such a small cart, repeatedly slipped off – into the mud. We trudged past the entrance of the "secret" tunnel below the airport, dug by the Moslems, where many mayors of world cities had to crawl through in order to attend the meeting. "What am I doing here," I thought. "I am almost sixty-six and killing myself in this by God and all people forsaken land, I really am crazy. I really should write that book at last."

From 1958 on I had dealt with Eastern Europe and Yugoslavia. I saw dozens of colleagues come and go. The older I got, the more stories I had. During those free moments at party congresses or other events of importance (a war for instance) we would meet as colleagues together to relax a little and occasionally I came up with such a story ("Grandpa tells a story"). "You should really write it down, your memory is still good," they used to say. "If you wait too long, it might be too late." I wanted to, but I did not have time. The war in Yugoslavia swallowed me up. Until they threw me out of Yugoslavia in October 1994 as "an enemy of the Serbian people."

Hoping that they would rectify the decision, I moved to Ljubljana in December in expectation of that decision. Regarding sources of information, I was in the right spot: one day after publication I even received the Belgrade dailies and I was able not only to receive the Slovenian, but also the Croatian and Belgrade TV. But after a couple of months I had given up hope to be able to return to Belgrade soon and I did not feel like starting a new life and to build up a new circle of friends and relations in Ljubljana "at my age." And the Dutch broadcasting organization was also not that fond of, "From our correspondent in Ljubljana" – it does not do it. One of my bosses wrote me, "You are there too far away from the front," while from Belgrade to "the front" it was five times as far as from Ljubljana. Moreover, the connections from the Slovenian capital with the front were much easier. But psychologically it was too far away. I remember that when I started my journeys to Eastern Europe, when practically nobody went into that direction, people would ask me, "Are you going all the way by car to Prague?"

"Why not," I used to say, "Prague is hardly 650 miles from Amsterdam. When you go on vacation to the south of France, you travel almost twice as far" and most people were then amazingly surprised, because Prague, Warsaw and Budapest also were psychologically immeasurably far away. For me, they became closer and closer; those countries became a part of my life. In the "communist" era, between 1958, my first trip, and 1989, when communism collapsed, I have been there, 136 times, of which fifty-nine were in transit – which was more than just a transit trip as this book will show. I did not include Yugoslavia. My first "communist" trip to that country was in 1955 – and I lived there from 1984 till 1994.

So I already doubted whether I wanted to stay longer in Slovenia – the wading along the airport of Sarajevo was the limit: I would go to Holland for at least a couple of months to reflect quietly what to do with the rest of my life. Drastic but in themselves happy private circumstances made me find myself two months later in the United States in Sandy, 15 miles south of Salt Lake City in Utah. So finally, I had the time and the peace to write "that book."

Fortunately, I did not have any record on hand, and I wrote the whole first version completely relying on my memory. Of course I have, like everybody else, forgotten quite a bit. But the things you do remember are issues, which have made the greatest impression on you. My memory works highly cinematically. Of the events I do remember, I still know exactly who stood where when he said this and that. The Nazi teacher in the corner by the window, when he saddled us up with Nazi propaganda; the place of the physician in the circle around the traffic victim; the day dream halfway up the Spaarne river in the canoe with its nose directed to the shipyard Konrad-Stork; the layout of my cell in the StB-prison in Prague. It is like a movie you watched thirty, forty years ago, most of which you have forgotten, but of which a few scenes remain inch for inch etched in your mind.

The reader of this book must, therefore, not think that my life was a sequence of the described events. In between were long periods in which in a manner of speaking nothing happened. Because of the nature of my work I might have experienced more remarkable things than the average contemporary, that is really all. The same is true for the critical voices I express concerning institutions. I will never forget that the management of particularly *VPRO-TV* and *NOS-radio*[1] have offered me possibilities that I would not have gotten otherwise. Of course I'm pleased to hear that history has set straight that which a number of talked-about cultures, criticized by me in this book, have distorted. But I don't agree with the headline above an article of Daan Dijksman in 1990 in the weekly *De Tijd, "Het gelijk van Dick Verkijk* – Dick Verkijk (pronounce: Verkike), he was right," how kindly it may be meant. The discussion was about

[1] From the early twenties until the end of the seventies/beginning eighties only PBS existed in the Netherlands, nonprofit organizations on religious or political basis. *VPRO* and *NOS* are two of those.

Eastern Europe, the Soviet Union and especially the dissidents, not, anyway not for me, about: who is right and who is not. My underlying motive all those years has been: profound moral indignation about what was done to human beings in those regions, and sadness that so many self-called leftists and *Realpolitiker* skimmed over it more casually than they should have done. What I wanted was to bring up facts about what was going on there just to take the chance away from them that they could ever say, "That, we did not know." And of course with the hope that my reporting would set people thinking who really don't know, and with the (lesser) hope that you could influence the policy makers.

Once, at the end 1968, I was visiting Agneša and Ladislav Kalina in Bratislava, Czechoslovakia. She was an editor of the weekly of the Slovakian Writers Union *Kulturný Život*, he a famous satirical writer. For years, both had been confirmed communists and been moving around in the "best circles." We ended up talking about the Slánský trial in the fifties at which many were sentenced to death and hanged. One of them was the Slovak Vladimír Clementis, who had been the minister of Foreign Affairs. Shortly after that the Kalinas, so they told me, were informally sitting together with other fellow party members. One of them was Viliam Široký, then the prime minister of all Czechoslovakia, but also a Slovak. The Slánský trial came up and Kalina very cautiously said to Široký, "How do you feel about the death penalty for Clementis, he used to be your friend, wasn't he?" Široký replied, "Communists do not have friends." And so it was. Such a system may build thousands of housing complexes and construct hundreds of new freeways – with such a morality it must go down (apart from the fact that the house-building and road-construction were also scanty). This had to be announced and I have tried to be one of the messengers. This book reflects what sometimes happened to me while gathering messages.

After writing this book I was "back in Holland" for a few months, tidying up my archive – like every journalist, I'm saving too much – being forced to look at everything. In doing so I came across material, connected to what I already wrote down. That's why I could here and there correct a date, add a detail, refine a fact. Moreover, I could check hundreds of names, dates and events with many friends, colleagues and institutions – too many to mention. On top of that, I had a big help of thirty years of visa stamps in eight passports, which told me to the day (and sometimes even to the hour), when and where I entered or left a communist country. Initially, I might have relied on my memory, in retrospect it is archive- and otherwise responsibly substantiated.

Finally, just a technical note that is dealing with the complicated ethnical and geographical division of (ex)Yugoslavia. There were in the old federation six republics and two autonomous territories. Nearly every nationality had its own republic or could fall back on its own republic. Most Serbs lived in the republic of Serbia. They were, as inhabitants of that republic, *Serbians*. True, all other Serbs living outside it did have the Serbian nationality, but they were not inhabitants of Serbia. When in this book I speak of *Serbs*, it is of Serbs *outside* Serbia. *Serbian* is used for those living *inside* Serbia.

Regarding the notion *Moslem*, it is even more complicated. One of the six republics was Bosnia-Herzegovina. But a "Bosnian" nationality did not exist, because more than half of the population consisted of Serbs and Croats, who already had a nationality. Serbs and Croats, who during the Turkish era were converted, were no longer called Serbs and Croats, but Moslems; 43% of the population of Bosnia-Herzegovina. But according to the atheist Tito they also ought to have a nationality and for that purpose they proclaimed the religious notion Moslem a *nationality* at a party congress in 1969. The present Bosnian government in Sarajevo has introduced the notion *Bosniak,* but I found it too confusing to use it in my stories, so that I have stuck to the old (nationality) notion of *Moslem.*

And for the curious: we were able to ease the walking, because a passing farmer put our stuff on his wheelbarrow and brought us for the total amount of one German mark (about half a dollar) to Hadžići. For the rest, we have reached Zenica by cab (the bus did not run of course) and by hitchhiking in seven and a half hour – a new record according to friends over there.

Haarlem/Sandy, February 4, 1997

INTRODUCTION FOR THE AMERICAN EDITION

This book was published in the Netherlands nine years ago and the introduction to it speaks for itself. That's why I don't have much to add to this one. I only want to emphasize that the names of all persons, cities and streets are the real ones (for the most part in the local spelling), which in my opinion gives the memoirs the necessary authenticity, otherwise readers could think it's a novel The headings of the chapters on purpose are very simple. I did not want to sensationalize the content by using crying headings. Besides, it underlined the continuity of events: similar headings for events, which are chronologically far apart from each other.

I have been a journalist since 1948 and covered Eastern Europe since 1958. Initially as a free lancer, but in 1966 I became a staff member at different TV and radio stations. In 1984 I left for Belgrade, Yugoslavia, continuing from there my coverage of Eastern Europe. Shortly after the collapse of the communist regimes in 1989 the war in Yugoslavia broke out – and I covered that war until they expelled me from Yugoslavia in October 1994 because they disliked my reporting and they considered me "an enemy of the Serbian people" although they never said this explicitly. Not until March 2, 2002, the chief of staff of the Serbian Ministry of Internal Affairs, Ivan Djordjević, officially notified the Dutch embassy in Belgrade that they had expelled me due to "biased and false reporting on the current social-political and economic situation in our country."

I did the translation myself, but it was corrected by my wife Catherine Stuy Verkijk, who did the main job, her daughter Melissa Willie and my cousin Philip Trommel to whom I am very grateful. For the Dutch edition I coined some words and expressions you could not find in a dictionary when I thought that they would be characteristic for a certain event or person. I tried to do the same for the American edition, so sometimes you will read some words and expressions you will not find in an American dictionary either. So if you chance upon one of those, and you are wondering whether this is correct English, it is due to my stubbornness – so do not blame the proofreaders!

Sandy, Utah – August 29, 2006

Map (in Dutch) of prewar Tito-Yugoslavia: six republics (Slovenia, Croatia, Bosnia-Herzegovina, Macedonia, Montenegro and Serbia, which had within its boundaries two autonomous regions: Vojvodina and Kosovo. The boxed part of this map is consistent with the map on the next page.

Map of a part of former Yugoslavia;
the names of places mentioned in this book are boxed.

FOREWORD

Foreword of Max van der Stoel, former High Commissioner on National Minorities of the Organization for Security and Cooperation in Europe and former Minister of Foreign Affairs in the Netherlands, for the Czech edition, published by Publishing House Doplnek in Brno, Czech Republic, in May 2002.

For almost half a century the Cold War dominated the political situation in Europe between the democratic states in the West and the Eastern Block, ruled by the Soviet-Union.

Journalists who kept on trying to do their duty in the communist countries, in spite of the many limitations imposed by the authorities, endured hard times. Unvarnished reporting of the suppressing practices in Eastern Europe aroused the danger of expulsion or even arrest.

Dick Verkijk was a journalist who could not be intimidated. In a rare combination of courage and ingenuity he succeeded again and again to gather essential information about the developments within the communist regimes. Besides, he had a well-developed political insight. Because of this, he realized earlier than many others the significance of [the Czechoslovakian opposition movement] *Charta 77* as an instrument to undermine communism and to prepare the restoration of democracy. In his own inimitable way he became the ambassador and advocate of *Charta 77*. His book gives an extensive report on that. That is why it pleases me that they will publish it in Czech.

Democracy has won the Cold War. Dick Verkijk always led the way. His book is a report on that. What he tells about his experiences also contains an implicit warning. We can only prevent a return of these horrors of a dictatorship if we are continually prepared to keep our democratic institutions healthy.

CHAPTER 1

The traffic victim and the doctor

He laid unconscious on the curb. The car, which had wounded him, had hit and run. I did not notice anything of the actual accident. When I happened to look out of the window, I saw that people had gathered around something on the curb, diagonally across the street from us, just in front of the *NSB*-family Bossers[2] on number 104. I walked outside and joined the growing circle of onlookers. The Bossers's curtains were, as always, closed. They rarely showed themselves. They knew that the neighborhood did not want to have anything to do with them. They respected that; they never provoked our anti feelings.[3] Traitors they were not.

Somebody went for the doctor, who lived a five, six hundred yards down the street. He came along immediately and examined the victim. The doctor wore a black shabby suit, sharply contrasting with the bizarre-big yellow Jew's star on his jacket. He shook his head doubtfully and stated that he only had the necessary instruments and medication at home, and therefore the unconscious victim needed to be transported there as soon as possible.

It was mid-1942, telephone communication still existed as well as the possibility to order a cab. It arrived very soon, too. It was one of those high, old-fashioned carriages from the beginning of the thirties. Those did not yet have an auto body, but a coach work. It had one of those wide-step-ins, so that we could lay the victim down on the equally wide rear couch without any problem. "Do get in also," we said to the doctor as if it was the old days. "No," he said softly and a little bit ashamed, "that's not allowed."

That answer we had already feared. On pain of internment in a concentration camp, Jews were no longer allowed to travel by private car, streetcar, train, bus, bicycle or cab. But, so we reasoned, also a little bit ashamed, "It is only a short distance, nobody will see it, after all." The Bosserses, we knew, would not say anything; besides, the curtains were still tightly drawn. But the doctor kept on refusing, finding it too risky. The neighbor, who had gone for the doctor, now went with the cab driver to see the patient off. The doctor had to walk

[2] *NSB* is the abbreviation of *Nationaal-Socialistische Beweging* (National Socialist Movement), the Nazi party in the Netherlands, founded in 1931 and prohibited in 1945.

[3] During the occupation of the Netherlands (1940-1945) the words "anti" and "pro" were common expressions to indicate whether you were anti or pro the Germans and the National Socialists.

– and we walked beside him for the sake of solidarity.

The cab was already waiting in front of the doctor's home. We carried the traffic victim in; the treatment could begin.

To this very day I don't know how it ended up for the doctor (to be precise: an animal doctor) and the traffic victim (to be precise: a sheepdog).

CHAPTER 2

The deportation

The car stopped. A military officer jumped out, yelling threateningly, "If you shoot anything, we'll shoot you to death." He jumped back into the car, leaving us behind in bewilderment. We had already been waiting in the burning sun for at least an hour.

That morning we had left Pančevo at five o'clock. In Pančevo, a little town six miles north of the Yugoslavian capital Belgrade, was an *UNPROFOR*-headquarters from where UN-convoys left for Bosnia. It was mid-June, 1992. The war in Bosnia was just two months old. A convoy would bring relief goods to Sarajevo that day; it would go through Northern Bosnia via Tuzla to the Bosnian capital. That meant: first through Serbian territory, than Moslem-Croatian territory, then again Serbian and then once more Moslem-Croatian. Such a UN convoy only gave bogus protection. You are allowed to drive behind them, but solely at your own risk and if something happens on the way, they are ordered just to go on. We could pass a number of Serbian checkpoints unhindered and without stopping in the slip stream of the UN column. But halfway between Bijeljina and Tuzla they stopped us. They let the UN trucks pass, we had to wait "until the commander has arrived" – a standard pretext for chicanery. We – this involved about thirty journalists divided over eight or nine cars. Sullen shoulder shrugging met our repeated questions where the commander was remained, because already then "the press" was considered "an enemy of the Serbian people." No sight of the commander, but after three quarters of an hour they allowed us to drive on. At the last Serbian checkpoint, just before Tuzla, which is Moslem-Croatian territory, they again did not allow us to continue, now because of fighting around Tuzla. The majority of us decided to return to Bijeljina, in order to try from there to reach Sarajevo via Zvornik. Some gave up and went back to Belgrade. Immediately south of Bijeljina: first checkpoint. While a soldier checked our documents, another uniformed Serb joined in. When he learned that Sarajevo was our travel goal, he said, "I am with a police car, I'd better drive ahead of you and bring you to Zvornik." He explained that he was a professional police officer "and on the way you could get checked by all kinds of nonprofessionals who could give you problems" – for that reason he would accompany us.

After thirty miles, at the checkpoint just before Zvornik, he asked us to wait. "I'll go downtown to find you an escort through the city and then you can drive on your own to Pale and Sarajevo." In short: we had come across a good Serb. But he never seemed to come back.

I had fallen asleep behind the steering wheel, when I was suddenly woken up by that military officer. A few minutes later his threat became clear: four busses passed with males of all ages. They were all sitting in the same posture: bent over, elbows on the knees, hands alongside the face with the thumbs against the temples and the index fingers against the forehead. Natural blinders, they were apparently not allowed to look up or back. *Rücksichtslose,* planned deportation. In absolute cooperation with Yugoslavia, because they were directly transported to Palić in Northern Serbia near the Hungarian border where a camp had been arranged for them. There was not any talk of maltreatment; they were very well taken care of and for the outside world promoted to "refugees." As soon as possible they were pushed off to Hungary, Austria and other western countries. Belgrade TV even made a TV report about it, but that was meant as a defense against an attack in the Hungarian media in which was apparently reported that Palić was a concentration camp where terror reigned. The Belgrade reporter asked the "refugees" how they were doing. Of course they all said – and in a way that was also the truth – that they were treated well. The reporter also asked where they came from. Nearly without any exception they answered, "From Zvornik." But not once the reporter asked, "What do you mean, from Zvornik, why are you here?", because he knew darned well that they were deportees, and precisely his silence at this point spoke volumes.

A couple of months later I spoke with the Serbian mayor of occupied Zvornik, Dragan Spasojević.

"How many Muslims were living here before the war?

"55.000," he answered

"How many now?"

"*Nekoliko* – some."

The deportation was completed.

CHAPTER 3

The raid

He stood with his back against the doorpost between the living room and the hallway, while his colleague went on searching the house. In the bedroom upstairs he turned over an umbrella stand to look whether weapons were inside. On the wall of my room hung the maps with the front lines. On the wall paper I had glued a little poster, distributed by the underground, which was warning for a raid, *razzia*, a word that stood above the text in capital capitals.

He also went into that room but did not react. In the attic he thrust the hatch to the loft open to look whether there would by chance be anybody hiding. But the guy in the doorway in his grim-green uniform, the reason his unit was called *Grüne Polizei* (Green Police) apparently thought it was enough. After all, they already had my father. "Bertie!" he yelled upstairs – with the intonation of: just come down!

When they had come to do the house searching half an hour before, I was reading in what we called in our home "the little chair": a kind of miniature love seat. I don't know why, but I simply remained sitting in that chair. I kept, however, looking at him in that doorway. He ate an apple, a luxury in December 1944. An apple, I'll never forget it. I was absolutely not nervous, rather apathetic. I also was not worried at all that the colleague of Bertie would find the underground papers that I had saved, our own *De Oprechte Haarlemmer* ("The Upright Haarlemer") included, of which we had just published the third issue. They were lying in the closet, not ten inches behind his back.

Actually, something was wrong here in what they were doing. In the *BEVEL*, "ORDER." they had put through the mail slot in the front door on the doormat early that morning, it was stated that men born between 1905 and 1928 had to show up in front of their homes "to be set to work." And my father was born in 1904, so he was one year too old. But the *Grünen* ("Greens") could not care less. Equally so about the fact that my father was lying in bed with a fever. They would probably have assumed that he was feigning. They took our neighbor, born in the same year, along as well, in spite of the pleas of his (not Nazi inclined) German wife. My father and the neighbor had bad luck in a double sense: they lived on the wrong side of the street. On the opposite side ordinary *Wehrmacht*-soldiers went from door to door. They banged on the door (bells did not work, because there was no electricity anymore) and when it was not answered, they just went to the next door. If someone did answer, they only

BEVEL.

Op bevel van de **Duitsche Weermacht** worden volgens de Verordening van den Rijks-
commissaris voor het bezette Nederlandsche gebied, No. 42/1941, betreffende de verplichting tot het
verrichten van diensten en betreffende de beperking ten aanzien van het veranderen van betrekking
en in overeenstemming met de Verordening No. 48/1942 alle mannen in den leeftijd van 17 tot 40
jaar (jaargangen 1905—1928) voor den arbeidsinzet opgeroepen.

Hiervoor moeten **ALLE** mannen van dezen leeftijd onmiddellijk na ontvangst van dit bevel met
de voorgeschreven uitrusting op straat gaan staan.

Alle andere bewoners, ook vrouwen en kinderen, moeten in de huizen blijven totdat de actie
ten einde is. De huisdeuren moeten geopend blijven. De mannen van de genoemde jaargangen, die bij
een huiszoeking nog in huis worden aangetroffen, worden gestraft, waarbij hun particulier eigendom
zal worden aangesproken.

Bewijzen van vrijstelling van burgerlijke of militaire instanties moeten ter contrôle
worden meegebracht. Ook zij, die in het bezit zijn van zulke bewijzen, zijn verplicht zich op straat
te begeven.

Er moeten worden medegebracht: warme kleeding, stevige schoenen, dekens,
bescherming tegen regen, eetgerei, mes, vork, lepel, drinkbeker en boterhammen
voor één dag.

**De dagelijksche vergoeding bestaat uit goeden kost,
rookartikelen en loon volgens het geldende tarief.
Voor de achterblijvende familieleden zal worden
gezorgd.**

**Het is aan alle bewoners der gemeente verboden hun
woonplaats te verlaten.**

Op hen, die pogen te ontvluchten of weerstand te bieden, zal worden geschoten.

...order, put through the mail slot...

asked whether men of the required age were in and when the answer was "no," they just went away. No house searching. My mother had, truthfully, also said "no" to the *Grünen*, but they did not want to put up with it.

Hans Cannemeyer, who lived on the other side of the Delft canal, did go to stand in best bib and tucker in front of his home. In his *Jeugdstorm* uniform[4]. They brought him also to the first assembly point on the Marnix Square, a thousand feet from our home. Meanwhile, I went outside. "Shouldn't you go and see your father on the square for a minute?" my friends asked me. I did not want to. I still don't know why. Mrs. Bossers, before the war our closest neighbor, who now lived across the street on number 104, had apparently, in spite of the permanently drawn curtains, noticed that my father had been picked up. She was the leader of the *Jeugdstorm* in Haarlem. Since the occupation we had not exchanged one word with her and her family. She did go to the Marnix Square and gave my father something for the road.

An apple.

---

[4] The national socialist youth organization in the Netherlands was called *Nationale Jeugdstorm*, literally translated: National Youth Storm. "Storm" in Dutch has nothing to do with rain or snow; it just
means: a very strong wind. It was typically fascist to use this word for an organization; it pretended
to symbolize strength and force.

The *Jeugdstorm* was the Dutch equivalent of the German *Hitlerjugend*, Hitler Youth.

Opgeplakt in de nacht van ... op ... Dec. ...

RAZZIA

Verleden week werd in Haarlem en omstreken een razzia verwacht. Het Duitsche heldenfeit te Rotterdam, waarvan wij eenige gevolgen meemaakten door de komst van een trein vol gevangenen, zou hier herhaald worden. Niet alleen hier, maar ook in den Haag, Leiden enzoovoorts. Met zekerheid werd de dag genoemd, waarop de Haarlemsche razzia zou worden gehouden. Maar zij kwam niet. Dus is zij uitgesteld. Maar niet. Wij zeggen dat niet om alarm te slaan, maar eenvoudig op grond van ervaring. Veel menschen hebben de gewoonte, in paniek te raken als er iets dreigt te gebeuren en roekeloos te worden zoodra de fatale termijn is verstreken, zonder dat iets is gebeurd. Dit beleid is het domste dat men voeren kan. De Duitschers hebben er dan ook, in den loop der jaren, aardig van geprofiteerd. Wij waarschuwen maar weer, in de hoop dat het althans een aantal arbeidskrachten aan den vijand onthouden zal. Als U voorzorgen hebt genomen en toegepast, handhaaf ze dan. Doe geen onvoorzichtige dingen, die U de vorige week vermeden zoudt hebben. De vijand slaapt niet. Hij heeft niet plotseling van slavendrijverij afgezien. Waarschijnlijk is de reden van dit uitstel, dat zijn Rotterdamsche „systeem" niet practisch was. Het gevolg van het oppakken in het wilde weg is natuurlijk geweest, dat de dagelijksche gang van zaken in het geteisterde deel van Rotterdam totaal ontwricht werd. Dat heeft nadeelen voor den vijand. Op verwarring, stoornis in de voedselvoorziening, met wellicht relletjes als gevolg, is hij niet gesteld. Hij heeft immers gebrek aan menschen en kan zich zulke dingen slecht veroorloven. Dus ligt het voor de hand, dat hij zich nu op een ander systeem van slavenjacht voorbereidt. Maak U niet bang bij deze gedachte. Als het blijkt, wees dan niet paniekerig.

Pas uw voorzorgsmaatregelen met kalmte en rustig beleid toe. Wie niet sterk is, moet slim zijn. Zij hebben de wapens, maar wij hebben de hersens. Wie die gebruikt, gaat rustig te werk en doet geen domme dingen. Wees kalm en neem geen onnoodige risico's.

DE VRIJE PERS

Underground warning for upcoming "razzia" (round up),
glued to the wall of DV's bedroom.

CHAPTER 4

Arrested – one

All at once, they stood in the room: three men of the State Security Service StB and Jiři, my youthful host. How happy I was that just an hour earlier I had burned in the fireplace a list with at least sixty names and addresses. That was, by the way, the first thing those StB guys did – go to the fireplace with spread-out hands to feel whether it was still warm.

It was Thursday, August 13, 1970. I had arrived in Prague the previous Sunday. I knew Czechoslovakia very well. After a reporting trip through Poland and the Soviet Union in 1958, they denied me entry to Eastern Europe, except Poland, but in the beginning of the sixties, when a kind of little liberalization went through those regions, I was reallowed to enter. Since 1963 I had been in Czechoslovakia with great frequency and had a good relationship with communists within the party, who strived for what later would be called "socialism with a human face." It goes without saying that I continued the relations with those people after the invasion of the Warsaw Pact countries on Wednesday, August 21, 1968. But after April 1969, when Gustav Husák took over the leadership of the communist party from Alexander Dubček, in the eyes of the new establishment they were no longer liberal communists but enemies of the state. And my status changed right along with it. My sympathies remained the same, but for the authorities I had drastically changed from a sympathetic observer into a liar. Nevertheless, I continued to come as often as possible.

From 1963 to 1965 I worked as a freelance journalist for *VARA-TV* [5] and after that until January 1970 for *VPRO-TV*. In 1963 I had made a few short reports in cooperation with the Czechoslovakian television. Jiří Sekerka was the cameraman, his wife Věra was the producer. We became friends because of that cooperation. After the invasion I worked different times "illegally" with Jiři, but eventually things got too hot for him and he went with me to Holland in October 1968. His wife and daughter came a month later. All three of them had received official exit visas, which was still possible until May 1969. They lived for six months in our home in Haarlem and then emigrated to Houston in the United States. At the time their son Jiři did not want to leave Czechoslovakia (later it turned out that he lost his passport, but had hesitated to tell this to his parents). Since 1970 Jiří Jnr. lived on 49 Zborovská

5. *VARA* is also a PBS station; see footnote 1 of the Introduction.

street, at the attic of a fled editor of the pre-1968 weekly *Reporter,* organ of the Czechoslovakian Journalists Union, which had played a dominant role in the liberalization of the party. Jiří lived there in a kind of commune with some six other youths.

I had come to Prague to experience the second "anniversary" of the Soviet invasion. On the first, in August 1969, they had followed us once already, which my then "illegal" cameraman Vladimír Tuma drove to a kind of Wild West trip across Prague to get rid of them. After his car stood safe and sound in his garage, he stated, "Of course, they know that you were with me in the car, but I absolutely did not want them to catch you in my car. Now they can't prove anything."

That's why I was totally prepared for the possibility that something would happen to me on that second anniversary. I had left even the slightest "compromising" stuff of any kind at home. I carried a notebook full of notes, none of which had anything to do with Czechoslovakia. It pleased me to know that, if they would detain me, they would be stuck with a notebook full of notes in my infamous bad handwriting, which were of no use at all to them, but they had to go through from cover to cover. One compromising little something I carried with me: a sheet of paper with some sixty names and addresses or phone numbers of relations. I consistently kept it in my pants pocket together with a matchbox. I locked the door wherever I was. If somebody whom I did not trust would come at the door, I would, so I had promised myself, burn the list, so that it would be destroyed before they would be inside. I also had prepared myself for a possible interrogation, because I was convinced that they would throw me out of the country before the day of that second anniversary. I did not have any illusion, that they would not trace me within a day. You check into your hotel, you are getting registered and the next day the StB knows where you are. That is why immediately after my arrival that Sunday evening I asked Jiří by phone to drop in for a while so that I could tell him the latest news about his parents, without the StB knowing that we had been in touch.

He came right away and brought a self-made small painting of the Charles Bridge with him. He sold these little works-of-art to tourists. It goes without saying, that this was not allowed as private initiative was a crime in the communist world and he had already been picked up several times, but he could not give it up. "Jiří Sekerka, 1970" he had proudly signed it. I gave it a place of honor in my room in hotel Evropa. He offered me to stay with him, so that I did not need to pay for an expensive hotel, but I rejected it.

I changed my mind when it was clear to me the next day that they would not leave me out of their sight for one second. My car was parked against the curb at Václavské náměstí in front of hotel Evropa and they had parked their car crosswise behind mine. If I wanted to leave with my car, they gently gave me space, and then followed me. Not with one, but with two and sometimes even with three cars. Every time they were the same cars, exclusive foreign brands like the Renault 16, which not one Czech could afford to buy, always carrying the same license plates. They do it very conspicuously and that's what they are after. They want to intimidate you to prevent you from getting in touch with anyone. Out of desperation I started to record what happened to me on tape, "I drive on Václavské náměstí, being followed by a Renault 16 with license plate ABA 36-92" etc., hoping later to create a kind of Prague diary for the radio. My first trip was to the Dutch embassy. At the time our ambassador was G. Jongejans who had experienced the hostage of the Dutch embassy in Beijing and who had made himself very popular among oppositionists and dissidents in Prague by simply inviting them for official receptions. I told him I expected to be picked up before the 21st and that because of that I would check in with him daily, personally or by phone. If I didn't, he could assume that something was wrong. So in a way, nothing could go wrong.

I decided that very Monday to go to Jiří the next morning and from there approach people of whom I suspected they would grab every chance to bring their message out into the open. But that meant that I have to leave my hotel unnoticed.

Tuesday morning I walked in a light-brownish outfit to my car and took out a plastic water can, looking out of the corner of my eye at the blockers. I went inside the hotel with the can, giving the impression that I was picking up water to add to my radiator. Back in my hotel room I put on my blue outfit in break neck speed, wetted and flattened my hair backwards (at the time I still had an impressive forelock) and took my glasses off. Behind the reception desk of hotel Evropa a staircase goes down, leading to a restaurant, which has its own exit to Václavské náměstí, some twenty feet to the left of the hotel entrance. In this way I ended up in the street. Slowly I bridged the 100 feet between the exit and the pedestrian underpass, went down the staircase, dove up on the other side, slipped through all kinds of small shop passages to the Národní street and took the streetcar there to Zborovská street. In a small attaché bag I had carried only the most essentials: a cassette recorder with tapes and a pencil. My list and my matchbox were in their safe: my pants pocket. I had even left my passport in my hotel room, so that they knew I would return there and *de jure* still stayed in that hotel room. It was obvious to me that they would enter and search the hotel room after they had lost me for a day.

The trick had worked, I had gotten rid of them.

Now I had some more flexibility, although it was clear to me that it would be short lived. Moreover, I did have the advantage that Jiří's phone was not bugged but, of course, the phones of a number of people I wanted to approach, were. My policy in all those "Eastern Europe" years has always been, "I am willing to be your messenger. If you don't want to speak out, with all respect, for *me* you don't need to do so." The situation between August 1969, the last time I had been Czechoslovakia, and August 1970 had drastically changed and even more than usual I emphasized that they should only do it if they wanted it themselves. I also added that there was a great chance that the StB would find out, because they had already been after me. A few, after having listened to me, hung up without saying anything, others said with regret in their voices they had to back out, but there were also a few who not only wanted it at all costs, but who would be very grateful if they could get the opportunity to have their say. And the "hanguppers" and "regretters" had been all, without exception, fervent oppositionists, who after the invasion of 1968 had been leaders of student strikes or otherwise had been in the vanguard of the resistance against the invasion. Husák's intimidations and arrests had already done their job very well. The pre-1968 famous TV anchorman Vladimír Škutina was eager to do the interview and would try to involve some others. We both agreed that it had to happen soon and next morning I went to see him by streetcar.

Škutina had three guests: Jiří Hochman, who until 1968 had been the editor-in-chief of *Reporter* and whom I used to know from earlier days, and two others in their thirties, whom I had never met before: Jan and Karel Šling, sons of Ota Šling, in the fifties party secretary of Brno, who in 1952 in the Slánský trial was sentenced to death and hanged.

Doing the interview was no problem, but how to get it safely out of the country? It was clear that I should not keep it in my pocket one second longer than necessary. "Go from here straight to the Dutch embassy and deliver it there," Hochman advised.

Although I knew that in cases like this, embassies were not allowed to cooperate at all, it seemed to me to be the only solution. "Ride along with me, I'll drop you near the embassy," said Hochman. Also riding along with us were the two Šlings, who meanwhile had given their addresses and phone numbers to me. About 2000 feet before the embassy I got off at Újezd street. At the time the Dutch embassy was closely watched. In July, they had arrested a Czech employee of the Dutch embassy, Hubert Stein. Nobody knew why. Questions about it from the Dutch side to the Czechoslovakian authorities remained unanswered. Whether it was the extra surveillance or a coincidence or that we had already been followed from the home of Škutina (we did not think so, we had not seen anything suspicious) – I did not know. But a fact was, that pretty soon after I had gotten out, a slow driving car followed me, somewhat

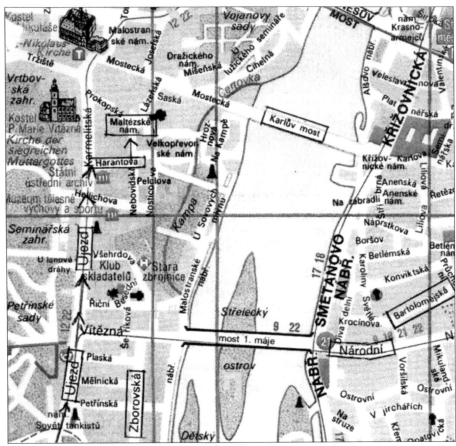

. . . with the cassette tape from the Újezd via the Harantova street to the Dutch
embassy on the Maltézské nám. (square). "Karlův most" means Charles bridge.
Some other streets named in the book are boxed.

later two men got out, who followed me on foot. I was scared to death, not
for myself so much as for my tape. I was convinced that they would stop me
before I would enter the embassy. I really did not know what to do. I went into
a small café to think things over. It had a kind of vestibule with a table and
a couple of chairs. I myself went to sit in the café proper. I was hardly there,
when four or five men entered. They sat at that table in that vestibule, ordered
nothing, just constantly looking at me. I was petrified, I did not understand
anything of it. Didn't they know that I was the same person their colleagues
had been watching at hotel Evropa? Apparently not, otherwise they would
stop me. Or may be they did know, but wanted to wait and see where I was
heading? I had ordered tea, thoughtlessly took a sip and burned my mouth
instantly. I literally did not know which way to turn. Yes, go to the embassy

or no, don't go to the embassy? But if not, then back to Zborovská? But then they would know right away where I was staying. Should I rather go back to hotel Evropa? But suppose they did not know that I was who I was? And so my thoughts ran around in circles. I think I sat there for a half to three quarters of an hour. So did the men in the vestibule. In the end I guessed that the least risky option for me *and* for Jiří *and* for my tape was to go to the embassy anyway. I got to my feet, passed close by the men in the vestibule, and turned right in the direction of the embassy. The men also got to their feet, most of them got into their car, one continued to follow me. So I thought. The cliché trick. I stopped at a shop window and looked interested at nothing. Some 200 hundred feet behind me he did the same. So it was true. The Dutch embassy was then located in a part of the old Nostitz Palace, in the heart of old Prague on the splendid Maltézské náměští. The palace has a big entrance gate to an inner court. In the left corner of that inner court was the door to the Dutch embassy. I hastened my step. He kept on walking some 100 feet behind me. A right turn into the small Harantova street that ends on that Maltézské square. The entrance gate is yet a hundred feet ahead of me, the man 100 feet behind me. I look back and see him almost panicky waving to a car, standing on the other side of the street, diagonally across the gate. I pass through fast, the car starts driving, takes a turn toward the gate, but I'm just ahead of him. The car apparently does not dare to drive into the inner court and I reach the door to the embassy unhindered. After the arrest of Stein they were more careful than ever at the embassy. They assumed that bugging equipment was installed on the premises of the embassy. Ambassador Jongejans was so careful that he even performed activities, not meant for other eyes, out of view of the window because he suspected cameras in a building across the street. We talked about this, that and the other, and meanwhile I wrote down on a small piece of paper that I had a tape with me. He wrote me back, "Give it to me when you shake hands with me when leaving." And so it came to pass.

Leaving. That meant: caught up again by the StB firm. This time only followed by a slow driving car. Back to Újezd, then left into a very small street with one-way traffic from the opposite side. It might work. They proceed fast to catch me again on the other side after turning left twice. But before they have completed the detour, I already had reached the park on the bank of the Motlava; some 300 feet farther on I sit down on a bench, kind of out of the way, behind a couple of trees and wait, a quarter of an hour, half an hour. I watch carefully whether I see the same person twice. Finally, I dare to proceed, alongside the bank of the Motlava, direction Charles Bridge. Nobody to be seen. Cross the Charles Bridge, already then a pedestrian area. Arriving on the other side, I immediately dive into a cab. I let him drive to my friend Hans Krijt, who already lives in Prague since 1948 in the Janáčkovo nábřeží, a street on the bank of the Motlava, parallel to the Zborovská. Even if they had jotted down the license plate number of the cab and questioned the driver, where he had brought me, the address of Hans Krijt would not be suspicious, because it was well-known at the StB of course, that we knew each other very well. Waited a few hours at Hans Krijt, nothing suspicious in the street and then on foot to the Zborovská.

The trick had worked again. I had gotten rid of them for the second time.

That interview had taken me the whole Wednesday and a mountain of nerves, but I was intensely satisfied-exhausted. Called a couple of people. Next afternoon the wife of the writer Jan Procházka, who had recently died, would come to the café down on the corner. Jiří would meet her down there. There was a back door in the café, which ended at the stair well of our apartment building. In this way she could come up to us pretty well unnoticed. The female Member of Parliament Sekaninová also wanted to talk to me. As one of the few she had voted in the parliament against "the temporary stationing of Soviet troops in Czechoslovakia," a proposal submitted by the Dubček-team at the end of August 1968. Mrs. Sekaninová had been a member of the communist party since her early years. During the war she had been doing time in a concentration camp for her conviction. After Husák came to power, she wanted to resign as a member, but then, so she had told me in 1969, "I discovered that you could not resign from the party, you could only be expelled. And that's what they did." Mrs. Sekaninová would call me that Thursday afternoon at 5.30 p.m. to arrange an exact appointment.

To bed. Room locked. List with matches on the night stand. I looked with some optimism forward to the next day. Wrongly.

Frequently we looked down from the attic window to see whether people of the StB would stand in the street. Around noon Thursday there they stood again: the conspicuously inconspicuous cars of the well-known foreign brand. Brazenly with the same license plates that I had already recorded on my diary tape.

"Apparently they know that I am here, I might as well return to my hotel now," I said to my friends of the commune. The appointment with Mrs. Procházková that afternoon at four could not be undone anymore, and I also did not want to miss the phone call from Mrs. Sekaninová. Besides, so I thought, they are not (yet) interested in picking me up, otherwise they would already have come upstairs. The longer they stayed away, the more this thought was strengthened. I wondered how they figured out my address, but I supposed that by bugging the phones of the persons I was speaking to, they also traced the calling number and the matching address. That's why I decided to return to my hotel that very evening; through the café, thus unnoticed, so I hoped. I had already made an appointment with film director Jan Němec for the next morning in the café of hotel Evropa.

At about three that afternoon, Jiří left to do some shopping and subsequently wait in the café for Mrs. Procházková. Not yet five minutes later a fellow commune member, who was repairing his motor cycle outside, runs upstairs with the message, "They have arrested Jiří and taken him along in a car." I had no clue whatsoever. Why Jiří and not me? I considered it as all the stronger evidence that at any rate they did not want me now. But I just made sure. Off my big list I copied on a much smaller piece of paper some fifteen names with phone numbers, among them the private number of the then editor-in-chief current affairs of *NOS-radio* Kees Buurman, the two Šlings, Mrs. Sekaninová, the dissident writer Ludvík Vaculík, the film director Jan Němec; all good acquaintances of the StB, who, if they would find the list on me, would not experience more trouble than they already had anyway. Of lesser-known people I had only written down the phone numbers without area code, it concerned relations outside Prague. The small list went to the pants pocket, the big one to the fireplace in the living room. It burned until nothing was left. The matches returned to the pants pocket.

And suddenly, at 3.30 p.m., they stood in the room. Three men plus Jiří; they had gotten in with Jiří's key. With intense joy I saw the apparent chief of the bunch walk to the fireplace. He did not say anything. Earlier he had waved an identity card the size of a credit card right in front of me and mumbled the Czech equivalent of "State Security Service." None of them spoke a foreign language. I understood I had to go along with them and my protests had no effect whatsoever, if only for linguistic reasons. They walked briefly through the house, and Jiří had to tell them whether I had hidden some stuff. He said no and so did not show anything about my diary-tapes that I had put on top of a closet out of precaution, out of sight. I had asked Jiří to bring it to the KLM office in case something would happen to me. Openly, for all to see, I had left my tape recorder with an empty tape in the room, suggesting that I had not recorded anything. It goes without saying that they took me along. Outside two cars were waiting for us. Jiří between two men on the rear seat of car # 1, I ditto in car # 2. We went to the "Bartelomějská" as the street was (and still is) called, where the StB had their headquarters at # 14. But in the communist times the name was synonym with the StB. Every dictatorship has its own street.

The arrival was highly encouraging. The message board was empty except for two small photos: one of Klement Gottwald, the first Stalinist president of Czechoslovakia after the coup d'état of 1948, and one of the master himself: Josef Stalin. Jiří and I were separated; not until fifteen years later I would see him back in the United States. "Empty your pockets," sounded the order. I took the matches out, but skipped the list. I was kept there under surveillance for hours. Nothing happened. The list was burning in my pocket even without matches. Would I ask to go to the bathroom? Better not, because that's the standard question of defendants when they want to get rid of "compromising" stuff. It could result in extra body searching. Wait for a better opportunity.

Finally, the chief returned. "Tomorrow we start with the interrogations, now you go to the cell," he lets me know. Two men took me by car, I sat alone in the back. In the meantime it had turned dark. Should I take the small list out and throw it away when I get out? But I was wearing very tight pants and had to lift myself completely off the seat in order to get my hand into my pocket. They would see it in their mirror. I rather wait until in the cell, then I would be alone and have the best opportunity to let it disappear unnoticed. Wished I had taken the risk. After arriving in the cell I had to undress completely, they checked all my clothes and at the same time turned my pockets inside out – and there my little list dropped to the floor. I was sure it could not do harm to those involved, but my goal, that nothing would fall into their hands, was not achieved. They did not blink an eye and they picked it up without reproaching me for my "omission" at the time I emptied my pockets. In the meantime it was nine o'clock in the evening and I had gotten pretty hungry. I asked them for something to eat and took up a modest position, "Just a slice of bread with a little bit of butter will do." They started laughing derisively. Dry bread I could get – and that's what I got.

I sat in cell 16, seven by twelve feet. Immediately right around the corner of the cell door was this open toilet with accelerator pedals *à la France*. In front of it a plastic curtain which, as it were, cut a triangle off the cell. Above the hole of the toilet was a faucet, which could only be operated from the outside. Every morning at six (get-up-time) it was turned on for half an hour. For the rest of the day you had to manage without running water. On the same side as the toilet was a wooden bed along the wall. On the bed a dirty straw mattress and an equally dirty horse hair blanket. In between a sheet which had not been washed for at least half a year, and you had to choose whether you wanted to sleep *under* the dirty sheet, to avoid the dirt of your blanket or *on top of it*, to avoid the dirt of your straw mattress. I chose the first option. After a couple of days I found under my pillowcaseless pillow a few pieces of moldy bread. Below the high barred small window on the shorter side of the cell stood a wooden table and in front of it a wooden stool without a back and arm rest. For the first three feet from the floor up the wall it was yellow ochre, the rest dark brown. (When years later in Brussels I watched a movie on the Slánský trial with Yves Montand in the leading role, I noticed that the decorators had used exactly the right colors). The lamp in the cell burned day and night.

On Friday morning they came around for me. First I had to go with them to the garage. There was my car. The previous evening they had asked for my car keys so that they could bring my luggage, car and all, to the Bartolomějská. Thursday evening my suitcase with my clothes had already been waiting in my cell but everything was noted. They took part of it. The searcher also wanted to take my watch, but the chief gestured that I could keep it – apparently a favor.

In the garage was my car. Two mechanics would search the whole car in my presence. They did it thoroughly, even the lining was taken off. I was scared to death that they would have planted something which they would then triumphantly produce as piece of evidence. But it all went correctly, they did not find anything (I really had nothing to hide) and they assembled everything neatly back in its place. We returned inside. I was guided past a row of interrogation rooms and from time to time my attendant opened a door to see whether any space was available. Behind one of the doors I observed a nervously smoking Hans Krijt opposite an interrogator. Finally an empty room. After a short while the chief entered. When I met Jan Šling in London in 1972, after he was expelled from Czechoslovakia, I described to him what the chief looked like.

"That must have been major Pichrt," he said.

Subsequently I wrote him down in my address book under the P, mentioning him *verhoormajoor*, interrogation major. Twenty-five years later I got the confirmation that it really had been Jan Pichrt. He was head of the department dealing with foreigners.

Pichrt started with telling me that he "knew seventy percent of everything about me." I considered it a bluff, because if you don't know everything, you also cannot calculate that you know seventy percent. I was pretty nervous, nevertheless, because I had no idea what was waiting for me. Fortunately, Pichrt made two blunders. I had immediately asked for the presence of a member of the Dutch embassy, because I was entitled to it. "You are not yet arrested, but only detained. That's why you don't have the right for assistance of the embassy yet." That refusal was no surprise to me.

"But," so I asked, "has the embassy been informed that I am held here?"

"That goes without saying," he answered.

Then, I was quite a bit reassured. The embassy knew, so the *NOS* knew, so action would be taken to get me free. It was a terrific moral boost for me. Retrospectively, it turned out that they had not warned the embassy at all. I still don't understand why Pichrt did not say, "Nobody knows that you are here, you have completely to rely on yourself." That would have made it much more difficult for me. That was blunder #1.

To prove that he knew "seventy percent" about me, he said, "And we also know that you defend Nazi generals." And that was blunder #2.

In 1966 the case-Kielmansegg had been played out in the Netherlands. Von

Kielmansegg was chief staff of the NATO-forces in Europe. During the war he had been assigned to the headquarters of Hitler in the *Wolfsschanze* in Rastenburg and now was accused of war crimes. I believed it and would make a TV documentary on this for *VPRO*. But during my investigation I concluded, among other things, that, based on interviews with unimpeachable witnesses like prof. Eugon Kogon and Fabian von Schlabrendorff, Von Kielmansegg not only did not commit war crimes, but even had played a role in the attempt on the life of Hitler in July 1944. Of course, so-called left wingers in the Netherlands could not accept that and the debates built up high and even got up to the parliament. And now that guy Pichrt wanted to tell me that I defended Nazi generals? Immediately, I rose above my timidity, got very angry and shouted, "As a fourteen-year-old boy I have made an underground paper against the Germans, do you really think I defend Nazi generals? I just defended him because he was *not* one."

Apparently he had not counted on such an outburst, because he quickly said, "Well, I don't want to interfere in the internal affairs of the Netherlands."

But I had, thanks to his two blunders, stronger than ever the feeling of, "I won't let you cut me down to size." That did not mean, that I was not scared any longer, because I really was, but I would not let them corner me, because of my fear. I asked him why I was detained. He did not answer explicitly but said generally, "You are here with the counter espionage service."

"But you know as well as I do that I am not a spy."

"I know, but it is about people here in Czechoslovakia."

I remembered the talk I had the Monday before with Mrs. Pachmanová. Her husband, chess master Luděk Pachman whom I knew very well, was already imprisoned for a year without an accusation. The StB knew that Pachman and I knew each other very well and so I could, being followed or not, visit his wife without problems. She had told me that most likely a trial was being prepared for September against her husband and five others, among whom Jiří Hochman and the writer Ludvík Vaculík, and that the StB wanted to try to construct a connection between the six and the arrested Stein of the Dutch embassy. Pichrt's announcement was reasonably unpleasant as it seemed that they had also reserved a little place in that group for me.

After this introductory talk, which took place through the German-speaking interpreter Ivan Schirmer (whose name I learned after 25 years as well), he left and left the interrogation to a lesser god. The interpreter showed a striking resemblance to Ernest Hemingway and in my mind I continued to call him Hemingway. Pichrt had told me that minutes would be made of the interrogation, which I would have to sign. I said I would sign only a German written record, but a translation would, according to Pichrt, take a lot of time, which would not be in my interest. The interpreter would read back in German paragraph by paragraph, so that I would know what was said in Czech in the minutes. At that moment I agreed to it. Fortunately, the lesser interrogation god was, in contrast with Pichrt, a very stupid man. It all lasted endlessly long, not only because of the translation, but also because the stupid man typed everything in slow motion. The questions were not too intelligent and I felt reasonably at ease. In the Dubček area a law was passed, which gave journalists not only the right, but even obliged them to remain silent concerning their sources. I was not sure about it, but I assumed that law was not yet withdrawn. When the Stupid asked about names, sources or whatever, I appealed to that law and added that we also had the right to remain silent in the Netherlands, speculating that they would not know that this was not true. That muddled on in this way until around four o'clock. Then Pichrt entered, glanced through the minutes and got angry, apparently because nothing had come out of the interrogation. "Back to the cell," he ordered. I protested against the conditions in the cell, but he irritated blew this off.

"*Konec* – over and out. Back to the cell. And if you have to report something interesting for our service, just ring the bell."

I had not discovered the bell yet. I found it later in front, left of the cell entrance on the blind wall. It was Friday, late in the afternoon. I had brought *one* book from the Netherlands, borrowed from the city library of Haarlem. They let me keep it: *Maigret in New York* by Simenon. It was rather thin and I already finished it that very evening. At ten p.m. you had to go to bed, at six a.m. you had to get up. The very first morning, I had made a very serious mistake. After being woken up, washing above the hole in the toilet and dressing, nothing happened. No breakfast or anything that passed off as such. So I stretched myself out on the bed once more. Every quarter of an hour a guard (sometimes a female, because we had those, too) looked through the famous hole in the cell door to see whether you didn't perform naughty deeds like hanging yourself or so. I laid there for not even ten minutes, when the cell door was thrown open with a lot of racket and I was ordered in a loud voice to get up. It was strictly forbidden to lie on your wooden bed between six a.m. and ten p.m. I really would think twice before I would commit that sin again on Saturday. So that meant sitting on the wooden stool-without-rests or pacing up and down. Or reading in Simenon. In a short time Maigret had been in New York twice.

The breakfast consisted of a dry piece of very old bread and something that somewhat resembled coffee, an Ersatz *à la* nineteen forty-forty five. The hot meal was made up of a small mug of reasonably good soup, a diminutively-small piece of meat and the famous Czech *knedlí,* a mortar-like squeezed-together mass of potatoes and bread. Under normal conditions they are already dry and only somewhat digestible with a tremendous amount of gravy. But these were drier than dry and gravy was not at hand. I couldn't eat them to save my life. In the evening there was again dry bread for a change, this time accompanied by a glass of milk. I was not interrogated that Saturday. It was clear that they would just let me sit there until I would press the cell bell button to report "something interesting" to them. I was firmly determined not to let it come that far, morally supported by the lie of Pichrt that the Dutch embassy was informed. I had plenty of time to think over how everything had happened and all of a sudden it flashed through me: Jiří's painting. Of course they had found that small painting in my hotel room with the full name of Jiří and the year 1970. They had figured out where he lived, had taken him along when he left his house, not yet knowing that I was there. They only found that out during Jiří's interrogation and then immediately dashed off to pick up me as well. When leaving the hotel, I had overlooked the fact that the painting actually contained a trail for the StB.

That Saturday lasted very long. So did the Sunday, by the way. I read Maigret once more. I also paced up and down quite a few times. No doubt, they had told the guards that some enemy of socialism sat in the cell. That's why I sang as a well-educated social democrat a great many times with great pleasure and in a loud voice "The Internationale" – of course in Dutch. One of my favorites was also, "We shall overcome some day-hey-hey-hey-hey." My cell was somewhere in the middle of a row, but I had no idea whether I had neighbors. In any case, I did not hear the slightest noise from other cells.

Nothing happened on the Monday after the Sunday either. The only human being I saw three times a day was the guard who, like it should, brought my food in silence. I was not even aired. I have to get sick, I thought, and then they have to bring me to a hospital. Although it was summer, it was pretty cool in the cell, which was located partly underground. After the guard had looked once more through his small hole (you could hear that, because he had to slide the small flap of the hole open), I climbed on my table once in a while. Then I could just look through the window which was practically at street level. I looked out on a courtyard. On the other side were apparently some offices of the StB, because in the morning the silence was slowly broken by *one* little sound, then a few, then a typewriter started rattling, then more: the sound swelled up in slow motion. It reminded me of the evening of the fourth of May 1945, when after curfew[6] street sounds swelled on in a much quicker pace. Then those sounds announced the liberation, which I hardly could say of the sounds in the courtyard.

As mentioned earlier, the cell window had bars, but you could open it your-

[6] During the greater part of the last year of the German occupation in the Netherlands there was a curfew from 8 p.m. to 4 a.m.

self from the inside. That led to my make-sick-idea. I exercised intensively and worked myself in a sweat. Then, I climbed, when the coast was clear, on the table, opened my shirt and stood stripped to the waist in front of the window, hoping to catch pneumonia. I admit – a peculiar idea, because you don't get pneumonia that quick. But I did discover that in the situation I had ended up in, you invent the craziest plans to get back out of it.

Tuesday morning. Again the daily swelling of the sounds. Again the same breakfast. And then at half past eight: the interpreter enters with two guards in plain clothes. I have to come along for interrogation. I feel like I am a little bit of a winner; they were the ones to buckle under first. First they bring me outside and I am allowed to walk around the block, just on the public street. Do the people around me see that I am not a free man? We arrive in the busy Národní street. There goes the streetcar in the direction of the Dutch embassy. Shall I suddenly run away and try to jump on the streetcar? If I see a car with a foreign license plate, shall I *then* run away, stop him with panicky gestures, so that he *has* to stop? That flashed through my mind, but I did nothing and kept walking on decently with them, because they would have been hopeless attempts, of course.

They brought me to a big office room. There, behind his desk: major Pichrt *himself*, with a Lenin button on his lapel. On the wall the same person but in a larger format. Stalin was not visible here. Against the back of his desk was another desk: I was put behind this. To my left the interpreter, Hemingway, on the right a female secretary for the minutes. In my cell, once more I had thought about the minutes in Czech I had signed. I had decided from now on only to sign minutes which were translated in German, regardless of how much longer they would keep me because of that. I said this to Pichrt and clarified myself, "You might write down in the Czech part, that I had planned an attempt on the life of Svoboda (the then-president of Czechoslovakia), and not read it back to me in German." He could do nothing else but agree, but, he said, "I'll come back to the attempt on Svoboda's life later" – so he did have a sense of humor, but it did remain the only time he showed it. In general he stated that I "maintained contacts with the top of the political opposition, of whom it was proven that they committed counterrevolutionary activities." His reasoning for that was quite funny. On August 21, 1969, at the occasion of the first "anniversary" of the Soviet invasion, a *Manifesto of ten points* (given to me by the author, the writer Ludvík Vaculík) was published, which demanded, among other things, that the Soviet troops should leave the country. Many had signed it and it was publicly presented to the parliament.

"In September last year [1969] you wrote in *Het Parool*[7] that you heard already in the beginning of August in Prague that the manifesto was going to appear. That means that you had a part in counterrevolutionary activities," according to Pichrt, and he predicted how many years of prison this carried. And so it went every time. I had helped the Sekerka family to escape the country. That carried two years. At a certain moment he asked, "Do you know the spy Stein?" The *spy* Stein. That's what it was. Stein was suspected of spying. I had met Stein once in a while at the Dutch embassy, but I did not really know him. That was also my answer. But now the conversation really went in an unpleasant direction. It reminded me once more of what Mrs. Pachmanová had told me. Next, they are going to make me the liaison man in the upcoming trial between those "counterrevolutionaries" and the "spy" Stein here and Holland, so it went through me.

One of the first questions Pichrt asked me, was, "People in the house where you stayed, have stated that you burned documents in the fireplace. What kind of documents were they?" In contrast with what he expected, I was delighted with this question, because I thought: I'll show you what you have lost. "That was a list with names and addresses of as many as sixty people whom I know here in Czechoslovakia. They all were absolutely innocent people, but from the fact you were following me, I concluded that those people could happen to run into problems if you would find the list. That's why I burned it." He did not react at all, but started asking "with whom I had been in contact in Czechoslovakia." I said that I did not intend to betray my friends and because of that I would not answer that question. Now he started reading out loud the list they had found. At the top was Šling and he asked me, how I got to know him. "I don't know him," I lied, "but I got his phone number from colleagues in the west who told me that he would be an interesting person to talk to. But I have not gotten around to that yet."

Again he did not react, I had a sigh of relief, apparently he did not know that I already had done that interview with Šling, Škutina and Hochman. To avoid further questions about that list, I added that this also went for the others on the list. Because I refused to mention names, he himself took the initiative.

"Did you have contact with...?" and then followed a name of an at that time well-known oppositionist. Some of them I knew very well, some of them I had met casually, some of them I did not know at all. In the meantime I had invented a standard answer. Again and again I answered, "I don't answer that question which is neither a denial nor a confirmation." And in between I asked him repeatedly, "What would you do in my case? Would you mention names?" It

---

7   *Het Parool* is a main daily in the Netherlands, founded in 1940 as an underground paper against the Germans.

The small list they found on DV was published in the "Rudé Právo" of August 21, 1970, in an article against DV.

goes without saying that I did not expect him to answer that question, but I assumed that he could hardly give another answer to himself but, "I would not have done it either" – hoping that in this way he would gain more understanding for my point of view. After some time he changed his tack and made the stereotypical remark, "You better tell us everything, because we know it all anyway," on which I gave the stereotypical answer, "If you already know it all, why are you asking me." He kept on acting correct, did not get angry, but did intimidate.

"You must know that for the time being you are only detained. It depends on the course of this interrogation whether you will be arrested or not. So you better cooperate."

In a way I had an easy time. The whole dialogue went through interpreter Hemingway. When I had said something in German, he first had to translate it into Czech. That gave me some time for reflection and so I said after his translation quite often, *"Und ich möchte noch hinzufügen ... –* and I would like to add...." By lack of knowledge of any foreign language, he also could not interrupt me and say for instance; "That is none of my business, I want to know what..."

Extra time was lost, because after the translation the major had to dictate to the secretary what she had to write down in the minutes in his own Czech. On top of that, I had gotten permission to make notes in my own confiscated notebook, which they had temporarily made available to me for that purpose. At half past twelve I drew the major's attention to the fact, that this was the point in time when the prison food was distributed and that I rather would not miss that. He interrupted the session immediately.

Around half past one the interrogation was continued, after they again rounded a block with me. Pichrt still had not answered my repeated question what I was charged with. So I asked it once again. He got up, walked to an office space behind him and came back with my tape recorder. He put it on the table, pushed the button and I heard myself saying, "I am being followed by a Renault 16 of the secret service, ABA 36-92." It frightened me. So they did find the tape on top of the closet anyway. It could not be anything else than that Jiří still had been forced to disclose where the tape was.

"This is obviously a tape, meant for an intelligence service," said Pichrt. Of course, he knew very well – and I told him so – that this was not true; it was clear from the whole context that it was about a journalistic diary. His surprise was a part of the intimidation by which he wanted to show me that he could have me convicted because of it if I did not mention names. It remained a bizarre verbal battle. Of course, they knew quite a bit of my relations with oppositionists, because I had written about it or done TV interviews with them, and they knew that I knew that they knew. But in connection with the upcoming trials it mattered much to them to have black-and-white minutes with a statement signed by me that I had been "in contact" with so-and-so in Czechoslovakia. So far I had been able to parry every reproach and prevent the mentioning of names. In earlier days I had been very nervous in general at exams and such, which sometimes resulted in operating below my capacities. True, at this exam I felt a great deal of tension, but I felt elevated far above my examiners. I despised the executors of the little and great terror in Czechoslovakia and I think that this gave me the power not to lose my head and to stand firm.

Finally, Pichrt played his last trump, "We also have a higher quality of interrogation."

"What do you mean?" I asked.

"You know very well what we mean."

"With physical violence?"

"Of course not, we don't do that here," he answered, but he left aside what he actually meant with that "higher quality of interrogation." It was five o'clock. After seven and a half hours he had enough for that day. On one point I was not yet reassured. As mentioned before: what I said was translated into Czech by the interpreter, and then the major made in *his* Czech the text for the minutes. I could follow the Czech language more or less and I had the feeling that his Czech was full of Stalinist conspirative insinuations meant for me. While

I had refused to sign – I really had not signed those Tuesday minutes – I still wanted to build in an extra safeguard. I therefore said that I wanted to produce a piece of my own in which I wanted to put down my position in my own German. The major immediately agreed.

"I'll give you five sheets of paper and you also give me five sheets back. When you have finished your story, just push the button of your cell bell," he said.

Back to my dry slice of bread and milk. I was thinking the whole evening about what I was going to write. It was clear why he wanted five sheets back. They did not only want to get hold of the final text, but also on every deletion, change or addition. It could have been a great deal worse if the toilet paper in the cell would not have been completely unsuitable for the purpose it was made for, but because of its hard glossiness it made an excellent writing paper. On Wednesday, I spent all morning with my toilet paper sheets (with my back to the door). Many changes, deletions, new considerations. I assumed I was going to be interrogated for days to come. I lied a lot, of course, but nothing is as difficult as to lie coherently. You have to anticipate every reaction to your falsehoods and set those against another falsehood. I did not know whether I could keep this up if all periods I ever spent in Czechoslovakia would remain the subject of the conversation. That's why I wrote in my statement that I no longer would answer any question dealing with the period before August 9, 1970, because apparently I had not committed any crime in their eyes, otherwise they would have detained me earlier. Furthermore I noted that I had not violated any Czechoslovakian law after August 9, 1970, and that, if they could prove me wrong, I would apologize for that. I copied the text with intended changes on one of the five sheets and put the rough draft on the toilet paper in my pocket.

Around two o'clock I rang the bell. The guard came and I handed him my five sheets. One hour later the cell door opened again. The guard said in broken German, *"Alle Ihre Sachen einpacken. In einer halbe Stunde Sie gehen hier weg.* All your things pack and in half an hour you go away." My first thought was: are they possibly going to release me? But subsequently: maybe it's going to "the higher quality of interrogation." Or they might be so dissatisfied with the interrogation I am not "detained" any longer but "arrested" – and then you have to go to Pankrac, the real prison. There I will be searched again. What to do with my rough draft of toilet paper? I did not dare throw it into the toilet with the accelerator pedals; who knows they have invented a way to find out whether there is important material in their drain pipe. I knew of only one method: I went and stood with my back to the door, put the toilet paper sheets in my mouth and washed them down with the water in my mug. No safer place than my stomach.

Indeed, after half an hour the cell door opened again. It looked bad. Not only the interpreter, but also the two guards in plain clothes. They did not say anything, so I asked the interpreter, *"Was machen Sie jetzt mit mir? –* what are you going to do with me now?"

"Jetzt gehen Sie zu Ihrer Hinrichtung – now you go to your execution," Hemingway answered.

"Das ist aber ein blöder Witz – That is really a stupid joke," I remarked.

He was honest enough to say, *"Verzeihung, das hätte ich nicht sagen müssen –* sorry, I should not have said that." But he left aside what really was going to happen.

"Werde ich denn freigelassen – will I be released," I hopefully asked.

"Aber nein, – certainly not," he answered, with a heavy intonation on *"nein."* So it was clear: I was going to Pankrac. In that case I will see Luděk Pachman, I thought. While walking through the long cell corridor heading for the staircase-up, I could not resist asking once more explicitly where we were going. And finally he made himself clear. With a threatening voice, as if he had a highly unpleasant message for me, he said, *"Sie werden über die Grenze gesetzt –* you will be put across the border."

No honorary lap this time. We went straight to the office of Pichrt. He read an expulsion order to me which among other things said that I "had misused [my stay in Czechoslovakia] for illegal journalistic activities" and that I, on top of that, had violated the journalistic custom by performing "illegal intelligence services." I protested on the spot against those accusations and quoted Pichrt's own words that he knew I was not a spy, but it was all in vain, of course. I could appeal, but only within fifteen days and I could not wait for the answer in Czechoslovakia. I had to leave the country before half past six p.m. in Rozvadov. Meanwhile, it was four o'clock. Prague-Rozvadov is 115 miles and the roads were smaller and worse at the time than even now.

"If you are not at the border on time, you will be arrested."

"Two and a half hours is much too tight. I could easily crash into a tree."

"That is none of my business. The time is half past six."

Some formalities had still to be completed and the interpreter said, "The commissioner (that's how Pichrt was called) *in person* will make a cup of coffee for you because of the high level of the interrogation."

Which came to pass. I had to sign a list for all the stuff what was returned to me. Nearly everything was there, even my tape recorder. Of course not the tape, nor a picture of Pavel Zajić, who had set himself on fire in Brno just as Jan Palach had done in protest against the occupation; a membership card of the *Dubček fan club,* which I had gotten from its president, whom I had interviewed in 1969, and a kind of die-stamp relief-printed portrait of the first

Krajské oddělení pasů a víz
PRAHA
PRAHA 1, Bartolomějská 14

Č.j.: PV - 11.370 / 4 - 70   V Praze dne 19. srpna 1970

V e r k i j k Dick

P r a h a

V e r k i j k Dick, nar. 4.7.1929, holandské státní přísluš-
nosti - zákaz pobytu na území ČSSR.

Provedeným šetřením bylo zjištěno, že jste zneužil svého pobytu v ČSSR k nedovolené žurnalistické činnosti, vymykají-
cí se běžným zvyklostem. Ke krytí své nepřátelské činnosti jste
v Praze získal soukromý byt, který sám ve vlastnoruční zprávě
presentujete jako krycí adresu, se které provádíte svoji činnost.
Ve zprávě určené k odeslání do zahraničí cestou nejvyšších před-
stavitelů holandského velvyslanectví v Praze a representace holandské letecké společnosti KLM v Praze jste se dopustil osočo-
vání několika čs. občanů tím, že jste jejich vlastní osobní vo-
zidla s uvedením státních poznávacích značek označil jako vozid-
la československé státní bezpečnosti, která Vás sledují. Dále
jste porušil platné předpisy tím, že jste nesplnil přihlašovací
povinnost na této krycí adrese. I při další své činnosti jste
porušil platné zvyklosti běžně používané v žurnalistické činnosti tím, že jste provozoval nedovolenou zpravodajskou činnost.
Ke krytí této činnosti jste měnil svoji podobu i svoje celkové
vzezření.

Tímto jednáním jste porušil čs. právní předpisy a proto
se Vám podle § 3 odst. 1 zák. č. 68 / 1965 Sb zakazuje další
pobyt na území Československé socialistické republiky a ukládá
se Vám, aby jste opustil území ČSSR dne 19. srpna 1970 do 18,30
hodin přes hraniční přechod Rozvadov. V případě, že ve stanove-
né lhůtě území ČSSR neopustíte, budete vyhoštěn.

Proti tomuto rozhodnutí je možno podat odvolání ve lhůtě
15 dnů ode dne doručení u zdejšího úřadu. Vzhledem k naléhavosti
obecného zájmu vylučuje se podle § 55 odst.2 zák.č. 71/1967 Sb
odkladný účinek odvolání.

Náčelník:

*Expulsion order by the "Bartolomějská," dated August 19, 1970, signed by J. Karel,
without any doubt a fictitious name.*

president of Czechoslovakia, Masaryk, which Jiří had given to me.

"Why don't you give back that portrait of Masaryk, wasn't he the first president of your country?"

"Don't start arguing with us, your time schedule is tight enough."

Upon leaving, I said to the interpreter, "Please, ask mister commissioner once more whether, if he were in my place, he would have mentioned names."

The interpreter translated, Pichrt answered something back and the interpreter said: *Der Herr Kommissar hat Sie begriffen* – Mr. commissioner has understood you." And finally he said, translating Pichrt, "We will take revenge on your friends for what you have done here."

In spite of that, Pichrt shook my hand for a long time, he absolutely did not show any hard feelings, although he actually had not achieved anything, and on the rebound I gave him in Czech the routine farewell, *"Na Shledanou* – (until I) see you," which, of course, did not have my highest priority as long as he remained in office.

They told me that I had to keep on driving behind a car of the StB until his guys would give me a signal that I could continue on my own. Furthermore, I was most strictly forbidden to call anybody on the road. This prohibition was superfluous, because in those days it took a half a day to call from outside Prague to Prague.

And there I went. Now the StB was not following me, but I the StB. It was extremely slow going. Only after some fifteen miles in snail-tempo I got the signal: drive on. After that, they kept on driving behind me with their *Tatra* for a while. At the border the red-haired guard from the Dubček era was still on duty. Checking me, he acted very laconically, "You still have a quarter of an hour," he said, and while taking a glance into my car, he added, "And they probably checked everything in Prague, I suppose."

Exactly on time I crossed the border, six pounds lighter than when I went in. In the German border town Waidhaus I called my wife, "I am free again," I shouted.

"What do you mean, free?" she asked. And then it appeared that nobody knew that I had spent six days in the prison. How was that possible? Ambassador Jongejans explained it to me later. When I did not report on Friday (after I was picked up on Thursday), Jongejans had hesitated to inquire at the Czechoslovakian authorities. Other reasons than an arrest could have prevented me from checking in with the embassy and Jongejans thought "let sleeping dogs lie," as he formulated it. Saturdays and Sundays the embassy is closed. But when I did not check in again on Monday, he called the Czechoslovakian Foreign Ministry to report me "missing" and did they know where I was? They claimed not to know anything about it, but they would investigate. A few hours later they called back, saying that I was detained because of a violation of the Czechoslovakian law and that I would be expelled from the country. Jongejans suspected that the involved ministry really did not know anything and that they in turn had checked with the StB. According to him a demarcation dispute arose between the StB and the ministry, which was angry, because the StB had not reported to them that they had locked up a foreigner. The ministry must have ordered them to release me immediately. That's why on Tuesday the StB made just one last attempt to drag something out of me. My conclusion then, that they were the first to buckle under, turned out to have been totally wrong. They were forced to do so and at the decision of their own ministry even dragged on for a day for that extra interrogation. I think that indeed, without the intervention of Jongejans and via him the Czechoslovakian ministry, they simply would have left me without interrogation, hoping that I would open my mouth in the end of the day.

On August 21, 1970, the day of the second "anniversary" of the invasion, a four-column article appeared in the party daily *Rudé Právo* under the headline, *"Journalist or spy?"* It said, that during 1968 and 1969 I had been many times in Czechoslovakia and that in 1968 (during the invasion) I "had filmed with no small effort abusive, provoking activities at Václavské náměstí and surrounding areas" and that I "had done interviews with representatives of revolutionary student committees, specifically of the law faculty" and that in doing so I had made propaganda "for the ultimatum-like demands" of those committees. "When and wherever anything or something happened, Mr. Verkijk was there – as long as it was directed against the realistic policy of the party or the government of our state." The writer of the article, Jiří Hečko, also summed up all those with whom I maintained contact: Luděk Pachman, Ludvík Vaculík, Jan Procházka, Vladimír Škutina, Jiří Hochman and Karel Kyncl. Pachman, Vaculík (the author of the *Manifesto of ten points),* Škutina and Hochman were correct – that all related to interviews I had made before my arrest. Jan Procházka and Karel Kyncl I had never met, but Pichrt did ask me about them, to which I had given him the aforementioned standard answer. The most important thing was, that Šling was not mentioned – so indeed, they did not know that I had done that interview. Jan Šling told me after his expulsion that in opposition circles exactly that incorrectly summing up of names and the lack of his name had led to their conclusion, that the interrogation had not gone anywhere. None of the above mentioned had been interrogated as a result of my arrest; no one on the small list either, so friends reported me from Prague. The dreaded trial never took place either. Pachman was even released after a short time. Only the absolutely innocent Stein got an (unrelated) trial; in July 1971 he was sentenced to twelve years imprisonment. In World War II he had fought in the British Army. Immediately after 1945 he returned to Czechoslovakia and

Žurnalista, nebo špión?

ter své činnosti, svědčí nejvýmluvněji ta skutečnost, že před zadržením nasimi bezpecnostnimi organy znicil některé písemné kompromitující materiály. Kromě jiného seznamy našich občanů, se kterými ho pojilo staré přátelství nebo se kterými chtěl navázat styky

Je zvláštní, že mezi těmito osobami, které sám nazývá zajímavými lidmi, není ani jediný s kladným vztahem k současnému stranickému a státnímu vedení. Ti byli totiž vždy pro pana Verkijka, který o sobě prohlašuje, že vyšel z rudého hnízda a že je velmi levým přítelem socialismu, krajně nezajímavi. Obdivoval jen komunisty typu Dubčeka. Proto také nosil legitimaci řádného člena pražského Dubček klubu číslo 227.

Někoho by mohlo při čtení tohoto článku třeba napadnout, zda naše bezpečnostní orgány se nedopustily nějaké svévole a zda nešikanují cizího státního příslušníka, který se třeba z pouhé nevědomosti dopustil nějakých běžných přestupků.

■ Zpověď pana Verkijka

Dejme slovo samotnému panu Ver-

Simca (jiné pozn. značky než včera) stála za mnou. Vrátil jsem se zpět do svého pokoje, kde jsem se převlékl do jiných šatů, vzal si jiné boty a jinou aktovku. Svoje vlasy, které normálně česu do výšky, jsem úplně namočil hřebenem a udělal si vlevo pěšinku. Hladce jsem je sčesal všechny dozadu. Při pohledu do zrcadla se na mne dívala zcela jiná osoba. Možná, že pouze proto, že bez brýli vidím neostře. Postranním východem přes restauraci jsem opustil hotel. Tento trik byl účinný. Nyní se nacházím na krycí adrese. Je to místnost s haraburdím, patřicí jednomu Čechovi, který před dvěma lety utekl na západ...

...Moji známí nespatřili v okolí ani jedno z vozidel STB — čs. tajné služby, která jsem výše uváděl.

Zítra schůzka s C., který byl právě propuštěn. Nevím, zda tuto osobu již nyní mohu jmenovat...-

Tolik z magnetofonových memoárů pana Verkijka. To snad také zcela stačí. Kdyby mu bylo něco kolem dvaceti let, mohli bychom shovívavě říci, že si zde zapracovala jeho bujná fantazie, bohatě odkojena bondyovkami a jinými »veledíly« buržoazní propa-

Part of an article in the "Rudé Právo" of August 21, 1970, reporting on my expulsion with the in-between-headline: "Journalist or spy?"

became a member of the communist party. In the beginning of the fifties he was arrested and sentenced to fifteen years "because of espionage," of which he had served nine years. In 1966 he got (with permission of the communist authorities) a job at the Dutch embassy as an interpreter. In 1968/69 his house was a meeting place of "dissidents," the real reason why he was arrested again and again sentenced "because of espionage." At the end of March 1976 his imprisonment was interrupted for health reasons; on February 23, 1977, he was rearrested during the furious campaign against *Charta-77*, an opposition movement founded (by Václav Havel, for one) on January 1, 1977[8].

The article in the *Rudé Právo* was also very stupid. It gave so many details about my work activities that it could only raise sympathy for me. Not only had they printed, as part of the article, the list they had found on me, but also my membership card of the Dubček fan club with my home address in Haarlem on it. Promptly I received different letters and cards from Czechoslovakia. The authors did not dare to disclose who they were. On one of the cards was a pronouncement of Komenský, "I am with you, be with us."[9] Another, signing with "Bob," wrote a letter of four pages, "How is it possible that our authorities have treated you as a crook. I am ashamed and offer my apologies," so Bob, who described himself "as a simple 28-year-old worker." At the end he says, "Maybe the time will ever come that I openly can tell you my name." It is possible now, but I am afraid that the now 64-year old Bob from ex Gottwaldov will forever remain Bob to me.

I had to kind of smile about the conclusion of the article. "The end of an Eastern Europe expert", it said in an in-between-headline. That's up to me to decide, I thought. But when shortly after that I wanted to go to Poland, where I never had experienced any problem whatsoever, an entry permit was denied. The then director of *NOS-radio*, Herman Felderhof, went to the Polish embassy in The Hague about it, where he was bluntly told – the Poles always have been the communist odd man out – that it was OK as far as they were concerned, but that the Russians were forbidding it. Thanks to the Russian advisers at the StB in Prague I had ended up on a KGB list. And that this would reach far, I would experience later. Eastern Europe was closed for me. So they thought.

[8]   In spite of a lot of research at the Dutch embassy in Prague and the ministry of Foreign Affairs in The Hague, I could not find out whether he served the full twelve years. Surely he has died in the meantime (he was born in 1906).

[9]   Jan Amos Komenský (1592-1670) was a famous Bohemian educator and theologian, also known under his Latin name Comenius, who during the Thirty Years War (1618-1648) went in exile in Poland and the Netherlands, where he died. Every contemporary Czech knows his name and is familiar with his works.

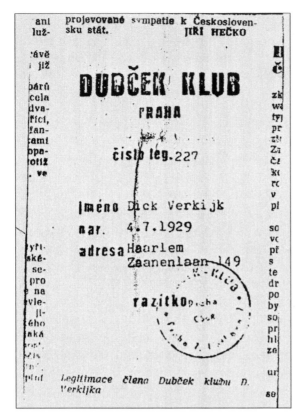

DV's membership card of the "Dubček fan club" as published in the "Rudé Právo"

After my return at a press conference I had to deal with, for one, an admirably persistent colleague of the social democratic broadcasting organization *VARA,* named Ad 's-Gravesande, completely cloaked in the outfit according to the latest leftist fashion, shoes with high heels included. Sternly he asked me whether it was true that I had traveled on a tourist visa, because this was unbecoming, of course. Timidly, blushed in the face, I had to admit it. Still I had the feeling that he did not blame his *VARA*-colleagues, who used (absolutely rightfully so in my opinion) secret roads and cunning methods to try to get into Franco Spain, for possibly using a tourist visa. But I must admit, that was antifascist and that is something else.

It goes without saying, that I could not make public that I still had an interview lying around somewhere in Prague, much less that the Dutch ambassador had taken care of it. For that matter, I had received a peculiar letter from him. At the top it said, "Copy," although it was unclear of what, because the letter was addressed to me. It did not say from whom it came, but in view of the (typewritten) text it was absolutely clear that ambassador Jongejans was the author. The letter did have a date, *"Praag, 20/8 –* Prague, August 20." The

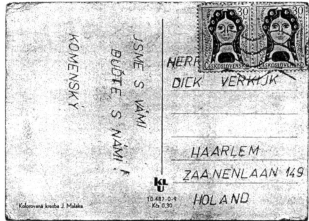

A few (obviously) anonym responses which DV got from Czechs and Slovaks after the Rudé Právo and later on the Czechoslovakian TV had campaigned against him. In the paper as well as on the screen they had shown his membership card of the "Dubček fan club," which he got in 1968 from the board president when he interviewed him. DV's address was mentioned on that card. The writer of the postcard in Czech quotes the famous 17th century Czech philosopher Komenský (Latin name Comenius): "I am with you, be with us," and he wishes DV much happiness and good health for the coming year.

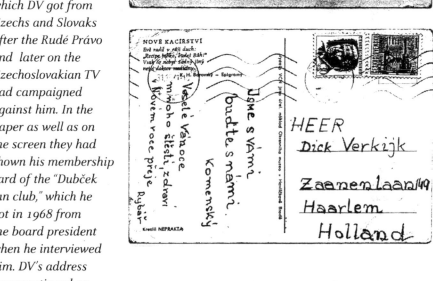

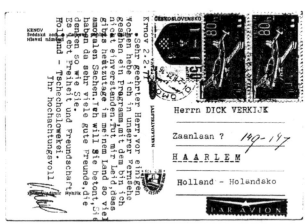

first line said, "Congratulations on the good outcome of the interrogation." He asked me to report to him what they had asked me and especially what they had *not* asked me. Further he warned me not to go to any country behind the Iron Curtain "the many coming years," because "this time they already attempted to catch you, they only did not succeed to catch you at the *moment suprême*." In another East European country they could easily arrest me and extradite me to Czechoslovakia, so he continued in his warning. I was already surprised at the time that Jongejans, one day after my release, knew that the interrogation of the StB had not gone anywhere. Thanks to the Freedom of Information Act I had the opportunity to read the secret memoranda 25 years later, sent by Jongejans to the Foreign Ministry in The Hague. On August 11, 1970, he says to have learned "via-via," that the interrogations (by the StB) of Stein "go in a civilized manner." It seems that if the Netherlands did not have a mole, they certainly had a *molette* at the StB, who kept the Dutch embassy generally informed about what was going on there. I am strengthened in this opinion by this sentence in the unsigned letter of Jongejans, "If you don't burn this letter immediately after reading, I'll never look at you again."

A good month later Jongejans came to Holland. He told me that he had kept the tape all the time in his inside pocket. He did not even trust the embassy safe. And just as well. On a night in September the embassy was burglarized and the safe cracked.

The interview with the four oppositionists lasted nearly 45 minutes and was transmitted on October 12, 1970; the original sound through the radio, the translation through the sound station of the television.[10] It is also broadcasted by among others BBC, NBC, Radio Norway and the text had also been requested by Time-Life.

A few days later: visit at Jongejans. A little bit of discussing about might-have-beens. "It has been worthwhile," he said, "but you should know, they will never forgive you that they got you in their hands and that they could not lay a hand on that interview and did not even know that you had done it." I did not dare to bring the letter up, because I could not find it in my heart to burn it and by bringing it up it would unavoidably provoke the question whether I had burned it. So I was happy that Jongejans did not bring it up. Now, thirty six years later, I dare to admit that I still have the letter.

In the memorandum from Jongejans on my case, a reference is made to a file stored at the Foreign Ministry under, "Expulsions Czechoslovakia." I was allowed to consult that, too, but a few months of the year 1970 are missing – one of them August; so my file is at large.

---

[10] In those days there was not that much TV in the Netherlands and we could use a station that was only transmitting test images.

VELVYSLANECTVÍ ČESKOSLOVENSKÉ SOCIALISTICKÉ REPUBLIKY
AMBASSADE DE LA REPUBLIQUE SOCIALISTE TCHECOSLOVAQUE Den Haag, den 26.11.1970.

C.
No. 3273/70/Ry/Ka

Titl.
Dick Verkijk
Zaanenlaan 149
H a a r l e m.

         Wir teilen Ihnen mit, dass laut der Erklärung
der tschechoslowakischen Behörden Ihrem Widerruf gegen dem Verbot
des Aufenthaltes in der ČSSR nicht entgegen gekommen ist.
         Wir machen Sie gleichzeitig darauf aufmerksam,
dass Ihre weitere Interventionen von der tschechoslowakischen
Behörden nicht in Kenntnis genommen werden.

                   Leiter der Konsularabteilung:

*An official letter from the Czechoslovakian embassy to the Netherlands shows
how far and without any scruples that country had distanced itself from a
constitutional state. It was a response to DV's protest against his expulsion and the
accusations against him, which was based on the laws of the country itself. The
chief of the consular department on November 26, 1970, let him know "that the
Czechoslovakian authorities will pay no attention to [your] further steps."*

The irritation of the StB showed a couple of months later. On the 7th of
January 1971, a 45-minute documentary against me, nicely announced in the
Czechoslovakian TV-guide was broadcasted under the title *At a secret address*.
It was a James Bond-like story full of half-truths and whole lies. But for one
sentence I am most grateful to them. In an outraged voice the commentator
said about my behavior during the interrogations, while images were shown
of the minutes, "He literally said, 'I don't want to betray my friends.'" It was
incidentally so easy to look through those half-truths and whole lies that I suspected the maker actually had wanted to sketch a positive image of me. But Jan
Šling, who had watched the film, said that the makers of those kinds of films
were too stupid to understand that they achieved the opposite of what they intended. All my life I have had two wishes: to ever lay a hand on those minutes
and to ever find out who interrogated me and what the background was.

Announcement of a documentary against DV in the Czechoslovakian TV guide, on January 8, 1971, aired under the title Na Krycí Adrese (At a Secret Address). Below the announcement a picture, "secretly" taken by the StB at Václavske náměstí. DV can't remember who the man is on his left, although he apparently has a vivid conversation with him. DV suspects that he is a Dutch colleague, also because of the pipe he so good-naturedly smokes. The man on the hood of the car is Carel Roosen, chief of the KLM office in Prague, who always took care of "the bread roll for the pilot." DV guesses that the picture is already taken in the fall of 1968, when it was not yet that difficult to go to Prague. According to the caption in the TV guide the photo dates from 1969.

On my first request to the new Czechoslovakian authorities after the *velvet revolution*, they reported to me that nothing had been found on me in the files of the StB. In the beginning of 1995 a friend of a friend turned out to work at the office which is delving through all of the StB files. He still found a five pages "evaluation" about me, but according to Czech law he is not allowed to hand it over to me. In an official letter of the "Committee for documentation and investigation of crimes of communism" of February 10, 1995 (signed by the president of that committee, the former Charta-77-spokesman Václav Benda) it is confirmed that Jan Pichrt, head of the StB Foreign Department, had interrogated me, and that "Hemingway" was called in reality Ivan Schirmer. He had died in the meantime. Pichrt was still alive. He was an attendant at the Police Museum in Prague. In March 1995 I went there. Initially, they denied that a Pichrt worked there. Another employee was brought in, who suspiciously asked why I was interested in Pichrt. I would not be surprised if they had parked more former StB collaborators in that museum. I had a Czech acquaintance with me who mumbled something on my behalf to the effect that we were old acquaintances of his. The colleague told us that Pichrt was ill. It seemed to be true. In the meantime, I figured out where he lived. Without notice we went up there. After we had ringed the bell, a woman came to the outside yard wicket gate. She told us that she was the daughter of Jan Pichrt and that the day before her father had been brought to the intensive care unit of a hospital because of an acute problem with his diabetes. But how did I get to know her father? Carefully I said, that we got acquainted 25 years ago. She invited us in and there I told her briefly how I got to know him.

"That's what I was afraid of," she sighed, "but I am not responsible for the deeds of my father."

I said that I absolutely had not come out of feelings of revenge or to express accusations, but that I simply for the sake of history wanted to speak with her father about what had been the background at the time. Whether she had a picture of her father, I asked. She showed me one, but I hardly could identify him and if I would have met him on the street I absolutely would not have recognized him.

"He was not a bad man, all his life he has worked at the StB and he believed in it. We have lost forty years of our life," she sadly said – by which she meant: forty years we have believed in the wrong thing. She was a journalist just like me and worked at the daily *Svobodno Slovo*.

"Wouldn't you like to write something about the Netherlands on a regular basis in our paper?" she asked. And that out of the mouth of the one, whose father 25 years earlier put me under lock and key because of my journalistic activities. It could hardly be more bizarre.

I also went to look for a minute at the former prison of the StB in the

Bartolomějská. Now it's a kind of youth hostel, the cells are lodging rooms. Practically nothing has changed. Even the little holes are still in the doors. I enter my former cell. The high window is still there, only it is twice as big and the bars have disappeared. And so has the French toilet in the corner. I start to shiver.

Epilogue 1

After he was dismissed from the hospital, I had the opportunity to contact Pichrt through a Czech colleague. Initially, he let me know he was willing to receive me "because I have nothing to hide." After I had sent him at his request some questions, he backed out and said in a letter that he had been "only a simple employee" and certainly knew nothing about "the events concerning the Dutch embassy" (among other things I had asked him why he had asked me during the interrogation about Hubert Stein) "and even if I would have known the answers, I am not so sure if I could have made them available to you, because they could be part of confidential information, something which is being observed by any retired functionary all over the world." Still he wanted to say that I was detained "because you probably had no journalistic accreditation." The order came from a "higher unit" to which he added the information "that it was known that your activities in the *CSSR*[1] were not in agreement with the status of a journalist who you were alleged to be." But then all of a sudden it shows that Pichrt's memory still works very well, "The circumstances of your arrest – shortly before, you had burned certain docu-

---

z těchto důvodů musím Vaši nabídku na osobní setkání a natáčení rozhovoru na video kameru odmítnout- s přihlédnutím i k té skutečnosti, že se necítím plně zdráv a nebyl bych tedy ani pro Vás ani pro paní redaktorku Hodíkovou "důstojným protihráčem" do novinářské debaty vedené v intencích otázek, které mi byly zaslány.

       V dokonalé úctě

                    Ing. Jan Pichrt.

P.S. Tento dopis zasílám na adresu pí. Hodíkové a omlouvám se, že jej píši v češtině, spoléhám však na její pomoc s překladem (tak, jak tomu bylo doposud u Vašich dopisů mně),za což jí tímto děkuji.

Letter, dated September 7, 1996, of former StB-agent Jan Pichrt to DV, signed by him "with the deepest respect."

---

[1] Pichrt uses here the old abbreviation for "Czechoslovakian Socialist Republic."

ments in the fireplace, of which the security service had no idea what they could have been – were the cause that the suspicion against you increased that you committed illegal activities. On top of that came your personal remarks that you had been able to avoid police pursuit by disguise, which created the question what the reason was for your conspiracy." He could not remember the questions he had put to me, only "that they were based on orders from [his] superiors." I was accommodated in a cell for preventive custody. "Not any law was violated, not even concerning the length of your detention and you got the same food as all other detainees." Actually my case, according to Pichrt "came under the 'central' (the headquarters) and my superiors have asked me at different times about the course of the interrogation. And if there really was talk, as you say, about a 'higher quality of interrogation', that could have meant then that you would have been transferred to the central."

The funny part of his argument is the typical dialectical reasoning. I was mainly arrested by incriminating myself *after* my arrest. In his eyes I still was the one at fault, which did not prevent him from signing his letter "with the deepest respect."[2]

---

[12] Letter of September 7, 1996

CHAPTER 5

Arrested – two

Without problems I had the visa received from the Cuban consulate in Rotterdam. In August 1979, I would go to the conference of the non-aligned countries in Havana. It would be a nice opportunity to take a closer look with my own eyes at the Cuban form of communism, so much praised by the famous, also internationally well-known Dutch author Harry Mulisch and his fellow Castro-adherents. Moreover, Castro's thesis, "The Soviet Union is the natural ally of the non-aligned countries" would be challenged by none other than the Yugoslavian leader Marshal Tito himself. That was in the period that you could not notice that much of the "eternal solidarity" between Yugoslavia and the Russians.

I barely had the visa in my pocket, when the Cuban consulate called with the question "whether I would mind coming around for a minute." At my question whether something was not right with my visa, they denied this emphatically. They called on a Friday and I would leave on Wednesday the following week, although the conference would only start on the following Monday. They invited me for the next Monday. I pretended not to have time and said to call them back later to tell them when I would come to Rotterdam. Apparently, they understood that I understood, because on Monday a telegram arrived at the *NOS-radio*, saying that my visa was withdrawn. My chief Cees Cabout (not particularly the type to spend money like water) agreed with me to go anyway. "You have that visa in your passport, I am fed up with the moaning of those countries, you simply go."

If they were not allowing me into Cuba, I would fly on to Nicaragua, where they had just chased away dictator Somoza. I did not fly directly to Cuba. I made an in-between stop in Houston to look up my Czech friends Jiři and Věra Sekerka for the first time in ten years, who, as mentioned before, had emigrated from Prague via Haarlem to Houston. Jiři Sr. was now a cameraman at a local TV station; she worked as a secretary at an oil company. They lived in a magnificent house in a so typical American subdivision. Own swimming pool in the yard. They would never have reached that prosperity in Prague. But still: that homesickness for the small alleys in Prague, the café's and coffee houses, where it still smelled of the Austro-Hungarian double-monarchy – this homesickness remained. Taking into account the circumstances in far away Czechoslovakia things were going reasonably well with their son Jiří, who had been detained for only one day and had not experienced further problems because of my stay in his commune. He was ill frequently, but the physicians could not find anything special.

At the time, you could not fly directly from the United States to Cuba, you had to go via Mexico-City. On a Sunday I landed from there at the airport of Havana. Passport and visa check. I was allowed through. All hotels were requisitioned for the participants and visitors of the conference. With some other colleagues, who had arrived on the same plane, I was brought by a special bus to "our" hotel, "Nacional." My name was checked at the reception desk by an excellently English-speaking lady from the Cuban Ministry for Information. Yes, I was on the list, I got my special hotel badge and was lodged in room 856. Next day: accreditation at the press center. We had to pass three red tape hurdles, in the form of three wooden tables, each equipped with a male human. I passed the first check point unhindered, the second table also authorized. But at the third things went wrong.

"You are not on the list," the third table said.

I expressed my amazement about that. I had a visa, after all.

The third table also thought that it was due to a misunderstanding, and that it would turn out alright. But for the time being I did not get a badge for the actual press center, so I came only as far as the corridors. The next morning the third table not only said that the problem was not yet resolved, but that pending the solution I could not even remain in the corridors of the press center. Actually, I was turned out of the house. Out of sheer necessity I was forced to do my work from my hotel room. Well, this was not a problem. Yugoslavia played a crucial role at that conference. For that reason a very strong delegation of the Ministry of Information of Belgrade had come along to Havana. The head of the delegation was Tatjana Lazarović, whom I knew very well from my innumerable journalistic travels to Yugoslavia. She stayed in the same hotel as I and through her I got much more information than any of my colleagues, who did have entry to the press center. So from a journalistic point of view I did not feel handicapped at all.

On Thursday the lady of the Cuban Ministry for Information came up to me, saying that the director of the hotel wanted to speak to me for a moment. With an apologetic face he said, while the woman acted as an interpreter, that I had to leave the hotel, because it was only for accredited journalists – and I was not accredited. It was clear that the lady, who acted as an interpreter, actually was the one in command. They took away my hotel badge. I asked where I was supposed to go, because all hotels were, after all, reserved for people who had something to do with the conference. They were of the opinion that this was my own business. Oddly enough they did not say *when* I had to go.

An office of the European Broadcasting Union had been set up in Havana especially for the conference, and I asked them to intermediate. I was considering asking the colleagues of Reuters, who had their own office in Havana, to give me a roof over my head in case of need. I also acquainted the Dutch embassy with my problems and some time later I was called by the then spokesman of the Dutch Foreign Ministry Jan Willem Bertens who urgently requested me to leave Cuba as quick as possible "because it is live-threatening for you." That was not the first time and it also would not be the last time that such news befell me, but I always take it with a grain of salt – but even so, I decided to leave for Nicaragua. That had to go via Mexico-City and the first upcoming plane went on Sunday afternoon at five p.m. The man of the European Broadcasting Union called, telling me that someone at the Cuban Foreign Ministry would sort out what was going on with me. I decided to consider this as a confirmation of the status quo.

The problem now was to bridge the few days until Sunday. I got a lot of support with that from Karel Roskam, then of *VARA-radio,* and Fati Mourali, a Tunisian working for *Radio Nederland Wereldomroep,* the nonprofit world broadcasting station of the Netherlands. When I met the hotel director in the lounge, I translated my optimistic explanation of my status with, "The case is being sorted out, for the time being I am allowed to stay." He could not be happier. I wanted to be noticed as little as possible in the hotel, so Karel, Fati and I did a lot of sight seeing in Havana and Saturday we left by bus for the former house (now a museum) of Ernest Hemingway in Cojimar, located quite a bit outside Havana, and the rest of the day we were lying on the beach. You were not allowed to enter the hotel without a badge, but my colleagues surrounded me tightly and smuggled me in every time. Everything seemed to go alright; even that early Sunday morning, when I was searched for and found by the lady of the Cuban Ministry for Information. She took me aside and told me that I had to leave Cuba. It was not my fault that I had been admitted to Cuba, but it was a misunderstanding. They would pay the round trip Netherlands-Cuba and they would also pay the hotel bill. I told them that I would leave for Mexico-City that afternoon, it all worked out very well. Until around twelve o'clock. Again I had to go with her. Now to another room, where two gentlemen were waiting for us. One was an interpreter, because all of a sudden the lady did not speak English anymore, but exclusively Spanish. The atmosphere was much fiercer, too. I was not supposed to be in Cuba, I was *persona non grata* and had to leave the country immediately. The airplane ticket I had to pay for myself, the hotel bill as well. Now I was certain that the KGB list reached as far as Cuba. I acted dumb. "Why am I an undesirable in Cuba? I have never been here and I have never written about Cuba, what could be the cause?" I asked. That was not the point, I had to go. "Do I have to *leave* the country or am I being *expelled?*"

"No," they answered, "you are not going to be expelled from Cuba, you have to leave it." Actually they said, without explicitly realizing it, that the cause did not lie inside Cuba, but outside Cuba. In the middle of the conversation a third gentleman walked in. He whispered something into the ear of the lady. She stood up and said, "We have to go immediately, your plane can leave any minute." But this was not true at all, we had hours left. I wanted to drag out the time and said that I still had to pay my hotel bill. No, that was not necessary, there was no more time for that. I had to pack my suitcase immediately and go along with them. Lugging my suitcase through the corridor, accompanied by the lady and the interpreter of the two gentlemen, we accidentally ran into my Dutch colleague Wim Janssen of the daily *Trouw*.

"I have to go with them, I don't know where to, probably the airport. Warn the Dutch ambassador," I said. Wim walked outside with me and saw me disappear in a waiting car. The seat felt familiar to me: in the back between my two attendants. We drove super-fast. With some relief I saw that we indeed were headed for the airport. We entered the well-guarded airport through the exit. My two attendants did not need to show any documents or anything; apparently they were old acquaintances.

"Wait here," they said, and left through a door. After some time they returned. The hastiness was gone. I had not only to hand over my luggage, but my briefcase as well, which I had wanted to take along as carry-on luggage. "You will get it back later," That was the way it was, but without my notebook with my notes about the conference. They brought me to the departure hall. I came to sit next to a Flemish/Belgian woman with her child.

"What are you waiting for?" I asked.

"For the *Iberia* plane, heading for Madrid," she answered, "it was supposed to leave at one p.m. but it has been delayed for hours because of hurricane David." So that's what they had wanted to put me on. Thanks to hurricane David it did not work out. The first plane leaving Havana was mine for Mexico-City. For some time I sat and waited anxiously in the departure room, and I only relaxed somewhat when ambassador J.A.M. Verdonk dropped by to see how I was doing. But I only felt really OK, when the plane to Mexico-City got off the ground.

CHAPTER 6

Arrested – three

It is the end of September, but there was still a tropical heat in Belgrade. I'm sitting in a T-shirt and shorts on the elevated patio of my rental home in a small back street in Zemun. For centuries Zemun was the border town between the Ottoman Empire, of which Serbia was a part, and the Hapsburg Austro-Hungarian double monarchy, to which Croatia belonged. The checkpoint was on the bridge across the river Sava – so it was at the same time the dividing line between Serbia and Croatia. Now the town has grown together with Belgrade. Yet it still has its own atmosphere and relatively many Croats are still living there. Nobody cared about this. Until 1991 when the Serbs started ed a war with Croatia. "Keep your windows closed, the place is full of Croats," a Serbian acquaintance once warned me. All of a sudden all Croats were fascists, child-killers, arsonists, throat cutters. It was the Belgrade television itself which said so, so it was true. Well, not all Croats. Every Serb or Serbian did have a Croatian friend – and *he* happened to be a nice guy. But all the other ones... In short, the well-known story of the anti-Semites who all knew at least one good Jew.

The bell of my yard-door rings. I answer the door and there are these two men in plain clothes. The eldest waves an identity card the size of a credit card right in front of me and says he is with immigration service. Could they come in for a minute? They come and sit down with me, outside on the patio. Their extraordinary kindness arouses suspicion. They ask for my accreditation card (every permanent correspondent in Yugoslavia is officially accredited at the Ministry of Information). They look at it and pretend to be very amazed when they see that it is expired, although it is exactly the reason why they came. They put the card in their pocket. Then they ask for my passport. My permission to stay expires the end of January 1995 and is therefore still valid for four months, but my passport disappears in their pocket, too. Then the classical words, "Would you mind getting dressed, you just have to go with us to the police station." I go inside, they politely remain waiting, and before getting dressed I call the Dutch embassy. I tell our *chargé-d'affaires* (due to the war and in protest against it, the western ambassadors were called home) Robert Engels that I have to go along with two men in plain clothes and that I suspect that they will withdraw my permission to stay. I get into the waiting car, but this time both of them are sitting in the front and I am in the back by myself.

At the police station I have to wait in the corridor of the department, where every year I have to extend my permission to stay. I have lived in Yugoslavia for nearly ten years at this point, so I have gradually gotten to know this office. I wait for hours. Now and then I see the eldest of the pair coming out of a door with my passport and going into another one and the other way around. Finally, the time has come. Would I mind coming in for a minute?

"I have a not so pleasant announcement for you," so the eldest, "your permit to stay has been revoked and you have to leave the country within six days."

He hands me an expulsion order, in which it says, that I am going to be expelled based on the law which regulates the stay of aliens; the word violation did not appear in it. I ask for a closer explanation, but unfortunately he cannot supply it, because he is only the executor of the decision – a standard pretext. I can appeal, but only within three days, and I cannot wait for the answer in Yugoslavia. The exile applies for five years.

It is the rounding off of a string of events, which already pointed in that direction for a long time. For months a campaign had been waged against foreign correspondents, whose reporting about Bosnia was stigmatized as "anti-Serbian." The bombardments on Sarajevo were not true, neither were those on Dubrovnik, stories about ethnic cleansing were lies, as were those about systematically blowing up of mosques. Radovan Karadžić was the defender of the Serbian people against the aggression of the Moslems who intended to make all of Bosnia a fundamentalistic Islamic state, which thanks to Karadžić and Mladić and their co-heroes was prevented at the last minute. Who thought and wrote differently from the official media was considered to be not "objective." I was not only counted as a nonobjective, but even considered as an "enemy of the Serbian people."

In December 1992 I had participated in Holland in a full evening's TV program with the theme, "Yes or no international military intervention in Bosnia." That program was almost completely rebroadcasted by the official Belgrade television under the motto, "Just look how anti-Serbia the media in the West are." With in-between "enlightening" comments and here and there "small" changes. There is a Serbian lobby in the Netherlands under the leadership of Jovan Grbić, who also calls himself a correspondent of *SRNA*, the press agency of the "Serbian Republic" in Bosnia. Those Serbs passed on to Belgrade, probably through the Yugoslavian embassy in The Hague, all what is being published in the Netherlands in "anti-Serbian" articles and programs. In this way that TV program ended up in Belgrade, too. On this program I had expressed explicitly to be in favor of a military intervention of the international world "to keep the fighting parties separated." But in the translation they had deleted precisely this sentence, one of those "small" changes. In the Serbian propaganda at the time a military intervention meant: waging war against the justified cause of the Serbian people and bombardments on Belgrade. Not surprisingly, the first thing I heard from an employee of the International Press Center after my return in Belgrade, was, "What do I hear now, you said on television that Belgrade should be bombed." Essentially, she was well-disposed toward me and therefore honestly dismayed about my comments. I gave her the correct explanation, but it goes without saying that I could not do that to every Yugoslav.

It was worse in Radovići. It is a small village in Montenegro on the Adriatic coast, close to Kotor. Since 1989 I have an apartment there, where I frequently used to go to. I was on friendly terms with the population, in the shops I was greeted as an old acquaintance. In April 1993 I went there again for a time. I saw an acquaintance, sitting on the window sill of the local supermarket, but before I could say hello to him, he shouted to me, "How dare you still come here!" He did not want to give nor hear any explanation, he just ran off. The personnel in the supermarket looked at me with hostile eyes, they did not exchange a word with me. At the post office I ran into somebody I did not know, but apparently he did know me.

"You have said on Dutch television that all Serbs have to be hanged," he snapped at me. He also was not interested in a further explanation. The people I really knew well and in whose homes I was a regular visitor remained loyal to me and I did and could explain to them the ins and outs of the matter. Fortunately, that also trickled down to the other villagers.

Two events have diminished my unpopularity in Radovići. On Easter, which is an important religious event in the Orthodox world, I went with an acquaintance to the Mass and walked around the church three times together with all the other church goers. That story was going around in the village and somebody doing that, could not really be anti-Serbian. But the extremists remained active, as it turned out exactly a year later when I was in Radovići again. One morning it turned out, that they had secretly and in the darkness deflated two tires of my truck and thrown away the valves. On top of that they had scrawled on my door with white (as turned out later indelible) paint the famous Serbian national symbol: a cross within the open sections four Cyrillic S-es (two of which in mirror writing), an abbreviation of (in English): Solely Solidarity Saves the Serbs. They had thrown the leftover paint over my windshield and hood *(see photo 24)*.

For many of the villagers that smear-party really went too far. They addressed me on it and at their oft-repeated question, who of all people could have done it, I always answered, "Those were neither Serbs nor Montenegrans, they were cowards." That answer really was to their liking and the antipathy disappeared somewhat. The acquaintance, who earlier had asked me how I had the nerve to return here, now came to me on his own and said voluntarily, "They say I have daubed your car, but I really did not do it." I believed him and we were on speaking terms again.

I rather expected the perpetrators to be in the circles of the Radical Party of the extreme mister Šešelj. It is a Serbian party, but it had also a branch in Montenegro. Its spokesman Jokšimović had a vacation apartment in Radovići also. Together with others he even had organized a petition among the villagers with a request to the authorities to expel me from the village. After the paint-party I warned the police and at the same time also mentioned the petition – and an officer really took some action. The result was that most of the villagers withdrew their signature.

But mister Jokšimović and his ilk had still other strings on their bow. One day I was called by a restaurant owner who, although being very nationalistic too, was still well-disposed toward me. Would I mind coming by for something very important?

On the terrace of his restaurant he told me that Jokšimović and some other villagers had been consulting in his restaurant about the best way to eliminate me. Because of the chance of getting caught easily they found it too dangerous to shoot and kill me in my own home. What remained: to stage an accident with a commercial truck or put a bomb under my car. They had talked so loudly that the restaurant owner could follow the conversation. I was convinced that they had talked that loud on purpose because they knew that the restaurant owner was a good acquaintance of mine, who without any doubt would warn me. Most likely they hoped that I would get scared and run for it. Now the last thing I am buckling under to is intimidation; so I stayed. But of course you never know. I informed the Dutch embassy so that they would know who was behind it if something would happen to me. Furthermore, every time I left by car I just looked under it to see whether something special was visible there. I did not worry about that commercial truck because such an attempt is only possible when the potential victim drives the same route every day.

Before I had left for Radovići, I had to finish some administrative business. My accreditation as a correspondent would expire in April 1994. I had applied for an extension – a matter of routine – but on the date of expiration I still had not heard anything. I called Tatjana Lazarović, but a new gentleman was now in charge. He said that the matter was still pending, but that there was nothing for me to worry about and that he expected an answer the very same week. I said I did not like it very much to drive to Montenegro in these unsettled times without a valid accreditation, but he just waved the problem away, "You still have your old accreditation."

I had barely arrived in Montenegro when the bombshell was dropped. The accreditations of a dozen colleagues were withdrawn. I was not on the list.

And I also did not feel the need to inquire from the new gentlemen how it did work. Both my addresses were known at the ministry, I had applied for an extension, I did not need "to worry about anything" and I "still had my old accreditation." Yet it was not easy "not to worry about anything" when a couple of weeks later the opposition paper *Borba* published a new list of journalists whose accreditation was withdrawn "respectively not extended." Because now I was on it. Technically, I assumed that the paper had made a mistake; after all, officially I had not heard anything, so I continued my work normally.

At the end of June I returned to Belgrade. A few days later the new gentleman reported by phone. Would I mind dropping by at his place, he had something to talk about with me. I asked him what it was about, but he said he did not know. Well, OK, I'll come – and we made an appointment. After an hour or so I had second thoughts. I called the new gentleman again and the following dialogue developed:

I, "We have an appointment for Thursday."

He, "Yes."

I, "You don't know what it is about?"

He, "No."

I, "Then I anticipate the following dialogue. I walk in at your place, I say 'Good day, Sir', you say 'Good day, Sir', then I ask about what I have to come to talk about and then you say: 'I don't know'. Well, I'm not showing up for that."

Profound thinking on the other side of the line. After a long interval the new gentleman says hesitatingly, "I was ordered to tell you that your accreditation will not be extended."

"Why not, what have I done wrong?"

"I don't know why, I only know that you don't get an extension."

"Well, so now I know. Then there is also no need for me to come in."

End of conversation.

Shortly after that the great sensation: the Serbian president Milošević issues a statement in which he rips Karadžić to pieces. The president of Yugoslavia, Zoran Lilić, who did not look like he could ever have thought of a meaningful word himself, talked in an interview about "gangs in Bosnia who committed terror against other nationalities," about "the hell" in which the citizens of Sarajevo have to live and quite a great number of other qualifications which up to then were labeled as "anti-Serbian." The text, of course, was not from Lilić but from Milošević. I drew some hope for myself from the new development and decided to play a little joke on the new gentleman; again by phone. When he answers, I ask, "When will the accreditation of Milošević be withdrawn?" He reacts bewildered and asks me to repeat the question. After I did this he asks, still bewildered, "What do you mean?" I explain it to him, "I don't know why my accreditation is not being extended, because you don't want to tell me, but all the other colleagues lost their accreditation, because their reporting about Bosnia would have been anti-Serbian. But mister Milošević is now saying exactly the same thing that all those colleagues have said earlier. That's why I'm asking: When will the accreditation of mister Milošević be withdrawn?"

He gets angry. End of conversation.

It seemed to me the time had arrived to undertake some other steps to undo the decision. What I had done was to inform the leadership of the Dutch broadcasting, but everybody had stuck to my explicit wish to hush it up. It appeared to me that in this stage a reversal of the decision *after* publicity would be out of the question.

For years, I had a good connection with professor Mihajlo Marković, a Marxist philosopher who in 1975 because of his liberal views was dismissed as a professor at the University of Belgrade. He belonged to the famous Praxis group, an international society of like-minded liberal Marxists around the monthly *Praxis*, published in Yugoslavia. In 1975 *Praxis* was prohibited; the Serbian members of the group were being removed from their functions, the Croats were left alone. Ever since, Marković belonged to the opposition and our contacts intensified in 1984 after my move to Yugoslavia. He was the president of a human rights group that devoted itself to freedom of expression. In those years at least once a week I got a bulletin, on behalf of the group signed by him, in which there was again (and rightfully so) a protest against this or that infringement of that freedom in then still communist Yugoslavia.

After the U-turn of Milošević in 1989 from communist to nationalist, Marković made a still greater skid: he became the ideologist of the meanwhile rebaptized communist party to Socialist Party and actually the right hand of Milošević. Marković revealed himself (and not only he, but a great many of the intellectual oppositionist circles) as a fierce Serbian nationalist, who for instance wholeheartedly agreed with the elimination of the parliament of Kosovo and all infringements on the freedom of the press which went with it. Ever since, our contact did diminish, but we were still on friendly terms with each other. When I asked him whether I could drop by to talk about "a problem" which was bothering me, he immediately said "yes." We talked at least an hour about Yugoslavia in general in the beginning and only after that I brought up the actual reason for my visit and explained to him what my predicament was. Marković's face set and he said, "They must have their reasons for that." Of course, he understood perfectly well what I came for, but he did not say, "What can I do for you?"

So finally I asked him myself. "I am in no way considered a good-fitting party member anymore, so I don't have much influence anymore," he said, pointing to the fact that he had expressed himself against the condemnation of Karadžić by Milošević. When he learned that my permission to stay was still valid for six months, he advised me to just keep on working. He noticed, though, that I did not find this the ideal solution and after some talking back and forth he was willing to do "some inquiring" at the Ministry for Information.

Now a funny chain of conversations developed. At my request he started with Tatjana Lazarović. He made himself known as "Academic Marković," said that I was at his home with him and that he wanted to know what was going on with my accreditation. Tatjana said, she only knew that my accreditation was "not yet extended," but referred him to the new gentleman. Marković repeated his introduction and the new gentleman, electrified by it, hurried to put him through to a higher figure. The electric shock skyrocketed, "Academic Marković" really was a household word: five calls and four minutes later we landed at the vice-minister. Also, he did not dare to make any statement either. He said that the minister, who was busy now, would call Marković back within ten minutes. Well then, this did not happen. Not after ten minutes and not after twenty. I already was at Marković's for a couple of hours and decided I had better leave. I urged him to try to arrange at least a conversation between the minister and me so that I could defend myself against possible reproaches. I simply found I was entitled to that after covering Yugoslavia for forty years, ten of which as a permanent correspondent. He endorsed it and would inform me about what the minister had said.

Marković never called back.

And now I am sitting in the police office with in my passport the invalidated permission to stay, and a new visa in which it says that I have to leave the country by October 5, 1994, at the latest, and that I am not allowed to return before September 27, 1999. For forty years I felt like a friend among friends in Yugoslavia. In spite of my absolute aversion of any form of dictatorship, I had sympathized with their system of workers' self-government, although I have always been aware that it had never worked well. And I was also an opponent of the break up of Yugoslavia. That was not one of the least reasons why I was opposed to the policy of Milošević. I saw in him – and since 1989 I had said that in no uncertain terms – the great cause of that falling apart. That turned out to be fatal for me. I felt deeply hurt that I would be expelled from the country as a scoundrel.

But I had not given up yet. Six days was not much time. Of course, I warned the Dutch embassy, the Dutch Union of Journalists and some other essential organizations, but still accompanied with the request not to bring anything out into the open for the time being. First I wanted to try to arrange something in private through my own stations. I tried my luck and called Marković once again. He said he could not do anything. The uncle of a good friend of mine was the federal Minister of Justice. We would approach him. I knew a few people at the department "Foreign Affairs" of the Socialist Party. They promised to intervene. Late Wednesday afternoon I had received the deportation order, the Thursday seemed to produce some kind of result. The head of the department "Foreign Affairs" of the Socialist Party, Vladimír Krsljanin, said to me that it was impossible to reverse the deportation order. But, so he said, "go to Holland, immediately apply again for an accreditation and we guarantee that the decision will be positive."[13] Did they say that, hoping that I would leave quietly and that they then would have gotten rid of me? Promises in Yugoslavia are, like the dinar, strongly devaluated. In the course of Friday morning it did not look like keeping it in private would have any effect. At two in the afternoon we decided, after consultations with the Dutch embassy, to take the public line. It was the introduction to five hectic days. Official protests and interventions from all sides. Without result. Wednesday the last day. What should I take along? In Radovići I had a fully furnished apartment; paintings, posters, a part of my archives. That was literally unreachable. The rental home in Zemun was fully furnished as well. What *could* I take along? I decided on only one suitcase with stuff for a month-on-the-road.

A few Serbian friends came to say good-bye. They cried. Others I said good-bye to by phone. They cried. They cried because "an enemy of the Serbian people" was going to be expelled from the country.

Back in Holland I applied for and got an audience with the Yugoslavian *chargé d'affaires* Djordje Lopičić. He remarked that "it was not the first time that you were expelled from a country" – a peculiar equalization of his Yugoslavia with the authoritarian regimes in Eastern Europe – and he was substantially influenced by mister Grbić and his ilk. "What would you say if I found that The Hague should be bombarded," he said. And it went without saying that I was an enemy of the Serbian people. "History will prove that Milošević is an enemy of the Serbian people, not me. Vuk Drašković (leader of one of the opposition parties in Serbia) is thinking exactly the same. Or does he also happen to be an enemy of the Serbian people?" I remarked. And yes, Drašković was also an enemy of the Serbian people.[14]

And so I was back again at my Dutch base in the Zaanenlaan of Haarlem, where my parents had started to live in 1935, when I was not yet six year old.

---

[13] Krsljanin has still the same function in the Socialist Party and was one of the main advisers of Milošević concerning his trial in The Hague.

[14] Vuk Drašković was after the fall of Milošević in 2000 and until the Declaration of Independence of Montenegro in 2006 the Minister of Foreign Affairs of the Republic Serbia and Montenegro.

CHAPTER 7

NSB[15]

My parents come from The Hague. Already for hundreds of years both family trees are rooted in that region. I was born there myself on July 4, 1929. My paternal grandfather was a telephone repair and service man, my maternal one was a shoemaker, but he really was *making* shoes, not just repairing them. My father worked as an advertising salesman at *De Vooruit*, the The Hague edition of the social-democratic publishing house *de Arbeiderspers*, established in the Dutch capital of Amsterdam. In 1931 he was transferred to Haarlem, where *Het Volk* was published, as well as the Haarlem edition of *de Arbeiderspers*.[16] Especially my mother as a true "The Hague-girl" could not settle down in Haarlem and within four years we moved four times – the last time to the Zaanenlaan. It was a newly built home, which they bought (with a mortgage of course) for 8,000 guilders, an equivalent of $ 3,000. That was in February 1935, I was not yet six years old. We lived at number 149.

After a few weeks we got neighbors, at number 147. I saw a boy in the front yard of the new neighbors, standing next to their wicket-gate. I went outside, walking to our wicket-gate. Shyly we looked at each other.

"What's your name?" I asked.

"Kees," he answered.

"And what else?"

"Bossers."

So this was Kees Bossers, as old as I was, but a head taller. There was really not much need for that, because I was just a little squirt. Kees and I were going to be bosom buddies. We played with each other, we were regular visitors back and forth, ate at each other's houses. Also, our parents became friends *(see photo 1)*.

It was maybe 1937 or 1938 when at Kees's house I noticed on their dining room table a small wooden shoe. I had never noticed it before, I think it was not standing in its usual place. It was completely black. Only on the nose was an image. It was a white rimmed triangle, the left side was black, the right side red. There were three letters on it. The part where you would have put your

---

[15] See note 2 of chapter 1

[16] There always has been a strong social-democratic press in the Netherlands. *Vooruit* means 'Forwards', *Het Volk* 'The People' and the *Arbeiderspers* " Worker's Press."

foot in was closed, but it had a slit where you could drop in pennies and dimes. It seemed kind of a gloomy wooden shoe to me and I asked Mrs. Bossers what it was intended for. "You are still too young to understand that, you will learn one day," she answered.

Of course, I also asked my mother.

"That is of the *NSB*," she said, but with that I came away none the wiser. Apparently, it was something like the *SDAP*, of which we were a member, but then kind of different.[17]

Once, around the same time, Mr. Bossers asked my parents whether they would allow me to go somewhere. I did not understand why he asked, because we did quite a lot together back and forth. I did find it kind of strange, though, as I went along on the back of Mr. Bossers' bike, that Kees was not with us.

"Kees is already there," explained his dad. That "there" turned out to be a huge tent somewhere in Haarlem. It was teeming with kids in black trousers and blue shirts with sea gulls on them. It was not a meeting, but a "tombola" which, I suppose, had to raise more money than the prizes had cost. Then I came to learn the word "grab bag," a barrel with sawdust in which for one cent you could reach around and grab something. I did reach in, but I really don't remember what I pulled out of it. Mr. Bossers stayed with me, we met Kees, also in uniform. I was about the only one without such a suit. At a certain moment there was singing, I think as a round off, and arms were stretched. I felt like a complete stranger, I did not like it. The neighbor never asked me again to come along and I have never gone to something like that again.

My parents were confirmed social-democrats. Even my grandfathers on both sides were at the end of the 19th century already followers of Domela Nieuwenhuis, the first anarchist-socialist in the Netherlands, and they were among the first members of the *SDAP*. All my The Hague relatives were *SDAP*, by the way. My parents were not fanatical at all and I decided by myself to become a social-democrat, maybe due to the general atmosphere at home, but certainly not due to indoctrination. How tolerant they were is shown by the fact that they had permitted the neighbor to take me along to an event of the *Nationale Jeugdstorm*, the national socialist youth movement "Youth Storm" – because that's what it had been of course. Shortly before the war the Bossers-family moved across the street to number 104, but we remained good friends and Kees and I bosom buddies.

The May days of 1940. Of course, I was horrified that the Germans invaded

---

[17] *SDAP* was the abbreviation of *Sociaal-Democratische Arbeiderspartij*, the pre war Dutch social democratic Labor Party, one of the fiercest opponents of the national socialist *NSB*.

our country.[18] But I understood only vaguely that the parents of Kees were "interned" in connection with it – another new word to me. That's why I found it totally logical that Kees stayed with us for the time being. I did not realize, and I am sure neither did Kees, that we had complete opposite interests concerning the outcome of the war on the *Grebbeberg*, the main battlefield in the center of the Netherlands. I cried buckets when the capitulation (again another new word) was announced and later on I took new hope from that lonely Dutch soldier. He walked in the middle of the street, in full marching gear, his long, old-fashioned rifle over the shoulder. And he repeated only one sentence, over and over again, while walking on as if in a stupor, "Officially false rumors, officially false rumors." Only much later I understood that he was completely rattled by that capitulation report. Fortunately for Kees it really was a capitulation, because it meant the return of his parents. History teaches quickly. Even as kids, or maybe just as kids, we made a simple distinction between good and evil. Not only did we sing, "Holland has fallen by treason," we also believed it. You did not associate with members of the *NSB* anymore. A good month later my parents, little sister and I visited them one more time. It was just after France had capitulated as well. Enthusiastically, Mr. Bossers showed me on the atlas how fast the Germans had defeated the French. Copies of the German propaganda weekly *Signal* were lying around and although no unkind words were said on a personal level, it was the last contact, nevertheless. Yet, Kees lent me a book about the "French times," dealing with the occupation of the Netherlands by Napoleon-Bonaparte at the end of the 18th and beginning of the 19th century. Ironically, it was swollen nationalistic pro-Orange[19]. In January 1996, clearing out the house of my mother

---

[18] The Germans invaded the Netherlands on May 10, 1940. The Dutch army could not match the *Wehrmacht* and, after a heavy bombardment on the civil population of Rotterdam, it surrendered on May 15, 1940.

[19] In 1568, the "Eighty-Years-War" for independence against Spain started, which reigned over the Netherlands at the time. The initiator was William of Orange, "the father of the fatherland." He is the ancestor of the present queen Beatrix of "the House of Orange." During the German invasion Wilhelmina was the queen of Holland. In the last minute she escaped to live in exile in England. From the very beginning of the German occupation every gesture of sympathy with "the House of Orange" was out of the question and punishable. Before the war the national socialists in Holland were very "pro-Orange," because they saw it as a potential possibility for an autocratic state. After the occupation they made a U-turn, because the queen symbolized the resistance against the Germans. The social-democrats, on the contrary, were republicans at heart and therefore had been before the war against "the House of Orange". But they also made a U-turn after the occupation, because they wholeheartedly supported the queen's role as symbol of the resistance. So in every respect a changing of the colors on both sides.

after she had died, I found it back in a forgotten corner. Swollen nationalistic they stayed, the Bosserses, but the orange color had disappeared; except on the caps of the *Jeugdstorm*. Their astrakhan headgear, model-*Wehrmacht*-cap, was still held together on top with a strip of orange fabric.

Kees was no longer our street playmate. We never told him so, he also felt that himself. Once, a few months after the occupation when we were playing some games in front of my house, he joined us. In his *Jeugdstorm* uniform. Immediately we formed a circle around him and started a discussion with him in the course of which we made "anti"-remarks without any fear. Fanatically he defended himself, but he went home when one of us, Jaap Veen, teasingly pointed out to him the contradiction between his convictions and the orange part of his *Jeugdstorm* cap. It was his first and his last attempt; his exclusion would be for eternity.

He belonged to the few of the national socialist kids who went a step further than the *Jeugdstorm*. In 1941/1942 he left for the *Reichsschule* ("Empire School") in Valkenburg, a small town in the south of the Netherlands. It was a German training camp for a kind of Dutch branch of the German *Hitlerjugend*. They were not only wearing soldierlike uniforms, they also got a military training. In 1944 they retreated with the *Wehrmacht*, I assumed fighting, to Germany where he disappeared into nowhere.[20] *(see photos 2a, 2b and 2c)*

Often the *NSB*-members were the black sheep of the family. But the Bosserses were an exception, at least from her side of the family. Her father was a member, as well as her brothers, sisters and in-laws. Her brother, Chris van der Linden, was a gifted professional photographer. We met each other at birthday parties and I found Chris a sympathetic, gentle uncle. The picture he made of my then two-years-old sister is still the official portrait within our family. And yet, this sympathetic, gentle Chris volunteered for the SS and left for the Eastern Front. Uncle Chris with a rifle, I just could not imagine it – and I don't understand it to this very day.

---

[20] According to Himmler the *Reichsschule* was a "training institute for future leaders of the Greater German Empire." The students were members of the German *Hitlerjugend* and the Dutch *Jeugdstorm*. The classes started on September 7, 1942; 66 German and 57 Dutch boys. The teachers were either Dutch SS-men or SS-orientated. In the beginning of 1943 78 Dutch boys were attending the school, of whom more than sixty became members of the *Hitlerjugend*. All students were tested for "race characteristics" by *SS-Hauptsturmführer* Aust. On September 19, 1944, the school was evacuated at the order of *Reichskommissar* Seyss-Inquart (Hitler's governor in the Netherlands) and the whole group pushed off ahead of the front to the northern German province Schleswig-Holstein, so not "fighting" as I had assumed during the war. Still in January of 1945, seven Dutch boys of the *Reichsschule* volunteered for the SS.

How did we find out that Kees left for Valkenburg and Chris for the Eastern Front? After all, nobody had any contact with the Bosserses. And yet, we had never seen either Kees or Chris in their uniforms. But that was the funny thing during the occupation; it seemed as if these kinds of facts were blown on by the wind.

Kees had chosen his way, based on the atmosphere in his home. So did I, based on the atmosphere in my home. A way, which stood at odds with his.

Both, we were ten years old then, being forced at too young an age to make fundamental choices. I had the good luck, not the wisdom, to make the right – he the bad luck, not the non-wisdom, to make the wrong choice.

CHAPTER 8

Occupied

Cor Gerritsen was a "handyman" at the Haarlem branch of the *Arbeiderspers*. Long face, reddish, backwards combed, curly hair – an example of an educated working class guy. As a ten-year-old boy I did not have the foggiest notion of ages. Everybody older than twenty was the same age to me – except my grandmas and grandpas, because they were very old. I know now that Cor was only 35 in 1940. Regularly, he brought us a copy of *Spartacus,* an illegal magazine of the *Revolutionary-Socialist Labor Party* of Henk Sneevliet[21]. I had never heard of Sneevliet, neither had my father, I guess, who was, by the way, no revolutionary socialist at all, but that was not important in those days. As long as it was against the Germans that was all that mattered. Cor always transported his *Spartacuses* conventionally in his bicycle bag on his luggage carrier. My mother already had asked him once in a while whether that was not very dangerous. But he had brushed that aside. It was only 1941, who had experience with illegal work? The mere fact that I, an eleven-year-old boy, was acquainted with these illegal activities, shows that caution did not have the highest priority.

One day my father came home, completely upset. The Germans had arrested Cor Gerritsen. When they searched the house, his wife had just been able to flush incriminating material down the toilet, so my father told us. Yet they had taken Cor along. The first thing my father did was to burn the *Spartacuses* he had saved so far. Shortly after that the consternation and the dismay: Cor Gerritsen was executed, along with a few others (it was the Sneevliet group, so I would learn only after the war).They belonged to the first Dutchmen who were executed because of illegal resistance activities[22] *(see photo 30)*.

The death of Cor Gerritsen, whom I personally knew because of his countless visits, the dismay of my parents and the harshness of the Germans made an indelible impression on me. What's more, it apparently was also a part of my inherent character, that I was interested in more than just playing in the street. Already in the Winter War 1939/1940 I had read with great intensity

---

[21] Although you would expect that the German occupation would have been called "illegal," it was just the other way around: from the very beginning the expression "illegal" and "illegality" was a name of honor and used for every activity directed against the occupiers and their collaborators.

[22] Cor Gerritsen was arrested on February 24, 1942, and executed on April 13, 1942.

in *Het Volk* the reports of the war which was waged on the Karelean isthmus by the Russians against the Finns. I still see the picture in the paper of, as the caption put it, "frozen Russians," before me. Frozen Russians! One in the foreground, on his side, in a fetal position. I looked at that picture maybe twenty times. But my sympathy went to the underdog, the Finns. I did not know anything about communism, let alone the evil deeds of mister Stalin. But a big country that attacked such a small country – that went against my feeling of fair play and consequently I stood on the side of the Finns. How intensely indignant I was about the bombing of Helsinki, on the "civil population," the umpteenth new word that I learned by it.

At home we had what was called in those days "radio distribution," nowadays called cable radio. It was very popular in the Netherlands. At the outbreak of the war there were more than 405,000 connections out a population of nearly nine million. A good 1,025,000 families had their own radio sets. Right away in 1940 the number of cable connections dropped dramatically by no less than 100,000. Officially the number of radio set owners rose by 40,000 – most likely it had been even more.[23] Why? The cable radio was immediately "equalized," a euphemistic expression meaning that all the media were supervised by and from one ideological center which, of course, did not relay stations of the free world. Most popular were the BBC broadcasts in the Dutch language, in popular speech, "the English station." To receive it, you had to buy a radio set, so my parents were one of those 40.000 or more. But most of the time I was the one looking for that station "in the 21-, 31-, 41- or 49-meter band," as it was always announced, and "biking" back and forth between those meter bands. That "biking" was a dire necessity. The Germans jammed the broadcasts, but it went in a kind of wave movement. If the jamming got too strong on one wave length, you quickly switched to another one, hoping that the jamming would be less there. In the course of the day you could scrape together the complete news in bits and pieces.

A cold winter evening in January 1941. The English station is on. I am sitting in the wash tub in front of the fire in the living room for the weekly bath. And then that report: Tobruk has fallen, the English put the Italians to flight. The warm water, the terrific news – the delight penetrates all my pores. I always listened very intensively – even to opinions and comments I only understood partly. Our new neighbor at number 147 was Jan Smit, head of the Haarlem Registry Office. They did not have a radio set and when Mr. Smit

---

[23] At the end of 1941 the number of radio sets had been increased by 150,000 and the number of cable radio connections dropped with 220,000. Data from *Radio Hilversum 1940-1945* by Dick Verkijk, Amsterdam 1974.

came home from work on his bike and I was playing in the street, he always asked me, "And Dick, any news?" – and then I very seriously told him what I knew. Once, I could not have been twelve years old yet, I had listened to a whole discourse on the economic problems of Germany. I had not understood most of it, too, and I hardly knew what the word "economy" meant. But the conclusion had gotten across very well to me and when Mr. Smit came with his standard question, I answered very jauntily, "Economically the Germans will never be able to carry on." Mr. Smit nearly died laughing about it and from that time on, he always asked me teasingly "whether the Germans would be able to carry on economically."

In the first weeks the occupation also literally knocks at our door. My *Junoschool* on the square of the same name behind the houses across our street becomes a German barrack and the German quartermasters have to be lodged in the surrounding neighborhood *(see photo 40)*. An officer-quartermaster of the *Wehrmacht* goes from house to house to see whether somebody has a room left. Our attic room is found suitable, billeting is compulsory. One day I return from school, which is already housed in another building, and my mother says, "Just go and look in the attic." The room is empty but at the table stands a gas mask tin with a German helmet on it. A peculiar smell is hanging around, most likely the polish for the German boots. A quarter of a century later a little girlfriend of my nine-year-old daughter is visiting whose mother has given her a cheap kind of perfume. It has exactly that *moffen*-smell: the gas mask and the helmet are back on that table.[24]

The *mof* is not allowed to accept anything from us, not even a cup of tea. "They are afraid of getting poisoned," the neighbors tell each other, who are also saddled with a *Wehrmachtsangehörige*, an army member. In our doorway hangs a copper colored relief-stamped printing with a broken rifle and the text, "*Nooit meer oorlog* – War never again." The *mof* asks what it means. "*Nie wieder Krieg*," my father translates with pride in his voice. The *mof* laughs condescendingly and makes a gesture of: how on earth can you be so foolish. And when we carefully indicate that we hope for the temporary nature of the occupation, he reacts, "We are only leaving when you eat pebbles with grass." He stayed for only two weeks, then my school was equipped as a barrack. Although the billeting was compulsory, they had promised to pay for it with a guilder (half a dollar) a night. But as to paying they were pretty reluctant.

[24] *Mof* (plural: *moffen*), mostly used in combination with "rotten" (*rotmof*; rotten *mof*), was the term of abuse more than a nickname for a German. It already existed before the war, but got an extra meaning during the occupation. Then it was strictly forbidden to use this term; you could go to prison for doing so. The closest American/English equivalent is "Kraut."

My father wanted his money at all costs, and he complained at least two or three times to the *Ortskommandantur,* the City Headquarters, on the Grote Markt, the Great Market, in the center of Haarlem. In the end, they paid him his fourteen guilders.

In no time the barracks were expanded. The adjoining middle school, the houses opposite the school complex and the houses opposite us in the Zaanenlaan were also requisitioned. The whole complex was fenced off with barbed wire, in the houses opposite us the officers came to live. Nearly until the end of the war we had to look out on it. And to listen to their infamous song, *Erica,* when they were marching in and out the barracks, their *moffen-koppen* rattling on the street.[25] But how intense was our *Schadenfreude,* malicious pleasure, when they were getting trained against the cold after the invasion of the Soviet Union. In those severe war winters they bumped by on the double, only dressed in short, black shorts and white, sleeveless T-shirts, stumbling over the rock-hard frozen snow-clods.

National-socialism was really very quickly noticeable in every fiber of society. In 1941 I attended the secondary school *HBS-B* on the Santpoorterplein.[26] Our principal J. Thie was anything but a hero. He did not resist any German measure. Propaganda posters of the *Arbeidsdienst*[27], later of the *Waffen-SS,* were hanging on the big notice board as well as the infamous poster "English airmen don't know mercy," with which they tried to talk us into believing that the English bombarded on purpose civilian targets, in particular hospitals and schools. To give that propaganda more credibility, concrete measures were taken, with which we school kids were extremely pleased. In 1943, the Germans had stipulated that in case of an air-raid warning the students, who had classes downstairs, had to sit under their desks. Those on the upper floors had to go downstairs and sit in the corridors with their book bags on top of their heads. And all of that to protect us against those "merciless air terrorists." Haarlem was situated directly in the approach route of the Allied bombers on their way to Germany. They did nothing else but fly over, but still every time an air-raid warning was given for it, and in that year Haarlem had more air-

[25] To spare the soles of the German soldier's boots, they had them hammered in with round, blunt nails, popularly called *moffenkoppen,* kraut heads. It goes without saying that this was also a forbidden term.

[26] In the Dutch school system at the time the "primary school" was from 6-12, the "secondary" from 12-17 years, equating junior and senior high school.

[27] The *Arbeidsdienst* (Labor Service) was a direct imitation of the German *Arbeitsdienst*; a military training institute with shovels instead of rifles. Without any doubt it was meant as a precursor of a Dutch national-socialist army, had the Germans won the war.

raid warnings than all other cities in the Netherlands: 150. That is an average of three times per week. And every air-raid warning lasted for hours, because it took quite some time before those thousand bombers, in bunches of forty to fifty, had passed over. And, of course, they had to return, too. It goes without saying that it was a feast for us. We were not allowed to react to the air-raid warning sirens, but only to the electrical school bell, which was to be turned on by the janitor. But there was a difference of only a few seconds. And then off we went. Either under the desk, or in the corridor, so-called with our book bags on top of our heads. We were sitting there for hours, not with the book bags on our heads, but under our behinds, which was somewhat more comfortable than on the hard corridor tiles.

The school program became a total mess. After a few weeks: an air-raid warning again. But no janitor's bell. We pointed out to the teacher the life-threatening situation in which we found ourselves. He brushed our objections aside: no janitor's bell, no danger. That was the end of our air-raid-warning-feast. The principal had taken the heroic decision to no longer respond to the German measure. It never had any consequence. A great number of the principals never executed the absurd order. Also without any consequence.

A quarter of a century later I learned that the North Vietnamese authorities had given orders that school children in case of an air-raid warning had to sit under their desk as a protection against the "American air terrorists," who aimed in particular at hospitals and schools...

One morning in 1942, right in the middle of a lesson, we were told to put on our coats, because we would go to a movie. The whole school went in procession to the theater *Cinema Palace* in the Grote Houtstraat, still a good half hour's walk. Students of other schools were present in the theater, too. The light was turned off and here we got dished up a propaganda movie, *der Hitlerjunge Queck*, the Hitler Boy Queck. Only in 1996, I learned that the movie was made by Hans Steinhoff based on a novel of the same name written in 1933. (In 1943 Hans Steinhoff also directed the anti-English movie *Ohm Kruger,* much applauded by Goebbels, who personally wrote the final scene.[28])

Der Hitlerjunge Queck plays in pre-Nazi Germany. Queck is a member of the Hitler Youth, but his surroundings are against it. He meets with all kinds of unpleasant experiences, especially of course from communists, and he came to meet a nasty end. The purpose of the movie was that you would identify with the underdog, in this case the *Hitlerjunge*. Two scenes are indelibly printed in my memory. Scene 1: Two "communists" are sitting in the waiting room of a

[28] After the war it was shown in the Soviet Union as an "anti-imperialistic" movie with only a slight adaptation and dubbed in Russian.

hospital. Queck enters in his uniform and sits down next to the communists. They make a wry face, get up and move to another spot. We greet this scene with loud cheering. Scene 2, also the final scene: Queck is chased by a bunch of murderous guys, of course again communists. Queck seems to escape and hides himself at a deserted fair ground in a merry-go-round which is covered with a canvas. You see the potential murderers prowling around at the ground. In vain, it seems. Then Queck touches a button which sets the drum of a music mechanism in motion. The drum roll is fatal to him. The "communists" find him, beat him up and he dies in the arms of fellow-*Hitlerjunge* – accompanied by the hymn of the *Hitlerjugend*, "*Die Fahnen flattern voran* – the flags flutter in front" – Queck, *der Hitlerjunge,* is dead. It sounds cruel, I'm aware of that, but his death is received by us with a standing ovation.

They never dragged us to something like that again.

At school we had an *NSB-* teacher Smolders, who at the very first lesson we got from him after the movie event furiously said that we had behaved "scandalously." But we would see what was going to happen yet. The whole school system was going to be changed. It would become much more Spartan. We would have to be at school already at seven in the morning and then do athletics for a few hours. More attention would be paid to physical matters, anyway – we had to become a strong generation. He was a fanatic, always wearing his "wolf's sting"-pin at his lapel.[29] Because of his Nazi convictions he was later on appointed as a principal to another secondary school. His successor, a "botany and zoology" teacher, Postma, was an "anti." Of course, he did not say that, but you knew it. The whole teaching staff was now *NSB*-free.

My first confrontation with the persecution of the Jews was also at school. Fellow classmate Max Herz had to leave school. We felt bad about that, so did he, but on both sides it was taken rather laconically and as a matter of fact, considered as something temporary. The second had to do with my father. He was a member of the social-democratic trade union for salesmen *Mercurius,* a part of the general social-democratic trade union *NVV* which, already two months after the occupation, had gotten a *NSB*-supervisor: H.J. Woudenberg. My father was the (unpaid) secretary of the Haarlem branch. After consultation with Henk Meijer, a paid member of the central board, he continued to stay in office. Incidentally, Henk Meijer was living on our street and was unadulterated "good" – he was the father-in-law of A. den Doolaard, a well-known Dutch writer at the time, who had already before the war written anti-Nazi books and articles in *Het Volk*. He had also been able to escape at the last minute and ended up in London. Very soon he would be famous as the commentator "Bob of Radio Orange," the radio station of the exiled Dutch government

---

[29]   The "wolf's sting" is an old rune sign, used by the *NSB* as a fascist symbol.

in London.Henk Meijer followed the general policy of the leftist movement in those days: stay in office to prevent being replaced by members of the *NSB*. So my father stayed in office. Until his Jewish colleagues were thrown out of the union – that was too much for him: he resigned.

On the Delftlaan, a street around the corner, the (Jewish) family De Vries was living. Jettie was our age and played with us in our street. All of a sudden she had disappeared. The whole neighborhood knew why, "They have left for Switzerland." My reaction was ambivalent. On one hand: yes, of course, for Switzerland, very good, as if it was quite logical to go to (unoccupied) Switzerland just like that. On the other hand you realized all too well, that you could not leave for Switzerland just like that at all. But you did not doubt the good outcome of such a journey. For us kids it was all so unreal. Sometimes the most complicated things were possible, the most simple ones excluded. We learned to live in an absurd world, to deal with the most horrible events, which absolutely did not mean that we were accepting them, and we were bewildered about the visible separation between Jews and non-Jews when "the star" was introduced. You did not see much of it in Haarlem, but once I went with my mother to Amsterdam – in 1942, I guess. We were riding by streetcar along the Damrak, the main street going downtown from the Central Station, and I did not believe what I saw. I was sitting on the left side and looked out of the window – and saw an ocean of yellow stars. I don't remember anything of the train ride to Amsterdam, nor what we were going to do in Amsterdam – I only see that image in front of me: the swarming of people with yellow stars on the left-hand side of the Damrak.

In those days a junk dealer from Amsterdam used to call at the house – with his yellow star. Apparently, my mother sold him something from time to time, otherwise he would not have kept on returning. He spoke with an Amsterdam accent and when he wanted to convince my mother that he really, honestly and truthfully was giving a good price, he always said, "reallonestrumam." What he was called, we did not know, nor where he lived in Amsterdam. In the family circle he was called, "reallonestrumam." "Reallonestrumam has been here again," my mother used to say when in the evening she reported a new sale to my father. But our Amsterdam junk dealer was not allowed to travel by train at all.

"Don't you think it is dangerous to travel by train?" my mother once asked. He shrugged his shoulders and shifted a small case in his left hand over the star on his worn-out beige tweed coat – to show that he was hiding his star when riding the train. Suddenly it was all over. "Reallonestrumam" did not show up again. Never again. Was he picked up in the train, after all? Or a "normal" victim of the raids?

In Haarlem you saw increasingly fewer yellow stars. So-called "full-Jews" either were in hiding (in Haarlem one/third of all Jewish citizens) or forced to move to Amsterdam. From there they went through the transit camp Westerbork in the eastern part of Holland to the final station: Auschwitz. Finally, the so-called "mixed marriages" (of Jews with non-Jews) were also forced to leave for Amsterdam. The Van Dantzich family of number 161 was one of them. The whole neighborhood felt bad for Mr. Van Dantzich, because he so visibly suffered under and was literally weighed down by that star on his coat. He did not dare to hide it completely, nor did he want to show it openly. He kind of tinkered a briefcase against it. With the departure of the Van Dantzich family the last "Jew's star" vanished out of my image.

In retrospect, on one point I have not been particularly on principle: I very often went with friends and girlfriends to the movies, even though it was "forbidden for Jews." I must confess that it did not even occur to me to make the consideration: yes-going/no-going – otherwise I might have backed out. As children we found the discrimination of our Jewish fellow schoolmates and neighbors terrible and yet we passed by the signs with "Forbidden for Jews" thoughtlessly, without the feeling that we suffered from a lack of solidarity. Some parents forbade their children to go to the movies, not because of those signs, but because they did not want them to be exposed to Nazi propaganda of the *Wochenschau*, the weekly *UFA* news reel, and of the shorts. We considered it a ridiculous argument, because who would really go for that propaganda? Shortly after the invasion of June 6, 1944, we went with our steady group of friends to the movies, especially for the *Wochenschau*. The Allied forces had just conquered Bayeux (a few miles inland) and we were dying for pictures of the Allied soldiers on Western-European territory – even if those would be wrapped in German propaganda. And we were gloating over the twisted commentary that made it appear as if the Allies were wiped out, whereas the film pictures, shown in chronological order, made it perfectly clear that the Allies were going forwards and not backwards. Within our group was a girl who was pretty spontaneous and whom we had impressed in advance to keep quiet. But Tini Buis, that's how she was called, expressed loud sounds of protest when the *Wochenschau* showed pictures of British prisoners of war who, with their hands up, were being brought in by soldiers of the *Wehrmacht*. I pulled at her jacket to silence her. Ten years after the war she emigrated to the United States. At the fiftieth anniversary of the liberation, which I absolutely wanted to experience in the Netherlands, for the first time in 51 years I again saw the pictures, to which Tini had reacted so loudly, in one of the many commemorating documentaries. A week later at a reunion of our war-children-group I saw Tini back: for the first time in forty years. A few months later we were married.

Even things which after the war turned out to have been true, we did not believe, because to us everything that the Nazi's said was a lie. But once I was kind of impressed. That was when they showed a long pipe at the *Wochenschau*, which a soldier put on his shoulder. He aimed at a tank, pressed the button and from the back of the pipe came a jet of fire. The tank, not far from him, burst open. *Panzerfaust*, Tank Fist, it was rightfully called. Bazooka. To me it seemed like a tremendous weapon.

CHAPTER 9

Resistance and "resistance"

Recently the myth came into existence, "Shortly after the war they made it appear as if the Dutch people as one man heroically resisted against the Germans." This was never claimed, that's why it's a myth. It did not stop the creation of the counter-myth, "The Dutch people failed miserably." Well, this is not true either – and consequently this allegation is a myth as well.

Practically everyone was anti-German in the years forty-forty five. The war and the certainty that the Germans would disappear very soon were the talk of the day, even in 1940 when that certainty was based on nothing more than the *wish* that it soon would be over. When you were in a shop – and they were always crowded in those days – everybody talked openly "anti." Nearly nonexistent were the fear and the reticence I later found in Eastern Europe where almost no one dared to make critical remarks in public, although the punishment for "anti"-remarks in the German time was considerably more severe than under the communist regimes – with the exception of the Stalin-time. Dutchmen are no trigger-happy hoodlums and – once more it has to be repeated – the Dutch landscape does not lend itself that much to imagination-appealing guerilla warfare. But nowhere else in the occupied countries were so many illegal papers but in the Netherlands: 1176. Easily a good twenty men were engulfed in running even the smallest, local, illegal paper: producer/editors and distributors. So close to 25,000 Dutchmen engaged in it; nearly half a division to translate it in military terms. And from 1943 on there were 300,000 *onderduikers*, hideaways.[30] The punishments for the hiding of *onderduikers* were draconian. By no means were these punishments

---

[30] *Onderduiker* (plural: *onderduikers*) derives from the verb *onderduiken*, literally translated: to dive under. Originally it comes from the fact that people, whom the Germans were searching for, hid themselves literally under the floors of homes. There are no American-like basements in Dutch homes. Very often hatches were sawed out in the floor and in case of danger the person looked for, literally "dove under" the floor in the crawl space between the soil and the floor. Later, when *onderduiken* was a mass phenomenon, they went into hiding in the countryside, but also out there on the farms, special hiding places were constructed. Under the so-called *Arbeitseinsatz* every male of working age was forced to work in Germany, unless he had a (German) "permit of indispensability" for the Netherlands. Hundreds of thousands did not go or did not return from their leaves and "dove under."

always executed, but you never knew. And making an underground paper was good for the death penalty. A hideaway stayed mostly with a family; four persons on average. When there were young kids in that family, you had to teach them to keep quiet. In other words: some 1,2 million Dutchmen were engaged in hiding 300,000 fellow citizens – by all accounts this comes easily to one and a half million. Oh sure, not a spectacular resistance, but it withdrew 300,000 men from the German production process for two years. And these are only two examples. Based on documents of the *Nederlands Instituut voor Oorlogsdocumentatie* (the Netherlands Institute for War Documentation), I have calculated that altogether from a minimum of 1,830,000 to a maximum of 3,370,000 Dutchmen were involved in some kind of resistance against the occupation, of whom 330,000 tot 450,000 served as hosts to Jews in hiding – of a population of 8,834,000.

The Dutch people resisted the Germans as one man? Absolutely not. But did the Dutchmen for a great majority fail? Absolutely not either. Among the vast majority there existed an anti-German consensus, which provided, as it were, a safe haven in which the relatively high percentage of anti-German-activists-no-matter-in-which-form could move around. But what about the Dutch Jews? After all, in spite of all those helpers, nowhere in the Western-European-occupied countries was the percentage of deported and exterminated Jews as high as in the Netherlands, wasn't it? With this, the wrong argument is made: of the 140.000 Jews 115.000 perished, consequently "the Dutch people" have failed. The criterion ought to be: how many Jewish Dutchmen wanted to go into hiding, how many could not find a roof over their head and perished *because of that?* The vast majority of the Dutchmen (Jewish and non-Jewish) did suspect around 1942/43, when the deportations started, that it was going to be very difficult for the deportees, but industrialized mass murder, like it happened in Auschwitz and Sobibor, was beyond our power of imagination at the time.

In the fifties a serial on the German occupation was shown on the Dutch TV. Once they interviewed a former member of the resistance, who was sent to Auschwitz as a political prisoner. Still during the war, he was released and it goes without saying that he returned to his underground circle of friends. He knew about the gas chambers, he knew how the Jews were being killed. He told his friends about it. They listened to him without any comment. Only after the war, when the existence of the gas chambers was common knowledge, they approached him again on this subject, the former member of the resistance was telling in the interview, and they said, "When you showed up with that story during the war, we did not want to say it in your presence. But after you left, we said to each other: 'He has gotten such a mental blow because of that concentration camp that he does not know the difference anymore between truth and fantasy." They simply had not believed him. And yet it concerned people who expected the worst possible of the Nazis, but that they would be able to do such things, was beyond their power of imagination, too.

Telford Taylor, the American chief prosecutor at the trial of Nuremberg in 1946, writes in his book *The Anatomy of the Nuremberg Trials* that his co-prosecutor Robert H. Jackson in his statement spoke about "'incredible events' so incredible, indeed, that despite compelling evidence of the death camps as Auschwitz, which leaked through in America during the war, few people had believed such reports. One such person was Jackson, who now described himself as 'one who received during this war most atrocity tales with suspicion and skepticism'. I was another who had shared this attitude, and, judging by the shocked reaction of Jackson's listeners, most of them were also erstwhile skeptics."[31]

In September 1944, a postwar friend of mine, Ab Caransa, and his father were transported by freight train from *Theresienstadt* in Czechoslovakia. Where to, they did not know, so he writes in his book *Dag meneer Blom* (Goodbye Mr. Blom):

"After 36 hours we noticed that we were close to Breslau, the present Wroclaw. Then we knew; we are on our way to Auschwitz. Nobody in the cargo wagon knew exactly what Auschwitz meant, but everybody had occasionally heard about it. Nobody had, however, the slightest imagination whatsoever of what precisely was going on there." After arriving in Auschwitz, both passed the selection, still not realizing what this meant. They saw chimneys and asked fellow prisoners, who already were inmates of the camp for some time, whether the chimneys were part of factories. They got evasive answers. "Until somebody said: 'Every missing person has disappeared through the chimney.' We did not understand. Then they explained."[32]

Even he, who was in Auschwitz, who saw the crematoria, saw the gas chambers and got the hint that human beings were disappearing through the chimney – even he still did not understand what was going on. September 1944. Because even with the unimaginable in front of your eyes, the unimaginable remained unimaginable.

Should the Dutchmen in 1941-1942 in the Netherlands have known more than the September-1944-Dutchmen in Auschwitz? Even if in 1942-1943 the horrible truth would have become common knowledge, it would have been too late, because the deportations were already over and done with.

Holland was the only occupied Western-European country with a civilian

---

[31] Telford Taylor, The anatomy of the Nuremberg trials, page 169, New York, 1992.

[32] *Dag meneer Blom*, Ab Caransa, Haarlem/Netherlands, 1997.

Nazi administration, all other countries had a military administration, which left much more to the older, prewar administrators. Of course, also there were *S(icherheits)D(ienst)* bodies (the German Secret Service), but nowhere except in Holland could they set up such an efficient investigation machinery, just because of that civilian Nazi administration. And the Nazi's in Holland played their sinister game with great shrewdness. Jews who would not register as such but go into hiding, would, if detected, be sent to a concentration camp, so they threatened, implicating that the ones who did register would "only" go to a labor camp. That's why many Jewish fellow citizens also did not *want* to go into hiding – rather the "certainty" of a "labor camp" than the possibility to end up in a concentration camp. That has nothing to do with naiveté. Naive is to suppose that we (Jews and non-Jews alike) could know the truth at that time. On the basis of the knowledge *then*, realistic choices were made. Only in retrospect it turned out to be an *apparent* realism. It is true, many found it too dangerous to take in Jewish *onderduikers* and underground help assistants sometimes had to go by many addresses. But how many Jews have perished, because no address could be found for them and the help assistant had to say, "I can't find anybody, just report to the Germans." According to me this has been a high exception. And if this is true, it means that also in this respect the Dutch society did not fail.

The consensus was that, if a German soldier asked the way, you showed him the wrong one. We kids also participated in that, but you really had to take care to get away before he noticed that he was fooled. At the end of our street there runs a canal which was converted in the war to an anti-tank-moat *(see photos 34 en 35)*. In a common effort a friend and I once pushed a "Spanish rider" (a construction of steel beams against tanks) into the water of that moat. Of course all this did not amount to anything, but you wanted to do something "against."[33]

One Saturday evening in 1941 *Radio Orange*, the London-based radio station of the Dutch government-in-exile, asks us to scatter V's around or to chalk them on walls the next day. The V for *Victorie, Vrijheid* and *Vrede* (Dutch for victory, freedom and peace)
  I make seven of them. The next morning my father and I bring my cousin,

---

[33] In Dutch they were called *Spaanse ruiter*, for us during the occupation a well-known apparatus. Apparently not for the Americans. The famous WWII reporter Ernie Pyle describes June 12, 1944, in his report on the invasion how he saw on the beach of Normandy "those great six-pronged spiders, made of railroad iron and standing shoulder-high, just beneath the surface of the water for our landing craft to run into", but he has no name for it. Only later they would be called a "hedgehog."

who had stayed with us for a couple of days, to the station. I drop one "V" secretly in the Extended Cronjéstreet, formerly Julianapark.[34] A little bit further down the street: another one. And then the highly unpleasant surprise: right across the whole width of the Cronjéstreet hangs a banner, "V = Victory, because Germany wins on all fronts."[35] They had simply taken over the action. Yet I do throw down the other five, too. Fortunately more clumsy "V"'s lie on the ground. Those are the good ones. The nice ones are the bad ones.

Once more, I have reacted to a broadcast from England. That was on the day the capitulation of Italy was announced, on September 11, 1943, also a Saturday. It was a warm, summery evening. We played on the street. We were beside ourselves with joy. We had to do something. Someone came up with the idea to pick flowers from somebody's yard, ring their bells and say, "Congratulations on the capitulation of Italy, here you have a flower from your own yard." For a reason I really don't recall, I was considered to be the best-suited person for this job. At random we picked homes, I rang, recited my text, handed the flower over and it was kind of appreciated. Again I ring a bell: a WA-man answers the door[36] in best bib and tucker including sword-belt and black boots. Here I was with my little flower. I gathered up my courage and gave the NSB-er the full text, "Congratulations on the capitulation of Italy, here is a flower from your own yard." But then I got out of there as quick as I could. The WA-man did not leave it at that. He ran after me, I heard the rattling of the ironwork on his boots behind me. Every time when he was close to me, I made a U-turn and got a small lead again. Every time I hoped to reach home, but he kept catching up with me. Finally he got me. He grabbed me by the collar and dragged me to his house. There, he forced me to pick up the flower and let me go with a sturdy kick on my behind. It was indeed the last flower I offered that night. My parents had their weekly bridge-evening with their friends and fellow-party-member-couple Geerlings and when I told them what had happened to me, my indignant mother wanted to go to that WA-man to lecture him, but my father and her bridge partners could convince her that this would not be a wise act. You did these kinds of "anti-"things by reason of that com-

---

[34] During the occupation all the names of the royal family were erased from history. So it was ordered to change the names of all the streets, parks, avenues named after them. Juliana was the daughter of the then exiled queen Wilhelmina. That was the reason that *Julianapark* was changed to *Extended Cronjéstreet*.

[35] From the grammar point of view it was such an illogical construction, that very soon everybody joked, "V = Victory, because a canary is also yellow."

[36] *WA* was the abbreviation for the militia of the *NSB*, an imitation of the *SA* storm troopers of Nazi Germany.

mon consensus. You simply did not count on such a *WA*-man. People used to call at the house to offer things for sale with the recommendation: the profit is for the *onderduikers*, the hideaways. So in 1944, I bought a metal cover for my ID card at the door, also "for the hideaways." It was even made by them, the salesman told me. Maybe it was not even true, but it is characteristic that it counted as an excellent sales argument. By the way, I still have that cover and my ID card has been preserved in excellent condition inside it. It's now displayed at the permanent exhibition "Child in Wartime" in the Municipal Museum in The Hague.

The Germans also were familiar with that consensus. One day a friend of mine and I walk in the street, being somewhat tiresome. He has a paper in his hand reading out loud in a reciting style. On the other side of the street a *Wehrmacht* soldier comes and rides up in the opposite direction on his typical German bike. He doubles back in a curve, summons my friend to come over to him and punches him in the face just like that. Amazed we ask him why he did it. "You called me a *mof*," he says to my friend. We deny it, truthfully and most emphatically, because we hardly had noticed him. But he took it for a fact that my friend had cried *mof*. Apparently, he was, knowing the Dutch, so keen on it that he also heard it when it was not even said.

At my school the same consensus prevailed. And we also showed it. On Wednesday and Saturday the *Jeugdstorm* and the *WA* had their meetings. From about 1942 they went to school in their uniforms; altogether a dozen of about 300 students. Our school's inner court had a yard in the middle. Normally, during the recesses we would gather around, walk every which way or stand and chat in small groups. Not on Wednesday and Saturday. Then the *Jeugdstormers* and the one *WA*-man of the highest grade walked squeezed together around the yard. In front of them a gaping space. Badgering, all the other pupils walked close together, at quite a distance from the *NSB*-bunch, behind them. This was not agreed upon, it just happened as a matter of course. The *NSB*-children responded in the only right way – they pretended as if nothing was going on. The teacher's room on the first floor looked out on the schoolyard and quite often we saw that he teachers radiantly observed, behind the curtains, those twice-a-week demonstrative processions. But our scaredy-cat-principal was, of course, scared to death again that it would get out of hand. Because all of a sudden there was a new regulation: we were no longer allowed to go outside during the recesses on Wednesday and Saturday.

But in the classrooms the uniforms led to problems, too. Generally, our classrooms had one-person-desks. But in "botany and zoology" we had two-seaters. *NSB*-teacher Smolders had already left and Postma had taken over his job when the *Jeugdstormers* came to school for the first time in their uniforms.

The lecture starts. Frits Groen, sitting next to *Jeugdstormer* Frans Schifferstein at the second desk-in-front, raised his hand. When Postma asks him what it is, Frits says, "I don't want to sit next to someone in a *Jeugdstorm* uniform." Queck revisited. Profound silence and great tension in the classroom. How would Postma react? He is confronted with an immense dilemma, but he tries to avoid the problem by calling something to the effect of, "Stop nagging." And he wants to continue the lecture. "Sir," cries Frits, "I really don't want to sit next to him." Postma tries again to sidestep the problem with a wave-away-gesture. But Frits insists and says for the third time that he does not want to sit next to that boy. Most likely, all this time Postma has given the matter feverish thought and he has found a brilliant solution. Quasi-angry he says to Frits, "Now I'm fed up, for punishment you go and sit at the very rear all by yourself." Frits stands up, satisfied, and goes off to his "punishment"-place.

It goes without saying that just because of that consensus the war time for *NSB*-children was a highly unpleasant period, regardless whether they were convinced members of the *Jeugdstorm* or forced by their parents. In the summer of 1944 our family with some cousins and friends (among them my schoolmate Joop Jonkman) was camping on the campground *Saxenheim* in Vierhouten, a small village in the center of Holland – already before the war our regular spot. We got in touch with three girls, seventeen, eighteen years old, who had rented a house trailer on that campground. I thought I vaguely knew the darkest one of the three and when they told us they were also from Haarlem, all of a sudden I saw the dark one before me in a *Jeugdstorm* uniform – most likely, I had spotted her around the home of the Bosserses. I was not sure, so I carefully asked her, "Do you happen to know well Frans Schifferstein?" Timidly she said "yes."

"Then you are a member of the *Jeugdstorm*," I concluded.

She understood that she had to won up and did not deny it. And then all three turned out to be members of the *Jeugdstorm* – one was Elly, daughter of "Bakkers Wallpaper" in the Cronjéstraat, one of the better-known *NSB*-members in Haarlem, the second was called Lottie Koning and the dark one Thea Meesters. They begged us not to tell anybody that they were *NSB*.

"Everybody is giving us the cold shoulder, and for once we were longing for a nice vacation without anybody knowing we were *NSB*-er," they said. And then that peculiar vacation mechanism started working. In the Haarlem society at home, we would have turned our backs on them. But they and we alike had just stepped out of our normal society for a little while: we promised to keep it a secret *(see photo 5)*. But it turned out to be superfluous. *Saxenheim* was full of (permanent) *onderduikers*, hideaways, we all knew it, and everybody knew for instance "Piet (Pete) the marine," who openly prided himself on his fighting in the May days of 1940 in Rotterdam against the German *Fallschirmjäger*, paratroopers.[37]

On a sand flat just outside the campground, popularly known as the *Gobi desert*, was literally an underground accommodation established in case there would be a raid, and the managers of the campground checked the political reliability of every unknown vacationer. The girls already had been weighed and found wanting. The management asked my parents to warn us that those girls were "at fault"[38] – but that's what we already knew. On the other hand it has to be said that the girls knew darned well that there were hideaways at *Saxenheim* – there were dozens of youngsters around who clearly fell in the age category *Arbeitseinsatz* and actually ought to be in Germany.[39] Opposite our tent three *onderduikers* were camping, also having contact with the *NSB*-girls. They were warned by the camping management as well, but they did not break off the contact either. For their part, the girls also held on to the unwritten vacation-consensus: they have not betrayed anybody – they were already glad that they could go around "inconspicuously."

For the same reason *NSB*-ers often did not wear their party badge, because they could in a manner of speaking smell the dense smoke of contempt when they did wear it. This fault was so widespread that the *NSB* leadership required their members to wear their badges on their lapels. It really was different in Eastern Europe. There the communists were wearing their badges provocatively and arrogantly and in many cases the reaction to that was submission by the noncommunists, most of them were too frightened to show their contempt.

Relying on that consensus may also go all wrong. It would have been September of 1940; I had just started in the highest grade of the elementary school. We were taught by the principal Mr. Van Eerden. He told us a story the content of which I have entirely forgotten, but he ended it with the exclamation, "Long live the queen," to which he immediately added laughing, while covering his mouth, "O gosh, I'm not allowed to say this." A classmate, Cora Cannemeyer, told this at home. What nobody knew, however: the Cannemeyer family was *NSB*. They belonged to the prewar "secret"members and had not yet openly

---

[37] On the first day of the German invasion on May 10, 1940, strong forces of German paratroopers came down in Rotterdam. Dutch elite marines very successfully defended the bridges over the river Meuse. It was one of the few places of the war theater where the Germans could be stopped. It was the main reason for the merciless bombardment of Rotterdam on May 14, 1940.

[38] Everyone on the wrong side was simply called *fout*, "at fault," the others *goed*, "good."

[39] See note 30 page 87.

stood up for their membership. Mr. Van Eerden was called on the carpet by the Germans for his exclamation and was so frightened ever since that he made all kind of concessions to make up for it, among other things by making tremendous efforts at school for the collection of food stuff among the pupils for the Nazi welfare organization *Winterhulp*, Winter Aid, a straight imitation and even a literal translation of the German *Winterhilfe*. After the war he was heavily blamed for this, suspended as a teacher, fell ill from misery and passed away shortly afterwards.

Cora, already a good singer at school (often we played together "leading roles" in school plays), became after the war an internationally famous classical singer, only all of a sudden her surname was Canne Meyer. *(see photo 3)*

You clutched at every straw which seemed to confirm that the occupation would soon be over. The February strike of 1941 was one such straw. I still feel the excitement, the liberating feeling, the vibration of solidarity that went through the strike region. Would this be the end of the occupation? And the profound disappointment when the strike was put down. And the new hope during the April/May strikes of 1943.[40] Buses were still operating in those days; equipped with a small trailer carrying a wood-burning stove generator, because buses were running on wood-gas. The red buses of the *Brockway* company were running in our neighborhood. From a side street they turned into ours. I went to sit on the neighbor's small low yard wall, a kitty-corner from my home, and peered to where the bus had to come from, hoping he would not show up, because that would mean that *Brockway* was also on strike. The buses did not run that regularly because of the problems with the wood-burning-gas-producing-generators. But still, my hope was building up the longer it stayed away. And how awful the distress: there it came, after all.

Sometimes fines were imposed on cities when in German eyes the population had been up to something "anti." And I was terribly embarrassed when Amsterdam did, and Haarlem did not get a fine.

---

[40] After riots in Amsterdam in February 1941 between the WA and Jews, the Germans arrested about 400 Jews in a raid. In protest a general strike broke out in Amsterdam, the first and only strike in occupied Europe against the persecution of the Jews. It spread quickly to other cities. The Germans proclaimed martial law, executed some people and within a couple of days their harsh measures put the strike down. Even more widespread was the strike in April and May 1943. Shortly after the occupation the Germans had released all Dutch POW's. In April 1943 all members of the former Dutch army were ordered to report to be transported again as POW's to Germany. The strikes were a protest against the order. It ended in the same way as the February strike. The third and last one was the rail road strike of September 1944. See note 44 on page 99.

Woensdag 6 September 1944

Westfront: De Canadezen hebben de stadrand van Boulogne bereikt
en Calais omsingeld. Armentières werd bezet. In België werden Yperen, Kortrijk en Gent bezet. Het 1e en
7e Amerikaanse leger naderen elkaar steeds meer. Het
1e leger rukt nog steeds op naar Aken. Bij Mons(Bergen)werden 25.000 Duitsers, waaronder 3 Generaals ge-
vangen genomen. De verslaggevers maken uit de voort-
durende stilzwijgendheid over de gebeurtenissen in
Nederland op, dat er een hergroepering plaats heeft
en de voorraden aangevuld moeten worden. Ook moet 't
bevrijde gebied van Duitsers gezuiverd worden. Generaal Eisenhower bevestigt het bericht van de Minister
President Gerbrandy, dat Nederlands gebied is bezet.
Hij zegt niet welk gebied. Charleroi werd bezet. Het
3e leger heeft zich met de Amerikanen uit het Zuiden
verenigd. Nederlandse troepen van de Brigade "Prinses
Irene" en Nederlandse ondergedokenen bij Parijs zijn
op weg naar Nederland. Amerikaanse verkenningstroepen
zijn op Duits gebied doorgedrongen en hebben zich na
een geslaagde verkenning teruggetrokken. Volgens een
Reuter-correspondent waren de Geallieerden 6 km van
Metz. Geallieerde vliegtuigen wierpen 3 millioen pam-
fletten waarin werd aangedrongen om te capituleren
boven het afgesloten kustgebied uit.
In Zuid, we kunne nu wel zeggen Oost-Frankrijk werden
Chálon-sur-Saône en Arbois, 45 km ten Zuiden van Be-
sançon, bezet. Volgens Duitse berichten hebben de
Duitse troepen zich op Dyon teruggetrokken.

Luchtfront: Nadat de Duitse troepen 't verzoek om te capituleren
hadden afgeslagen, wierpen Geallieerde bommenwerpers
1500 ton bommen op Le Hâvre. 3500 ton kwamen op Brest
neer. Emden gebombardeerd door "Lancastres". Vannacht
bombarderen Musquito's Hamburg. Van deze twee laatste
bombardementen keren twee toestellen niet terug. In de
buurt van Koblenz en Amsterdam werden treien bescho-
ten door Geallieerde jagers.

Oostfront: In twee dagen zijn de Russen 200 km opgerukt en hebben
de Joego-Slavische grens overschreden, waarbij Turnu-
Severin en Prahovo bezet werden. Hier 80 km van Bel-
grado. In de Transsylvanische Alpen werden Pitesta
en Campoelceng bezet, terwijl 't Roemeense Legerbe-
richt er melding van maakt, dat Russische troepen,
die in Zevenburgen oprukken, in de buurt van Klausen-
burg zijn. Bij Warschau werd Ostrolenka bezet.

Slowakije: De Geallieerden hebben Slowakije wapenen gezonden.

Engeland: Een covooi van 150 schepen uit Amerika aangekomen.
Verduistering in Engeland voor 't grootste deel afge-
schaft.

België: Winterhulp blijft bestaan. Naam veranderd in Nationaal
Hulpcommité. De kooien van het leeuwenhuis in Antwerpen zitten vol Duitse officieren, verraders, Polen
en Russen, wier zaak onderzocht zal worden. Enige verraders zijn al aangewezen en daarna voor 't gerecht
gebracht. Waarschijnlijk zullen zij gefussileerd worden.

The 25th issue of "'t Nieuwbureau" of September 6, 1944.

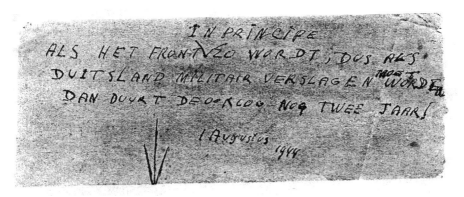

DV's "prediction," pinned on the wall above a map with the front lines if they would go according to his "strategic" understanding. It says: "If the front in principle develops like this - that means: if Germany has to be defeated militarily, then the war will last another two years! August 1, 1944." Although an ardent saver, DV could not find the map back in his archives. He had sketched the future front lines on the map of Europe, every line indicating a time lapse of fourteen days. The calculation was based on the speed with which the Allied and Soviet Forces had advanced until then. Ten days before, the attempt to kill Hitler and to overthrow the Nazi regime, had failed. That explains the adding "in principle," because in his "wisdom," he did not exclude the possibility of a successful second attempt which could have shortened the war.

So we slowly grew closer to the idea that we ourselves had to do something substantial against the occupation. In June 1944 the friend, with whom I had thrown the "Spanish rider" into the water, started a newspaperlet called 't Nieuwsbureau, The News Office, with the news he gathered from "the English station." He was Dik van den Haak, then 17 years old, three years older than I. I lent a hand in the production, it was typewritten with carbon copies and only meant for acquaintances. They knew that we were making it, but because the circulation did not amount to anything, we were not worried that much about it. However, it was kind of unpleasant that a jovial neighbor, when he met us in the street, very kindly but also rather loudly greeted us from his bike with, "How are you doing, gentlemen of 't Nieuwsbureau'?" He was the father of Tini Buis, so it was obvious whom she had gotten it from.

Meanwhile, I had become much more realistic about the course of the war. The front in France got completely stuck after the invasion of Tuesday, June 6. One day in August 1944, I had kind of philosophically looked at my maps of the front on the wall, here and there indicated with a few lines how and at what speed the rest of the war would go off according to me and written down on a small piece of paper, "If the front lines go off in this way, [....] the war will last for another two years." And I pinned it to the top of the map.

Things were moving so slowly that in August we left anyway for a vacation in Epen, a little village in the province of South Limburg close to the Belgian border with a sort of illegal boy scouts group. By train and buses, which were already shot at by Allied planes. To them, the Netherlands was a war zone, to us – and to the adults as well – France was something very far away.[41] Still, I don't understand even now that our parents let us go, all the more since South Limburg was again a good 150 miles closer to the front than Haarlem.

Well, we were going to notice that Holland was a war zone. One day we went by bus from Epen to Valkenburg, a 30 miles ride. A narrow, winding road; I was seated next to the driver on one of those spring seats in the front, admiring his steering skill. Late in the afternoon of that same August 10, 1944, we returned. Halfway, in Wittem stood a burned-out bus – it was ours of that morning, shelled by an Allied fighter. The driver, whom I had admired so much, had been killed, of my spring seat was nothing left but a steel frame.

We had only just gotten back home in Haarlem when the Allied forces in Normandy broke through the German defense lines and a few weeks later Epen was liberated. Subsequently, I got a little bit more optimistic about the length of the war. In those days my father worked in Groningen in the North-Eastern part of Holland. I wrote him a letter, undated, but the postal stamp says: August 22, 1944. The postal stamp itself shows a head with a German helmet, around which is written: *Frontzorg* ("Front Welfare"). Plus the slogan of those days, "Front Welfare is a duty of honor," with the mention, "Pay into giro account # 106156." *Frontzorg,* as it was called in bad, German-like Dutch, was supposed to take care of relatives of Dutchmen who had volunteered as SS-men to fight at the Eastern front against "bolshevism." Propaganda was everywhere, even on the postal stamps.

My letter is extremely short and deals exclusively with the war. After my question whether he had arrived well ("No shooting or anything of the kind?"), I announce to him:

"In France it's over. Almost the entire German army is encircled. The few, who escaped, are fleeing to the German border. In the South of France they withdraw on their heels to the south-west of France. The English are nearly there, though, coming from the North. Montgomery has said: 'The end is in sight.' Toulon is surrounded. Toulouse is occupied by terrorists. In Paris a handful of Germans is nearly defeated by the patriots!!!! More news I don't have. A sturdy hand from your son Dick."

The Germans called everybody in the resistance "bandits" or "terrorists" – so

[41] At that time the distance from my home town Haarlem to the front line was a good 350 miles.

to us, they were names of honor. As the letter turns out, they were synonyms for patriots.

Pretty soon, though, the offensive lost steam and Dik and I decided (on his initiative) not to wait any longer for the arrival of our liberators, but to try to cross the lines, so that we could help with the liberation on the other side. We prepared our trip all week long. Unnoticed by our parents, we collected piece by piece some clothes and food and hid that in his house across the street at number 116. We took a tent along in case we could not spend the night on a farm. We left on October 25, 1944, at four o'clock in the morning, right after curfew[42]. We had told our parents that we would go for wood[43], so they would not find it strange that we set off so early. I put a good-bye letter to my parents between the dishes for lunch time, so that they would not find it earlier than at noon. In that letter I wrote that we had left in southern direction "with the goal to reach the English lines." To put their minds at ease, I said that our plan was worked out into the finest details and that we had thought of everything, "even *Ersatz* tea is in our possession." I also wrote that they would be notified "by the *De Vrije Pers*, Haarlem edition ('The Free Press', a frequently read underground paper), after we have reached the English lines. So don't worry." How would that message have gotten through? Our schoolmate and neighbor-boy Henk Meijer Jr. was the brother-in-law of the (aforementioned) Dutch writer A. den Doolaard, the famous "Bob of Radio Orange." We would have contacted him and asked him to announce via Radio Orange that "D. and D." had safely arrived, with the request to *De Vrije Pers* in Haarlem to publish it. I concluded the letter with, "See you in a liberated Holland and in a liberated Haarlem!!" To underscore the importance of this last sentence, I used the red typewriter ribbon....

Our goal was less daring than it sounded. We had looked at the map to see which town was likely to be liberated soon. That was in our view Kesteren, a very little town in the center of the Netherlands, and we would wait there for the liberation. It was a couple of days walking, though.[44] At the end of the

---

[42] There was a curfew from 08.00 p.m. till 04.00 a.m.

[43] In the last eight months of the occupation there was a lack of everything. The only fuel for heating and cooking (although there was not much to cook; see chapter 14) was wood. Even this was scarce in the heavily industrialized North-Western part of the Netherlands and very soon you could hardly find any of it.

[44] At the request of the Dutch government and the Headquarters of the Allied Forces the Dutch railways went on strike in September 1944 as part of the airborne operation around Arnhem to break the German communication system. The strike lasted till the end of the occupation on May 5, 1945. That also meant that there was no public transportation left in that period. Bicycles were confiscated by the Germans, so the only means of transportation left was your own legs.

```
                                        Haarlem 25-10-'44

Beste Mam,Pup,en Nettie,
        Dik en ik zijn vanmorgen om 4 uur vertrokken in Zuidelijke
richting,met het doel de Engelse linies te bereiken.
    Ons plan is tot in de puntjes uitgewerkt. We hebben ongeveer f. 100.-
bijelkaar gescharreld. We hebben om alles gedacht,zelfs thee-surrogaat
is in ons bezit. We hebben een nood-tent bij ons,indien we niet bij ienbc
kunnen slapen. Zaterdag een week geleden hebben we het plan al opgevat.
Toen hebben we alle wat wat gepakt en zodoende hebben we alles bijelkaar
te weten. Ik heb ook een pakje cigaretten meegenomen,want als je het ge-
ruild had,was mij toch een-vierde deel te beurt gevallen en dus heb ik
een-vierde deel van het te ruilen materiaal "gerequireerd".
    Ook heb ik wat suiker,boter,en een paar blikjes groente-soep meegeno-
men. Ik hoop,dat je het niet erg vindt.Je krijgt bericht,als we in de
Engelse linies zijn aangekomen via "De Vrije Pers", uitgave voor Haarlem.
Maak je dus niet ongerust.
        De hartelijke groeten,ook aan de meisjes,jongens en andere be-
kenden uit de buurt.
                Een stevige poot voor jullie en een kusje voor Nettie.
                Tot ziens in een bevrijd Nederland
                          en in een bevrijd Haarlem!!

        O. Z. O. ! ! !

                                Jullie zoon,
                                    DICK

P.S.  't Beste met je hand,hoor mam.
                D.
Vergeet vooral niet de groeten aan de meisjes en jongens te doen!!!!
                ADIEU.
```

The letter from DV to his parents October 25, 1944, in which he writes that Dik van den Haak and he are on their way to "the English lines." "O.Z.O!!!" at the end of the letter was the abbreviation of the underground slogan during the occupation for "Oranje Zal Overwinnen", "Orange will be victorious."

Kleverparkweg we had to go straight through the railway underpass. But Dik absolutely wanted to turn left, along the Schotersingel. OK, no problem, there we could cross the little bridge to the Bolwerk and then take the other railway underpass. But at the little bridge Dik wanted to turn left again – as a matter of fact back home. And then the truth came out: he had lost confidence in the whole affair, his backpack (with a tent) was too heavy. I offered to take that heavy backpack over, but he wanted to return at all costs.

At half past five a.m. we were back at our starting point, the fiasco was complete and the hangover tremendous. The first thing I did was to take the letter out from between the dishes, so that my parents would not find out, that our trip to the English lines only came as far as the Kleverparkweg, not yet three miles from our home.

The hangover lasted only for a short time. Not across the lines? Then we had to do something else.

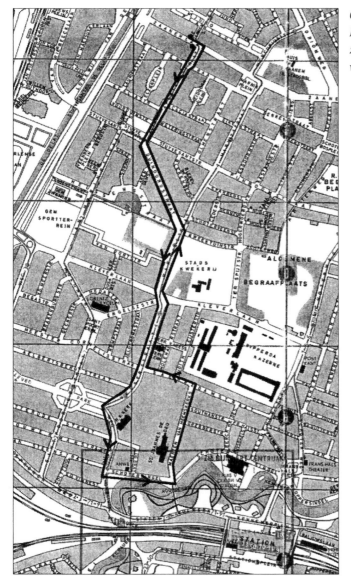

Our futile trip "to the English lines" - a 2 x 3 miles round trip within Haarlem...

CHAPTER 10

The Upright Haarlemer

The question what to do after the fiasco was quickly answered. There was no electricity anymore, so the people who had not turned in their radio set in 1943, were also cut off from the Allied news broadcasts now[45], and the best thing we could do was to stencil *'t Nieuwsbureau* in a much larger circulation. Before the war Dik's father had been a board member of quite a few organizations and, consequently, had a duplicator at his disposal and a reasonable supply of stencils and stencil paper to go with it. Only, the name had to be changed, because too many knew who made *'t Nieuwsbureau*. The name *De Oprechte Haarlemmer* (The Upright Haarlemer) came to my mind, named after the oldest daily newspaper in the world, founded in 1656 under the same name, and of which the publication was prohibited by the Germans in 1941. At the same time, we would continue to publish *'t Nieuwsbureau* in a typewritten form, because it would be too suspicious if this would suddenly no longer appear at the very moment the publication of *De Oprechte Haarlemmer* started.

It was related to yet another risk. On May 15, 1944, the first copy of the school paper *De Omroeper* (The Town Crier) had appeared at the initiative of a senior of our *HBS* Jaap Willems. It was entirely a non-political paper, but in those days not anything was allowed to be published without the permission of the Germans, so the editors remained anonymous.

---

[45] Because of a lack of fuel, we did not have electricity and or gas since September/October 1944. During the occupation the BBC and The Voice of America also broadcasted in the Dutch language, as did Radio Orange of course. Those broadcasts were very popular in spite of the fact that it was strictly forbidden to listen to those stations. If you were caught listening you were sent to a concentration camp. Of course, the Germans and their collaborators used the radio for intensive Nazi propaganda. But they were that much aware of their failure to convince the Dutch people and also of the fact that everybody kept on listening to the Allied stations, that they confiscated all radio sets in July 1943. You had to turn them in and you got a receipt for that. All radio sets had already been registered in the beginning of the occupation, so it was known if you had one and therefore they could easily check whether you had turned in your radio. Again the penalty for disobeying the order was: concentration camp. Nevertheless, many Dutchmen hid their set and kept on listening, even more secretly than before. But this last opportunity disappeared when the electricity was cut off. So the need for Allied news grew immensely and made it more necessary than ever to make underground papers with that news. *(See also "P.S." on page 108).*

It was stenciled by Dik van den Haak, but it had to be sold normally at school, of course. I acted as a kind of liaison officer between the anonymous editors and the students. There was only one signed contribution to the first copy. It was a, by the way very awkward, little poem, meant to pay tribute to the new school paper. The "poet" was me. The paper was a big hit: right away we sold a hundred copies.

After the third edition I was called on the carpet by scaredy-cat-principal Thie. He wanted to know who the makers were. I refused to tell him. But he insisted, explaining he only wanted to speak with the editors, and he guaranteed me that nothing would happen to them. In those years school principals were quite an authority and after quite some back-and-forth-talk, I finally mentioned the name of only Jaap Willems. Immediately he was summoned by the principal and only to him he disclosed the reason of his action. In the third edition an article was published with the title, "To arms – a declaration of war on the mosquito." Malaria was not found anymore in the Netherlands, so the article, "but the possibility of a focus of malaria-infection has been created since on the order of the Germans large pieces of land are inundated with freshwater." The author, probably Jaap Willems, had, as a support, even added a poem of his own, "Kill" with the opening line, "Down with the mosquitoes."

Until this very day we keep on saying that there was no hidden meaning whatsoever in the story, but scaredy-cat-principal Thie was of the opinion that whenever *mug* (Dutch for "mosquito") was written, *mof* was actually meant and that we had said, "Kill the Krauts." And he prohibited the paper.

I was deeply ashamed that I had dropped Jaap Willem's name, especially given the consequences it had and I firmly resolved that I was not going to let it happen ever again.

To avoid a comparison between *De Omroeper* and *De Oprechte Haarlemmer*, we started using other stencil plates for the headline letters. Moreover, there was a time difference of six months between the last copy of *De Omroeper* and the first of *De Oprechte Haarlemmer*, so we did not consider it too big a risk.

We would come out once a week with a circulation of 150 copies with a size of two to four pages. And so on Wednesday, November 1, 1944 the first number of *De Oprechte Haarlemmer* appeared, not even a week after the fiasco "English lines" *(see photo 28)*. Also co-producer for the first two weeks was Ton Kerkhoff, but he had to go into hiding and disappeared to Edam, a famous cheese making town a few miles North of Haarlem.

We followed the same division of labor we used with *'t Nieuwsbureau.* Dik listened to the radio, jotted down the news and put it on a stencil – and I was his handyman. We received all the stations we wanted through a crystal receiver, for me still a greater miracle than television. Without electricity you

1e Jaargang No. 1   Woensdag 1 Nov. 1944

De Oprechte Haarlemmer.

WEEKOVERZICHT.

WESTFRONT.

De vrijmaking van de haven van Antwerpen is bijna voltooid. Na de bevrijding van Zuidzande, Cadzand en het retranchement zijn de Duitsers nu uit geheel Zeeuws-Vlaanderen verdreven. De tussen Ellewoutsdijke en Hoedekenskerke gelande Canadezen, bevrijdden, na eerst met de vanuit Noord-Brabant over de Krekeraksche Dam oprukkende troepen contact gemaakt te hebben, geheel Zuid-Beveland en bereikten de Sloedam tussen Walcheren en Zuid-Beveland. Thans staat de bevrijding van het zo zwaar beproefde Walcheren voor de deur, waar de Duitse troepen en artillerieopstellingen deze week zulke zware bombardementen moesten doorstaan, dat men daar niet veel rekening meer mee hoeft te houden. Sedert Maandag is geen enkele vuurmond op Walcheren meer in actie geweest.

Dit was de belangrijkste overwinning van deze week, uit militair oogpunt gezien. Voor ons in Haarlem echter, is de opmars door Nrd.-Brabant het voornaamste.

Nadat het Duitse front bij 's-Hertogenbosch over een front van 30 km ineen was gestort, rukten Britse en Polse troepen snel naar het Westen op. Daardoor waren de Duitsers genoodzaakt Tilburg, dat door deze manoevre dreigde omsingeld te worden, te ontruimen. Maar ook vanuit de omgeving van Antwerpen rukten de Canadezen in snel tempo naar het Noorden op. In allerijl proberen de Duitsers nu hun 40.000 man, die door de snelle opmars van Geertruidenberg afgesneden dreigen te worden, over de Bergsche Maas te evacueren. Alleen ten Noord-Westen van Bergen-op-Zoom verdedigen de Duitsers, die blijkbaar vast besloten zijn de daar liggende Zuid-Hollandse en Zeeuwse eilanden zolang mogelijk te houden, zich heftig. Zij wierpen zelfs parachutisten in de strijd.

Zo kunnen we thans zeggen, dat achtereenvolgens: Den Bosch, Bergen-op-Zoom, Tilburg, Breda, Roosendaal en Oosterhout deze week werden bevrijd. Met spanning kijken we naar één van Nederlands grootste meesterwerken: de Moerdijkbrug. Want dat is het doel van de snelle Geallieerde opmars, om die belangrijke post onbeschadigd in handen te kunnen krijgen.

Ten Noord-Westen van Roermond begonnen de Duitsers een afleidingsmanoevre. Nadat zij erin geslaagd waren, Meyel te heroveren, en tot Asten en Liesel door te dringen, en een poging om een bruggenhoofd over de Zuid-Willemsvaart te vestigen mislukt was, wierpen de Geallieerden weer uit het veroverde gebied terug en vernietigden 15 van de 50 aanvallende Duitse tanks.

Verwacht mag worden, dat de Geallieerden, na de zuivering van Noord-Brabant, een offensief in de Betuwe, die tot berstens toe met Geallieerd oorlogsmateriëel is gevuld, zullen ontketenen. Tussen Opheusden en Dodewaard werden reeds enige Geallieerde aanvallen ondernomen. Vandaar uit zullen zij dan, met of zonder Moerdijkbrug, naar Dordrecht en Rotterdam oprukken.

Aan het overige deel van het Westfront maken de Geallieerden zich voor nieuwe acties gereed.

OOSTFRONT.

In het Noorden maakten de Russen een begin aan de bevrijding van Noorwegen door de bezetting van Kirkenes en Neiden. Zij overschreden de Noorse grens over een front van 80 km en maakten contact met de achterhoede van de vluchtende Duitsers.

Engelse vliegtuigen bestookten vanaf vliegkampschepen schepen langs de Noorse kust en brachten er 6 van tot zinken. Ook de duikboothaven Bergen kreeg een goede beurt. De Russische vloot beschoot de haven van Vardö. Dit alles ter ondersteuning der oprukkende Russische strijdkrachten.

In Oost-Pruisen kwam het front, na een grote overwinning, weer tot stilstand. De Russen rukten nl. onder de 57-jarige Generaal Tjermanowski over literally pluck the radio waves out of the thin air through that little crystal.

Because of the larger circulation, we had to set up a rather modest distribution apparatus, of course. The 21-year-old Erica van Nunen, whose father had died in a German concentration camp in 1943 (of which they had exceptionally received word), took the biggest part of the edition and she in turn raked up sub-distributors. We did not know who they were and we did not want to know. I myself took 50 copies: 25 for my own distribution area and 25 went to my half-a-year-younger schoolmate Joop Jonkman.

We got busier all the time with our paper and soon it was our daily work, especially after we decided in December to have it appear twice a week: on Monday and on Thursday. It was inconvenient that we had only one head phone at our disposal, which meant that I could not listen in. We put an appeal in our paper for a second one and we received one within a week. Now, both of us could listen; he made his notes in a completely self-invented kind of shorthand system, and while listening, I shifted the needles behind the woolen threads on the maps on the wall, which depicted the front lines.

We were extremely cautious. We had a steady group of friends of a dozen boys and girls, among whom the mutual ties got closer as the war lasted longer. But we never told them – and they never knew – that we produced that paper. Joop Jonkman did not know either. To him I acted as if I got the papers from somebody else, too. Twice a week at a fixed time he came to pick up his part at my place – at least a good twenty minutes walk from his home.

One day, we had big problems with the stencil machine and when he came knocking for the papers, I still was messing around with that stencil machine in Dik's attic. My mother disclosed where I was and told him just to go there and find me. Dik's father called me downstairs and suddenly I saw Joop in front of me, asking for his papers. The only thing I could do was tell him that I myself had not received them yet, and that he should return to my place in an hour or so. And so he did, faithfully, an extra walk of two times twenty minutes. Only after the liberation did he tell me that he understood already then that I was one of the producers "because you had black ink on your hands, but I did not want to tell you, because, otherwise, you might have worried" – a 14-year-old boy; we were precocious in those days. I seriously reproached my mother for her "lack of caution" and impressed on her mind never to do anything like that again.

And not less than 52 years from date, Joop Jonkman told me that "on a Thursday" he got his papers extra late – it had to have been that same day – and that he returned home after the eight o'clock curfew. The risky spot was the Rijksstraatweg, a wide main street he had to cross in order to get from my Zaanenlaan into his Zaanenstraat. About a quarter past eight he got home

– but nobody answered the door: his parents were not in. After another ten minutes, they returned. They had been seized by panic and had left to look for him, because they thought he had been arrested.

Initially, I put my papers through the mail slots in the front door, chosen at random, but later on I had a fixed route in the neighborhood, where I put them in the mail slots of people I was more or less acquainted with (and of members of our circle of friends as well). Only in the darkness, of course, which toward the springtime fell *after* the curfew of eight o'clock in the evening. The chance to be seen was very slim, because in those war times, due to mandatory black out, dark really meant totally dark; you could not see your hand in front of your eyes unless it was full moon and a cloudless sky. Yet, looking back, it was not very smart that I, being a co-producer of a paper, also had a distribution area. If I would be caught, they would be right at the source. I had prepared myself for it, though. If they pick me up, so I thought, they undoubtedly would first take me to my own home. When I would pass by the house of the Haak-family, I would start very loudly to cry and howl, so that they could hear inside that I was caught and clear the attic of all compromising materials. But still, I am not sure whether I would have dared to do that. Fortunately, I was not put to the test and during that time only once I thought that someone was follow-ing me. I kept on going as usual, on the Delftlaan, and took a left turn, into the Wilgenstraat, to put my newspaperlet through the slot of the Mooiman-family. Then, I made a U-turn – straight in the direction of my "pursuer." I am follow-ing the text now of a school essay which I found back by cleaning my archives after I had written the first version of this chapter. I had totally forgotten that I had described that event already earlier. The essay dates back to 1947 and carried the (most likely compulsory) title "Relief."

"What did it appear to be?" so the text of 1947:

"It was a man who, like me, edged his way through darkness and Germans, equally skinny and skittish, at least judging by his face, or rather by his conduct. I believe that he was more frightened by me than I by him."

The essay also notes that I set off with my papers that evening somewhat later than usual "because even the six-o'clock-news was in there."

We not only got those head phones through our readers, but also money. How those channels were running, I don't know even today. Of course, there was among that group of distributors always somebody who had to take someone else into his confidence. That was a risk, but it was impossible to run a pa-per without that. Our paper and stencil stock was not endless and we needed money to buy paper. We asked for it by appealing to our readers and we got it

– through those unfathomable channels. Of course, it happened anonymously under a certain motto, and then we published that motto with the mention of the received amount so that the sponsor could see that it had ended up with us.

Dik could not leave home anymore after the order of the Germans that every male between 16 and 40 years had to report for work in Germany, heralded in Haarlem on December 6, 1944, by a door-to-door raid. He was "within the age," fortunately I still was "under the age."[46] Consequently, I was the only contact with the outside world and Dik also had to stop the typing and shorthand classes we had especially started to take in order to be able to work somewhat more efficiently. I did continue, though, passed my typing exam, and could because of that occasionally take over Dik's task. Slowly the work expanded, more and more often we came out with four pages. I looked for and found other friends who were willing to take on a distribution area and one of them, Jan Veling, a contemporary and schoolmate as well, asked me to do something in return: whether we were willing to include in our distribution apparatus De Typhoon (named after the American fighter plane). But, mind you, we were talking here about some thousands of copies each time. De Typhoon was a printed paper, produced in the northern part of the province of North-Holland, just above the North-Sea canal, which connected Amsterdam with the sea and cut the province in two. I told him I was not able to decide right away, but when I reported to him a couple of days later that we agreed, it had to be canceled: the ferry across the canal was taken out of service which cut off the supply of De Typhoon.[47]

Meanwhile, our circulation increased to 350. Since at least three persons per household could read the paper which on top of that went from hand-to-hand, we estimated that we provided approximately 3000 to 4000 people with the latest news. We felt happy, the hangover of the fiasco was over. We finally even managed to cross the lines, though in a more abstract way. During our vacation in August 1944, we got to know a few girls from Maastricht, the in the mean time liberated capital of the province of Limburg, and we wanted them to know how things were going on in Haarlem. Again, we looked at the map to find out which town, village or hamlet was about to be liberated. St.-Willibrord in the province of Brabant, so we thought. In a letter Dik sketched a picture of the situation in Haarlem and we put it into another letter to "the priest of the Catholic Church in St.-Willibrord." We did not know that priest at all, but we were convinced that he was "good." We asked him to save the letter until St.-Willibrord was liberated and then send it through to Maastricht.

---

[46] There existed standard expressions "under the age" and "above the age" to indicate whether you were either young or old enough to escape forced labor in Germany.

[47] According to a document in the City Archives of Haarlem this happened in March 1945.

Indeed, the small village was liberated pretty soon thereafter, and we learned after the war that the letter had arrived fourteen days after it was sent off. The report even appeared in a Limburg newspaper.

And it turned out to be very good that we did not go to Kesteren. Not only because there was heavy fighting between October and December, which brought severe damage to the town, but also because the liberation did not come there before May 5, 1945, either.

We were not the only ones in our age group to run a paper. I already had my suspicions about some classmates doing "something"also. After the war those suspicions appeared to be true: tens, maybe hundreds of my contemporaries have done the same thing we had – especially because they were the only males in that last year, who could go outside, being "under the age."

In the meantime the liberation was long in coming. The only liberating sound came from the Allied bombers, who flew over day and night on their way to Germany. It was accompanied by a less pleasant sound: that of the German anti aircraft guns. There was probably one positioned on my old school playground of the now German barracks across the street. You heard the blaring blasts of the firing and like an echo in equal rhythm the, somewhat softer, exploding of the grenades in the air. That was going on already for years now. The shooting had become part of our daily (and nightly) life.

P.S.

Just days before the proof prints had to go to the printer, the *Salt Lake Tribune* on November 23, 2006, published an AP article, written by Arthur Max, which confirms what is said in note 45 on page 102: when you were caught hiding your radio you ended up in a concentration camp. The article is dealing with the decision to open the archive of Nazi prison camps, located in Bad Arolson/Germany. Arthur Max found there "a plain manila envelope" with data and possessions of "Cornelius Marinus Brouwenstijn, a Dutchman who vanished into the Nazi gulag at the age of 22 for illegally possessing a radio." He died "sometime between April 19 and May 3, 1945" - so just a few days before the liberation. Not surrendering his radio, meant to him the death penalty. It is impossible to find out how many shared his fate for the same reason.

The picture that goes with the article shows, among other things, his ID card, identical to mine, mentioned in chapter 9 page 92.

CHAPTER 11

Invasion – one

Machine guns rattle close by. Somewhat further up a tank fires off a grenade. In our hotel Pim Korver runs panic stricken, aimlessly, upstairs – and down again. I crawl to the front of the building to look why and at what they are shooting. I don't see anything. The guns of the three tanks across the street are threateningly but silently pointing in our direction.

Prague 1968. On Wednesday, August 21, the Soviet Union and the other Warsaw Pact countries except Romania invaded Czechoslovakia. At eight o'clock in the morning my neighbor had knocked on our window and had cried out to me, "The Russians have invaded Czechoslovakia." I could not believe my ears. I had experienced "the Prague Spring," knew the people who for years had carried up the materials to realize that Spring, and "the socialism with a human face" was in half a year's time so rooted in the Czechoslovakian society that it seemed impossible to eradicate it. I took offense personally. The *VPRO*-TV, for which I worked at that time, immediately agreed that I would try to reach Prague.

We did not have our own cameraman at hand before long, but we found the Rotterdam free lancer Pim Korver willing to come along. Right away, the Czechoslovakian ambassador Pospíšil gave us a visa and toward eight that evening we were at the German-Czech border in Waidhaus/Rozvadov, but despite our visa, we were not allowed to enter. The red-haired border guard, whom I still knew from previous trips, was very kind and on our side, but he had an explicit order to keep foreigners out. It was only a temporary measure, he said, but we had to be patient for a while. In the meantime, foreigners streamed in the opposite direction: leaving was allowed. One of them: Shirley Temple, an idol(et) of my childhood. The child-actress of "On the good ship 'Lolly pop'," now senator of some American state. Sunday, around noon, the border was thrown open. Nowhere a route sign in sight anymore, all street name signs had been removed: the Czechs and Slovaks showed for the first time in history how to perform passive resistance against a foreign intruder.

The Russians had put a ring around Prague and did not allow anybody to enter. The closer we came to Prague, the more nervous Pim Korver got. At the indications of locals, we had found a sort of hidden short cut to Prague. They also had advised us to glue a paper with the symbols "USA" and "CD" on the car "because they dare not to do anything against Americans." I found it a bit exaggerated, because my real license plate clearly indicated that we came from Holland. But Pim Korver insisted that we follow the advice, and so we promoted ourselves to American diplomats. Via a higher road, passing by the famous Barrandov-film studio's, we arrived unnoticed in Prague. We had to be downtown, on the other side of the Motlava, and the Russians had their check points on the bridges, too. Only the pedestrian bridges were free. So Pim would go on foot across the Charles Bridge with his camera outfit, I by car one further down. I would wait for Pim at the other side of the Charles Bridge. Of course, on "my" bridge there was no check whatsoever and there *was* a Russian on the Charles Bridge, "but he happened to be busy with somebody else, and I could go on just like that," according to Pim. We went to my favorite "niche," hotel Evropa on Václavské náměstí, say the Broadway of Prague. Pepi-the-receptionist started crying when he saw me. "Would you ever have thought this?" he sobbed. No, I had to confess, I would never have thought this.

The restaurant of Evropa is on the backside of the hotel, past the check-in desk. It was toward six, we had a bite. But the personnel did not allow us to go outside or even to the front door of the hotel. "At seven they start shooting," they said. And so it was. There was an undeclared curfew, starting at seven. We "tourists" (all of a sudden all journalists had become "tourists") tried with tooth and nail to chat with the crews of the tanks, facing our hotel. They were nice and kind, but toward seven they pointed to their watches: would we be so kind as to return to our hotel? And then the senseless shooting party started: in the air, alongside the gutters of the sidewalk, not at people because they got out of there. You also were not supposed to leave your car on the street "because the Russians flatten it with their tanks," according to the story. It had happened, but very seldom. Yet, to be sure I had put my car in the underground parking garage of hotel Alcron in a side street opposite hotel Evropa.

Filming – given the circumstances it would be very confusing to use the word "shooting" – , filming was an ordeal. Namely, another rumor which went around was, "When the Russians notice that filming is going on, they shoot at the cameraman." But I had come here to shoot something. Pim was not too happy about that. He never had experienced a war, did not know what shooting was, and was on top of that very worried about what could happen to his equipment, because his whole professional existence as a free lancer stood or fell with that. And when we were making the first shots I could feel him think, "You can talk easily, but if they shoot, they shoot at me and you get off free." That's why I told him that I wanted to run the same risk as he did. I laid my two hands on his shoulders, positioned myself close beside him, held my head nearly against his and then I asked him to film, under the motto, "If they shoot at you, they shoot at me, too." But it remained a highly laboriously way of working.

Incidentally, a colleague of *VARA-TV*, Milo Anstadt, was in Prague when the Russians invaded, together with his cameraman and sound technician. After one or two days he and the sound technician had left for Holland with unique material, but did not return. While I was working with a cameraman who asked for nothing more than to return to Holland, Anstadt's cameraman Dick Kool, walking around kind of forlorn, was eager to get cracking. At the time, the telephone only rarely worked, but the telex of the *KLM*-office, practically the neighbor of hotel Evropa, performed excellently. By telex I asked Herman Wigbold, chief of *VARA-TV* program *Achter het nieuws* ("Behind the news"), whether he agreed that I could go on and work with Dick Kool, giving Pim Korver the opportunity to go home. It turned out that, given the circumstances, all the PBS-stations in Holland, had started participating in a joint program, so there was no problem whatsoever. Pim Korver went by train through Vienna to Rotterdam, I continued with Dick Kool who had not experienced a war or shooting either. But the cooperation with him was excellent, he easily kept a level head.

One shot I will never forget. On Václavské náměstí stood one of those wooden hut-on-wheels of Public Utilities along the curb in front of our hotel. To us, it seemed the safest place to interview Praguers at random. Dick positioned himself with his back against that hut. Now we were covered in the back. I stood a little bit nearer to the housing side, my back turned halfway to the camera. While interviewing passers by, I watched regularly, and I may say: pretty skittishly, left and right, whether a Russian patrol was popping up. Everything OK. Until suddenly out of the corner of my left eye a Russian patrol loomed. They had crossed the street right on the level of the left side of the hut and had, after having passed it, turned right. The interviewed man did not notice anything, and the patrol, three men with the rifle barrels downwards, was apparently unaware that filming was going on.

Dick Kool had not noticed anything either; he only saw all of a sudden in his viewer three Russians passing behind the interviewed person. But he keeps a cool head, lets us disappear out of the picture and pans right along with the Russians, zooms in on them so that they remain prominent in the picture and then pans back to us. To me, it's the nicest shot ever made.

Filming was problem A, getting the material out of the country problem B – possibly even bigger than A. In the first week of the invasion there was no air connection between Prague and Amsterdam. But I was lucky. I was asked at the Dutch embassy whether I was willing to bring a stranded Dutch tourist to the border. Immediately, I agreed under the condition, though, that he was willing to take along my film material. This willingness he had. At Monday around noon we left for Rozvadov with our first films, shot since our arrival the day before. I did not have that much time, since I had to be back at seven p.m. A few miles before the actual border crossing there was, dating from former days, a kind of pre-check-point. It was manned by a Czech border guard, who warned us that the actual border was already being guarded by Russians. According to him the Austrian-Czech border at Furth im Walde, about 20 miles to the North, was Russian-free. So we just drove up to there. And indeed, no Russians. My hitchhiker made the last 100 yards on foot to the Czech border post, in his backpack among other things my film reels. Shortly afterwards I saw him leaving the custom's booth, he gave me the agreed signal that everything was OK and continued toward Austria. I had told him that he could fly from the closest airport, being Nuremberg, to Amsterdam at the expense of my TV-station. The next day the reels were in Holland, the very same evening it could be broadcasted.

It goes without saying, though, that I also had to return. I had lost quite some time, having been forced to make the detour to the other border post, and it was way past seven, when I entered Prague. In one of the suburbs I was stopped by a Russian patrol. I was ordered to show my passport (and I know for sure that they could not read it since they only knew the Cyrillic script) and the evidence that I was living or lodging in Prague. They made a shoot-sound and -gesture, from which I deduced the question of whether I had taken guns along, and I answered, "Njet." They asked something else, but I did not immediately understand what. For some time I had taken TV classes Russian, but because of my work I had missed quite a few of them. Yet, over the years I had acquired an East-European gibberish, kind of "Esperanto-Slavic." One of the Russians stamped on the ground and produced a noise that sounded like *podpolje*. Finally I understood: whether I had taken "underground" material along. "Njet." They still would like to check this and that, though. In a storage space under the floor behind the rear seat of my station wagon they found a *Rudé Právo*, the official organ of the communist party of Czechoslovakia. Ah, that was "underground". In my Esperanto-Slavic I tried to clarify that it concerned an official paper. But in those days every piece of printed paper was illegal to them. They confiscated it, but I was allowed to continue.

Right before a bridge across the Motlava, a Czech *Skoda* with a Czech license plate approaches me from the opposite direction. An arm out of the window waves me to stop. Much to my surprise, the arm is attached to a Soviet officer. He does not step out, but asked me who I am. The answer, "a Dutch tourist," apparently satisfies him, I'm allowed to continue. Through a few side streets I wind up at hotel Alcron and dive into the parking garage. Still, I have to cross the immensely wide Václavské náměstí on foot. There is nobody on the street, I cross, on purpose in no hurry; by all means, no running. I reach the other side in one piece. I enjoyed my dinner.

At one essential point, the invasion went wrong for the Russians. The massive passive resistance of the population prevents even the hardest die-hard of the communist party from saying that he "called the Russians for help." Indeed, more than that: those who were suspected (and who were, as it turned out later, all-too-happy with the invasion) stated openly not to have done so. That's why the Russians felt compelled to recognize as a negotiating delegation the arrested party top like party secretary Alexander Dubček and president of the parliament Josef Smrkovský. These negotiations took place in Moscow in the course of which Brezhnev and his ilk literally threatened the Czechs and Slovaks with a bloodbath if they were not willing to give in. Tuesday a "compromise" was reached. The imprisoned leaders would remain in office, but Czechoslovakia had to be "normalized," which meant re-introduction of censorship and some other unpleasantries to go with it. The most important and most fundamental concession of the Dubček-team was, however, their consent for "the temporary stationing of Soviet forces in Czechoslovakia" – which so far, like Romania, had not gotten Soviet troops within its boundaries. To me, it was clear right away: this was the end of the "socialism with a human face," the end of the attempt to unite democracy and socialism in another way than in the West. The liberal communists were allowed to keep up appearances for a while and in a TV-broadcast I compared them with some mayors in occupied Holland, who also made fundamental concessions, though remaining in office, "to prevent worse," a policy which initially had also glued my father to his chair as an unpaid secretary of his trade union in Haarlem. The Czechoslovakian negotiators have *under*estimated the passive resistance in their country, partly due to lack of information about the real situation. I wonder what would have happened if they would have remained firm. Would the Russians really have committed the bloodbath they threatened the Czechoslovakians with?

In a coffee house next to the building of the Czechoslovakian Writers Union (which was occupied by the Russians) in the Národní street, I had a meeting with writer and party member Ivan Klíma. In 1965 I had gotten a lengthy interview with him for the Dutch weekly *Vrij Nederland* ("Free Netherlands"), in which he developed ideas, which were being realized in the Prague Spring three years later.[48]

"Don't you find it strange," I asked, while we were looking out on a Russian gun in the middle of the Národní street, "you are a member of the communist party and Brezhnev is a member of the communist party and yet, you are opponents?"

"Neither of us is a communist," he answered, "we are social democrats and they are fascists."

---

[48] See Appendix page 377.

The Czechoslovakian leaders may have *under*estimated the passive resistance, the population in turn heavily *over*estimated the positive results of the negotiations. That the initially arrested leaders had been released and would return to office was considered as a victory by the vast majority and they did not realize that it was the beginning of the end. That's why the entry of Smrkovský was so tragic. Smrkovský was possibly even more popular than Dubček, not at least thanks to his pro-democracy statements during the Prague Spring which had been much more concrete than those of Dubček.

At the time, the parliament's building was closed due to renovation and the sessions were held in a building at the corner of the Gorki square and the Jindřišská street. Smrkovský, after his return from Moscow on August 28, would go straight from Prague-airport to the parliament. Thousands and thousands of Praguers were waiting for him. I had gotten permission from the employees of a State Bank branch opposite the improvised parliament's building, to film from their balcony, high above the crowd.

There comes Smrkovský, in an open car, waving his hands cheerfully. The people are cheering, they sing the national anthem and here I am, high on the balcony, gone to pieces because I know: it's all over, the people are laboring under delusions. I hardly could get a word out. Powerless. I stood there and looked at it. That was the attitude of the whole Western world. Unavoidable. Military intervention could have resulted in World War Three. Besides, the wrestling from the communist regimes was in de first place a task of the peoples themselves. By the way, I hardly met any Czech or Slovak asking for Western intervention. Yet, it was written in yards' high letters on a façade on Václavské náměstí: *Pomoc* – Help. But this was the façade of a movie theater, where they just were showing the Beatle's film "Help" when the Russians invaded.

On that dramatic Wednesday I interviewed Ludvík Veselý in the office of the *KLM*. He was the deputy-editor-in-chief of *Literární listy,* the weekly of the Czechoslovakian Writers Union.[49] This union, with the weekly in front, had played an essential role in the liberalization of the communist party. It does not make sense to stay here, it's over, was the bottom line of his story, too – and with his small car he left straight from the *KLM*-office for West-Germany. A year later, in the spring of 1969, I was told about the same by Jiří Hochman, editor-in-chief of *Reporter,* the organ of the Czechoslovakian Journalists Union, which had been no less of a driving force in the liberalization. "We have done our best, but it is obvious that the Soviet Union suppresses every deviation of its system with violence. Now, liberalization can only come from within the

[49]   Initially it was called *Literární Noviny,* but in 1966/67 it was prohibited. Shortly afterwards it resurrected under the name *Literární listy.*

Soviet Union itself. Our hopes are focused on Sakharov and his friends. But we shall have to be patient for another generation, before the socialism in the Soviet Union has gotten a human face. Only after that, things can turn out all right in Czechoslovakia," according to Hochman. In spite of that, he remained in Prague.

As early as 1968, some sounds did come from the Soviet Union. A statement of solidarity of seven Muscovites circulated in Prague. On the Red Square they had openly protested against the invasion – and, of course, had been arrested. One of the signatories was Larisa Bogoraz. Her first husband had been Juli Daniel, who in 1966 together with Andrej Sinyavski was sentenced to five years concentration camp – the first trial against "dissidents" in the Soviet Union. Her second husband would become Anatoli Marchenko, a "dissident" too, who already went and still would go in-and-out camps (see photo 18).

I continued to come as long as possible – until 1970. In the first year the "normalization" went a millimeter at a time. Very soon, though, it was not possible anymore to work with your own cameraman. In the year of the invasion I was back three times: in September, October and December. Initially, I worked with Jiří Sekerka. Later, after he had left with me for Holland, I shot with his colleague Vladimír Tuma. In those days, quite a few Czech cameramen cooperated with reporters from the West. It was not allowed, but they did it anyway. The Czechoslovakian secret service StB had taken sides with Dubček during the invasion and was in a process of rebuilding with a lot of help from the Soviets, but in that first year it amounted to almost nothing.

It was no longer a problem to send your film reels in. Pretty soon after the invasion air traffic was resumed and the boss of the Prague *KLM*-office Carel Roosen was more than a businessman. He turned his sympathy toward "the Czech cause" into deeds. He gave our film reels to the crew, who could pass the customs unchecked. "Bread-roll for the pilot," he called it. In that first year I have sent pounds of rolls with them. We were lucky that there was a *KLM* flight on Thursday at three p.m. At the time, *VPRO-TV* had a broadcast once a week: on Thursday evening. In October the students of the Law Faculty went on strike on a Thursday. Until noon I could shoot and do interviews. It went as a "bread-roll for the pilot " to Amsterdam and could be broadcasted the very same evening. Only: did this really happen? And in what form? The fashionable leftishness at the *VPRO* had already broken out under the regime-Jan Blokker. That goings-on with East-European oppositionists did not fit in it. But that's another chapter.

Over time, the StB suspected the cooperation of the *KLM*. In the documentary against me, in January 1971 broadcasted by the Czech television, a photo was shown of Roosen and me on Václavské náměstí – not too big a surprise because we had seen them take it in the fall of 1968 – and we had made fun of it. In August 1970, during my interrogation, major Pichrt asked me straight out whether the *KLM* had transported my films, but I had refused to answer "which is neither a confirmation nor a denial" – in the film and in the article in *Rudé Právo* it was represented as a fact. Most likely Vladimír Tuma had told them (had to tell them?), but they did not have evidence: never ever one step was taken against the *KLM*.

Should the Czechoslovakian army have resisted with arms against the invasion? You can't answer that with a simple yes or no. The Soviets knew Dubček all too well. In his way he was a loyal communist. A few days before the invasion (the plans must already have been prepared), a communist summit conference in the Slovak capital Bratislava had taken place, in the course of which Brezhnev had pretended to agree with Dubček's policy. Shortly afterwards, but still before the invasion, the Hungarian party leader János Kádár and Dubček had (at the request of Kádár) a secret meeting at the Slovak-Hungarian border in Komarno/Komárom. It goes without saying that Kádár at the time already knew more and he tried to warn Dubček in guarded terms. When it became clear to Kádár that Dubček had the fullest confidence in the agreements of Bratislava, he asked in some despair, "Do you still not know those guys in Moscow?"

"Those guys in Moscow" were convinced that the Czechoslovakian army would not get involved and that the invasion would be a piece of cake. If the leaders in Prague would firmly have let it be known, month after month, that they were willing to defend the new freedoms with arms in an emergency, it might have gone differently. Still, the story is going around that in Moscow the Politburo's decision to invade was made with a majority of just one vote. A firmer Prague position beforehand might have changed the vote.

After the invasion, they left it at a prohibition for Czechoslovakian officers and soldiers to have any contact whatsoever with their colleagues of the Warsaw Pact countries. A Polish tank unit was encamped in barracks somewhere outside Prague. At a certain moment a Czech soldier and a Pole, hanging out of his tank turret, got involved in a conversation. A Czech officer angrily approaches his private, prohibits him from continuing the conversation and subsequently spits at the tank. Says the Polish tank driver, "You do not spit at tanks, you shoot at tanks." It was not a Czech who told me this, but a Pole, who was outraged that the Czechoslovakians had not defended themselves.

The Russians were not totally sure whether the action would go off without violence. Across the middle of all the transportation means and tanks of the Warsaw Pact countries a wide, white stripe was painted from the front to the back – to distinguish them from the Czechoslovakian army fleet, after all, consisting of nearly identical equipment.

The war in Czechoslovakia remained limited to one week of senseless shooting at buildings, subjects or just shooting at nothing. The National Museum, at the end of Václavské náměstí, was heavily damaged: the façade was pockmarked by machine guns. The Czechs named that piece of art "El Grechko," created under the leadership of the Soviet minister of Defense Grechko, and in a variation on El Greco.

That was Prague-1968. I did not know what was still waiting for me elsewhere.

CHAPTER 12

Invasion – two

It was pitch dark on the totally desolated road from Knin to Split. September 1990. Knin, a town in South-Eastern Croatia, inhabited by an overwhelming majority of Serbs, had proclaimed itself to be an autonomous territory after a "referendum." It would be the first of a series of referendums by Serbs and for Serbs. They were on the level of asking redheads whether they had objections against redheads. Hence, the surprising result of 99,9% "no" is triumphantly put on the table as a democratic decision. The black-haired have not been asked anything – could not have been asked anything, because they have already been chased away.

Tudjman, president of Croatia since May of the same year, had announced Croatia to be independent, but it still was a part of federal Yugoslavia, and because of that units of the *JNA* (*Jugoslovenska Narodna Armija*, "Yugoslavian People's Army") were still present, spread out over quite a few barracks in the federal state.

On our way to Knin, during the day time, we did notice the Serbian checkpoint, but it was unmanned, so we just kept on driving. It was a gorgeous, sunny day and the guards must have been sleeping. *NOS-radio*, my boss since 1970, had sent Michel Simons to make a documentary together with me on the bizarre situation in Knin. In radio-city-Hilversum, I was not particularly known as a brilliant documentary-maker, although I was as a good atmosphere-describer. So, quite often a good documentary-maker was sent to set off with me to whom I did some talking on tape about the-how-and-what. Then he provided the side-sounds and the sound color – and at home welded it all together into a nice-to-listen-to piece of work.

In Knin, we had interviewed the Serbian leader Milan Babić among other things. Everybody, ordinary Serbs included, advised us against returning to Split in the dark, a good sixty miles south of Knin. I had asked Babić whether or not he considered it irresponsible to let civilians without any police training walk around with guns just like that and to let them man barricades. "No danger whatsoever," he replied. Every citizen or foreigner could just go into and specifically, go out of Knin – the barricades were only meant as a defense against Croatian intruders who were only out to kill Serbs.

"So you also guarantee us that we can return to Split in the dark without any danger?" Wholeheartedly he guaranteed us. It was something to try out, so we left.

Rocks and car tires loom up in the light of the headlights, seemingly thrown on the road surface at random, forcing you to go on slowly and zigzagging; it was obvious that we were approaching the barricade.

There they are. Three, four men – the rifle on the shoulder. We are ordered to stop. They go to Michel's side and are clearly put out, that we violate their unwritten rules by driving in the darkness. Suddenly they notice the lit tiny red lamp of Michel's recorder, which we had switched on to tape some "couleure locale." They get outrageous. One takes the cassette out of the recorder, fiddles his finger behind the tape and pulls it out of the cassette. Another walks around the car, opens my door, pushes his gun against my knee and cocks the gun demonstratively. Now it's my turn to get angry. I yell out to them in forceful terms, as far as my Serbian goes, that I have an official accreditation in Yugoslavia, that I am allowed to make recordings wherever I want to and that they just pulled a tape out of the cassette on which an interview with their chief Babić was recorded. At the height of the argument a quiet, properly dressed middle-aged gentleman jumps up from out of nowhere, calms down the men and asks us in flawless English what is going on. We explain it to him and offer him to listen to the tape with Babić. They return the cassette, the tape is fortunately not broken and Michel rewinds it with the help of a ballpoint. We put a headphone on the head of the middle-aged gentleman, Michel pushes the play button and the gentleman says, "Yes, that's our leader." He shakes hands with us and we can go.[50]

The next day we have a conversation with the director of the Split studio of the Croatian television and I express my astonishment that a handful of armed citizens can erect barricades unpunished. "No government can afford to tolerate this," I remark.

"Technically, it is no big deal, but we dare not take action against it because we are afraid that, if there would be even only one Serbian casualty, the *JNA* will intervene," he answered.

Tudjman, not remotely as shrewd as his alter ego Milošević, had committed two blunders. In the Tito era it was said in the Croatian constitution that Croatia was inhabited by "Croats, Serbs and other nationalities." The first act of Tudjman as a president was to scratch the word "Serbs" out of the constitu-

---

[50] Milan Babić on June 30, 2006, was sentenced to 13 years imprisonment by the *International Criminal Tribunal for the former Yugoslavia* in The Hague, Netherlands, for "ethnic cleansing, including murder of more than 200 civilians." He was going to be a key witness for the prosecution in the case against Slobodan Milošević, but in March 2006 he committed suicide. A couple of days later, Milošević died of a heart attach.

tion. The fact remains that the Serbs used to be disproportionately endowed with regard to the most important political and economical positions. In a way they had been privileged. These privileges were taken away from them. But one, who has enjoyed privileges for years, feels it as an injustice, indeed, when they are taken away from him, certainly if it happens in the untactful way of Mister Tudjman.

The re-introduction of the red-squared chessboard as the state coat of arms was his second blunder. In itself the coat of arms was centuries-old, but after the proclamation of the so-called *Nezavisna Država Hrvatska, NDH,* (Independent State of Croatia) in 1941 under the patronage of Hitler, the Croatian fascists, the *Ustaši,* had promoted it to the state coat of arms, again. Hundreds of thousands, mostly Serbs, have been killed under this symbol. To many present-day Serbs it still is the symbol of the horrors of the Second World War. Open to nuances they were not. For instance, to the fact that this was the coat of arms for hundreds of years; that the *Ustaši* had put a "U" above the chessboard and that the original one even made up the coat of arms of the *Socialistička Republika Hrvatska,* the federal state of the (communist) Yugoslavian federation. Nevertheless, you can conclude that when it comes also to this, Tudjman behaved like a bull in a china shop.

It goes without saying that it was, though, grist to the mill of Milošević and his ilk; the Belgrade horror fairy tales started right away. The "equalized" press and television acted as if the present Croatia was nothing more than the German satellite state *NDH,* they laid on thick the really horrible WWII murders of hundreds of thousands Serbs, those of the Jews and Roma were hardly addressed and those of antifascist Croats were totally overlooked. This frightening card was being played out with just as much verve as shamelessness. For instance, already in 1990, a reporter of the party paper *Politika* wrote about a town in Croatia "where the Serbs are treated exactly like in 1941, when the *Ustaši* invaded it. I had tears in my eyes." Definite lies – but they were being swallowed.

The massive Serbian propaganda made the Serbs in Croatia – and in Serbia-proper as well – ripe for believing all rumors about "those fascist Croats." A kind of "Crazy Tuesday" effect arose.[51] In town A the rumor went around that the *Ustaši* were killing Serbs in town B, thirty miles down the road. This would not happen in town A: just arm civilians and build barricades to keep those *Ustaši* out. As a matter of fact nothing at all was going on in town B. But here they in turn had learned that in town C, another twenty miles down the road from B, Serbs were being killed. So the Serbs in town B armed themselves,

[51] See chapter 14

too. And so between the end of 1990 and the beginning of 1991 the Serbian armed enclaves spread unchecked. Unpunished, Serbs could raid and occupy Croatian police stations to get some extra guns, but if the Croatian police here and there tried to regain them, all of a sudden the Yugoslavian People's Army intervened to stand "between the parties to prevent a civil war." De facto, from the very beginning the *JNA*, though an instrument of the federal government in Belgrade, has defended not the federation but the Serbs – and in doing so highly contributed to the funeral of that federation.

In the meantime, Professor Mihaljo Marković, the ex-dissident, had become the ideological right hand of Milošević, who no any longer called his party "communist" but "socialist." On Saturday, March 9, 1991, hundreds of thousands in Belgrade protested against the propaganda of Belgrade television which nearly ended up with the fall of Milošević. The insurrection was suppressed by tanks, two demonstrators were killed. The Socialist Party convened a press conference shortly after the demonstration on the "Croatian problem," in the course of which Professor Marković also expressed his indignation about "the genocide of Croatia against the Serbian people." When I asked Marković, "You are dealing with the genocide against the Serbs, but the only Serbs who have been killed since Tudjman came to power a year ago, are those of the ninth of March in Belgrade because of actions of the Serbian police," he answered, "Yes, but we should not forget the Second World War," and on my subsequent remark that I was not asking about the Second World War, but about killed Serbs in Tudjman's times, he owed me the answer. But the horror fairy tales continued, with catastrophic consequences.

In Croatia, the spring of 1991 was the indefinable twilight zone between war and no-war. At the end of June, Nicole Lucas of the daily *Trouw* and I traveled by car from Belgrade to Zagreb. Like Slovenia, Croatia had proclaimed itself independent. The Yugoslavian People's Army fought a losing battle in Slovenia but formally left Croatia alone. They had to keep up appearances that the Serbs in Croatia did the job themselves. The freeway Belgrade-Zagreb was totally deserted. It was so quiet that we were wondering whether it was possibly dangerous. We were not overtaken or passed anybody ourselves, and we met only two oncoming cars. A few days later the make-believe-war escalated to a real one – the freeway was cut off: Belgrade and Zagreb winded up on two different continents.

Until the end of June the skirmishes were limited to some shooting with handguns and raids, and only Croatian cops had been killed in the genocide against the Serbs. Just after our arrival in Croatia, the first grenades were being fired – from the Serbian side. It was in Tenja, a small, long-standing Serbian suburb, glued to Osijek, in the middle of Northern Croatia. One day later we were on the spot. A few miles away from the center of Osijek: the Croatian checkpoint. Within view the Serbian barricade. Can we go to the Serbs? At your own risk, the Croats say. We drive slowly toward the barricade. Nothing stirs there. On both sides of the street through no man's land: fire-wrecked houses. Halfway half a truck, hit by the first grenade in the Serbian/Croatian war. Sixty feet down a car, bullet-riddled by machine guns. I don't dare to continue, we turn around.

The next day we have plucked up new courage: we give it another try. Again the no-man's-land-street, again that truck, again that bullet-riddled car: a stiffened picture that underscores the threatening desolation of the area between two worlds. I have acquired a new tactic, which I would apply again at many barricades: I drive slowly and blow the horn loudly, to let them know that I don't want to approach them by surprise, and I hold my left hand high out of the window to let them know that I have nothing shootish in mind. We drive through the opening in the barricade, into which three tanks of the JNA are integrated, the guns pointing at the Croatian checkpoint. A nice illustration of the impartiality of that army, which is there to prevent a civil war, isn't it? We get involved in a chat with a few Serbian militants. Our guns and ammunition? We get it from the JNA, they frankly say. That's also visible because the ammunition chests, spread here and there on the ground, are carrying JNA inscriptions. The commander of the village, a stern but nice guy in his early thirties, intervenes: we are not allowed to talk to rank-and-file warriors. That speaks for itself, because most of them are not from Tenja at all – and that, of course, should not be out in the open. In the course of the day a few other foreign and Serbian journalists drop in and the commander decides to give a press briefing, his rifle slantwise on the table in front of him. He has only just started when from extremely close by the blaring short-but-powerful shots from some handgun sounds out. The commander jumps up, grasps his gun and runs outside. We let ourselves fall down on the floor or jump to the wall, away from the door opening. False alarm. The commander sauntered inside again. A co-warrior just had received a new pistol and liked to try it out. That's what children do with their new little toys.

It developed into a complete war, in which the central government in Belgrade almost openly participated. Just when, in September 1991, the battle started around Dalj, a small town on the Danube in Eastern-Croatia, I was with a few Dutch colleagues on the other side in Serbia, thus Yugoslavia. We crossed by ferry, casually used by the Serbian militia just as a logistical connection. No Yugoslavian authority in sight to undertake any action whatsoever against the on-and-off sailing, heavily armed Serbian rebels. Heavy fighting was going on at the Croatian side, ambulances slid along muddy, impassable paths to the embankment of the Danube where the wounded were transferred into a speedboat and sailed across to the Yugoslavian side. At the shot up police station of Dalj, already in the hands of the rebels, crying women learned that their son or husband had just fallen. It looked like a melodramatic movie, but it was the sad reality.

The war occupied me ever more, physically as well as psychologically, and after a really very shocking incident I longed for my apartment on the Montenegran coast of the Adriatic. There you were far removed from the war turmoil and could you take a breather for a while. So I thought. Until suddenly, on October 2, 1991, *JNA* units, mainly consisting of Montenegrans, invaded Southern Croatia – the second front was sparked off not even ten miles from my apartment. This time without the excuse "that the Serbian brothers, threatened with genocide, had to be protected," because you could not find this "minority" anywhere in these regions. They had invented something new: the Croats had invaded Montenegro, so we were dealing here with a clear case of "self defense." But the Croats in Southern Croatia had only a few gendarmes with light handguns at their disposal and the last thing the badly armed Croats needed was a second front.

Immediately I drove with my truck to Radovići: 390 miles of scenic beauty and road-technical catastrophe. It is nothing but twists along friendly hills, deep canyons and high mountain passes with as a final surprise the panoramic view far below you at Sveti Stefan near Budva, both jutting out into the Adriatic. Woe to those who literally and figuratively hacked this splendid country, once Jugoslavia, into pieces. If hell does not exist, it should be invented for these culprits.

The very day I arrived, I left for the combat area. Just past the resort Herceg Novi, not visited by any tourist since the war, is the Montenegran-Croatian border: Debelo Brdo, literally translated: Fat Hill. Up to that border (in prewar times absolute invisible and unnoticeable) everything is undamaged; immediately, right away after the very first feet, the heap of rubble begins. I know the road to Dubrovnik inside out and how many times didn't I enjoy the small restaurants along the road, eating *roštil* ("grilled"): the *JNA* has flattened everything with mortars and specifically tank grenades.

As the Montenegran television had reported the night before, on October 3 the front line lies between Gruda and the international Dubrovnik-airport Čilipi – three miles across the border. I drive into the area. No one to be seen. After a good mile I stop at the umpteenth ruin. At a distance I hear the typical war-sound – a mixture of muffled bangs and aggressive machine gun fire. I might as well drive on. After another mile I have to maneuver around a shot-riddled and burned-out car, lying in the middle of the road. It's like in Tenja: I don't dare to go on. Before you know it, you find yourself suddenly in the middle of the fighting. The odd thing is that I don't see any soldier either. The *JNA* had not attempted to shield the flanks of its road of advance at all. I turn around and drive back as quickly as possible. After two miles I spot on the right side of the road a lonely Montenegran soldier, kneeling behind a shrub, with his rifle at the ready directed toward Dubrovnik. I know for sure that he was not there on my way in. I stop and ask him whether Croatian snipers could be sitting here. "No, not here," he says reassuringly, "only three hundred yards down the road" and he points in the direction from which I just came. This was not a recommendation to try it once more – I go home.

A day later, it all went more official – and much safer. In Herceg Novi the *JNA* had set up an information center where you could get accredited and you got an army officer to go along with you when you went to the war theater. Mine was a captain in the Navy, Radovan Milosavljević, a extremely nice guy, absolutely not fanatic; he did not impose his convictions on me and when I was busy with my video camera, he never said: you are not allowed to take pictures here.

One day later, the *JNA*, has conquered the airport Čilipi, ten miles southeast of Dubrovnik, according to the evening news of the television. And then all at once adjoining Cavtat appears in the picture. The camera stands on a high hill and looks down on the tourist resort at the Adriatic. It would be a lovely picture if not for the big cannon in the foreground, shooting grenades and ripping the lovely picture apart. "The last resistance is about to be broken," reports the anchor man. Cavtat. One of my favorite spots on the coast. Two, three hundred years old small houses. Promoted from a fishing village to a tourist resort. Along the palm tree bordered boulevard restaurants and side-walk cafés. My first visit was sometime in the seventies. How often did I bring relatives and friends over here? And now they are shooting at my Cavtat.

When I arrive the next day around noon at the *JNA* information center, I learn that Cavtat has been "liberated" this very morning. "If you want, we can go there right away, " says my navy captain

War is a mess on the road. Our route to Cavtat is strewn with boxes, empty ammunition chests, cartridge cases of tank grenades, cars shot-to-shreds, a lonesome bike – by which you wonder what has happened to the rider. Left and right, as far as the eye can see: houses burned out and shot to pieces. "We did not want to bring our heaviest tanks into action to limit the damage as much as possible; we use our old Russian T-52's," my navy captain says, but he frankly adds, "We also do so, because we know that the Croats have no tanks." We arrive at the first place of some size: Čilipi. Not a stone left standing. This cannot be caused by tank guns only, it's all consciously blown up. The only thing that is upright and undamaged is the church.

"As you can see, we spared it," says the captain.

A little way further down: the airport. A totally plundered arrival and departure hall – an absolute empty space. Some bullet holes are to be seen in the windows, but fierce fighting had not taken place here. On a window is written in English, "Don't shoot, we want peace." When a few days later I pass by, all the windows have been smashed.

We turn left, toward Cavtat. The scattered houses along the winding road down: in ruins. I fear the worst. But what a relief: Cavtat itself is practically undamaged. A bullet hole in a window here and there, a few riddled cars, a bus shot into pieces and two mortar impacts, which only resulted in some roof damage. The boulevard lies there unchanged. Only, instead of sauntering tourists, a vigorously marching patrol: soldiers, with guns at the ready with the barrels right up, headed by a commander with his nose in the air – who, seeing me filming, leaves his patrol and marches straight up to me. Fortunately, my accreditation card did have his approval. At the end of the boulevard, they are just trying to pull down the Croatian flag, hanging on a high mast. It takes a great effort – but at last it falls down with a soft sigh. At the sidewalk cafés: only some sprawled sitting, loudly conversing soldiers; the occupiers, behaving like all occupiers: act as if you belong here.

After a week, warning posters of the local commander with the to me all-too-well-known announcements are hanging everywhere: at which time you have to be indoors, that you can't sail in the harbor with your boat without permission, that it is punishable to undertake activities against the *JNA* and yes, also this: that you are punishable if you know that others want to undertake activities against the *JNA* and you don't report this to the commander.

Those were the days swarmed with truces, meant for eternity but of which the real length usually did not last longer than a few hours. During one of these truces the Swedish photographer Jon Magnus, who had dropped in on me, and I were allowed to go to the farthest point of the "truce line." Two hundred yards before that point we made a stop for a while because we had an excellent view of the Croatian territory on the other side of a bay in the Adriatic. Right behind us the several meters-high name sign "Cavtat," pitifully hanging slanted because one of the supporting legs was shot bent. While standing there, we heard some mortar fire and little fountains, still hundreds of yards away from us, jumped up out of the sea. But we would go a good two hundred yards down yet to see a valley bridge, which was blown up by the Croats. "But keep driving on the left side of the road because the right side is not yet mine free, " my navy captain warned. We were maybe halfway when the bangs became frighteningly louder. Suddenly, panic stricken, fast-running soldiers appeared around the bend of the road, yelling, "Back, back." Because of the mines I could not turn around, so I backed up as fast as possible, while ear deafening bangs could be heard above the sound of the engine. What was it about? *JNA* soldiers had used the opportunity of the truce to repair the valley bridge. Obviously, in order to be able to advance more easily because truces are there to be violated. The Croats were aware of it, tried to prevent the repair and shot at the soldiers. But in the evening the television reported "that a Swedish and a Dutch journalist had witnessed that the Croats had violated the truce." Quite a few times, I would return to Cavtat. Very soon Dubrovnik was completely cut off from the outside world. The *JNA* had literally passed it by, taken the upper road and conquered some towns further on. They did shoot at Dubrovnik but mainly aimed at the outskirts. The Montenegrans had cut off the water supply, there was no electricity anymore and the food situation was also getting critical. That's why delegations of Dubrovnik and the *JNA*, throughout all the truces and shootings, frequently conferred under the supervision of European observers. That took place in Cavtat because it was easy sailing from Dubrovnik to Cavtat, a twenty minutes trip and in normal times a beloved tourist outing. The negotiations always amounted on paper to something and de facto to nothing, thus the usual pattern.

It seemed to me, though, an exquisite chance to get into isolated Dubrovnik. At the arrival of yet another delegation I asked the mayor of Dubrovnik, Pero Poljanić, whether I could go along with him back to Dubrovnik. He had no objections whatsoever. I informed my navy captain Radovan of my attempt: he wished me good luck – I already said he was a nice guy.

It was already dark when the "negotiations" were finished. I walked along with the Dubrovnik delegation and in the crisscross I slipped along on the boat and twenty minutes later I stood on the absolute pitch black quay of the marina of Dubrovnik, world famous because of the Yugoslavian tourist poster of better days. This time a successful attempt to cross the lines and dressed in an outfit, which was also familiar to me: the suit I wore, my cassette recorder and a tooth brush. The only hotel still open was Argentina. Here, all foreigners were accommodated: a few journalists, European observers, a UN representative and Bernhard Kouchner, the French under-minister for Human Affairs, who in 1999 would become the UN governor of Kosovo. Outside hung a huge flag of the United Nations, in the hope that the hotel would not be shot at.

After a few days of rambling around, one thing was clear to me: the military defense of Dubrovnik did not amount to anything. From Argentina on the southeastern side of Dubrovnik a road, maybe two miles long, runs steeply upwards. There on the top were the *JNA* guys with their cannons and rocket weapons, right at the spot from which that picture was taken for the world famous tourist poster. Between Argentina and the *JNA* was no defense line whatsoever. Compared to that, the situation at the northwestern side was considerably better. There is the district-Lapad with the big harbor of Dubrovnik, a good four miles from the southeastern point. The main street on the northern side of the harbor makes a right turn at the end and just around the corner was the front line. There were at least twelve land mines lying here and there on the road, and I estimate the number of men put there for defense at at least four. A Dutchman, living for years in Croatia, who had volunteered for the Croatian militia, confided in me that Dubrovnik did not have more than ninety fully fledged soldiers at its disposal. To Kouchner I advanced the not-too-daring thesis, that the *JNA* could conquer Dubrovnik in half a day. "Half a day? In a quarter of an hour," he answered. Obviously, it was a political decision not to occupy the city.

The historic town center of Dubrovnik had gotten only a few impacts then, but everywhere around it was in a few weeks time hit by hundreds of grenades. Most of the damage was limited to windows, roofs and attics, but the tourist centers like hotels were gun-shattered into obliteration. What was left in terms of hotels was overcrowded with refugees; also in our hotel refugees were accommodated. Even Serbs were living in a half-destroyed hotel. They got the same treatment as their Croatian partners in misfortune.

I stayed for a week in Dubrovnik and at that time, the end of October/the beginning of November, it was relatively quiet. I did not hear any grenade impacts and there was only some sporadic shooting with machine guns. After that week, the mayor and his delegation were again going to negotiate. Now, for the first time, the trip would go overland to the Army headquarters in Kupari, halfway between Dubrovnik and Cavtat – and I got permission to ride along with them. We went around the bend in Lapad – the four defenders had pushed the twelve mines aside a little – and a good hundred yards down was the Yugoslavian check point, which let us pass without any problem. Via the splendid upper road we crossed the destroyed landscape with the all-too-well-known picture: not one house which was not shot-out or burned down. The members of the Dubrovnik delegation, coming here for the first time since the blockade, were too dazed to say anything; they just muttered somewhat under their breath with drawn faces. In Kupari, we were awaited by a multitude of journalists who had come from the opposite side, accompanied by my navy captain, who greeted me as a lost son. The mayor of Dubrovnik watched kind of surprised by that heartfelt greeting between that *JNA* officer and me, whom he had not exactly gotten to know as an advocate of the Montenegran invasion. "I was already worrying about you," so Radovan, "if you had stayed away one more day, I would have warned the Dutch embassy."

I did not wait for the result of the negotiations, the driver of Radovan brought me with his car to Cavtat and then, off I went with my own truck to

Radovići, where I could keep on following the war turmoil on television: heroic stories about brave soldiers. And stories full of compassion when things
went against them, not at the front but with the weather: images of sad soldiers in their tiny tents, because it rained, and then it is impossible to wage
war. Once, when the temperature went below +70 degrees and in addition
even the wind strengthened, the suffering of the brave soldiers was absolutely
immeasurable. Nice-weather-soldiers they were, who wanted to march on, enjoying the sunshine, the sleeves rolled-up, the bullet strings crosswise over the
chest. There was not much discipline. Some took the weekends off, others just
did the opposite. The guns were carried loosely in the pockets. For their weekend off, many had, in order to get home, to take the ferry across the bay of
Kotor and once, a soldier emptied his machine gun, straight into the air. That's
what he thought. But he hit the lower part of the wheelhouse of the captain
who shouted from his window whether there wasn't something else he could
do. Not a few came from the front with their "own" car, with no license plate.
They had stolen it from a fled Croat. Sometimes loaded with other looted stuff.
The increase in the number of unlicenced cars in the region kept pace with the
number of miles the front shifted westwards.

On Friday, December 6, the old historic town center was shot at, according
to the news media, denied, however, by the JNA. On December 7, a group of
journalists (all but me "Small"-Yugoslavs) went at the invitation of the JNA
press center to the spot-of-the-poster-picture. Far below us Dubrovnik was lying, at first glance undamaged. I even could distinguish hotel Argentina. On
the spot itself: cannons and rocket weapons. The soldiers on the top denied,
too, that they had shot. "We have noticed it came to blows among themselves,"
so they said. They also alleged that the Croats had set fire to car tires to make
the press believe that fires had broken out in Dubrovnik. I wanted to have
a look for myself. Now, this went easier. After many negotiations they had
agreed that twice a day, a boat would sail between Lapad and a hamlet in the
bay of Lapad which was in the hands of the JNA.

Sunday, December 8. A small boat, the Croatian flag on the masthead, moors
at the "hostile" landing. An armed Croatian militia man gets off first and starts
a lively conversation with his also armed "enemy" of the JNA-army. We are allowed to go aboard and seven minutes later we stand on the quay of Lapad,
the commercial harbor of Dubrovnik. Hitchhiking, I reach the entry gate of the
historic town. And then the grumbling rage takes possession of me. Not one
of the premises alongside the famous Stradun is left undamaged. Already on
the centuries-old pavement between the gate and the clock tower, I count more
than 40 grenade impact holes. The famous 14th century Franciscan monastery
got 23 hits. Next to it, two historical premises are completely burned down, a

fate they shared with some eight other ones in side alleys. Yesterday, up there, appearances had been deceptive. The war in Yugoslavia is fought with mortars. Their grenades don't penetrate walls, they do go, however, through windows and roofs. From a far distance, everything seems to be alright, only from close up you notice what damage they have caused. All shops along the Stradun are blown out, all attic floors shot to shreds. So is the barber's shop where just a month ago I had been shaved, it is one big heap of rubble inside. The rubble of pulverized stones and broken glass grind under my feet. And so do my teeth, and I say out loud, "This is barbaric." A seemingly "nonjournalistic" subjective reaction, seemingly, because it is based on objective observation. There are events, incidental as well as historical, in which not-taking-sides equals deceit. And I am happy to be able to say that Montenegran friends explicitly came to tell me how ashamed they were of that bombardment on Dubrovnik.

As early as Saturday, I had learned that officers of the JNA were invited by mayor Poljanić to come and see for themselves what the JNA had caused. I even had asked permission to come along, but it had been refused. A cameraman of the (Small-)Yugoslavian television did go. The mayor himself showed the officers (who were in plain clothes, of course) and the cameraman around. They did not say a word, the mayor told me later. The cameraman took plenty of shots. Not one millimeter, though, was broadcasted in Montenegro or Serbia because according to the "equalized" media over there the shooting never took place. However, there has been a dialogue between Dubrovnik and the JNA by telex, in which the commander of the JNA, Pavle Strugar, alleged that a unit started shooting without orders from the army leadership. This was a downright lie. The UN representative in Dubrovnik told me that Sunday, that after the shooting started at nine o'clock in the morning, he immediately by his satellite phone warned the UN headquarters in Geneva, Switzerland, which in turn at once notified Belgrade. But the shooting just kept on going. From nine to one with a frequency of six grenades a minute and from one to five of one a minute; a total of 1700 grenades on an area of not yet 0.6 square miles.[52] A mistake or a shooting without an order can take place for half an hour, an hour at most, not for eight hours.[53]

---

[52] My calculations and data are based on personal observation and talks to UN-, EU-, and Red Cross functionaries on the spot. According to a later official publication of mayor Poljanić, there would have been twelve hours of uninterrupted shooting, by which two thousand grenades landed on the historic town and immediate surroundings, of which four hundred did not explode.

[53] The *International Criminal Tribunal for the former Yugoslavia* in The Hague, Netherlands, considered the bombardment as a war crime. In 2004, Pavle Strugar and his chief of staff, Miodrag Jokić, were brought to justice. Strugar pleaded not guilty and was sentenced to eight years' imprisonment. Jokić pleaded guilty and got seven years.

Life in Dubrovnik was highly unpleasant at the time. There was hardly any food, no running water, no electricity, no heating. It also happened to turn bitter cold in December. There was a terrible storm blowing and the temperature lay around the freezing point – something very rare in that area. The hotel people did what they could. Every day they poured fresh seawater in your bathtub. But just try once to brush your teeth with seawater. Yet Dubrovnik appeared to be just a little prelude.

CHAPTER 13

Invasion – three

Heavy explosions. White spots which slide in half bows along the black sky like in a slow-motion movie. Baghdad 1991 revisited. But this is no repeat of the famous CNN report. Not Baghdad on television, but Sarajevo in reality. It's Wednesday, April 29, 1992, three weeks after the beginning of the war of the Serbs against the central government in the Bosnian capital.

The first shots fell on Sunday, March 1. The foundation for this was laid in December 1991 by the European Community. The nagging of the German minister for Foreign Affairs Genscher did not only lead to the recognition of Croatia. No, it befell the European leaders to ask the Bosnian government as a political snack-in-between to just inform them whether they also wanted to be recognized as an independent state or that they would rather remain a part of (Small)Yugoslavia. But please do answer within two weeks.

They were not happy at all in Bosnia that Yugoslavia was falling apart. With its three different nationalities, Moslems, Serbs and Croats, Bosnia itself was actually a small Yugoslavia. The falling apart of greater Yugoslavia could therefore very easily mean the falling apart of Bosnia. That's why president Izetbegović, a Moslem, wanted to postpone as long as possible the answer to the question of which side to take in the disintegrating Yugoslavia. Neither was it a coincidence that the TV station *Jutel*, created in 1989/90, was based in the Bosnian capital Sarajevo. It was addressing all of Yugoslavia and was in the beginning relayed by the stations of all six republics. It was managed by the former star reporter of Belgrade TV Goran Milić, a Croat who always started his *Jutel* broadcasts with, "Good evening, Yugoslavia." More and more, this became an anachronism, but *Jutel* kept up, even after one republic after the other pulled out and stopped relaying the broadcasts. So did Serbia, although it continued to pay lip-service to the pursuit of one Yugoslavia. Izetbegović knew that "yes" to independence would mean troubles with the Serbs who, after all, wanted to stay within "Yugoslavia," at the time consisting of nothing but Serbia and Montenegro, and that "no" would produce troubles with his own Moslems and the Croats, just because Yugoslavia was nothing but Serbia and Montenegro, and that joining *that* Yugoslavia would mean Serbian dominance. And now he had fourteen days to tell what Bosnia wanted. Hastily a session of the parliament was convened. The Croats and the Moslems had announced they would vote in favor of independence, the Serbs said they would boycott the session and they declared their representatives to be a separate parliament of only the Serb community. In absence of the Serbs the parliament said "yes." So now the EC could proceed toward recognition. Wrong. It demanded first from Bosnia that it organizes a referendum to find out whether the Bosnian population really wanted independence. Still bigger problems for the central government. With all speed this referendum was organized. It took place on Saturday, February 29 and Sunday, March 1. The Serbs boycotted it, so it became an easy victory for the advocates of independence. But even if all the Serbs would have voted against it, the government's proposal would still have gained the majority. Monday, March 2. Meeting of the EC summit, which, of course, would finally decide for recognition. Wrong. The result of the referendum was still considered too uncertain. Postponement of the recognition until at least the next session – a month away. Still bigger problems for the central government.

Sunday, March 1 in Sarajevo. A Serb couple gets married. They drive to the church. A Serbian flag sticks out of the window of a car in the wedding procession. Somebody shoots at the car: the father of the bride is killed. Serb nationalistic die-hards and their supporters know: the murderer is a Moslem, he has nationalistic motivations, this can't remain unanswered.

The answer comes on Monday, March 2. Hundreds of heavily armed Serbs erect barricades around and in the whole city, check passers-by, refuses to let Moslems pass, and fire with live ammunition if something does not please them. To this very day it is the official Serb-Serbian version, that the Moslems started the "civil war" in Bosnia with the murder of the father of the bride. And that is a very logical way of reasoning, of course. Let us place this into an American situation. A black guy in New York shoots a white fellow citizen to death. It was clearly a racist act, because he yelled, just before he fired, "Filthy pale face!" Then it is absolutely logical, isn't it, that the whites of New York, to prevent that the whole white population of the United States would perish under a black genocide, erect barricades on the Brooklyn Bridge, in Manhattan and elsewhere in the city, manned with hundreds of heavily armed whites, who have the right to deny entry to every black fellow citizen and to kill him if he does not obey or neglect the order, "Stop."

Yet, tens of thousands of citizens of Sarajevo, Serbs, Croats and Moslems alike, found these kinds of actions not that logical. One of the barricades was erected on the Maršala Tita, the Marshall Tito Boulevard, half a mile away from hotel Holiday Inn. Toward the evening those tens of thousands advance to the barricade on the Maršala Tita, unarmed and without banners. They yell only one slogan, *Hočemo mir* – We want peace." I don't know what comes over me, but I find this so impressive, that I walk along with them in the first ranks.

We approach the barricade, the Serbs fire like madmen with rifles, revolvers, machine guns; over the heads, in the air. Six hundred feet before the barricade the procession stops. The ad hoc leaders of the demonstrators confer about what to do next. I approach them and advise them not to go on "because they will shoot to aim." The striking answer is, "We give them five minutes more to leave, if not, we will go on." They wait five minutes, the Serbs continue firing, the procession proceeds. And then the Serbs really fire aimed. Many demonstrators throw themselves on the ground, I go and stand as the third person behind a thick tree, from where I see that the persons in front simply keep on walking. A guy in his twenties crawls next to me on the ground to look for a safer place. All of a sudden he cries out in pain, a bullet went right through his shoe into his foot. I hoist him up, put my arm around him and bring him to the rear. The first ambulances were already approaching; he could get in right away. Only much later I realized that from the moment that the guy was hit, I did not pay attention anymore to the shooting. Because of the incident both of us had, as it were, taken leave of the demonstration, we no longer belonged to it, so also the bullets could not have been meant for us anymore – that must have been the subconscious thought.

But the demonstration succeeded. It turned out that demonstrators from the other side had gone up to the barricade, as well, and the Serbs made a run for it; they were not ready for a blood bath then. Elsewhere they gave up, too, the civil war seemed to have been averted. The ordinary television as well as *Jutel* did a terrific job. While it was as clear as day that Serbs had been shooting, the Bosnian television said, "Citizens of Bosnia, stay calm. It's not Serbs who are shooting, it's not Moslems who are shooting, it's not Croats who are shooting; it's idiots (*glupani*) who are shooting." In a live broadcast Goran Milić brought the parties together by telephone, in the course of which Karadžić promised there would be no more shooting. This really was a big difference with the propagandists aka reporters of the Croatian and Serbian television, who were ready in a flash to call the other side a murderer, even if there was nothing wrong, just to incite hatred. These hate-inciters too should have to answer to the Yugoslav Tribunal in The Hague and eventually be sentenced.[54]

The Bosnian television went to great lengths to prevent hatred, appealed to reasonableness and common sense. I recall a report on a reception center for the first refugees. They were Moslems from little towns in the surrounding area of Sarajevo, who, after that barricade-business, were afraid that Serbs

---

[54] Rightfully the Belgian-born radio journalist Georges Henry Joseph Ruggiu was sentenced to 12 years imprisonment in June 2000 by the UN Criminal Tribunal for Rwanda for inciting people to commit genocide in 1994.

would harm them. A well-known writer, a Moslem himself, begged them to return. "Don't be afraid, the Serbs won't harm you, it's over, just go home" – and home they went, as the report showed. The Serbian leaders scornfully called the Bosnian television a "Moslem station," and demanded their own Serbian program. It was a fact, though, that Serbs, Croats and Moslems had already for years made television programs together and were dead set against the *apartheid* policy of the Karadžić-Serbs.

The barricades may have been cleared, but it remained a bizarre situation. Holiday Inn was Serbian property and actually the Serbian headquarters. The Serbian leader Radovan Karadžić walked in and out, accompanied by heavily armed Serbs in full military uniform, which was absolutely illegal. The Bosnian police, standing in front of the hotel entrance, did not do anything against it. Once I met one of these heavily armed gentlemen in the elevator. Quasi naively, I asked him what kind of uniform he was actually wearing. He remained silent. After repeating my question, he stuck up his thumb, fore- and mid-finger in silence – the Serbian symbol. I told him that he had no right to carry weapons and that he did not belong in this hotel – but to be sure, I preferred to not get off at the floor where my room was. A few days later I met him again. "*Opet* – Again?" I remarked – and he witheringly looked at me. I also submitted a complaint with the hotel management against the presence of those brothers in arms, but it was of no use, of course. I had not expected it, but my point of view is that you should never put up with things like that. It should be made clear to the involved, in this case those illegal soldiers and the hotel management, that their behavior is not acceptable. Silence and timidity strengthen their enjoyment of power and arrogance. A few days later at a press conference, president Izetbegović promised me that the police would take action against the illegal-arms-carriers in the Holiday Inn – but this did not change the situation either.

The war was only being postponed, not canceled. Not until April 4 had it "really" started. Supported in all possible ways by the *JNA*, the Serbs conquered the greater part of Bosnia at a terrific pace to the detriment of the Moslems and the Croats who hardly had any weapons at their disposal. Two weeks after the beginning the Serbs had their positions consolidated so much that the bus service Belgrade-(close to) Sarajevo could be reopened. Nicole Lucas and I took one of the first buses and it ran punctually. Exactly according to schedule at six o'clock in the evening, we reached Pale, the new headquarters of Mister Karadžič and his gang. Not yet all territories were "pacified," but the driver went through it at excessive speed, just to be sure. The next day we could hitchhike with a British team along a mountainous wooded path, leading from Pale to Sarajevo, because the main road was closed due to the war. At that time it was rather easy. In the city itself the situation was absurd. He who went by car to the Serb quarter Ilidža, had to submit to a heavy Serbian check. But the streetcar still went normally from "Moslem" to "Serb" territory. The streetcar track ran parallel to the highway, and from your window you could see the cars being checked while the streetcar passed without any checking.

On April 29, we went to dinner with a Turkish colleague in a Croatian restaurant, a twenty minutes walk from hotel Evropa where we stayed. Just when we were enjoying our dessert, grenades started to fall. It was half past seven and the restaurant closed at eight. We had no choice, we had to leave. In the meantime the sound of machine guns had joined the explosions of the grenades. In that initial period of the war, Serbian Holiday-Inn-boys were still scattered within the Moslem territory, shooting in the darkness at members of the Bosnian militia or police. At the time, there still was electricity in Sarajevo, but the authorities had turned off the streetlights because of the bombardment. We kind of sidled along the walls to the wide street, where the Presidium lies. We had to cross it in order to reach our hotel. By that time, we were more worried about small arms than about grenades, because these were coming down on an area 1500 to 1800 feet away from us and not in the direction of our hotel.

We stand across the street, opposite the Presidium. Fast running, Nicole starts to cross the terribly wide *Maršala Tita*. I warn her not to do so. And there we go to the other side, on purpose not hurrying and by no means fast running. Now through the parallel street yet, the "Street of the Yugoslavian Peoples Army" (of all names!), to the hotel. We know that halfway a soldier stands at guard. See him, we don't, because it is pitch dark. We put our hands up and call out in English and Serbian, "Don't shoot, we are journalists and we have to go to hotel Evropa." The soldier answers out of nowhere, "OK." – and at long last we enter the safe haven of hotel Evropa. The shooting with tanks, mortars and machine guns continues until one o'clock in the morning.

Another part of the absurd situation is that the *JNA* is still located in barracks in the heart of the Moslem territory. On purpose, the Bosnian government, unlike the Slovenian and Croatian, had not blockaded them and I had a good connection with Major General Žarković, substitute of the commander for Bosnia, Milutin Kukanjac. This was a bullyish broadsword, Žarković, on the other hand, was a very refined gentleman, who had studied philosophy and did not think much of any of the leaders in Bosnia, not of Karadžič either. "I know him only as a ping-pong champion," he said, disdainfully. At the same time, he was an advocate for one Bosnia. He provided us with an official paper, signed in the name of Kukanjac, that we had preference to fly with an army plane from Sarajevo to Belgrade. Friday, May 1, we would fly: Nicole and I, and our Turkish colleague. He was especially in a funk, because already then, Turks

```
Pukovnik Magazin !


Molim te da prioritetno, u prvi avion staviš ove ljude:

-Nicole Lucas
-Murat Akgun
-Dick Verkijk
Pored pasoša poseduju novinarsku kartu.


                                    K O M A N D A N T
                                    Generalpukovnik
                                    kanjac Milutin        (
```

Request by the commander of the "JNA", the Yugoslav People's Army, in Sarajevo,
Milutin Kukanjac (signed by his deputy Žarković) to the commander of the airport
of Sarajevo, to let Nicole Lucas, Murat Akgun and DV fly along with the first plane
leaving for Belgrade. They could not get on the first, but they did on the second.
Later on, it turned out to be the last one: May 1, 1992.

could never do anything right in the eyes of the nationalistic Serbs of Bosnia.
It was chaos at the airport. Hundreds of Serbs pushed each other aside for a
seat, just to get away from Sarajevo. But you had to be on a list. Our paper was
good enough to get on the list, but it was questionable whether we could fly
out that day. Finally the plane from Belgrade arrived. It was jam-packed, we
could not go along and had to wait until the same plane would return once
more. That took two hours. But we got it. With hundreds of others we were sitting on the floor of the cargo plane without windows. Forty minutes later we
stood on the military airport of Belgrade. The next day the airport of Sarajevo
was closed by the Serbs.

We had been flying on the last plane from Sarajevo to Belgrade.

We also wanted to be there, when, two months later, the first plane would land
again in Sarajevo. The UN had given the Serbs an ultimatum: as of July 1, the
airport had to be open for delivery of aid supplies for blockaded Sarajevo. If
not, the UN would take it over forcefully. Since it would start from Split, we

could not fly along, so that we had to go to Sarajevo by car. Not only Nicole would ride along with me to Sarajevo, but Raymond van de Boogaard of the *Nieuwe Rotterdamse Courant* and Veronique Pasquiers of the Swiss paper *24 Heures* as well. We would join a UN column which would leave from Pančevo near Belgrade. But in Sarajevo the dangers had increased dramatically: Serb snipers covered many streets in the Moslem area and at the same time the road from Pale to Sarajevo had become unsafe, especially the last part across the airport – there, in no man's land, you could be fired on by Moslem-Croatian as well as by Serbian snipers.

On the day before our departure, in Sarajevo, a French colleague was hit by a grenade, by which he lost a leg. Raymond was well acquainted with him and that was the limit for him; he pulled out. So did Nicole, later in the evening; a completely legitimate and respectable decision, about which you should not make a fuss. Veronique did not change her mind, otherwise for sure I would absolutely have stayed home as well – trips like that you'd rather not undertake on your own.

And to our great relief, in Pančevo it turned out that dozens of other colleagues would hang with their cars behind the UN convoy.

After quite some driving back and forth, thanks to that correct Serb police officer of the old school, we had reached Zvornik at the Serbian-Bosnian border. He had left for Zvornik to get us help, but it took quite a long time before he returned. Meanwhile not only the buses with deportees passed us by, at the same time we were also harassed by a Serb "volunteer" in full uniform, probably a member of the "White Eagles" or "Tigers," the infamous murder gang of Arkan, a professional criminal, who in Serbia had risen to be a "respected" politician. Our "Eagle" drove up in a normal private car and stopped when he noticed our waiting column. He was obviously intoxicated and behaved extremely unpleasantly when he learned that we were foreign journalists. We were "liars" – that kind of language. We had to open up our cars and when he noticed spare cans of gas, he stated that it was not allowed to transport them. All chicanery, because he knew darned well that you could not find gas anywhere and for that reason see to it that you have at least enough gas with you for a round trip Belgrade-Sarajevo – and then you have to easily count on 600 miles. The ordinary police officer, guarding the checkpoint, did not dare to interfere. Fortunately, the drunk militant left without causing any further trouble. But I did complain to our correct Serb, when he returned shortly afterwards. He took it seriously, asked for the brand and license plate of the car and subsequently went to the checkpoint to call somebody. "I ordered to have him arrested," he reported laconically. And he had an even better message. He had to bring some bigwigs to Pale and we could continue to drive behind him, and so accompany us to Pale. That worked out beautifully. We maybe encountered seven or eight checkpoints, for a while he chatted with the guards – and on it went. Toward evening we drove into Pale.

The next morning: the sand-path-like back way across a mountainous forest-area where it is reasonable safe until Lukavica, a military headquarters of the Bosnian-Serb army. There starts no man's land, there it gets dicey. Also, there begins the great hesitation. Mutual consultation. Drive on right now? Wait for a UN UNPROFOR car from Sarajevo and drive back with them? And the eternal question: Do you tape a "Press" or "TV" sign in capital letters on your car, or is that exactly what *not* to do? Does it provide protection or does it just attract the snipers? I decided it would be the least dangerous simply not to do so. The decision was to break up the team and that everybody should do what he thought was best. One part drove on right away, one part waited, but when no UN vehicle showed up, some still went on their own. Some idiot, coming from Sarajevo, had painted his car white and fashioned the letters "UN"with black tape on his doors. I found that driving behind a fake UN car was even more risky than going on my own. We were in luck – after half an hour of lonesome waiting, two armored APC vehicles of UNPROFOR drove onto the barracks terrain. They brought a UN officer, who came to confer with the Serbian army leadership. It would not take long, so the drivers, and then they would go back. And yes, we were allowed to drive behind them. A good hour later we stood on the parking lot of the UNPROFOR headquarters in Sarajevo – maybe two hours later than the first group of drivers-on, but surely, given the circumstances, in the safest way.

In those two months the situation had become much grimmer. Formally, the *JNA* had withdrawn from not just the city, but from all of Bosnia. It was called back by the government in Belgrade, where Serbia and Montenegro had created the Federation of the Republics of Yugoslavia which was meant to replace the old Socialist Federation of the Republics of Yugoslavia (*SFRJ*). The *JNA* of the *SFRJ* became the *JA* (Yugoslavian Army) of the *FRJ* and thus all of a sudden stood on foreign territory, called Bosnia. Hence, the "call back." In fact, it did not amount to anything. They ordered the personnel of the old *JNA*, born in Serbia or Montenegro, to come back to the motherland. That amounted to only 15% of the total personnel constituent (so they alleged). All of their equipment remained in Bosnia, all army stocks included. Eighty-five percent of the men and one hundred percent of the equipment of the old *JNA* were from now onwards called the "Serbian Army" of the "Serbian Republic," as the Serb-Bosnian leaders had baptized the territory they had conquered. Once, when I asked at a press briefing in Belgrade the then minister of foreign affairs Jovanović whether, given that 15% arrangement, you still could speak of a real withdrawal, he answered, "It would have been in defiance of human rights if we would have forced people, born and bred over there, to come to Yugoslavia." I countered, "The *JNA* was under the jurisdiction of your government. You could have called back the *JNA* in Bosnia as a whole, disband it and then let every ex-soldier go wherever he had wanted to" – but according to him, also this would have been in defiance of human rights. The only ray of hope in this official point of view was that, after all the infringements on human rights Serbs and Serbians had committed and still were committing in Bosnia, the subject "human rights" once again was part of the government's policy in Belgrade. This new view did have as a consequence, though, that with the equipment, left behind for ever so humane reasons, the soldiers, left behind for ever so humane reasons, were able to shoot unfettered at Sarajevo with the bullets and grenades, left behind for ever so humane reasons. Based on that ever so humane decision unlimited shooting on civilians was possible – and on us. The Karadžić-Serbs (the overwhelming majority of the Serbs in Sarajevo did not want to have anything to do with these overheated nationalists) had lost the battle in the center of the city and had withdrawn into a few adjoining districts. They had replaced their headquarters from the Holiday Inn to Pale, along the normal road ten miles from the center of the town. But the hotel stood scarcely two hundred yards away from a sniper's position in the district Grbavica, just on the other side of the river Miljačka, which runs straight through the city. They kept the main entrance of the hotel covered, so you only could get in through a back entrance. The main entrance was on the side of the hotel and the Serb sniper's position was in line with that side. So only in the linear direction of that side could the Serbs take the main entrance under fire. The lobby was on the side as well, separated from the outer world by a huge glass wall. That lobby was relatively safe, because between the front of the hotel, facing the Serbian position, and the lobby, there was not only a thick front façade, but also a great many evacuated shops and halls. To the Serbs, sharp shooting apparently was a kind of leisure activity, because after six p.m. it was the most dangerous on the streets. The Holiday Inn, where practically all foreigners lived who professionally had to be in Sarajevo, had an underground parking garage. That was very nice, the disadvantage was, though, that its entrance also was on the side and that you had to cross a little part of the Serb field of fire in order to get in. So it was extremely unwise to come home after six.

On a late afternoon elsewhere in the city there was a briefing by the Bosnian minister of Defense. A dozen colleagues were present, but I turned out to be the only foreigner and then immediately you are bombarded as a kind of guest of honor. The briefing ran into overtime and I wanted to go home. No, I had to stay, because a meal was being offered. Fortunately, it was nothing lavish, just a simple meal. Once again, I wanted to leave. No, because there was still a small gift waiting for us. It kept on going and going. I was sitting on a hot seat, had no interest at all in that gift, but it was clear that they would be displeased if I left. At last – the small gift: a pair of Reebok-like gym shoes.

In the meantime it's way past seven and I take to my heels. Through a couple of side streets I reach hotel Holiday Inn and dive into the parking garage. I did hear a lot of rattling of some automatic gun, but this in itself was nothing new. Once downstairs you are safe. You can reach the lobby by cutting through the hotel.

There it's unrealistically cozy. I approach a couple of colleagues, who tell me in dismay, "Do you know that, when you drove to the garage, the bullets ricocheted only ten inches away from your car?" I had absolutely not noticed anything. Only then it really sank into me that I would not have noticed anything either, if they really had aimed well. It would have been a high price to pay, though, for a couple of gym shoes.

When I am in Sarajevo, I cannot resist going for a while to the spot where in 1914 Gavrilo Princip shot Archduke Ferdinand to death, which was the reason for World War I. On a stone is a cryptic text, which does not speak about murder, but suggests that the Serbian nationalist actually deserves praise for his action. His footprints are on the curb on the spot from where he discharged his shots. The stone is fixed to the façade of a building that has been remodeled into a small museum with unique documents about Princip and his attempt. I go there once again to have a look: everything gone. The memorial stone smashed to smithereens, just like the footprints. Besides being hit by one or more Serb grenades, the museum is totally looted; all documents have disappeared. The destructions were caused by Croats and/or Moslems for a change, who wanted to erase any memory of that Serbian nationalist. I have taken along a few of those smithereens on which some letters were still visible, so the plaque is not completely lost for history.

In Sarajevo the war was close all the time. In manifold aspects. In a small river behind the UN headquarters almost right under a bridge, lie three swollen corpses, stuck behind a couple of rocks. I passed there very often and every time my view was irresistibly attracted to that horrible image of those totally dehumanized human bodies. I could not establish how long they were lying there, but they weren't taken away until the fifth day after I had seen them for the first time.

In a different way, the trip to the airport was unpleasant as well. The arterial road to it, the Maršala Tita and the Vojvode Putnika nicknamed the "Snipers Boulevard" ran for miles at about two hundred yards from the Serbian territory with side streets ending up in that territory. At the end of those streets, there they were. Now it was essential yet to get out as fast as possible. Fast meant: 70 to 80 miles per hour. There was not that much traffic, but who did drive, tried to do it as fast as possible. So it's not surprising that the cynical question went around in Sarajevo what you would die of first: a bullet or a car accident.

Only on the third of July, I could make the first trip to it, after the Serbs had buckled under and handed the airport, as well as the control over the entry road, over to the United Nations. On that Friday the third of July, it really was an impressive event to see the first Hercules plane land. There were also journalists on it, who were grounded straight away, because there was no transport from and to the airport. I took a bunch of them in the bed of my truck – and this would not remain a one-time-event.

Two days after the arrival of the first plane a big surprise: Raymond van de Boogaard walks into the Holiday Inn. Nicole and he had decided to come to Sarajevo anyway, together with and in the car of Gert van Wijland and Marjolein Sebregs, a Dutch freelance married journalist-couple, permanent correspondents in Belgrade. But considering the way we had taken still too risky, they had made a tremendous detour through Croatia and Slovenia until initially Split – close to 600 miles.

All of a sudden, in Split Gert and Marjolein had enough of it. Some weeks earlier they had experienced that Moslem units invaded the Holiday Inn in order to chase away the Serbs and the subsequent shooting had gotten to them. They made a U-turn and went on vacation in Austria – with the car. Then, Nicole and Raymond could get a ride from an American colleague to Mostar (another 125 miles) and Sarajevo (another 100 miles). In Mostar, Nicole got so depressed by the ravages (then only caused by the Serbs; a year later when the Croats started their war against the Moslems, they would go ahead and do it all over again), that she could not handle Sarajevo on top of that. And so Raymond still ended up in Sarajevo as the only one of the Dutch team left.

By this it's not meant to say that the one is "tougher" than the other, only that journalists in former Yugoslavia were working under great stress and often with cold sweat in their hands – and that more than once the moment for everyone came, that he had to completely distance himself from it, and which he also could, a privilege which was not granted to the inhabitants of Sarajevo and other war areas.

Of course, there were also reporters whom I use to call "fire-reporters" – in good American: smoke jumpers. In the "Eastern Bloc" I met them quite a few times. When an incident of some dimension took place, their editorial office sent them to cover it. I don't want to claim that they hardly knew where they were, but often those ad hoc colleagues did not have the slightest clue in which context they had to fit into the incident. It may sound chauvinistic, but this fault occurred the least among European colleagues, the most often among Americans.

Well then, with every load of aid supplies along came loads of "fire-reporters"as well: the Holiday Inn nearly got fully-booked up, also because they did not rent out the rooms at the front where you looked out at the Serbs (and they at you!). Once, one of those "fire-reporters" came to check with me whether it was true that the Croats were Orthodox and the Serbs Roman Catholic. I have tried to explain to him that in principle exactly the opposite was true, but that most of them on both sides had not taken part in that religion for nearly half a century and that in all those years religion hardly had played any role in the mutual relations between the people in Bosnia.

But the "fire-reporters" were in luck: to the "incident" of the first aid goods, a second one at seven o'clock in the evening of Tuesday, July 7 was added: Serbs were heavily shooting with machine-guns and mortars in the immediate surroundings of the hotel. We were ordered to either go to the (shelter)basement or sit below a lean-to in the lobby. I chose the latter, meaning the lean-to, because I wanted to record some sound and for this reason also see a little bit of what was going on, but in the long run the grenades fell so close by that I had to lie flat on my stomach behind the bar and actually regretted that I had not gone to the basement. One grenade landed on the roof of the underground parking garage, some sixty feet away from the main entrance. A part of the glass wall, already considerably damaged, fell into the lobby. Mortar grenades cause an ear deafening, cracking explosion, its shrapnel effects are murderous, but they produce hardly any air pressure. If one is coming straight through your window, you are finished, but if it clashes against the wall next to your window, you have a lucky escape. Like the bullets of the snipers, the grenades came from Grbavica and followed the same path as well, parallel with the side wall of the hotel, so there was no danger that one could go straight through the glass wall and end up in the lobby. That's why after the first fright I once again went to sit upright at a table with the (wide) bar between the glass wall and me. At another table a waiter was quietly making out his day-account on the basis of his receipts under hellish explosions; new customers were hardly to be expected this evening. The hotel management had postponed the serving of the one-dish meal until after the shooting would be over – that was at eleven o'clock. American cameramen came to tell us, that a car just in front of the hotel had gotten a direct hit, but that the driver was apparently unhurt, because he jumped out of the car and ran off. The next day I saw the car: there was nothing left of it *(see photo 37)*.

Those cameramen applied a more and more used method: you put your camera with a wide angle lens in the direction of a spot, where you guess something is going to happen, press the button and your videotape runs for an hour. You don't need to stay there yourself, so you are not in danger. After an hour you take the risk to quickly put in another tape. At the end of the shooting you look to see whether something special has been taped. You can apply this system in only certain cases. Most of the cameramen work with their cameras on their shoulder – and in a war situation those are the most vulnerable colleagues.

The shooting is over. In a safe corner of the hotel, a restaurant was improvised. The manager has hastily called for a piano and had managed to get hold of a pianist, so that it just would look like everything was normal. The pianist plays the usual, but this time really very applicable dinner-babble-music, "Stranger in the night." Raymond, who just arrived that day, had had enough. "The real news has already passed, I don't feel like being shot to death for just nothing," he says. The next day I bring him to the airport. A few days later Veronique and I also went back, now with a whole convoy of different journalists. Crossing of the airport runway area is seen as the most dangerous thing to do. At an irresponsibly high speed we chase across the concrete, two, three separate shots sound. That's all. Quickly, the UN guards push the barriers open at the end of the airport, so that we can drive through without stopping, along the narrow country road to Lukavica. There we are safe.

March 1995: once more I'm back in Sarajevo. There is a kind of peace. The Serbs have given in to an ultimatum (which in my firm belief the UN would never have carried out, but it seemed just like the real thing) and have withdrawn their heavy weaponry to fifteen miles from the center of the city. Life normalizes a little bit. Small coffee houses have reopened. But as far as electricity, gas and water is concerned: sometimes it's there, sometimes it's not. I am staying in a private home. The host runs the bath as soon as there is some water – to have at least a small supply. In a partly destroyed hall there is an exhibition about how Sarajevo survived the siege. I see a glass of water with a thin layer of oil on top of it, on which a little wick floats – a tiny spot of light in the darkness. I see a little, metal cylinder with a little grill in it – a super-frugal cooking-stove. The filled-up bathtub, the oil light, the little cooking-stove – I see the hunger winter.

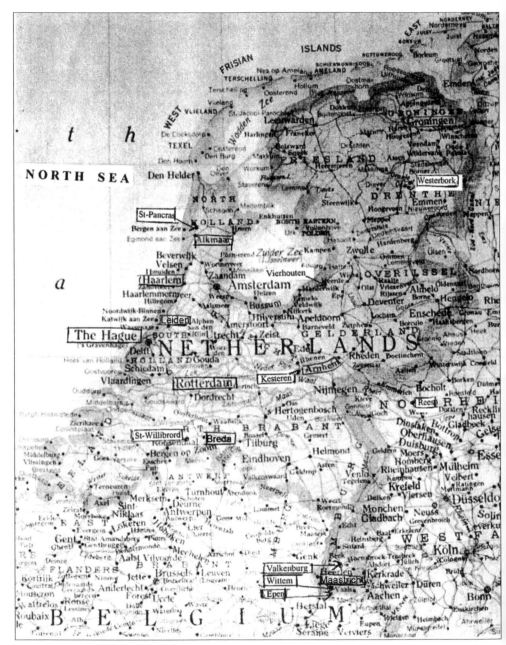

Map of the Netherlands and part of Belgium (to the South) and Germany (to the East); the places mentioned in this book are boxed.

CHAPTER 14

The Hunger Winter[55]

The glass of water with one millimeter of turnip oil on top of which a tiny little wick floated, which produced a three millimeter high tiny flame – that was the last spot of light we still had at home. Never ever will the cliché expression "the dark days before Christmas" be so realistic as in the Netherlands of 1944.

We were sitting around the table, my mother on the short end, my seven-year-old sister and I opposite each other on the long end, but close to the short end in order to be as near as possible to that last tiny light. My father was picked up during the raid of December 6 and was somewhere in Germany. Where, we did not know. We had hardly anything to eat. My father had become kind of sickly in mid-November and we had not been able to go "to the North" to try to get some food from the farmers. He had not yet recovered when he was picked up and for us the period of "grass and pebbles" had come, as it was announced by the *Wehrmacht* officer who was billeted with us in 1940 for two weeks.

It was a dark tunnel without a light at the end. "Children," my mother said,

[55] After the failure of the Battle of Arnhem in September 1944, the Allied offensive came to a stand still. The relatively not so densely populated area of the South-Eastern and North-Eastern part of the Netherlands had to be liberated town by town and mostly house by house. That method would have been a disaster, had it also been applied to the North-Western part. It was highly densely populated and it would cost an enormous loss of lives of the civil population there. So the Allies in cooperation with the Dutch government-in-exile in London decided to wait for the capitulation of Germany in general.

There was not much agriculture in that part of Holland. On top of that, the Germans wanted to punish the Dutch for the railroad strike. Transportation of food was forbidden. So about three million people, completely cut off from the outside world, were victims of the arbitrary policy of the Germans. Food became very scarce and very soon – November, December – the rations were cut down to one pound of bread of an extremely bad quality and two pounds of potatoes per person per week. Nothing more. It is very difficult to imagine, that nothing more really meant nothing more. Also in the fall, electricity and gas were cut off. Heating possibilities went down to zero. Citizens went on foot with hand carts to the agricultural areas "in the North" to beg some food from the farmers there in exchange for bed linens, jewelry, and even wedding rings, but very soon these sources were also exhausted. Quite often the Germans improvised checkpoints where they confiscated the precious food. So-called "central kitchens" (kind of soup kitchens) were organized, where "one thing is for sure: as good as we had it before the war – that good we will never have it again." We did not doubt this for a second. We did not have heating, unless we lit our "tiny emergency cooking-stove," as it was called (16 inches high, diameter 10 inches) with a few small branches to cook some sugar beets. That's why we went to bed early, half past seven, eight o'clock. Also that evening. We stumbled into the hallway, I kept the "lamp" in my hand. In the hallway: an awkward movement, I bumped up against my mother, and the glass slips out of my hand. Total despair, all three of us cry: we lost our last light.

Just a short time earlier everything still looked so beautiful. On Monday, September 4, the BBC reported that the southern Dutch town of Breda had been liberated. It was an incorrect report, but precisely that got a flow of rumors going which went into history as *Dolle Dinsdag*, "Crazy Tuesday." In Rotterdam they were sure that Breda was liberated, in The Hague they said the same of Rotterdam, in Leiden of The Hague and with us in Haarlem of Leiden. As firm members of the *SDAP* we never had gotten, of course, the national red-white-blue flag.[56] So it had to be produced in a flash. At the drug store around the corner I bought red and blue dye. From an old sheet, my mother cut three equal strips. One went into the pan with the red color, the other in one with blue. It had to be boiled through and through, otherwise the color would not soak in. I was scared to death that the English (to us all future liberators were "the English") would arrive before the flag was finished. After the boiling, the strips had yet to dry. I hung them up in the back yard on the

you could get some watery soup, mostly made of (spoiled) cabbage leaves once a day. You could only get the two pounds of potatoes you were entitled to "if available." If not, they were replaced by sugar beets. A popular food in those days were tulip bulbs, which contained starch and had a nice sweet taste – they were considered a delicacy.

It was known in the Allied camp that after mid-April there would be absolutely nothing left to eat and it was feared that millions would die. Eisenhower's headquarters decided therefore to let bombers drop food. They told the Germans that the planes were unarmed, would fly at a very low level, and that anybody, who would fire at them, would after the war be treated as a war criminal. The Germans accepted the conditions and so American and British bombers dropped food during full war time, which saved the life of countless Dutchmen, although much of this food could only be distributed after the liberation. In the Dutch history that period between September 1944 and May 5, 1945 (when the Germans in the "Fortress Holland" capitulated) is named *De Hongerwinter*, "The Hunger Winter." More than 25.000 people died of starvation during that period.

[56] Before World War II the red-white-blue flag was not considered by the social-democrats as the symbol of the nation, but of the Royal House. Republicans at heart, the social-democrats could not accept that. That's why in my parental home no flag was present, but this attitude had drastically changed due to the occupation of the Germans, who had strictly forbidden to use the flag or to show anything with the colors red, white and blue.

clothesline, the white strip meanwhile in the center. If you stood on the street in the front of our home, you could see through the windows the separated red, white and blue hanging in the back yard. We were absolutely sure that the liberation was not a matter of hours, but of minutes. So it's not surprising that I ran nervously back and forth between the back yard and the street, on the one hand hoping that the English were going to come, on the other hand that they would wait a little until the flag strips would be dry. My God – how dry was that flag going to be!

The *NSB*-ers were no wiser than we were and the majority took to their heels, in the direction of Germany. However, the *NSB* family Bossers, who had not been seen in their home at number 104 for a long time, did just the opposite: they returned, minus their lost son Kees.

The rumor turned out be what is was: a rumor.

Not yet fourteen days later, the tremendous disappointment changed into new hope: the airborne operation near Arnhem on Sunday, September 17, and the spectacular railroad strike connected with it. But when this also ended up in failure and the Krauts on top of that were able to start the Battle of the Bulge, I again started to believe in my calculation that the war might last until August 1946.

On Christmas Day, an unknown man pays us a visit. Somebody from the neighborhood, also picked up in the raid but sent back to Holland as *arbeitsunfähig* – "unable to work." My father had asked him to drop by our place. From him we learned that all those Haarlem people picked up in the raid had been brought to Rees, close to Emmerich. The man lied that it was not all that bad "and when you eat your soup you can feel the fat on your lips." My mother said she was very grateful to him "that he had given her such a good Christmas." In those Christmas days, this angelic liar brought home "tidings of great joy" to many fellow neighbors.

Nevertheless, the situation at our home was so depressing, that I proposed to go to The Hague to our relatives to celebrate New Year's. My mother did not want to go, but I found her argument, "I want to be home when your father returns" absolutely unrealistic. "He will not come back before the war is over," I said. But we shared the opinion that our relatives in The Hague had to know that my father had been picked up and therefore she agreed that I went alone. That meant: thirty miles on foot, other connections did not exist.

On Thursday, December 28 I set off early in the morning, armed with a backpack with some clothing, my guitar (which has been my inseparable friend for years) and one slice of dry bread. Halfway I overtook two men with a carrier tricycle, who had picked up some food somewhere "in the North." The oldest one, an estimated 25 years old, was sitting on the saddle and pedaled, the other, somewhat older than I, was towing in the front with a rope. I asked them whether they would allow me to put my backpack and guitar on their carrier, if I would help them tow in exchange. They agreed. I don't recall much of the younger one, but the face of the older one is still sharp in my mind, because of his dark appearance and black eyes I supposed him to be of Jewish origin. He had a beard of a couple of days and looked exhausted. He was wearing a leather Lindbergh-style aviator's cap and the chin straps, loosely hanging alongside his head, reinforced the Jewish image I got of him. He said his name was Frederik. They also had to go to The Hague and lived somewhere in the Laak-district, where we arrived after seven in the evening. From there it was still a good half an hour's walk to my uncle, a brother of my father. Exactly at curfew time, eight o'clock, I knocked on the door.

The Hague was a very dangerous city in those days. Wernher Von Braun's V-2's were fired from there to London, but approximately half of them did not go further than The Hague and surroundings. One was fired off just before midnight on New Year's Eve. We were just ready to wish each other a Happy New Year and listened anxiously to the rattling grunt of the engine. At the stroke of twelve the engine cuts out. Deathly silence. We stand stock-still, tens of seconds. And then: an enormous bang, but at a reasonable distance. Great relief, because it did not fall on our heads.

The next morning we pay a New Year's visit to another aunt and uncle, who lived on the third floor of an apartment building in the Nijkerklaan. We were just sitting down, when my uncle yells, "A V-2 is coming, clear out!" We run downstairs and seek hiding under the staircase in the doorway. I had not seen anything, but my uncle did: a V-2 approached very low, rotating around its longitudinal axis, right in the direction of the apartment building. When we stand under the staircase, it skims over the roof with a still throbbing engine and lands not a good half a mile further on a block of houses which is completely wiped out.[57]

The Germans were aware of the fact, that their V-2 was far from perfect, because everywhere in the city they had hung up posters, on which was announced that you would get the death penalty if you would take home V-2 parts. One hung in the shop window opposite my uncle's home and reading it, I was scared to death. Because it was a fad among us kids to collect war souvenirs, especially pieces of shrapnel of anti-aircraft grenades. But how could you

---

[57] The V-2 on New Year's Eve landed on an evacuated part of The Hague, the one of January 1, 1945, crashed on the Indigostraat, corner Kamperfoeliestraat. Thirty three houses were destroyed, 38 people killed. The distance from the Nijkerklaan to the place of the impact appeared to be 900 yards. (File Municipal Archives/The Hague).

know here in The Hague whether you picked up a piece of just ordinary war metal or a V-2 part? So I rather left everything untouched on the street.

I did not want to stay too long in The Hague. My mother was alone with my little sister and at the same time I could not let my newspaper-customers wait. In a few days' time I had informed most of my relatives about our situation and on Tuesday, January 2: 30 miles back to Haarlem. Again somewhere half-way I got a luxurious ride. A married couple with a horse and carriage was on its way to a place north of Haarlem, which meant that they practically passed by my house. At the intersection of the Rijksstraatweg and the Zaanenlaan they dropped me off. On the coach box there had not been room for me and I had been sitting extremely uncomfortably below the couple on the squared foot support for hours, but it already had been a real treat that I did not have to walk half the distance from The Hague. Just another half a mile – and I would be home. After a few hundred yards a boy, totally unknown to me, came up to me, enthusiastically shouting, "Your father has come back!"

It turned out to be true. My mother's intuition had triumphed over my re-alism. On that very same January 2, early in the morning, he suddenly stood in front of the door. From the day he was picked up, he had not been out of his clothes. In Rees three pumps had been available for 3000 men, where you could wet your face a little bit every day – and after some time two pumps were out of order. In theory it was a labor camp, but in fact a prisoner's camp. If you did something the Krauts were not pleased with, you were beaten up on a buck especially set up for the occasion. They hardly got any food, although they had to accomplish a hard job: digging anti-tank-moats with a shovel. They were housed in roof-tile-drying-buildings. These were big, covered sheds without proper side walls, because the secret of drying roof tiles is, that they have to hang in drafty spaces to speed up the drying process. They slept on wet straw, with the snow blowing in through the nonexistent side walls. My father had been declared *arbeitsunfähig*, because he had caught pneumonia. Physically he was in very bad shape, but psychologically even worse. "They are all going to die, they are all going to die," he repeated all the time.[58] He had de-veloped a frantic fear of German uniforms. When he noticed one only 300 feet away, he literally walked around the block. He also was scared to death that they would find my underground papers and he actually thought that I had to throw them away. The compromise was that they were hidden in the pipe of the stove. The "emergency cooking-stove," which was connected to that pipe via the ordinary heating stove, needed only a little bit of air to draw anyway.

[58] I a few months time, at least 321 died in the camp due to maltreatment, illness and starvation. Thanks to the underground movement, hundreds could be saved.

But not surprisingly, the saved copies are a bit brownish-discolored.

By the way, the return trip from Germany was not without danger. Of course, they had to go most of the way on foot, but since they were the *Arbeitsunfähigen*, the "unable-to-work-persons," they were allowed to use *Wehrmacht* trains if available. Hans Cannemeyer, who on December 6 went to stand so proudly in his uniform in front of the door, was also sent home due to illness: he was killed in an attack by an Allied fighter plane.

Still, we were not able to go "to the North," because my father's pneumonia had to run its course. Shortly afterwards, I fell ill, intestinal flu or something like that. I had a high fever, which according to my relatives went up to 104 degrees. I myself know little about it, because I passed out. I laid downstairs on a camp bed, I lost control over everything and after a few days I returned to the world because of a vaguely pleasant feeling, caused by a complete cleansing of me, as well as of my sheets: the crisis was over. The brother of Dik van den Haak, Rob, brought the newspapers to me, so that Joop Jonkman would not come in vain. But Joop himself also brought along something for his sick friend: an apple. And when my mother and sister also were knocked down by intestinal flu (fortunately, they had not gotten it as bad as I did), so all four of us were stuck in bed, he showed up every day to bring our ration of food from the "central kitchen."

It was not until the end of February, my father had recovered so far that we could go "to the North" to scrape together something to eat. We had laid our hands on a handcart and at a farmer's place in Sint-Pancras, a small village near Alkmaar 20 miles north of Haarlem, we could fully load it with white cabbage. It was quite a self-conquest for my father with his deadly fear for everything German, that we went that far away from home. Neighbor Smit, chief of the City Registration Office, had given him a real, false identity card: real, because it was an official copy and not counterfeited; false, because his birthday was not mentioned as 1904, but 1903. Yes, but, as a matter of fact, 1904 actually would have been OK, too, and the Germans really didn't care about that part, so would they care about 1903? That matter only came up on our way back. A few hundred yards ahead of us, around Alkmaar: German checkpoint. We stop. My father hesitates: should he show his real, 1904 ID with the *arbeitsunfähig* statement to go with, of his 1903 ID, but then without that statement, because this says that he was born in 1904. We are deliberating endlessly, but still, he cannot come to a decision and I also don't know what's the best thing to do. We stood there for at least half an hour, considering first one thing, then another. We were so busy with each other that we literally lost sight of the cause of the problem. When after some time we again look in the direction of the checkpoint, the Kraut turns out to have disappeared – and we returned home safe and sound.

Fuel was as big a problem as food. One of our sources was the estate *Schapeduinen* of the Bierens de Haan family in the affluent neighboring village of Bloemendaal. Once a week I go there with my mother. They do some wood trimming then and give you the trimmed wood free of charge. Again it's a trimming day, March 1945. We are seated on a bench, besides my mother and me another lady is also waiting for the twin brothers Bierens de Haan. They have not taken one step out of the house yet, or one of them jumps back inside with a "Goddamned," and the other dives behind a big bunch of branches, behind the bench we are sitting on. A second earlier they had seen what we are also now seeing: an open *DKW* with *Wehrmacht* and *SS*-soldiers is racing up the driveway. A few are sitting on the front fenders and shooting with their revolvers. They jump off the car and invade the enormous country house from all sides. All but one. A *Wehrmacht* officer. He stands guard, right in front of us. While his colleagues are searching the house, he paces up and down. Every time we shift along with him to deprive him as inconspicuously as possible from getting a view of Bierens de Haan, because the faggot is pretty transparent. "Why don't you go home?" the officer asks us, but we respond that we keep on waiting for some wood. For at least two hours we sit there, freezing to death. When the officer walks away a little bit, we confer whispering with the Bierens-behind-the-faggot. Finally, the search team comes outside, they have caught the brother, who had fled inside. His shirt hangs loosely out of his pants, a Dutch *SS*-man holds a revolver in his hand and shouts loudly that they have found it in the house. Hence, the prisoner is being kicked into the *DKW*. The officer gets in and they leave. When the coast is clear, Bierens de Haan #2 runs quickly into the woods. That day we went home without wood. Later on we learned that Bierens de Haan #1 was brought to the prison in Haarlem pending his transport to elsewhere, but that he was liberated in time by friends of the underground, dressed in German uniforms.

They still were very well off in the semi-barracks across the street from us. That was highly visible. While we were nibbling on a tulip bulb or a sugar beet – or sometimes even on nothing – every day, we saw at some 50-foot distance soldiers behind the barbed wire passing by with steaming potatoes, destined for the gentlemen-officers, who had nestled in the houses of the chased-away fellow neighbors. But I have to admit that one day I took advantage of their stock. At the end of February, beginning of March, the barracks, already partly evacuated earlier, were completely vacated. The *Wehrmacht* could not or did not want to take along everything. A soldier stood at a ladder behind a wall they had erected to screen their barracks complex on the Junoplantsoen from the rest of the neighborhood. From his high position he threw loaves of bread across the wall. From our house I saw it happening and ran to it full speed and amid dozens of others, actually succeeded in catching a loaf. It was such a rock-hard sour German bread. A collaborator's bread, I admit, but it was again something to nibble on.

For one reason or another it was known that we were not that well off. Baker Swart, the father of my primary (female) schoolmate Aagje, got wind of it also. Once a week my little sister and I were invited to eat there. Knowing myself, I can hardly imagine that I did not make anti-German remarks there, but remembering it, I do not. It goes without saying that I did not breathe a word about our underground paper. And this was a good thing too, because right after the liberation baker Swart was picked up and his business confiscated: he turned out to have been a "secret" member of the NSB.[59] For my sister and me he did his best. Was it a redeeming of feelings of guilt? Was it honest compassion? If I had said something "anti" at all, then he did not do anything with it, because we never got any problems from it.

Because of the *De Oprechte Haarlemmer* I was a daily visitor at the Haak's and from time to time I was allowed to stay and eat there also. In July 1943 or 1944 when it still was relatively "good," I once asked for my birthday "a whole loaf of bread." I myself don't remember that anymore, but my parents remembered it very well, because to their sorrow they could not fulfill that wish. One time I was allowed to eat as much as I wanted. That was in February/March 1945 when we, thanks to the Swedish Red Cross, got a whole loaf of bread per person. Nine slices of bread I ate, spread with the also Swedish margarine – and I did not get sick.

Of course, producing and distributing that paper did not shorten the war by one second, and maybe our readers were also kept informed about the war events by other underground papers, but for us personally it was of the greatest importance, especially in that endless, cheerless and hopeless hunger winter. You were dealing with something more than just material matters and you had the feeling that you were taking some action against those bastards who had dragged us into the total downfall. In this way you could forget the daily, miserable fight for survival more easily.

We had a second moral support. Around 1943, a close-knit group of friends had been formed, which in the hunger winter became even closer: seven girls and six boys. In those in every aspect dark last seven, eight months of the war, we gathered very regularly in the evening between six and eight – and some-

---

59 Some members wanted to and could remain "secret." It was especially used by shop keepers, because they rightfully were afraid of losing their customers if it was known that they were members of the NSB.

times even after curfew. We took turns, first at one person's home, then at the other. Mostly in pitch-darkness, but sometimes someone still had a bicycle with a tire at his disposal and having put it on a stand, we pedaled the bike in turn, with the generator on the rear wheel, and so we produced at least some kind of light. Two of us played guitar and we sang songs along with it. At a prosperous household, you got a tulip-bulb-cookie to eat. Also then, we could forget everything and really have fun. One day, in February or March, all of us went to a concert of the *Haarlemse Orkest Vereniging*, the Haarlem Symphony Orchestra, in the ice-cold Concert Hall of Haarlem. I don't remember who the composer was, or how the music sounded, but the title itself remains stamped in my memory: *La Vita Nuova* – the new life. Whether you were a member of the *Kultuurkamer*, the Culture Chamber, or not, was not checked anymore[60].

That concert was quite an experience. There was in interacting common feeling between musicians and audience of: we don't let them walk all over us. In spite of everything, there was, at least according to my feeling, a great mutual solidarity during that hunger winter.

For a long time, we still went to school, although the number of students went down every day. One day schoolmate Frits Honig had suddenly disappeared. Picked up shortly after the December raid when he was stopped and caught with a false ID (so he told me fifty years later), which was meant to make him a couple of years younger, so that he would seem to be "under the age." Factually, he was seventeen, "within the age." After a few months he returned to school – he had been in the infamous concentration camp Amersfoort, geographically in the center of the Netherlands, but politically, of course, a German *SS*-camp. A shy, tiny bird, all skin and bones, a bald-shaven head. He did not want to (or could not) speak to anybody – he just stood there, huddled in a corner. After a couple of days he went back home. It took two years before he recovered. And it took him fifty years, before he dared have a look at the memorial site in Amersfoort – but after just a few minutes he was through with it. And he still cannot talk about it.

More and more Haarlem became the border of the civilian territory. September 19, 1944, the whole area on the West (sea)side of the Delft canal, two hundred yards from our home, and the area north of the Jan Gijzen canal, two miles from our home, were declared a restricted area. Everybody had to leave his home. On the bridges across those canals thick concrete *Mauermuren*[61] with

---

[60] All artists of any kind were obliged to be a member of the *Kultuurkamer*, the Culture Chamber. It was, like many other institutions, a direct imitation of the German *Kulturkammer*. It was even written with a capital K in stead of a C, as it should be in Dutch. Non-members were forbidden to perform.

narrow pass-throughs, were constructed. Because of incomprehensible reasons you were still allowed to pass through those areas, but it was forbidden to live there. Not surprisingly, many of the involved, especially in Bloemendaal, simply remained in their homes, curtains drawn *(see photo 32)*.

February 12, 1945. Rietje Geerlings, daughter of the bridge partners and *SDAP* friends of my parents, drops by our house completely shaken. She just comes from the "Mauerwall" on the bridge over the Jan Gijzen canal. The Germans had rounded up all the passers by there and stood them in a circle. Eight men were taken out of a German assault van, put in a row and shot to death. Also she as a fifteen-year-old was forced to watch. Shortly afterwards they stopped Hannie Schaft at that same point.[62] She underwent the same fate, only she was murdered "neatly" in the dunes.

Fourteen days before the liberation.

---

[61] We had given them a nickname, based on a combination of the German and the Dutch for wall: *Mauermuur* – Mauerwall, plural: *Mauermuren.*

[62] Hannie Schaft is the most well-known member of the resistance in the Netherlands. She was executed in the dunes west of Haarlem, used by the Germans as an execution place. Hundreds shared her fate. They are all reburied after the war in a "Cemetery of Honor" near the spot where they were executed. Hanny Schaft is a key figure in the novel *De Aanslag* by Harry Mulisch, published in an Amercian edition under the title, "The Assault."

CHAPTER 15

The frightened tiny bird

Wednesday, September 25, 1991. Two Dutch colleagues, Runa Hellinga and Henk Hirs, along with their Belgrade Serbian female interpreter, an Austrian female journalist and I drive to a new act of the war theater in Yugoslavia: Šid on the Serbian-Croatian border. The *Jugoslovenska Narodna Armija*, the Yugoslavian People's Army, had a couple of months earlier invaded Croatia, which in June had proclaimed independence. The conquering was executed under the pretext "to prevent a civil war" and to "save the Serbian minority from genocide by the Croats."

From a cozy sidewalk café in Belgrade to the war is only fifty miles. Not yet an hour's drive against the sun and we are there. For a change once again there is a truce. But the activity of the *JNA* before and in Šid is immense. A gigantic army force is being built up. We are hardly able to squeeze our way alongside hundreds of trucks and tanks. Šid is just inside Serbia, four miles north is Tovarnik in Croatia. The day before it was "liberated" by the local Serb militia. We are allowed to go there, but because it's still kind of risky, the female colleagues stay behind in Šid. Henk, his Serbian interpreter and I crawl on a trailer behind an army tractor which hops around all the tanks to Tovarnik. Also in Tovarnik, the streets are jam-packed with tanks and trucks of the *JNA* and it is totally obvious: a large scale offensive is being prepared here, but until then Vukovar, 15 miles North-East of Tovarnik, was nothing more than a name out of hundreds. A few weeks later it would look like Stalingrad after the battle of 1943.

We were taken to the local Serb militia commander. He and his pals have put up themselves in the living room of a run away Croatian family. The carpet is already dirty due to the frequent walking in and out, the furniture stands topsy-turvy, but the cups still stand nicely in the china cupboard against the wall. "Is there a Serb majority in this town?" we ask. No, it is two-third Croatian, but before the Second World War more Serbs than Croats were living here. That explains it. Slowly we had become familiar with this kind of illogical logic. It happens on all sides. You always do find a year in history in which your group had the majority or that the territory was yours – and that justifies chasing away, conquering, murdering and everything else thinkable or unthinkable.

The vast majority of the Croats did not wait for the "liberation" and has fled. A great deal of the houses is damaged, shot at with tanks, not with the rifles of a few local Serb rebels. It's obvious that the *JNA* once again has "intervened to prevent a civil war." The commander asks us to come along with him to their newly installed "police station," but first we do have to tie white ribbons around our arms: the Serb identifying mark to prevent attentive militants from taking us for *Ustaši*, because there still are Croatian snipers in the village and it goes without saying that they don't wear white arm ribbons. *Ustaši* was the name of the fascists, who were in power during WWII in Croatia, at that time a satellite state of Nazi-Germany. In the Serbian propaganda the Croats again were called *Ustaši* to suggest they were fascists. In an opposite way the Croats called the Serbs *Četniks*, the name of the Serbs who also were supposed to have fought on the German side during WWII.

We walk to the "police station" across the street, talk a quarter of an hour with the commander and a few of his fellow warriors, when outside a loud fight breaks out. Intuitively we know that it is not just a fight. We all run outside – the Serbs and we. Arriving outside, we see an armed Serb. Across from him: four citizens, their age varying between 35 and 65. The oldest and the Serb have a heated argument, the other three just stand around. Then the Serb lifts his rifle and aims at the oldest. I yell at the top of my voice in Serbian, "Don't shoot, don't shoot!" But he shoots, nevertheless. The man turns halfway and falls then forward as if he stumbles over something. I want to go up to it, but Henk stops me, "Stay out of this, otherwise they will shoot you down, too," he rightfully warns. In the meantime the Serb also shoots the other three down; they collapse wounded.

The commander says, "Come on, let's take that one guy along and ask him what it was all about." At my question whether he shouldn't first take care of the wounded, he answers that I did not need to worry, because "they are only shot in their legs and an ambulance will bring them to a hospital shortly." We return to his headquarters, together with the Serb who had just done the shooting. He sits opposite us, not at all a macho-killer but a frightened tiny bird who looks at us with big eyes. He had found the four in a basement and "one of them has two sons and they are *Ustaši* who live in Zagreb and the other one has three sons, also *Ustaši* living in Zagreb." The commander puts a hand grenade on the center of the table and says, "That one guy wanted to throw a hand grenade at him (he points at the frightened tiny bird), that's why he shot."

"But what about the other three?" I ask. The commander immediately understands the implication of the question and says, "Maybe we will find some more hand grenades down there." Henk and I had not seen any gesture of the oldest one during the fight, that in the least resembled a throwing movement. They simply were four Croatian citizens, who were in hiding because they were afraid of local Serbs – not unjustified as it turned out.

After ten, twelve minutes the conversation was over. We went outside again and there the four men were lying in exactly the same position. No ambulance in sight. On the other hand, dozens of soldiers and officers of the *JNA* had arrived to watch, but they did not do anything. A local armed Serb militia man with a Red Cross armband went to the oldest, turned him over and observed that he was dead. He felt the pulse of two of the wounded, who did not say anything but were still moving. The third wounded man still did some talking and leaned on his elbow, his shirt was soaked with blood. Another officer of the local militia gave some order and then the victims were dragged one by one on their backs by their shoulders to a walled inner court. They tried to hoist up the least wounded one, but he collapsed, so he was dragged in the same way to that inner court. That local officer went along. Shortly afterwards three shots sounded: the three wounded were slaughtered. The officer returned outside and apparently only then he noticed us for the first time, because he asked inquisition-like, "What are those two civilians doing here?" I hurried to say that we were guests of the commander, who was still with us and confirmed it. Henk and I knew what both of us were thinking of: the TV-team of our Soviet colleagues which a few weeks earlier had disappeared somewhere in the war zone without a trace – as was their car. Henk's Serbian interpreter used all her charms to cut the tension. The officer asked where we wanted to go. "To Šid," we answered. All right, he would provide a Red-Cross car, but, he added threateningly, *"Vi nište videli ništa"* – you have not seen anything which in Serbian sounds extra severe because grammatically it is a double denial, so that you can underline the denial verbally two times, literally, "You *not* have seen *nothing.*"

The car, provided with a jumbo-sized Red Cross, was fully loaded with weapons. The officer sat down next to the driver in the cab, connected by a little hatch to the back part where we were sitting on a bench in line with the car. Near the tailgate left of us an armed soldier was seated, to the extreme right our Serbian girlfriend, constantly chatting through the hatch with the officer about this, that and the other. In Šid we were allowed to get off.

The next day we met Ewoud Nysingh of the Dutch daily *De Volkskrant* who a few hours after us, had also been in Tovarnik. The Serbs showed him four corpses in an inner court; "Those are Serbs, killed by the Croats," they had told him. We have checked everything extremely precisely and it is beyond any doubt: they showed him the corpses of the four Croats. And this proved indisputably that, indeed, the three wounded were slaughtered.

The Dutch ambassador at-large Henri Wijnaendts, who on behalf of the president of the European Community Hans van den Broek went to extreme lengths to achieve some kind of peace in Yugoslavia, happened to be in

Belgrade. We informed him about the murder and next day, so he told us later, he also acquainted the Serbian president Milošević. Shortly afterwards Henk and Runa also told the whole story to general Milan Pujić of the ministry of Defense when they were with him for an interview. You never should give a chance to legends like *Wir haben es nicht gewusst* (we did not know it), a phrase that was used by Germans for a long time after the war.

Just in those days a new independent TV-station was founded: Studio B. One of their reporters asked me whether I would be willing to tell on camera what I had experienced in Tovarnik. I do have to admit that I hesitated to say yes. Yet, given the Serbian propaganda by which *the* Serbs were the victims and *the* Croats the psychopathic murderers, I thought some counterweight could be useful. At any rate, the broadcast had a noticeable consequence: the storage of my fifth-wheeler on a Belgrade campground was canceled "because I don't want to have anyone on my campground who is saying that Serbs are murderers," so he told a Serb, without knowing that this was a good friend of mine.

Henk and I let our jobs be our jobs for two days. As a matter of fact I wanted a little rest at my Montenegrin apartment in Radovići, a small village on the Adriatic coast, 400 miles down south, far away from the war turmoil. A few days later I was there – but, as I already described, not for a little rest.

CHAPTER 16

Liberation – one

It is eight or nine minutes past half past eight on Friday evening the fourth of May 1945. I'm already in bed upstairs, and my parents and my little sister as well.

Outside voices sound. At first a few, but very quickly increasing in numbers. How is that possible? You have to be inside at eight. I get out of my bed, open the window. To my amazement: dozens of people on the street. One of them is neighbor-boy Jaap Veen. "What's going on?" I shout. "The Krauts have capitulated. We are free!," he shouts with joy. "That's not true, it must be a rumor," I answered without any hesitation.

I did not tell him why I was so sure, but at Dik van den Haak's place I had just listened from a quarter past eight to half past eight to Radio Orange. Nothing about capitulation and liberation. Right away at half past nine, I had returned home. The first part through the back alley. Then, I had to cross the street. A look to the left and right. No Germans? No. Then fast-run home. Undress and to bed.

Now everything in the reverse order. Dress at full speed and back across the street. Of course, Dik had also heard of "the rumor" and had immediately started to scour the ether. Knowing what he had to pay attention to, he had understood through a BBC-Norwegian broadcast that the Germans, indeed, had capitulated, to take effect the next day. So it is true!!

We are completely at a loose end. We do the silliest things. Now everyone has taken to the streets. Gone fear of the *moffen*. Our steady group of friends and all other neighborhood peers hook arm-in-arm and sway back and forth right across the width of the street-and-curb up to the front yards on both sides: back and forth, back and forth. A waving strip of at least 100 feet: the street is ours again. We are bursting of hunger, we are as thin as a rail, but we keep on running back and forth tirelessly. Until suddenly the story goes around, "They are pulling down the *Mauermuur* on the Stuyvesant Bridge." That's the bridge across the Delft, since the evacuations on September 19, 1944, the end of civilization. Also here, a narrow pedestrian's passage was left open in the wall; the district behind it was immediately popularly called "The Crimea" – which after the war would also become the official name. But shortly before the end of the war that passage was closed with bricks. En masse, we advance to the Stuyvesant Bridge. The story turns out to be true: with pickaxes, neighbors are

DE OPRECHTE HAARLEMMER

1e Jrg. No. 34 — VERSCHIJNT IEDERE DONDERDAG EN MAANDAG — 5 Mei '45

DE BEVRIJDING

Goddank, zo is de bevrijding dan toch nog onverwachts gekomen. Toen de onvoorwaardelijke overgave gisteren bekend werd ging een golf van vreugde over ons land. Mensenmassa's stroomden de straat op en hosten door de stad. Onmiddellijk werden vele vlaggen uitgestoken. Op vele plaatsen begon men de uiterlijke kentekenen van de Duitse overheersing te verwijderen. In Haarlem-Noord stroomde een grote menigte naar de zich aan het einde van de Stuyvesantstraat bevindende "Mauermuur". Een enthousiast stadgenoot kwam, zodra het nieuws bekend werd, met een grote moker op de muur af, om dit obstakel, waaraan hij zich al zo lang geërgerd had, even uit de weg te ruimen. Onder de toejuichingen der samengestroomde menigte brak hij met geweldige mokerslagen de stenen één voor één weg. Van alle kanten kwam men met fakkels aandragen om bij te lichten. Vlaggen werden op de muur geplant en men zette het Wilhelmus in. Velen zongen het nog wat vals, omdat zé het zo'n lange tijd niet hadden kunnen zingen, anderen wat zacht omdat zij nog niet geheel van de angst voor de Duitse slavendrijvers bevrijd waren, maar tenslotte vergat men dit alles in de vreugde der bevrijding, zodat het gezang tot een orkaan aanzwol. Maar nog moest men zich voor de fanatieke Nazi's in acht nemen en op last van de Ondergrondse werden de Uiterlijke kentekenen van vreugde verwijderd en ging men uiteen. Overal hoorde men schoten. Waren het D. die blij waren, dat de co.log ook voor hun was afgelopen of fanatieke Nazi's? Men wist het niet en schonk er ook geen aandacht aan. Alles zonk in het niet voor de vreugde van de herwonnen vrijheid, die vijf lange jaren door de vijand onderdrukt werd.

Een zware last is van ons afgewenteld. De vijand, die nog een maand geleden het hele gebied tussen Rijn en Oder in zijn bezit had, is in een bliksemsnelle opmars ten val gebracht en zal niet meer opstaan. De kopstukken der Nazi-Partij zijn dood. Hun namen staan in de Geschiedenis met bloed geschreven. De storm in Europa luwt, de zon breekt weer door de wolken. Zij zendt haar stralen ook over het verhongerde en getrapte Nederlandse Volk, dat zich klaar maakt voor haar opbouwende taak in een nieuwe en betere wereld.

Gisteravond deelde Montgommery in zijn communiqué mee: De vijand in de Vesting Holland, N.W. Duitsland en Denemarken heeft onvoorwaardelijk gecapituleerd. Hedenochtend om 8 uur wordt van Duitse zijde bevel gegeven om de wapens neer te leggen. Dönitz is op weg naar Noorwegen, waar hij de belachelijke strijd voortzet.

Liberation issue of "De Oprechte Haarlemmer", May 5, 1945, with the title "De bevrijding," "The liberation." The drawing is made by Rob van den Haak, the same who walked a couple of months earlier through the same "Mauer"wall (see also photo 33).

busily chipping away the bricks. Every piece that falls is greeted with jubilation. In an amazingly short time the passage is a passage again, not yet four hours after we had just only *heard* that the Krauts had given up.

Toward midnight, dead-tired but intensely satisfied we return to Dik's place. After all, we have to produce our liberation paper. Dik's 15-year-old brother Rob, who had designed from time to time maps of the front for our paper, made a marvelous drawing of the demolition of the wall, Dik made a report to go with it and after a night of work at full tilt our paper was ready in a special circulation of 500 copies. The next day we distributed them downtown, they were torn out of our hands and we had to print several hundreds more copies.

At last, the bone-dry flag can be hoisted. There is no food at home anymore, the central kitchen does not work anymore and a whole week long I don't eat anything. But I don't notice it, I live on my emotions. These run so high that I lose my voice and for days I can only produce some hoarse sounds. After one week the papers announce that we are going to get two pounds of crackers per person. That must be a misprint. But it wasn't, we really get eight pounds of crackers for our family.

Saturday, May 5, Boeli, a part Indonesian boy with a dark face, walks along our street. Next to him a peer with such an intense white face – never in my life I have seen somebody that white. He had been a Jewish person in hiding, outside again for the first time in three years. And who joins on Sunday our group on the street: Jettie de Vries. No, they had not "gone to Switzerland" at all. They had spread that rumor around on purpose. Actually, they had gone into hiding in the dwelling-house above the family shop De Vries in the Cronjestraat which was, mark you, "aryianized."[63]

Tuesday, May 8, we meet a legend, a voice that turns out to have a body to go with it, "Bob of Radio Orange", aka A. den Doolaard, who in an army uniform visited his in-laws. He is the guest of honor at the street festival that evening and Dik van den Haak does an exclusive interview with him in *De Oprechte Haarlemmer*, the first in liberated Holland.

But there also are other kinds of meetings. Aagje Swart and her mother join a kind of liberation parade at a street festival on the Junoplantsoen, while her

---

[63] Already in 1941 all Jewish property got confiscated. Jewish owners had to transfer (without being paid) their shops to a non-Jewish administrator, even in Holland only named with the German word *Verwalter*, who was appointed by the Germans. They were either Germans or Dutch national-socialists. This procedure was officially called "aryanization." The De Vries family had the same kind of helpers as the Frank family had in Amsterdam. When our school restarted in September, 1945, it turned out that schoolmate Max Herz had also survived the war.

dad just has been picked up because of his *NSB* membership. And some three days after the liberation, a man on a bike is approaching me at the Stuyvestant square. On his lapel he is wearing an Orange-ribbon. On a bike, how is that possible?[64] And all of a sudden I see who he is: Mr. Bossers. We see each other and shyly say hello to each other. Shortly after that, he is picked up, as is his wife. My father does some kind of research on their situation and it turns out that Mr. Bossers had resigned his membership in 1943. What's more, he had participated from conviction in the railroad strike (he was stationmaster in Haarlem). Mrs. Bossers was seriously ill. Also because it was known they had not been traitors, my father, not yet fully recovered from his short stay in Rees, went to great lengths to get them free. He succeeded, first him, then her – already in the summer of 1945 they were, no, not home, because their home including furniture was confiscated; now, a civil servant of the Haarlem legislature was living there. They were staying with relatives. Skinny, with thin messy hair, she was lying on a camp bed. Their son Kees was lost.

Fall 1945. There's a ring at the door: Kees stands in front of me. In ordinary boys' clothes. He had God-knows-how returned from Germany to Holland, had no idea about the whereabouts of his parents and guessed it would be safest to drop by our place first; so it went in May 1940, so it went again five years later. Mrs. Bossers died (of cancer) in the beginning of 1946, Mr. Bossers first remarried a ticket-clerk of the railway. She was the daughter of Y.G. van der Veen, the director of *De Arbeiderspers*, who in July 1940 had committed suicide when the *NSB* took over the company. After this marriage failed, he married to the widow of a member of the former resistance, who was executed during the war. In 1946, the image of Kees Bossers, who really was not my bosom buddy anymore, disappeared, as it were, off my screen. I did not see him back until 2005. He did not want to say one word about his wartime past and it turned out that he had literally deleted it from his memory. He neither remembered that he stayed with us during the May days of 1940, because his parents were detained, nor that the first thing he did after his return from Germany in 1945 was coming to us, because he didn't know where his parents were. I handed him the book I borrowed from him in June, 1940. It carried an inscription of his grandfather which said, "For your ninth birthday." He gave it back, saying, "Keep it as a memento." Even that real part of his past was unwanted.

A few months after the liberation, I met his fellow member Frans Schifferstein close to the railway station in Bloemendaal. We passed each other at a distance and calling out in passing. I asked him how he was doing,

---

[64] All mens' bikes were being confiscated by the Germans, unless you were either a *NSB* member or had been able to hide it somewhere.

because he walked kind of bent over. His face that never had shown, with all impartiality, any sort of kindness, was now distorted with anger, "They kicked my stomach to pieces," he shouted grimly. And with "they", he was referring to the guards of the camp, in which he was apparently locked up for a while. My liberation was the decline of his world.

But the liberation seems to me also as an end. Still on that very same Saturday, May 5, after the first festive flush had passed, I said to myself, "What do I have to live for yet?" The somewhat older Dutchmen already had a past on May 10, 1940, for them the occupation was an interruption of the normal life, which they would pick up again after the occupation. We, on that date kids of about ten, had no past; we had just started to build a past, looking at the world around us. We had only one goal in life in those five years: the liberation. That's what we lived for and we did not think a second about what should happen after that. That whole goal in life fell away in one blow on May 5 and it gave in a way a feeling of emptiness. But this emptiness did not take away the joy at all: for me those hours on Friday the fourth of May between half past nine and midnight remain the greatest hours of my life.

The Dutch poet Leo Vroman, now living in the United States, wrote this poem just after the war:

Come tonight to tell me stories,
How the war has disappeared.
And repeat them thousand times.
All the time I shall shed tears.[65]

What a terrible kitsch. But how terribly true.

---

[65] In Dutch:

Kom vanavond met verhalen
hoe de oorlog is verdwenen.
En herhaal ze duizend malen,
alle malen zal ik wenen.

INTERMEZZO

If I had only thought right away of that key-numeral *five* on that tenth of May 1940, the day that the Germans invaded the Netherlands, then I would have been able to predict exactly the end of the war and the occupation. Just think about it: the war started on Friday (the *fifth* day of the week), May (*fifth* month) 10 (2 x *five*), 1940 (8 x *five*). It lasted until May 15 (3 x *five*), that means *five* days. The subsequent occupation lasted until May (again *fifth* month) 5, 1945 (9 x *five*). So the war and the occupation lasted *five* years minus *five* days. The symbol for freedom and liberation was the *Fifth* Symphony of Beethoven. And the *V*ictory we were hoping for for five years starts with the letter *V*, which is the Roman number for five. And I was ten (2 x *five*) when the Germans invaded Holland, and fifteen (3 x *five)* on the day of liberation.

Also after the war the number *five* continued to play a remarkable role in my life. When I had typewritten the last page of the manuscript for my book *Radio Hilversum 1940-1945*, it turned out to be page... *five* hundred *fifty-five*. And when was I expelled from Yugoslavia? On October (tenth month, so 2 x *five*) 5, 1994, with a return ban for *five* years after a stay for ten(2 x *five*) years. And believe me, I'm not superstitious yet.

CHAPTER 17

Liberation – two

Why was nobody going to Czechoslovakia? I was jumping up and down in my chair. It was February 1968 and I was editing a TV documentary on the German resistance between 1933 and 1945, an idea originated after the Von Kielmansegg case. In those days, there were only five broadcasting organizations in the Netherlands, due to historical reasons four "big" ones, which each had several broadcasts weekly and one small one, the *VPRO*, which had a broadcast only once a week. Unlike the "big" ones, the *VPRO* where I was a staff member had no current affairs program. We only made background documentaries. The big ones were supposed to cover the hot news.

In January, the Central Committee of the Czechoslovakian communist party had dismissed the Stalinist secretary general Antonín Novotný and replaced him with Alexander Dubček. What was being said by the communists over there since then was astonishing, but nobody at the Dutch TV was noticing it. Because you did have to kind of read between the lines of their statements – communists always have been masters at veiled statements and initially it was also applied by the "Dubček communists." To be able to read between the lines was not a matter of intelligence but of experience. I was one of the small horde of foolish hobbyists who considered and reconsidered every currant of the communist cake, subsequently drawing razor-sharp political conclusions from the slightest change in their jargon.[66] There were not a great many of those hobbyists working at the Dutch TV, but my feeling was that still enough simple human language emerged from Czechoslovakia that it should have alerted the current affairs guys.

March came around. Still, nobody was going there. It could not go on like this. I called the *VPRO* general manager Arie Kleijwegt with the announcement that I could not take it any longer. "The other broadcasting organizations are failing, terrific things are going on in Czechoslovakia, I have to go there," I argued. He agreed that I could forget about my resistance documentary for a while. Cameraman Jochgem van Dijk and I arrived in Prague on Friday, March 8.

---

[66] Over the years quite a few times I have been announced by the radio or TV as a Czechoslovakian expert, a Poland expert, an Eastern Europe expert, a Soviet expert – as the fluctuations of the events required. More than once, I reacted to that with the remark, "Expertise on these regions does not exist, only degrees of ignorance."

Receptionist Pepi of *Hotel Evropa* was as pleased as Punch when he saw me again.

The real breakthrough came on Saturday, March 9: the censorship was lifted. Censorship lifted in a communist country – that was not a communist country anymore. That very same day the party daily newspaper *Rudé Právo* published a big article about "the concentration camp Leopoldov" where political opponents of the regime had been imprisoned. And they put forth the question whether the last minister of Foreign Affairs of the democratic government, Jan Masaryk had committed suicide at his ministry in 1948 or was thrown out of the window by communist putschists – a subject that had been an absolute taboo for twenty years. There was a festive mood in the streets, the coffee houses were filled with cheerful, elated Praguers – I had not seen Prague like this ever before and for the first time I again had that overwhelming feeling of liberation as on May 4, 1945.

All of a sudden, everything was possible. Doing street interviews. That was absolutely out of the question in a communist country, now it was possible. The chief of the department of current affairs of the Czechoslovakian TV Kamil Winter openly said in front of Van Dijk's camera, "Over twenty years we did not always tell the truth." The Slovak writer Ladislav Mňačko said without beating around the bush, "We have lost twenty years, we have to start from scratch." Only after the lifting of the censorship, the rank and file Czech and Slovak really started to believe that something new was going on. A wave of enthusiasm went through the country: the Prague Spring had broken out. My communist relations, who had fought for years for those reforms, had won. Ludvík Vaculík wrote his *Manifesto of Two Thousand words*, in which he said – to the immense anger of the Russians – that the acquired freedoms must be, if necessary, defended with arms. A year later he would write, as a protest against the occupation, a *Manifesto of Ten Points*, but it would number – subtle Czech humor – exactly two thousand words.

It was out of the question that those, leading the Prague Spring, wanted a capitalist society. They did watch the West concerning its political democracy, but in an economic respect they focused their eyes more on Yugoslavia with its system of labor self-management. Though not the inventor, Dubček was still the bearer of the term with which the new era was characterized: socialism with a human face. A grim tragedy is hiding behind that seemingly gentle expression. It is, after all, the recognition on their part that their "socialism" previously had *no* human face, while to me, that expression is a pleonasm, because socialism without a human face can never be socialism, exactly the reason why I fought vehemently against that system, which used my phraseology to give a "progressive" flavor to a policy that did not much deviate from what the Nazi's had done.

Dozens of books have been published on the Prague Spring, so I'm not going to add one to it. Personally I felt during that spring as elated as the Czechs and Slovaks themselves. A socialist experiment was set up which could have a chance to succeed. Like during the Hungarian insurrection of 1956, workers' councils were spontaneously founded in factories. Four days long we worked day and night in a festive mood, not only in Prague, but also in Bratislava, the capital of Slovakia where attempts for liberalization already had started as early as 1963, partly due to some anti-Czech undertones which 35 years later would play a dominant role and lead to the partitioning into two independent states: the Czech and the Slovak Republics.[67]

The *VPRO* didn't have their broadcasting time until Saturday, March 16, and we were the first in bringing a 45-minutes documentary on the new situation: *Czechoslovakia without censorship.* Little did I know that I would have to make the sad part II: *Czechoslovakia "normalized"* not even six months later.

[67] See appendix page 376.

CHAPTER 18

Traveling in Eastern Europe

That use of my "phraseology" for a system, which did not deviate much from the one under which I was compelled to live from 1940 to 1945 – that irritated and at the same time intrigued me. I especially wanted to take a close look at the "cradle" of "socialism," the Soviet Union. But you could not go there as an individual traveler, you always had to go with a kind of "delegation," and I refused to be dragged along through the "achievements of socialism" as a part of an obedient "collective."

My chance came in 1957. In September/October the Soviet Union announced that tourists were allowed to visit the Soviet Union with their own cars. Two routes were released: Brest-Litovsk (at the Polish-Russian border)-Moscow-Yalta and Brest-Litovsk-Moscow-Leningrad. It was a good year after Khrushchev had unmasked Stalin at the 20th party congress of February 1956. That something was going on in the Soviet Union had already been shown somewhat earlier, when the Soviet Union officially announced that "the Jewish doctor's conspiracy" (invented by Stalin shortly before he died) had never existed, that the confessions were extracted forcibly and that the functionaries, who had executed it, had been arrested. When I heard that report on the radio, I literally fell through my knees from amazement, my arms thrown straight up in the air. Such a recognition had not taken place since the October revolution of 1917.

So now, you could go to the Soviet Union individually. You were obliged, though, to take along a "guide" from the state tourist office *Inturist*, but you were more or less able to make up your own program. I immediately decided to sign up for such a trip, but the winter period did not seem to me the best time to travel across the Soviet Union. Moreover, as a free-lancer I had to enter into contracts. It succeeded: I bought a used *Volkswagen* and at the end of April 1958 I left. In Poland the liberal communist Gomułka had come to power in October 1956 and on my way on I would stay for two weeks in the Southern part of Poland, on my way back in the Northern part.

I had only a little money at my disposal and I had rebuilt my little *Volkswagen* in such a way that I could sleep in it. Moreover, I had some addresses of Poles where I possibly could lodge, which I had received from a communist-orientated acquaintance, who once had participated in a communist Youth Festival somewhere in Eastern Europe. The travel in the Soviet Union cost about

$ 1,000, everything included, the guide as well. I had opted for the route to Yalta, the place of the famous conference.

Already in those days, the official Poles no longer belonged to the usual brand like in the rest of the communist "bloc," where they claimed that everything was spick and span. At the Polish embassy in the Netherlands, they warned me, "Take care for your car, because you run the risk they'll take the wheels off your car during the night." Now more than ever I decided to spend the nights in my *Volkswagen.*

But Poland was a relief. At all those addresses I have been, they received me with great hospitality and from there they sent me through to other acquaintances – and I did not lose my wheels. Also from the journalistic point of view, it was much better than staying in hotels. I was confronted with all kinds of day-to-day problems such as, "Sorry, we have no toilet paper" – a complaint that held out for more than thirty years.[68] And this was only one of the hundreds which all of them endured for thirty years, too. But the Poles have always had a *savoir vivre,* a "knowing-how-to-live," through all times. Friends regularly come together, never losing their sense of humor even under unbearable circumstances, and will be not brought to their knees. They also stubbornly cling to maintaining courtly etiquettes, the most remarkable being the hand kiss a man gives as he is introduced to a woman. On a trip across the *GDR,* East Germany, in July 1960 together with a colleague from India, Dilip Malakar, we were accompanied by the hard-boiled Stalinist, very German prewar communist Eugen Betzer, on behalf of the *MAA,* the ministry of Foreign Affairs. We repeatedly clashed and every time he snappishly reacted to the criticism I expressed. To tease him, I said, "I don't understand, in Poland I feel at home and Poland is a communist country, too." "Poland a communist country?" he muttered, "over there, they are still giving each other a hand kiss, that's not a communist country." And, as a matter of fact, he actually hit the nail on the head. You also notice it in the Polish language. In Polish the form "you" to address a person is unknown. They say, "Does Mister have..." or "Does Madam believe..." like in former days housemaids and male servants used to address their masters *(see photo 9).*

My new acquaintances took me along everywhere, and once again we were together with a dozen friends when one of them inquired in a friendly way how many communists we had in Holland. "Some three, four percent," I answered. "That means it's more than we have around here," he seriously responded.

---

[68] Barb Guy in the Salt Lake Tribune of August 6, 2006, describes the cordial reception of Cuban journalists in the Press Center in Havana, but, she adds, "they had no toilet paper there." I venture to suspect that this toilet paper problem reaches as far as the communist system is reaching.

Sometimes you did experience unpleasantries. At Easter we visited the neighbors of my hosts. We got some cream crackers, because the lady of the house was in the business of foreign trade and therefore managed to get hold of something. Her live-in aged mother regularly nudged her daughter, said something, upon which the daughter made a fending-off-gesture. But the mother kept on insisting. Finally our hostess said, "I don't like to do this, but my mother insists on telling you that you should not think we are Jewish because we are eating *matzos*." Apologizing, she said that only the older generation thought that way. In the springtime of 1968, at the peak of the so-called "anti-Zionist" action in Poland, which was actually plainly anti-Semitic, a Pole once told me, "Don't worry, if the government is anti-Semitic, we are anti-anti-Semitic."

In 1958 Gomułka was still very popular and considered an extreme liberal. "Please, don't write what all is possible here, otherwise our Gomułka will run into troubles with the Russians," said a female acquaintance who did not want to have anything in common with communism whatsoever. Professor Leszek Kołakowski, once a professor at the Party University in Warsaw, has the opposite opinion. At the end of the sixties he told me in Oxford, England, where he was a professor after his emigration in 1968, "Gomułka was not the beginning, but the end of the liberalization. The party had completely lost its grip on society, he took care that the party regained that grip." He was partly right, but in the day-to-day practice there was a world of difference between the Stalinist- and the Gomułka-era, surely in those first years.

The author Antoni Słonimski once told me an anecdote connected with Kołakowski which, by the way, was based on reality. After his departure for England, Kołakowski's name was not allowed to be mentioned, of course, and the censors were supposed to pay strict attention to that. But most censors are stupid robots. Słonimski once quoted Kołakowski in one of his books, but instead of Kołakowski he had written Skolakowski, counting on it that the censor would only consult the alphabetical list of prohibited writers. His gamble paid off well, the censor let it pass. For every ordinary human being it was clear who was meant. The corruption of his name had a funny side effect, too, because *Skola* means "school," so that Słonimski indirectly also pointed out, that you could learn something from the quoted scholar.

Poles always have been rebellious – and often successfully. In 1956 they had managed to stage their insurrection in Poznań to chase away the Stalinist secretary general of the party Bierut, in whose place came the still amply liberal Gomułka. I was not present then, but I did incidentally end up in a half-insurrection in Nowa Huta. Every "socialist" country had its "socialist city" – always dedicated to the heavy industry. Poland's "first socialist city" was Nowa

Huta, ex Stalincity, a collection of buildings thrown together a few miles outside Kraków in Southern Poland, included a blast furnace industry – a "steel
combination" in the communist jargon. It goes without saying that there was
no room for a church in a socialist city, but it equally goes without saying,
that the Catholic population found it impossible to do without a church. In a
typical Polish compromise, they had left a wide-open space where possibly a
church could be built and to mark that, a several meters-high wooden cross
was erected there. In May 1961, I was visiting some friends in Nowa Huta,
when audibly a commotion was developing in the street. We went out and
the commotion turned out to have been caused by a just-announced decision
of the city government that the cross would be taken away, because a Culture
House would be built on the empty spot.[69] The citizens of this "first socialist
city" did not swallow it and by dozens of thousands they advanced to the cross
to protect it against the demolition-happy authorities. It became a real insurrection, the city got completely cut off from the outside world and foreign
journalists, rushing in from Warsaw, were denied entrance. Police cars did patrol across the town, but did not dare to intervene. Yet, the anger – the Catholic
Poles did not want to have anything in common with communism and not
much was necessary to activate those dormant uneasy feelings – got out of
control and in the long run they started to turn over cars and set them afire.
My little *Volkswagen* was too dear to me to have it sacrificed to the people's
rage – and I returned to Kraków and wrote for the Dutch daily *Het Parool* a for
the regime critical story on the event. A few weeks later there was a reception
at the Polish embassy in The Hague in celebration of a "national holiday." I got
an invitation and the first thing the ambassador said to me when I entered,
was, "Congratulations, you were the only Western journalist present in Nowa
Huta." That ambassador was Dr. Jan Balicki, no Betzer, but an open minded,
tolerant man who represented his country in The Hague for seven years, from
the beginning of 1959 until the middle of 1965. He was of Jewish origin, to me
an absolutely irrelevant fact, were it not that he because of it had fallen into
disgrace during the anti-Semitic campaign after 1967, was dismissed from the
Foreign Service and had to lead a difficult existence somewhere in Lublin. But
the cross remained and with international aid, way back into the communist
era, a real church was being built on the same spot.

The Soviet Union was a different world. My trip there in 1958 would start on
May 15, but I thought it would be wise to cross the border at Brest-Litovsk
the night before. It was dark when I arrived at the Russians: on the bridge

[69] Every self-respecting communist city had to build a "Culture House," mostly used for communist or
communist-orientated events.

across the river Bug. The first thing the, incidentally kind, border guard said to me was, "You weren't going to arrive until tomorrow." I had to wait because the border was already closed. It looked like a border between two hostile countries. Big searchlights along the bank on the Russian side, which showed that this was fenced off with barbed wire. Now and then a border patrol with tracker dogs. From time to time a shot from a rifle or pistol. I was tired and fell asleep.

After an hour the border guard woke me up. "Just follow our car, then it will bring you to your hotel. We can leave the checking of your luggage for tomorrow." That was what you call accommodating. In the hotel I was for the first time confronted with two unmistakable Soviet elements which would accompany me for the next thirty years every time I would enter any Soviet building whatsoever: the immense smell of a cheap kind of furniture polish and the dust covers on every love seat or any other sit-on-thing, so roomy that it looks like the furniture is pregnant.

The next morning, I was woken up by my guide, Slava Zjilin, who had especially come from Moscow to accompany me from the first foot of Soviet territory. He was my age, 29, spoke in spite of a somewhat too thick "R" and somewhat too short "E" fluently German (for instance not *Pférde* ["horses"], but *Pfèrrde*) and revealed himself as a cheerful hard-liner. He had those very light-blue, nearly fluorescent eyes, high cheekbones, blond hair, in short: a typical Russian face. We did not need to return to customs, the customs came to us. Checking the car was a formality. That's why they did not find the four bibles I had received to take along from a Protestant Community in Warsaw for their brothers in Moscow ("If you can get this across the border, it's worth more than gold"). I might be an agnostic, an atheist I'm not.

The endless Brest-Moscow road. Six hundred miles, built by German POW's. Here and there blown out tires. Slava found this quite normal, "Our drivers only get new tires when the old ones are completely worn bald." Now and then a lopsided sunken American GMC truck, remnants of the tens of thousands of trucks, delivered by the United States in the beginning of the war, which remobilized the run-aground Soviet army.

As a foreigner I got special gas coupons: A-60 which entitled me to buy what Slava in all seriousness called airplane gas. The octane content was what the coupon already indicated: 60, and even my *Volkswagen* pinged away lustily when I stepped too hard on the accelerator.

That *Volkswagen* was, by the way, an object of interest. I was the third foreigner using the new tourist law. One Danish journalist had beaten me to the punch, but he did not go as far as Moscow. The second was Henri Nannen, editor-in-chief of the German weekly *Der Stern* (Slava had been his guide also) who had taken the same route as I: Yalta. But he drove with a kind of sports-

Mercedes and according to Slava my *Volkswagen* was the first in the Soviet Union (not counting the German *Kübelwagen*, in WWII the military version of the *Volkswagen*). Everywhere we made a stop, in Moscow as well, a crowd gathered around our small car. Of course, the first surprise was that it had its engine in the rear. The second, that the engine was so small. Their *Pobeda's* (which means "Victory"), a four-person compact car, had a truck-size engine which got 7 miles to the gallon. And this caused the third surprise: my small *Volkswagen*-engine got 36 miles to the gallon. As a matter of fact, they did not believe it, but Slava was honest enough to confirm it. He also had to convince them of the no less unbelievable fact that the *VW* could do 60 to 65 miles per hour. Then how much horsepower did it have? Thirty? Only that much? Head-shaking in disbelief *(see photo 8)*.

To accomplish the program I had formulated, getting up early was a must. If you wanted your breakfast at eight, you had to order it at seven. Waiting time for your dinner was one-and-a-half to two hours. Now legendary data, but I had yet to learn it. At noon we did not eat at all or we took a food-stand-snack and only late in the evening toward half-past eight we ventured to order a dinner. In Moscow we were seated among the ordinary customers, but everywhere else we were put in a separate room, even in a big city like Kharkov.

As much as this is possible in the Soviet Union, Slava and I became friends. On those hundreds of lonely kilometers from Moscow to Yalta (I still remember the sign, "Next gas station 453 km" – 300 miles), he sang Russian and I Dutch songs. He avoided political conversation, but he was willing to confess, that the unmasking of Stalin had shocked him deeply. He hinted he held no high esteem for (then the party leader) Khrushchev, all the more so because he did not uphold the decorum. "Sometimes he drinks seven, eight water glasses of vodka in succession," he said reproachfully. One evening, I ended up in a restaurant in a company of Russians. Slava was at home with his wife in his Moscow apartment, so there were no prying ears present and they were pretty frank. One of them said that Khrushchev was not that popular in the Soviet Union, but that he personally was very grateful to him "because he released all concentration camp prisoners. Without him I would still be there." But, so he added, he did not want to grumble: in the ten years he had spent there he had not grown older "because for ten years I have been frozen in." Now, he occupied himself with writing children's books. I would have liked to elaborate with him on it, but in spite of the de-Stalinization, in 1958 the time was not ripe yet to talk about Stalin's concentration camps just like that in a restaurant.

One point on my program was that visit to the Protestant brothers of the Warsaw Protestant church, because I had to get rid of my bibles. They had their own small building somewhere in Moscow. Slava brought me there and the minister turned out to be a very law-abiding Soviet citizen – at least in the presence of Slava. No, no church persecution; yes, religious education was allowed. There was also something to see in the building, so I let Slava stray off a bit. In an unguarded moment I quickly handed my four bibles over to the minister and told him from whom they came – but even in that unguarded moment he remained the law-abiding Soviet citizen. "I don't understand," he said, "we can import bibles without any problem." According to me, he fibbed which does not befit a Christian, but he probably thought I was an agent provocateur or yet more-probably he thought to be guarded even in unguarded moments, a possibility already put forward by George Orwell in his book *1984*.

I have done another naughty something in Moscow. I was staying in hotel *Ukraina* and along the street opposite the hotel ran a long fence, behind which I suspected construction activities. Until one day I could get a view over the fence from an upper floor of hotel *Ukraina* and spotted small huts over there. In a Slava-free moment I walked along the fence and discovered a door. And then it turned out that I had ended up in a district composed of hundreds of wooden huts, cut off from the outside world. One was open, ten by ten feet, sparsely furnished, the inside plastered with newspapers as a substitute for wall paper.

There was nobody around and I quickly took some pictures. A short time later one of the inhabitants showed up, and what I did not want to believe was still true: people lived in those huts without windows. The story I wrote about that in *Het Parool* was yet to bring me severe consequences *(see photo 20)*.

To me, Yalta was a highlight. It was there, that in February 1945 the legendary Conference between Churchill, Roosevelt and Stalin was held. Including the persistent legend that there "they divided the world, and the West sold the East European countries." The opposite is true: Roosevelt and even more so Churchill fought, sometimes as lions, to make the best of a bad job, and at least *on paper* they succeeded in laying down the basic laws and rights for all liberated territories. Very often it is forgotten that the factual *power* in Eastern Europe was already in the hands of Stalin by the victories of the Red Army. That all those countries became communist is not due to the "selling out" of Churchill and Roosevelt, but to the fact that Stalin did not stick to the agreements. Roosevelt and Churchill did not have too many illusions concerning Stalin's promises, but they did not have the *power* to force Stalin to fulfill his promises.

Though the agreements may have fallen into smithereens, the buildings where they had been made were still there. The conference building, a former resort of the Czar-family, was now a holiday resort for the workers, of course. The hall with the fireplace where the negotiations took place was now the dining room. And it was fascinating to stand in that inner court, where that famous picture of the threesome, the emaciated Roosevelt in the middle, was taken.

Consistent with what I had already thought, the general impression left from my first Eastern Bloc trip was that you could not speak anymore of an Eastern *Bloc* and that in Poland it was better and in the Soviet Union worse, and consequently the contrast between those two still greater, than I had expected. Better and worse especially in political respects. Open-mindedness and a lack of inhibition in Poland, conformism and cliché behavior in the Soviet Union. But there was also a great difference in the standard of living. The countryside in Russia and the Ukraine looked seriously neglected with ramshackle houses. Often, the children went barefoot. I did not encounter the spirit of, "We won't put up with it", which was so strong in Poland. Hundreds of explanations are to be found for these contrasts, but I don't find them that relevant anymore in 2006 – I limit myself to my observations of then.

Back at the border, underscoring the differences between the two countries by its barbed wire and nightly patrols, I said good-bye to my friend Slava. He had – by order – accompanied me literally until the last yard. I asked him for his address to be able to send him photos. And I asked him to write me, whether he had a son or a daughter, because his wife was nearly due. Just write to *Intourist*, Hotel National in Moscow, he said. And so I did. I really did send him the photos. He never sent news of himself.

As has been said before, since the de-Stalinization in 1956 you could not speak any longer of one Eastern bloc. It goes without saying that the structure of the party in each country of the Warsaw pact was the same. But in terms of the day-to-day effect there were enormous differences. At a conference for human rights of the CSCE (one of the so-called "Helsinki" follow-up conferences) in Ottawa in 1985, I talked about it with the chief of the Hungarian delegation Imre Uranovic. Generally, he stated that the Western World starts from the individual human rights and the Eastern from the collective ones. "OK," I said, "let me for the sake of discussion go along with you that such a common philosophy of that notion does exist in the communist world. But how do you explain then that on the basis of that common way of thinking, a dissident in Hungary only has to pay 1000 forint for producing oppositionist literature, while a dissident in the Soviet Union gets five years camp plus a seven-years-exile for the same offense?" Uranovic looks at me in resignation and answers, "They have [in the Soviet Union] still to learn quite a lot, but," he added, "I assure you that it all will be different under Gorbachev" (who had been in power for just two months at the time).

Based on those differences and also based, of course, on personal, often subjective experiences, I had a list of preference: 1. Poland; Hungary and Czecho–

slovakia together for second; 4. Bulgaria; 5. *DDR* (GDR); 6. Soviet Union; 7. Romania. I'm afraid that the low ranking of the *DDR* (*Deutsche Demokratische Republik* – German Democratic Republic) was partly due to the fact that their party jargon was spoken in the same demagogic tone and in the same machine-gun-German as was wielded by the occupying authorities in the Netherlands from 1940-1945. In the GDR a youth organization existed with the euphemistic name *Gesellschaft für Sport und Technik* – Society for Sports and Technics where teenagers got a *vormilitärische Ausbildung* – a pre-military training. When you saw the pictures of those uniformed children, instructed by the "comrades" of the *Nationale Volksarmee* – the National People's Army, and you put them next tot the pictures of the uniformed children in the Hitler-time, instructed by the "comrades" of the *Wehrmacht* – you had to look very carefully to notice a difference, in no small part due to the fact that the accompanying texts were hardly different; also under Hitler it was called *vormilitärische Ausbildung*. And the way Erich Honecker as the leader of the state youth organization *Freie Deutsche Jugend* (*FDJ*, pronounce: FD-yot – Free German Youth) yelled at his *"FD*-yotler" matched well with the way *"H*-yotler" (of the *H*-yot, the *Hitlerjugend*) were roared at. Language can be terrifying.

I once visited a camp-out of the *Freie Deutsche Jugend*, where at the entrance I was greeted by a 13-year-old uniformed girl. She jumped to attention, held her arm not stretched out but half-bent up (this was the *FDJ* salute) and shouted loudly, *"Freundschaft!* – Friendship!"

And I have also experienced the changing of the guard at Unter den Linden in Berlin at the "Monument against Fascism" in the ex *Zeughaus*, which used to be a kind of military storage building. A platoon of soldiers, dressed in practically the same uniform as the *Wehrmacht* and wearing helmets which seemed to be a compromise between the Soviet- and the *Wehrmacht* helmets, marched on in that all-too-familiar Prussian pass – each one stepping so close to the other that it looks like they are kicking each other's behinds – headed by a stiff-playing military band; along Unter den Linden as if it was 1939. It was reported by the TV and I went to the *Berichterstatter*, the reporter, and told him that I had to look at that for five years during the war, and that I had watched the spectacle with shivers running down my spine. But he said that this simply happened to be a German tradition which had nothing to do with national-socialism or the *Wehrmacht*.

On that trip in 1960 under the guidance of Betzer, I already had some highly unpleasant experiences, as well. To begin with Betzer himself: he was wearing a pin of honor, elongated, made of wood, painted half-red, half red-yellow-black. On the red part was written in white numbers: 1918-1923. That was, Betzer said, a distinction "because of participation in the armed combat against the republic of Weimar."[70] It did not occur to me immediately, but later on I understood why exactly 1923 was the end year. In November of that year, Hitler and his national-socialists perpetrated their putsch against the republic of Weimar in Munich. True, the coup failed, but seen formally it was from that year on no longer decent to identify yourself with attempts to kill that republic. That does not alter the fact that the German communist party de facto lustily continued to do so on the orders of the "Comintern," the "Communist International" based in Moscow, sometimes even in cooperation with the Nazis.

On our tour of the GDR I had seen concentration camps in Brandenburg and Eisenhüttenstadt (literally "Blast Furnace City"). In Brandenburg we just passed it by, but I intentionally drew Betzer's attention to it: he did not react. In "the first socialist city" of the GDR, Eisenhüttenstadt, ex Stalinstadt, we were guided by a local functionary – converted to communism after 1945. When we crossed the town, we saw, next to a blast furnace, a concentration camp: rows of barracks, barbed wire, watch towers.

"I see a concentration camp there," I said to the local companion. I was not supposed to call it that, it was a "labor camp." Those sitting there had resisted against the laws of the GDR and those doing so "stecken wir hinter Stacheldraht – we put behind barbed wire," according to the local companion.

"When I see the wings of a duck, the legs of a duck and the head of a duck – then I call that a duck. And when I see the barracks of a concentration camp, the barbed wire of a concentration camp and the watch towers of a concentration camp – then I call that a concentration camp," I responded. No reaction, neither from Betzer, nor from the local functionary who, by the way, had participated in the war against the Soviet Union as a soldier of the Wehrmacht.

A few days later we visited the former Nazi concentration camp Buchenwald near Weimar, which was still being used even after the war as a concentration camp, not only for Nazis, but for social-democrats as well who had resisted the merger of the SPD (Socialist Party of Germany) and the KPD (Communist Party of Germany) into the Sozialistische Einheitspartei Deutschlands (SED – the Socialist Unified Party of Germany). The in the fifties popular West Berlin Senator Lipschitz was as a social-democrat thrown into the camp by the Nazis before 1945 and after that, again as a social-democrat, by the communists – literally and metaphorically lumped together with the Nazis.

In Buchenwald we were given a special guide and, added to Dilip Malakar

[70] Officially the decoration was called: Medaille für Teilnahme an den bewaffneten Kämfen der deutschen Arbeiterklasse in den Jahren 1918-1923 – Medal for the participation in the armed combats of the German working class in the years 1918-1923.

and me, was a functionary from Egypt, which in those days formed together with Libya, the "United Arabic Republic," the UAR, under the leadership of Nasser. The guide told something about a certain cruel SS commander Schobert. After listing what horrifying things he had done, he said, "And where is Mister Schobert now? He lives in the Federal Republic of (West) Germany, in Düsseldorf." I knew quite a lot about Buchenwald, but the name Schobert did not sound familiar to me. "Who can that Schobert possibly be?" I asked Betzer later on.

"Not Schobert, Schubert, *Pistolenschubert*, Pistol-schubert."

"*Pistolenschubert*," I responded, "but he was the *Lagerführer*, the camp commander. The Russians arrested him after the war, sentenced him to life imprisonment, but released him after a year and let him go to West Germany. There, he was immediately arrested, got life imprisonment and lives now, indeed, in Düsseldorf – but in the prison." But to Betzer this was not relevant. Somewhat later the guide tells the story of Dr. Kurt Eisele, who did medical experiments on prisoners in Buchenwald. "And what does the Adenauer (then Federal Chancellor in West Germany) administration do?" he asked again rhetorically, "It let Eisele escape." I asked the guide whether he might be willing to tell where to he went. "That is not relevant," he answered.

"It *is* relevant," I remarked. "He escaped to Egypt and not with the cooperation of the West German government. They asked the UAR government, mind you, for his extradition, but it refuses to send him back to West Germany. Just tell that Egyptian that Eisele is with them."

This conversation went in German and the Egyptian understood only English. The guide did not show any intention of addressing the Egyptian about Eisele and that's why I myself started to explain it to him in English. But Betzer interrupted me with a dismissive gesture, quickly snapping at me in German: "Shut up, we are close to having diplomatic relations with the UAR and we have to be very careful. We'll talk about it later." This is indeed what we did and Betzer repeated, "We are close to having diplomatic relations with the UAR and we have to be very careful. That's why the guide did not say anything about the persecution of the Jews. When pure Arab delegations are being guided around here, they do tell something about it, but in a very special and careful way."

"Antifascism" in the GDR was not indignation about the past, but an instrument for the policy of today, a façade for propaganda against "The West" and especially against West Germany.

At the end of the tour, you are always requested to write down something in the visitor's book. My entry read, "I hope that all concentration camps all over the world will be closed down, also those which I have seen in Brandenburg and Eisenhüttenstadt."

No, the GDR and I never became friends and for that reason I went there with the greatest aversion. But once I had a lot of fun there. It was in January 1966. Jan Nagel, like me a radio/TV journalist, had just become a member of the central board of the *Partij van de Arbeid*, the Dutch Labor Party. He was one of the "fashionable leftishers" of those days and he wanted to put out feelers toward the GDR and proposed to the central board to send a delegation to that "first Workers and Farmers State on German territory." The Labor Party did not like the idea of an official delegation at all, but agreed to a half-official one. I really don't know what the criteria for the composition of the delegation were, but Jan Nagel asked his colleagues from the broadcasting organization *VARA*, André van der Louw and Wim Bloemendaal, and me to join him. We agreed and Jan Nagel got us an invitation.

One fine day, we left for Berlin in my Ford Taunus station wagon. In Helmstedt, at the West/East German border, we were waited on by an about 25-year-old colorless person of the *SED*. This was the beginning of the comedy. The first thing the colorless person asked was, *"Wer ist Herr Nagel? –* Who is Mr. Nagel." *Herr Nagel* makes himself known and he has to come along with the colorless person in this special, distinguished *SED*-limo; we, the ordinary Labor plebs, were allowed to follow them in my suddenly to a poor-guy's shrunk little Taunus. We were put up in hotel *"Johannishof, Gaststätte der Regierung der DDR –* guest hotel of the government of the GDR" in *"Berlin, Hauptstadt der DDR –* Berlin, capital of the GDR," a phrase they never failed to add. At the reception desk the second act of the comedy follows. Again the question, now from the receptionist, *"Wer ist Herr Nagel?"* Jan, somewhat more timid, steps forwards and gets a key. No questions were asked of us: three, apparently similar second-class keys are lying on the desk – those are for the three of us. It turns out that Jan has a complete suite, television included, at his disposal; our rooms are considerably more modest. It is clear: to the *SED,* a member of the central board of the Labor Party is a *Prominentler,* a VIP, who must be, in agreement with the communist principles of equality, considerably better dealt with than the commonplace ordinary rank-and-file members. Even with their historical-perspective on scientific-Marxism-based education, they could not foresee that André van der Louw would not only rise up to become the mayor of Rotterdam but even a minister of Her Majesty's Government, to which the career of Jan Nagel would pale in comparison. No – *Herr Nagel* remained the principal person.

Immediately the next morning, the third act of the comedy developed. We went to visit something very interestingly (I absolutely don't recall what) and it goes without saying that the director and a number of his collaborators of that interesting-something were waiting for us. And, yes, a new variant came out of the mouth of the director, *"Wer ist der Delegationsleiter* – Who is the leader of the delegation?" All three of us immediately pushed *Herr Nagel* forward who, normally never afraid to be the cock of the walk, was not feeling happy at all with the leading role forced upon him in the comedy. That unhappy feeling was to a great extent determined by the fact that of the four of us he had the least command of the German language. Or let me put it honestly: it was on the level of:*"Es ist coolt aussenseite"* ("It's cold outside."). If not for the unfortunate fact that no camera followed our footsteps, it is without any doubt that we would have deserved an Oscar for best supporting actors in the course of that GDR tour. For those not familiar with communist rites: every whether-or-not-a bigwig, receiving a delegation no matter where, holds an opening speech and a good-bye speech. And not only that: it is expected that the visiting delegation leader does it, as well. Therefore, we pushed Jan Nagel forward with satanic pleasure every time the well-known question was asked. Every time it took us the greatest effort to keep a straight face when *Herr Nagel,* stammering and stuttering, showered his broken German over his hosts, who pretended to understand him because, after all, he was a member of the central board of the Labor Party.

We experienced another satanic pleasure, but this time not related to Jan Nagel. One day we are told that we would go to Rostock to have a talk with Prof. Rudolf Schick about a special way of growing potatoes. I knew his name. He was the Chancellor of the University of Rostock and at the same time head of the Agricultural Institute there. But I still knew even more about him, but I kept it in reserve as a surprise, although I informed my fellow members of the delegation.

At the institute in Rostock, we were introduced to Prof. Schick. Yes, it is him. I had seen an old picture of him, but he was still clearly recognizable. We are seated at a table, Schick at the head of it, we on both sides, plus quite a bunch of functionaries. Not only those accompanying us, but also a few local ones. Prof. Schick gives a whole lecture about growing potatoes, which does not interest us at all. When he is finished, I took the floor as the first one (we had mutually agreed on it). I quoted on of his articles, in which he praised the achievements of socialism, the usual propaganda story. "But," I added, "on May 1, 1937 under number 4,865,857 you became a member of the *NSDAP* [the Nazi party] and in front of me I have an article in which you said then pretty much the same thing as now, only the word national-socialism is replaced by socialism" and I asked him for an explanation of how that could be. An icy silence fell among the GDR functionaries, but I have to admit that Schick reacted as if I had asked him why he was wearing brown shoes. "Yes, in former days I had that view, in the GDR, though, I came to a different conviction."

We always were on the road with a procession of cars, *Herr Nagel,* of course, in the first and the nicest. I shared one of the following cars with a few functionaries. For the rest of the tour through the institute they had remained silent, but once we arrived in the car, they burst out. "How dare you do something like that," they shouted. I acted as if I was utterly amazed.

"I don't understand you. Again and again the GDR reveals names of former Nazis, who have leading functions in the Federal Republic. I completely agree with it. I only think that the disclosures should not remain limited to one half of Germany." But that was something totally different. People like Prof. Schick had recognized their mistakes and therefore gotten a new chance. "Also in West Germany, you have repentant former Nazis," I replied, but, nevertheless, I think that they should not become a Chancellor of a university – neither there nor here." From their reactions I could conclude that I had not made new friends *(see photo 36).*

One time *Herr Nagel* failed. That was when I had made an appointment for us with the first dissident in the GDR, Prof. Robert Havemann. In 1932 at the age of twenty-two he had become a member of the communist party and after Hitler's assumption of power he was a member of a communist resistance group. He was arrested and in 1943 sentenced to death and had been sitting in the Berlin Moabit prison together with Erich Honecker. After the founding of the GDR, he was appointed as a professor of philosophy at the Humboldt University in Berlin. More and more, though, he defended in his lectures theses which later on would be realized in the Prague Spring in Czechoslovakia; publicly he declared himself an advocate for a plural party system. He was dismissed in March 1964, expelled from the party and was a private citizen now. He lived in the center of Berlin on the Straussberger Square number 19, part of the ex Frankfurter Allee, ex Stalin Allee, ex Karl Marx Allee, now again Frankfurter Allee. In the evening we should go to Havemann, Jan Nagel had different affairs which to my firm knowledge were of a strictly non-political nature. By doing so, he missed one of the most important parts of our trip. Havemann told us, that the former Nazis at the University had organized petitions against him. "They just let them to do the dirty work. They know they won't dare to refuse because of their Nazi past, and thus are open for blackmail," according to Havemann. One of the order-executors was Werner Hartke, president of the (East) German Academy of Sciences, in the Nazi-time *"Blockleiter"* ("block leader" a term, difficult to translate, but it implicated that you were kind of supervisor of a part of a quarter of a village, town or city) and a member of the *NSDAP.* It goes without saying that Havemann was strongly against "the wall." It was especially a pity that Jan Nagel did not hear this. Maybe he would not have come to the pioneering idea later on to consider the wall "as a historical necessity." Like André van der Louw, he belonged to the influential part within the Dutch Labor Party that was in favor of an unconditional recognition of the GDR and he succeeded in pushing it through in 1969 as the official point of view of the party, frustrating the policy of their political brethren in West Germany *(see photo 11).*

Every delegation visiting the GDR had to submit to an *Abschlussgespräch,* a round off discussion, at the end of the trip. So did we. Half a year before our trip I had made a documentary for the *VPRO*-TV, called "Twice DDR," using the fortunate coincidence that in the German language the abbreviation of *Das Dritte Reich* ("The Third Reich") also was *DDR.* In it I had made comparisons between the daily practice, political indoctrination, youth education, culture policy of both *DDR*'s, nearly completely based on both countries' own file footage. The only material I had added was about former Nazis occupying high functions in the GDR. The hypocrisy of the GDR on this point stuck in my throat considerably. That was my contribution to the *Abschlussgespräch* and I gave the disgusting example of Luitpold Steidle, who not only had been a general in the *Wehrmacht,* but also a member of the *NSDAP,* which was extremely rare among the officer's corps of the *Wehrmacht.* Now, he is the mayor of Weimar, I said, and as a mayor he is a host every time commemorations are taking place in the former concentration camp Buchenwald – and this is unacceptable. They did not lose a word on it. They did have a comment at my second remark, though. It concerned the drivers who every time we went out to eat, were put at separate tables. "With us, as social-democrats, it is customary that they eat at the same table with us." They hastened to state that this was also customary with them, but that they were never sure whether foreign delegations would appreciate that and to be on the safe side, they had the drivers eat separately. In the future, though, they would take my remark into account. It goes without saying that right at the end it came to the hands-shaking-routine. When the highest functionary shook mine, he said, "When you come next time, we will just have a talk about that documentary of yours." So they not only knew that the documentary was aired, they apparently also had a copy at their disposal. That's fine with me. But it is a kind of strange, though, that concerning Schick, who was mentioned in that documentary, they allowed me a shot at an empty goal. I think that by organizing our trip the one left-hand did not know what the other left-hand was doing.

After the collapse of the GDR in 1989, a report about this visit was discovered, written by a certain Niklas, a functionary of the East German Ministry of Foreign Affairs, in which he described my attitude as "self assured and aggressive."[71] In March 1967, Jan Nagel tried to organize a second trip for the four of

---

[71] Report of February 8, 1966, by Niklas (*MfAA,* , the East German Ministry of Foreign Affairs), *Bundesarchiv SAPMO, DY 30/*IV A2/20/493 (German Federal Archives), quoted in *Nederland en de DDR* (The Netherlands and the GDR) by Jacco Pekelder, Amsterdam 1998.

us. The GDR lets him know, though, that only three of them were welcome and that they refused to invite "the Nazi hunter Verkijk" for a second time, also taking into account "his [other] statements during his visit in 1966." Fair enough, Jan Nagel sent them a protest telegram, canceling the trip.[72]

Not only Prof. Havemann, another important GDR personality had also spoken out against "the wall," only a few years earlier, in 1964. With the difference, that Havemann had done it publicly, and the other only to me. That was Ernst Busch. To me, Busch was a legend. His metal voice seemed to have been created to sing the lyrics and music of Hanns Eisler, Bert Brecht and Kurt Weil, although he became most famous because of his role in the film *Dreigroschenoper* (Three Penny Opera) of the twenties, in which he performed in an inimitable way the leading song *Mackie Messer*, Mack the Knife. Not even Louis Armstrong could have done it better.

After 1933 he had fled to the Netherlands and worked for years for the social-democratic broadcasting organization *VARA*. In Spain he performed for the Republicans in their fight against Franco. Later on, he was interned in the Unoccupied Zone of France by the Pétain-Vichy-regime and after the Germans had invaded there also, he was arrested and sent to the Moabit prison in Berlin as well, where he was liberated by the Russians in 1945.

Once a militant singer, always standing up against injustice and suppression, in the GDR he became an obedient, conformist citizen. He lent his voice to the most vulgar propaganda with as an all-time low the song, *"Die Partei, die Partei hat immer recht, und Genossen, es bleibe dabei. Denn wer kämpft für das Recht, der hat immer Recht, Gegen Knechtung und Ausbeuterei* – The Party is always right and, comrades, it should stay that way. Because he, who fights for justice, is always right, against subjugation and exploitation."

Another all-time low was an ode to the first president of the GDR Wilhelm Pieck, "whose name is deeply engraved in the hearts of the people," and of whom it says somewhat further, *"Dein Leben gab Deutschland das Leben –* your life gave life to Germany." Lyrics from Johannes R. Becher, music from (none other than) Hanns Eisler, both also the composers of the East German national anthem.

Busch was not the only one, swung around from an unbendable fighter against injustice to a preacher of injustice, but I was terribly curious how such a process had developed in a person of the caliber of Busch. I spent two consecutive days in his VIP-house on the Heinrich Mann Street in the East Berlin district of

---

[72] Telegram of May 23, 1967 of Jan Nagel to Kurt Kann of the *Nationalrat der Nationalen Front*, the National Council of the National Front, and phone minutes of Kurt Kann of May 20, 1967, *Bundesarchiv, SAPMO, DY 6/vorl.979*, quoted in the same book (see note 71).

Niederschönhausen. Actually, I came away none the wiser and I was shocked by his cheap excuses. "How could I know," he said nearly desperately, "that good communists were being killed in concentration camps in the Stalin era – *umgelegt*" as he put it in German. For him also, *"Wir haben es nicht gewusst* – we did not know." He reacted irritated at my question how for God's sake he could sing a song like *Die Partei had immer Recht.*

"They always say that the *SED* or the communist party is meant by *Die Partei*, but it only says that the party who fights for justice is always right."

"But then, how do you explain the text, later on in the song, that the party is *von Lenin geschweisst und von Stalin gespeist* – forged by Lenin and fed by Stalin?" I asked.

"Yes, of course that was *Blödsinn* – nonsense," Busch admitted. And that terrible "Ode to Wilhelm Pieck" in honor of his 70th birthday, what about that? Yes, as a matter of fact they had recorded a record with a different text, but at the very last moment it turned out that the text had already been published at his 65th birthday.

"In one night Becher made a new text. I personally did not think much of it, but, you know, Becher was not one of our greatest poets," explained Busch.

Those half-truths were not that interesting, the most interesting was, that he, exactly by those answers and the way he formulated them, actually showed that he was ashamed of those songs. He simply had not *dared* to say no. Ernst Busch, who had defied hardships and prisons for the sake of his conviction, had become a chicken under a regime he himself had helped to create. Bert Brecht and he had also signed obtuse "peace petitions." I expressed my amazement about that as well. With great emotion he cried, "Brecht and I went very far with our criticism – to the edge of the grave," and both his forefingers measured out a distance of four inches. He did not want to be more explicit, but he meant to say that they had resisted internally. He thought that the wall, which was three years old at the time, was an absurdity and he called the then party leader Walter Ulbricht a "cultural nitwit." And Erich Honecker, in those days only the leader of the *FDJ*, was in his eyes "a nothing." But why did he not come out of the closet with his criticism instead of publicly supporting the regime in everything? He came forward with the usual bromide, "I don't want to play in the hands of the enemy." Busch was a disappointed man who was left with few illusions. "We are an occupied country, the Russians prescribe everything. But without the Russians they would have hanged me on a tree in 1953 [during the insurrection on June 17]."

To the outside world Busch remained the conformist who was not willing to drop out of the society he was living in, but not wanting to lose his self-respect completely, he still had maintained a kind of internal integrity. He had not sunk into total stupidity and was not willing to defend matters he himself considered indefensible. Without any doubt his frankness was stimulated, not only because I was a Dutchman (Busch was still fluent in Dutch) but also a social-democrat who worked for the *VARA*. He enquired whether S. de Vries Jr. and Eli Bomli (prewar and also for a short time postwar *VARA* phenomena) were still alive, and at my affirmative answer, he gave me a few of his records with a dedication to them to take with me. No, not of the always-be-right-party, but songs of the Spanish civil war which he had recently rerecorded.

He gave them to me as a present, too. Magnificent records. I would not like losing them.

CHAPTER 19

Television documentaries

At any rate quantitatively speaking, my trip to the Soviet Union and Poland was journalistically successful. In total, I had disposed of seventy stories about it, including a number of talks for *VPRO*-radio, the first ever made for Dutch radio from the Eastern block. In Moscow, I was even allowed to use the studio of the Dutch department of Radio Moscow. Editor-in-chief was Jan Wijnkoop, son of the illustrious prewar leader of the Dutch Communist Party, David Wijnkoop. He was very kind and helpful, and apparently pleased with a visit of a Dutchman, even though I did not share his opinions. A regular listener of Radio Moscow, I knew his voice. The voice of Rinske Hoff I knew even better. She was the regular speaker of the Dutch broadcasts and had such an iron voice. She spoke Soviet language in Dutch and for myself I had given her the nickname "the woman with the tractor-voice." She had been married to a Soviet officer, who had been killed in action during the war. Jan said, partly melancholically, partly proudly, that he still had a Dutch passport. He asked me whether he could do an interview with me for his Dutch broadcasts, it could be strictly apolitical. I told him frankly that I considered Radio Moscow a propaganda station and that I refused to collaborate with propaganda institutions, even if my contribution would be non-political. He respected it and I appreciate it that he still provided the technical facilities to record my talk for *VPRO* radio *(see photo 6)*.

But a second trip to the Soviet Union would not follow that soon. In 1959 I wanted to go to Czechoslovakia. I did not get a visa. On my question as to why not, the Czechoslovakian consul said, "You should write the truth about the Soviet Union" – and my remark that perhaps I should go to the Soviet embassy to apply for a visa for Czechoslovakia, most likely did not contribute to speed up the lifting of my entry ban. But we did not live in the computer and telefax era yet. At the Eastern European borders they did not know anything about the decisions of the "centrals," and when in 1959 I chose Turkey as an "alternative country" (I had a family with two children to support), I could go there and back across Bulgaria – which provided me with the necessary experiences and articles. In a way I had it easy, because hardly anybody went to communist countries in those days, so the most ordinary things you experienced contained a story. Still, from a financial point of view, 1959 was an extremely lean year and in 1960 I went to Poland again when it turned out that they did not care about that entry ban. At the Czechoslovakian embassy in Warsaw I got (no computers, no telefax!) a transit visa for Czechoslovakia and in Prague I went to the Ministry of Foreign Affairs to ask why I did not get a visa for their country. They promised to find out. I don't know whether this was of any help, but after some time my first entry ban for Eastern Europe was apparently lifted, because my applications for a visa were honored by country after country. It coincided, by the way, with an increasing, hardly noticed liberalization in the communist world. Nevertheless, journalistically I was getting into a fix. The first time in Poland you can write a story about "the trumpeter of Kraków" or about the rebuilding of the historic center of Warsaw. And in Bulgaria about the Rila monastery or the Black See pleasures in Varna. But the second time these kinds of stories drop out and pretty soon you can no longer write about what *is*, but about what *is changing* in those countries. So only the political and economic stories are left. From the financial point of view, this was too little to live on, so I had to look for other ways. On top of that, I was very much interested in the possibilities television was offering to make people wiser. For years I had written radio and TV reviews for the weekly *Vrij Nederland* and the press agency *Regionale Dagblad Pers* (a syndicate of regional dailies) and because of that I fancied to know something of those media. That's why in 1963, when I once more got a visa for Czechoslovakia, I proposed to Herman Wigbold, at the time editor-in-chief of the current affairs program *Achter het Nieuws* ("Behind the news") of *VARA* TV, to do some TV reports there. He did see something in it, but the then lord and master of the *VARA*, J.B. Broeksz, did not want to go for it at any price. He was afraid for all kinds of unpleasantries like confiscated cameras and despite my plea (via Herman Wigbold, because not everybody got access to such bigwigs as Broeksz) that matters in those regions were somewhat normalizing in that respect, he initially stuck to his refusal. It really would have been quite a step, because until then not a single Dutch-made TV report had been done in Eastern Europe. But Chief of the TV department of *VARA* was Gijs Stappershoef, somebody open to new ideas, and he knew how to wriggle out a compromise: we would ask the Czechoslovakian TV to put a cameraman at our disposal with whom I would work. Just before my departure at the end of August (to be precise: August 21, exactly five years before the Soviet invasion), they said "yes" – and I would face two premieres. It would not only be the first self-made Dutch report on Eastern Europe, it would also be my own premiere as a TV maker.

Just then, the Czechoslovakian TV had set up an institute especially meant for foreign TV stations: Telexport. During the first conversations with their representatives in Prague they said that they did have cooperated with teams "of the other socialist countries" but not yet with somebody of the Western television. So for them it was a premiere as well. Besides a few bureaucratic functionaries of Telexport, also present were the cameraman I was going to work with, Jiří Sekerka, and the producer, Věra Sekerková, Jiři's wife, both a couple of years older than me.

If I would have made my debut in the Netherlands, I would have said, "Hey, listen, it's the first time for me, so if something goes wrong: my apologies in advance." I found that I could not allow myself to do so toward the Czechoslovakian television and so I pretended that is was mere child's play to me. But immediately my word-perfectness was challenged when the cameraman asked me "how many meters I thought we would need." I had not the faintest notion whether that had to be 10, 500 or 3000 meters. "Well, you know," I said casually, "we are going to do three reports of about ten minutes each, so just figure out how many meters that will be approximate." That answer apparently sounded reasonably professional, because he nodded understandingly.[73] I had proposed three subjects. One: students from Africa, who studied at Prague universities with Czech scholarships. You see, there was a lot of envy among the local students, whose scholarships were much lower and who also were not allowed to travel to the West like their black fellow students. Because of that there had been race riots in Czechoslovakia. It goes without saying that I left these reasons out to the Czechoslovakian authorities. The second subject was Lidice, a town, like Putten in the Netherlands and Oradour in France, completely razed to the ground on June 9, 1942, in retaliation for an attempt made shortly before on the life of Reinhard Heydrich, the *Reichsprotector* for *Böhmen und Mähren* ("Bohemia and Moravia"). All citizens had been killed, some children who looked very "Aryan," were lodged with German families and educated as little Germans. Just nine children survived the massacre. Third subject: a collective farm. The subjects were approved, Věra would produce them. It was done very efficiently – after a few days I was called about whether I would report to the studio the next day, located in those days in the Jungmannovo náměstí. I did not know much about television making, but I did know that you set out with a cameraman. I assumed that producer Věra would also go with us and that my little Volkswagen would be big enough to fit the three of us plus the camera stuff. This turned out to be a misunderstanding. In front of the studio an *IFA* bus *Garant* of East German make waited. With: a driver, the – to me already known – cameraman Jiří, an assistant cameraman, a sound technician, a lighting technician, an interpreter and of course Věra. I felt like an actor at a premiere: an inclination to turn tail. It remained by an inclination, in truth, I let myself be bumped along in

---

[73] At the time, reports were made with 16-mm film reels in cans of 30 meters (2 ½ minute) or 120 meters (ten minutes).

the extremely badly sprung bus with my seven "staff members" to the first subject: the collective farm. Along the way I had asked myself hundreds of times how and what kind of instructions I had to give to the team and I had not come to a conclusion yet, as we stepped out somewhere in the countryside. Unintentionally, Věra was the saving angel. "I don't know how things are done where you come from," she said, "but around here the cameraman is somewhat like the director." My generosity was unlimited, "OK, let him go ahead." And so they pulled me through my first television exam *(see photo 7)*

The interpreter, Richard Schwarzbach, was a somewhat elderly man, who spoke an excellent German. Before the communist coup d'état of 1948, he had a shop in Philips radios but, of course, that was taken away from him under the communist blessings. It goes without saying: without compensation. Since then, he had been in all kinds of unimportant professions and now he was a freelance interpreter at the state travel agency *Čedok*. When I was alone with him for a second, he warned me that Věra might work for the StB; then, when I was alone with Věra and Jiří, they in turn gave me the same warning concerning him. None of them were working for the StB; all three of them had to report on their daily experiences with me. So it went – and so you knew. None of them was out to blacken me and in their presence I did not anything that could have confronted them with the dilemma: shall we or shall we not report it? An unspoken, seemingly complicated but in essence simple consensus existing among all involved.

The first cracks in Stalinist Czechoslovakia were already visible, introduced by the Slovaks. There had always been anti-Czech sentiments in Slovakia. Now, it expressed itself in the classic-dialectical way not directly against the Czechs. The reasoning was: Stalinism is a Czech political policy, imposed on us, Slovaks. The aspiration of the Slovaks for a liberalization of the Czechoslovakian communist party was partly inspired by those anti-Czech sentiments. Not surprisingly, it was in the Slovak capital Bratislava and not in Prague that for the first time protests against the Stalinism came out in the open. At the congress of the Slovak Union of Journalists in May 1963, Miroslav Hyško showed the incredible courage to point openly to the dubious role of Antonín Novotný at the preparations of the show trial against Slánský, Šling and company in 1952. In itself, it was no secret. At a special party conference in the beginning of 1953, dedicated to those trials, Novotný had been patted on the back "for his activities which led to the unmasking of the Zionist conspiracy of Slánský, Šling and their ilk." After the unmasking of Stalin in 1956, it was also officially recognized in Czechoslovakia, that the accusations had been false. But nobody had connected those two facts publicly yet, or dared to speak about Novotný's role, because he still was party secretary as well as the president. In June/July, Novotný had attacked Hyško furiously, but the latter had not been arrested.

In September I got an interview with Hyško through the Slovak television. A nervous wreck and chain smoking, he, nevertheless, repeated to me what he had also said during the congress. But he spoke at the same time about more independence for Slovakia.[74] After he had left, the TV functionary Jan Pitoňak, a confirmed party member, of course, put it much clearer, "Finally, after 19 years, we are talking again about our own Slovak state." When you deduct nineteen years from 1963, you end up in 1944. So even this confirmed party communist considered the fascist vassal state of Monseigneur Tiso as a kind of independent Slovak state. The same reasoning some Croats nourished with regard to "their" *NDH*, the Croatian variant of Tiso's state. The dreams (or the nightmares) would become true a quarter of a century later and it would take a good ten years more before these two states became genuine democracies.

I enjoyed very much doing television and apparently Herman Wigbold also seemed to be rather satisfied, because the following year I did some reports for *Achter het Nieuws* on Poland, based on the same proposition: cooperation with the local television, and for incomprehensible reasons we still were the only ones.

In 1958, I was for the first time in Auschwitz. Already then, it was a little bit of a commemoration site, but nobody visited it. I was guided around by a prematurely old lady in a brownish, worn-out long coat. She was an ex-prisoner herself – political prisoner mind you, otherwise she never would have survived. All the barracks of the annihilation camp proper, Birkenau, still stood there – hundreds and hundreds. The administrators had already arranged the now world-known display cases with the things they found after the liberation: thousands of pairs of glasses, hundreds of pounds of hair, hundreds of artificial legs and, most impressive of all, hundreds of suitcases with the names of the murdered owners on it; suitcases which looked at you as if they were human beings. On the terrain itself, I still found a wooden shoe with a piece of a car inner tube as a sandal strap, a porcelain head with barbed wire on it, part of the fence which stood under a deadly high voltage, a charred piece of wood from one of the gas chambers, which the Germans had blown up in 1944 in a failed attempt to cover up their crimes. I have saved them carefully, I don't have much of an artistic talent, but for years now I have a concept in my mind how to do "something" with it – but where in your house are you going to hang up something like that? In your living room? Can you still celebrate your birthday in such a living room? And is it not even worse if it hangs there so long that you actually don't notice it anymore, which as a matter of fact happens quite often with objects which sit in the same spot for years?

[74] See appendix page 376.

That not knowing what to do with it, is the main reason that I still have not done anything with it. About this Auschwitz I had written in 1958, about this Auschwitz I wanted to do a TV report. Kraków television put a cameraman at my disposal. I could not have been luckier. He was an absolute anti anti-Semite, not because the government was anti-Semitic, but from deep down in his heart. He had a girlfriend-assistant who had lost practically all her relatives in Auschwitz. With them, I made my report. Pouring with sweat, he lugged his lead-heavy camera from the beginning of the era along that immense terrain, but it was his heart more than the camera which shot the images. After the airing of the report in the Netherlands, I got a letter from somebody who had been in Theresienstadt together with a friend. From there, his friend was deported. To Auschwitz, he suspected. Now, though, he knew for sure. On one of the suitcases we had filmed was the name of his friend. If we would have made the film for only this one viewer, it already would have been sufficient.

Not long afterwards, still in 1964, at last other Dutch TV colleagues went in the direction of Eastern Europe as well.

I interviewed a lot of Germans for the above-mentioned documentary on the German resistance against National Socialism. But one of the most intriguing statements came from somebody who was not willing to be interviewed. Part of that documentary was the attempt on Hitler's life at his headquarters in Rastenburg on July 20, 1944. The story is well-known: Stauffenberg put his brief case with the time bomb against a wide, thick oak table leg on the side where Hitler stood. *Oberst* Brandt, deputy of general Adolf Heusinger, picked up the brief case and put it on the other side of the table leg. When the bomb exploded that table leg proved to be the rescue for Hitler, he escaped practically unscathed. Adolf Heusinger himself was also present at the conference, and when after the war protests came against his appointment as inspector general of the (West) German *Bundeswehr,* the Federal Armed Forces, he defended himself with the story that he had been "involved in the attempt on Hitler's life." Already an activist against the Nazi regime since the thirties, Dr. Fabian von Schlabrendorff had to scornfully laugh about it. At the time, he personally had gone to ask Heusinger's cooperation in the attempt, but Heusinger had refused. It's true that he was one of the members of the officer's corps who were no Nazi's and fundamentally disagreed with the way Hitler waged the war. But they had sworn an oath of allegiance to Hitler and according to them it would be in defiance of the "soldier's honor" to breach that oath and, although knowing that a conspiracy to kill Hitler was on its way, they were on principle opposed to it.

So, that knowledge was the whole "involvement" of Heusinger. I wanted to interview him on camera about the actual events in that conference room on July 20. He refused, but he agreed to speak to me off camera.

"When Von Stauffenberg entered I knew that he brought the bomb along," he said to my surprise.

"But if you knew it, could it be then that your deputy Brandt also knew it?" I asked. Heusinger answered, "I don't know whether he knew."

We can't ask Brandt anymore, because he was killed by the bomb. I have no proof of it at all, but I personally believe that he knew it very well indeed, and repositioned the brief case of Von Stauffenberg on purpose. What other reason could he have had? There was a conference going on, there was map reading, there was only a few seconds between the setting down and the re-positioning of the brief case – well, then you really must have a very urgent reason to immediately reposition a brief case, which had just been put down somewhere by somebody. Brandt in my opinion wanted to save the life of the *Führer*, succeeded and by doing so changed the course of history.

This is what I wrote in the Dutch edition in 1997. In the meantime Ian Kershaw published his famous Hitler biography. In the second part he writes, in de-scribing what happened on July 20, 1944, "Colonel Heinz Brandt, Heusinger's right-hand man (*and, as it transpired, connected with the conspiracy*), lost a leg and died later that afternoon [italics by DV]."[75] Remarkably, Kershaw does not mention that Brandt repositioned the brief case, something every witness agreed on. So Heusinger's evasive answer to me should have been, according to Kershaw, affirmative – as I already suspected at the time. More than ever, I'm convinced that Brandt, who probably was as much "involved" in the con-spiracy as his boss Heusinger, repositioned the brief case on purpose.

On June 22, 1941, the Germans invaded the Soviet Union. The *VPRO* accepted my proposal, introduced in October 1965, to make a documentary about it to be aired in June 1966, 25 years from date. Through its press officer Makarov, the Soviet embassy in The Hague was very enthusiastic about the idea and promised full cooperation. The whole winter I read all kinds of books on that "Operation Barbarossa" and its preparations in order to be well prepared for my task. I found a reasonable number of former Nazi generals willing to co-operate, but from the Soviet side I was left with only promises for the time being. I had presented them precisely with whom, where and about what I wanted to speak and in this respect there were no objections whatsoever – but the visa was long in coming. Also, we were not allowed to shoot with our own

[75] *Hitler, 1936-1945 Nemesis*, page 674, by Ian Kershaw (W.W. Norton & Company, London/New York, 2000).

1. Seven-year-old Dick Verkijk (right) playing checker with his bosom friend Kees Bossers, who later would join the national socialist youth organization. The picture is made by "Uncle Chris," who during the occupation would fight at the "Eastern Front" as a SS-volunteer.

2a. 1935, neighbor-boy Jaap Veen (left), Dick Verkijk, DV, (right) and his buddy Kees Bossers (middle) in front of DV's parental home on the Zaanenlaan 149, Haarlem/ Netherlands.

2c. The same Jaap, Kees and Dick in front of the same house (which is still DV's Dutch residence) - seventy years later.

2b. Seven years later the same Kees Bossers as a student (front row, third from left) at the (Nazi-)German Reichsschule in Valkenburg/Netherlands.

3. *Spring 1941, school picture, taken after a performance at a farewell party of the school. The picture is taken in the courtyard of the Berkenschooltje (Little Birch's school), a kindergarten to which the Junoschool was evacuated after this was "promoted" to Wehrmacht barracks. In the center "master Van Eerden" On the first row, far left, legs crossed, Cora Cannemeyer whose parents were (then still secret) members of the NSB, second to the right DV (like Cora in stage dress because of the performance). Next to him with the recorder Henk van Mechelen, who in 1944 would be killed during a heavy bombardment on Nijmegen/Netherlands due to a navigation error by the American Air Force. Extreme right upper row, standing on the wall, Joop Jonkman who, also in 1944, would be a distributor of De Oprechte Haarlemmer, the Upright Haarlemer. In the middle row, fifth to the left, squatting, Aagje Swart, daughter of the baker who in the "Hunger winter" of 1944, let my little sister and me eat at his place once a week and of whom it only after the war became known that he had been a secret member of the NSB for all those years.*

4. DV as a 10-year-old in the class room wit a dip pen. In the background a map with his future working territory: Germany and Eastern Europe.

5. At the campground Saxenheim near the village Vierhouten in the center of Holland; to the far right Thea Meesters, "the dark girl I saw all of a sudden before me in a Jeugdstorm uniform." Next to her an "onderduiker", a hideaway, an unknown girl who did not belong to the Jeugdstorm, then Joop Jonkman and behind him DV.

6.Jan Wijnkoop, son of the most famous prewar Dutch communist leader David Wijnkoop, together with his colleague Rinske Hoff, "the women with the tractor voice" in their editorial premises of Radio Moscow/department of Dutch broadcasts. Picture taken May 1958.

7. Literally DV's first steps as a TV-reporter/producer. The bus of the Czechoslovakian TV is parked at the lot of a collective farm in Lichočeves. Interpreter Richard Schwarzbach opens the door for Věra Sekerková, whose husband Jiři is just being hidden behind Schwarzbach. At the left, the director of the kolchoz looks into the distant future. The recording of DV's first TV-report can start; August 24, 1963.

8. Soviet-interest in DV's VW on the Sumskaya street, the main street of Kharkov; May 24, 1958.

*9. Interview with a pavior in Torgau where in April 1945, American and Soviet sol-
ders shook hands at the bridge across the river Elbe, which at the time was partly
shot to pieces, but now repaired and visible in the background. Behind DV, the driver
of our State-Volga, and behind him our watch dog, the very Stalinoid Eugen Betzer
("Poland is not a socialist country because there they are still giving each other a
hand kiss"); July 9, 1960.*

10. Interview with Nicolae Ceauşescu, spring 1975. To the far right the then second man in the hierarchy, Cornel Burtica, who was outraged that after the conversation DV handed a petition over to Ceauşescu. DV had put the envelope with the petition ready on top of his tape recorder in order not to forget to hand it over to Ceauşescu.

11. Jan Nagel with Lügen-Erich (Erich-the-Liar as he was called in Western Germany), the commander of "The Wall" at the Brandenburger Tor, January 1966. To Lügen-Erich, The Wall was already then a historical necessity. Not long after that, Jan Nagel thought the same.

12. Reunion of the contributors of De Oprechte Haarlemmer, 25 years after the liberation. In the center Dik van den Haak, to the right Joop Jonkman. At the left DV with his "inseparable (war)guitar."

13. Twilight period in 1987: the Pope visits Poland. Solidarity is still prohibited, but the leaders have gotten amnesty anyway. From right to left in Gdańsk: Konrad Bieliński, Jan Lityński, DV and his assistant Lino Boekelman.

14. General Sandalov (sitting, left), who was urged twice by general Strelbitski (sit-ing, right) to talk more leniently about Stalin - for the VPRO documentary Operation Barbarossa. Behind that twosome, cameraman Cor de Jager to the right and DV to the left ; May 1966.

15. *Nothing concrete is left from DV's meeting with Václav Havel in the kitchen, but the one in October 1994 (for a NOS radio program by Jaap Vermeer, second to the left), is recorded indeed. The chief of the protocol and the guests in their best suits, Havel just in his shirt.*

16. The "whisky-incident" between Jacek Kuroń and DV. New Year's Eve party-1980 of the (then ex) "opposantry" (three months earlier Solidarność had been legalized). Kuroń gives DV the bottle of whisky back, which DV clasps in his right hand, as he, through a bearded ad-hoc interpreter, lectures Kuroń with the left little forefinger held high.

17. Dinner in 1985 at György Konrád's place, when in Budapest within the framework of "Helsinki" a "Cultural Forum" was held. To the left in the foreground George Theiner, who in 1948 emigrated from Czechoslovakia, and editor-in-chief of the London-based magazine Index on Censorship. Hidden behind him then dissident Györge Bence, next to him Konrád, Maria Kovács (Bence's wife and active in opposition circles as well). With her back to the camera Judith, the wife of Konrád. Extreme right DV.

18. Anatoli Marchenko, who on the 8th of December 1986, died in a concentration camp.

20. Picture of the interior of a wooden hut without windows, in a kind of ghetto near hotel Ukraina in Moscow, of which the publishing in Het Parool resulted in a visa ban for Eastern Europe for a couple of years; May 1958.

On the left page:
19. With the newsreel team of the NOS in the Serbian quarter Grbavica of Sarajevo at the border line with the Moslem territory. Gerri Eickhof (in the foreground), cameraman Chris Ploeger and DV, all provided with bulletproof vests.

21. *With cameraman Paul van de Bos in the yard of the former Sudeten-German Nazi leader Konrad Henlein for the documentary on the German resistance against the Nazi regime, fall 1967, aired in 1968. I'm wearing the fur cap baptized by Jan Blokker as "bearskin cap," which he so hated that he prohibited me to wear it on screen. Of course, it was more about the bearer than the bear.*

22. *With cameraman Jaap Buis somewhere in France for the VPRO documentary "More than 1011" about an escape line from occupied Holland to Spain, organized by Jean Weidner, which saved the lives of at least 1011 Jewish Dutchmen (1967). Not even a year later Weidner turned out to be the employer of Shirhan Shirhan who assassinated Robert Kennedy.*

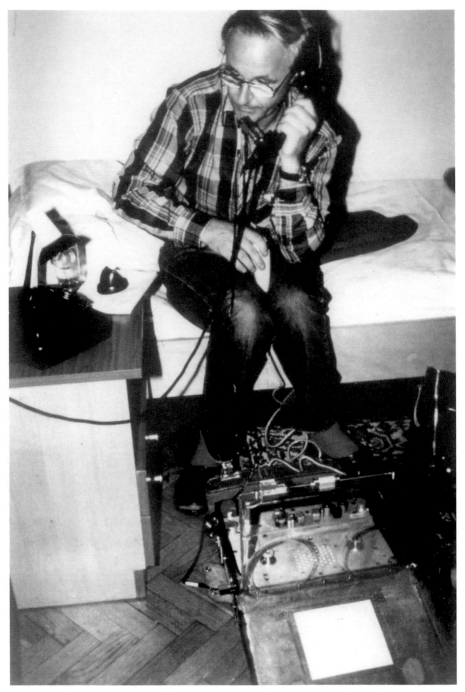

23. Report by phone through the "Nagra" recorder for NOS radio and TV during the strike in Gdańsk; August 1980.

24. *A paint-stained car and valveless tires - activity against DV by fanatics in the Montenegran seaside village of Radovići, where he owns an apartment; spring 1994. A Montenegran friend helps out by pumping up the tire*

25. *From left to right: Jan Lityński, Jacek Kuroń and Adam Michnik of the Polish KOR during a secret meeting with representatives of the Czechoslovakian Charta-77 at the Polish-Czechoslovakian border in a faraway mountain area; summer 1978.*

26. With a team of KRO-TV in a totally destroyed Vukovar; 1993.

28. *The home where De Oprechte Haarlemmer was produced. Right leaning against the wall Dik van den Haak, next to him his brother Rob who designed the maps for our paper. The picture is taken approx. 1941/1942. On the window glued paper strips, meant to prevent you from getting hurt by splinters of flying glass after a possible bomb explosion due to an air raid. During the war, every window all over the Netherlands was provided with those paper strips.*

Left page:
27. *First big demonstration for independence by 150,000 people in the Estonian capital of Tallinn on the 17th of June 1988, when for the first time since nearly half a century the old Estonian flag was openly carried along.*

29. With Milovan Djilas on his deck in his apartment in the Palmotičeva street in Belgrade (1979). (Photo Vincent Mentzel)

30. Cor Gerritsen 1905-1942

31. The moving meeting in Prague of the Czechoslovakian "dissident," prof. Jan Patočka (right), with the Dutch Minister of Foreign Affairs, Max van der Stoel (left), and some journalists. In the middle, with his hand in front of his face, DV, on March 4, 1977. (Photo Vincent Mentzel)

32. Rob van den Haak, carrying a lawn mower with a suitcase on top through the small opening in the Mauerwall, helping friends who had to leave their homes on order of the Germans. (This, and other pictures of the war time, are kind of vague because the quality of the films was pretty bad in those days.)

33. The other side of the Mauerwall. Bakers' carts and -tricycles are loaded with the piece-by-piece transported items of the evacuees.

34. *In 1943, the Germans reshaped the canal Delft, at the end of the Zaanenlaan where DV lived, into an anti-tank-moat. In the middle the contours of the dredge, deepening the canal for that purpose. On the rooftop of the home left at the end of the street, the air-raid-warning sirene.*

35. *After it has done its job, the dredge is towed away to the nearby river Spaarne. Both pictures are taken by Dik van den Haak from the attic window of Zaanenlaan 116.*

36. Rudolf Schick, talking to DV. who had a surprise for him in reserve.

37. . . . nothing was left of the car . . .

38. War criminal Walter Warlimont, as a general of the German
Wehrmacht . . .

39. . . . and when DV interviewed him for the
TV-documentary Operation Barbarossa; 1966.
(Both pictures taken from TV-screen.)

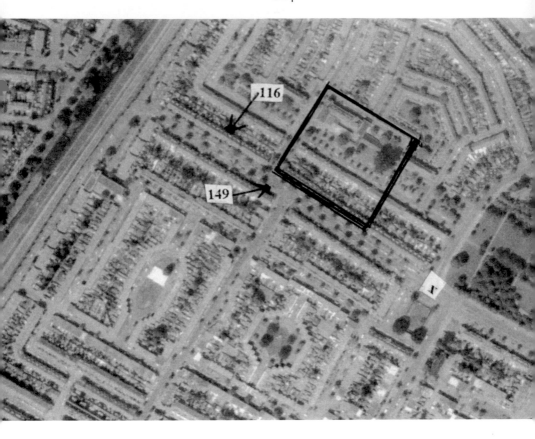

40. *Areal picture of the area DV lived, taken in 2001, but hardly anything has changed since 1940-1945. The arrows coming from "149" and "116" indicate the homes on the Zaanenlaan where DV lived resp. where the underground papers were made. Within the frame, the school buildings and private homes, requisitioned by the German Wehrmacht for their privates and officers. The "x" indicates the Marnix Square. The gray line in the left upper corner shows the canal Delft, which was from 1942-1945 an anti-tank-moat. On September 19, 1944, the territory left of this line became a "restricted area", to be vacated by all civilians except for the Nazi collaborators. A smaller strip along the North Sea coast had already to be vacated in 1942.*

cameraman, they did not trust us that much. The broadcast was planned for Sunday, June 26, 1966 and at the beginning of May, I still did not have my visa. In Germany and England we had already shot everything, and had it ready for editing. Only on May 10, the visa came through. I raced with my Ford-Taunus in two days to cover the 1600 miles to Moscow and only then did they start to organize everything, which was, fortunately, fixed in a short time. They gave me somebody from the Soviet television to go along as an interpreter, Vitaly Sseferiyants, and what they called "a military adviser": general Strelbitski. Sseferiyants was not such a pleasant person, but Strelbitski turned out to be a sociable grandpa whose comments mainly consisted of "*Khorosho, khorosho* – OK, OK."The first shooting took place in Orel. After coming back in Moscow the films, which I had brought myself from the Netherlands, was developed: wrong. It all looked pretty pale. I insisted on having our own cameraman. A conversation was convened with a fivesome of functionaries, whose origin was unclear to me. What matters was that they agreed to a Dutch cameraman, provided that before airing I would show the documentary to members of the Soviet embassy in The Hague. No censorship, indeed? No, no censorship. "In that case I have no objections," and I had to sign a document proving it. Within a couple of hours Cor de Jager, one of the two steady cameramen of the *VPRO*, got a visa and he landed the next day on the airport of Moscow. We filmed the German advance in reverse order – from Moscow to Brest-Litovsk through Smolensk and Minsk. I got a whole sequence of Soviet generals in front of the camera. But just Marshal Timoshenko, legendary to me, who already in July 1941 had pushed back the Germans near Smolensk, was not available – no reason given; nor for the non-cooperation of Ilya Ehrenburg, with whom I would have been very glad to speak about his great many radio talks in which he repeatedly had stated that the war was waged against the Nazi system and not against the German people. For three weeks we lugged across the Soviet Union, hectic, because the 26th of June was approaching with rapid strides. A fierce opponent of the Soviet regime, I found it to some extent an absurd situation that I was traveling around with a Soviet general-in full-regalia with whom I was, moreover, on good terms. But the film had a positive intent, which was best expressed in the dedication I gave to the film, "To the Soviet soldiers who were *also* killed in action for our freedom." Explicitly with the emphasis on *also* – to indicate that we should not only be grateful to the Western allies, but certainly not with the emphasis on *our*, because this would mean that the Soviet soldiers were also killed in action for their own freedom – and, unfortunately, this was not the case.

Once, it was not *khorosho* to Strelbitski. It was during an interview with general Sandalov. In 1941 he had been the commander in Brest-Litovsk, the Soviet border town at the German-Soviet demarcation line. In no uncertain terms he said he had known that the Germans would attack and that he also had reported it, but that Stalin had not been willing to believe the reports *(see photo 14).*

In 1966 the de-Stalinization was somewhat over the hill, one and a half year before, Khrushchev was dismissed and replaced by Brezhnev, and Strelbitski intervened; the criticism of Stalin was too strong, Sandalov had to weaken his statement. It was too suspicious to let the camera keep on running, but I could gesture to Cor de Jager at any rate to let the sound recorder run. After a short discussion, the struggling Sandalov promised to give a milder version of his opinion on Stalin's shortsightedness. We meticulously recorded it. But Strelbitski was still not satisfied. Again a short discussion. Sandalov resisted even more, but finally agreed to a third version. Yet, his criticism of Stalin remained in essence standing, and as if indicating that he had no intention to spoon up a fourth version, he finished his third statement, while making a throw-away-gesture with his hand, with, "And that's that!" We took the liberty to air all three versions, with each time in between a summary of those discussions between Strelbitski and Sandalov.

As the first Westerner I was allowed to browse through the historic film archives in Moscow and I had selected some never-before shown material. Among other things, the in the meantime stereotyped image of the Russian woman with a crucifix who stands along the side of the road when her town is being liberated from the Germans, letting a Soviet soldier kiss that crucifix. In another footage you can hear and see how a Soviet unit goes onto the offensive with the then famous attack-slogan, "For the fatherland, for Stalin." They would copy all that material for me, but it had not been done before we left Moscow. They would forward it, but just like with the visa case – it was long in coming. From early in the morning till late in the evening editor Hans de Jong and I were editing – leaving gaps in places where we wanted to put the archive material, if it would ever arrive. And really – five days before the broadcast it came in, copied on 35 mm extremely flammable nitrate film tape and sent by air plane, strictly forbidden because of the self-combustion of the material. On the door of our editing room we had to glue the announcement that behind that door work with highly flammable material was going on and that nobody was allowed to enter. Nothing was missing of what I had asked for – but one small piece. From the slogan, "For the fatherland, for Stalin," the second part had been cut off. True, the de-Stalinization was a little bit over the hill, but they also would like to forget that they fought for Stalin.

Only on the Sunday morning of the broadcasting day, the film was ready for airing. In the afternoon a delegation of the Soviet embassy showed up to watch the film. I had also addressed the preceding history of that attack in the documentary: the negotiations between the Soviet Union on the one hand and France and Great Britain on the other hand to come to an anti-Hitler coalition, the dismissal of the (Jewish) Soviet minister of Foreign Affairs Litvinov and his replacement by Molotov, with whom the Germans got along better, the non-aggression pact between the Soviet Union and Nazi Germany and the partition of Poland between Germany and the Soviet Union after the German invasion in September 1939. After that partition, Molotov had called Poland in the Soviet parliament "a monstrous miscarriage of the Treaty of Versailles." I had also incorporated this in the documentary. It was this our Sunday Soviet guests absolutely wanted to have deleted. They pretended to have the right to demand that by reason of my agreement in Moscow, but we pointed out to them that they had the right to see the film in advance, not to change it, unless it contained manifest inaccuracies. "Is it your opinion that Molotov did not say that?" I asked. No, they admitted that he did say that. "Then it stays," I stated. *VPRO* boss Arie Kleijwegt and I argued at least two hours with the Soviet delegation about other things they would like to see deleted, but we did not delete one millimeter. The conversation took so long that the documentary, which had the at the time unusual length of 110 minutes, only started half an hour after the planned time.

The Soviets were good sports. Apparently, they seemed to be happy with the general line of the story. A week later, Arie Kleijwegt, Vice Manager Bouke Poelstra and I, with our spouses, were invited for a dinner at the Soviet embassy. After the dinner, the women had to go to a separate room to talk about this, that and the other, so that the men could just talk among themselves about real matters, the proof that the then progressive circles were right in honoring their point of view that the conservative part of the Netherlands could at least learn something from the Soviet Union concerning women's emancipation. We had promised to send a copy of the film to Moscow. "Please, at least delete in the version you are going to send to Moscow those parts, against which we had objections, otherwise we will get a good scolding that we did not do our work right," the Soviet ambassador asked.

This concession we have made.

It was in those days unusual to pay for interviews. But we got angry letters from a couple of Nazi-generals, asking where their money was. *Panzergeneral* (Tank general) Leo Freiherr Geyr von Schweppenburg even threatened to sue us. The sentenced war criminal general Walter Warlimont demanded money as well. He was the highest still living chief of the *Wehrmachtsführungsstab*, chief of staff of the Nazi armed forces. His only superiors had been Hitler, Keitel and Jodl – the last two had gotten the death penalty in Nuremberg and had been hanged. Warlimont had been responsible for the so-called *Kommissarbefehl* (commissar order), which contended that all captured political commissars of the Red Army had to be executed immediately, and for the *Kommandobefehl* (commando order), the order to consider soldiers of commando units of the Western allied forces, who operated behind enemy lines, as partisans, even if they were wearing their own uniforms. In other words: they also had to be executed by firing squad. I had a long preliminary talk with Warlimont, but not on this subject. I had agreed with cameraman André Gunn that I would signal him to put in a new film reel (120 meters, ten minutes – I had learned my lesson!) when I was going to ask him about it. When I confronted him with his past, Mister Warlimont started fidgeting on his high, beautifully carved wooden seat in his capital villa at the *Tegernsee*, the Teger Lake, close to Berchtesgaden. The film reel was long enough to really give him the third degree. Packing up your stuff afterwards, suddenly turns out to be a lengthy procedure.

You always wonder how people of his caliber, education and intelligence could become so servile. Yes, he knew that such and such an army order was unfeasible, yes, it was clear to him that in a certain war theater there was more to be saved by a tactical retreat than by continuing to defend every meter. Yet, every time Hitler could talk him into doing the wrong things. Why? "It was as if Hitler ate the thoughts out of your head." Initially, he got life imprisonment in Nuremberg, which was reduced to eighteen years of which he served only six. Why was he found guilty? "The interpreters who had to translate our German in English were all former German Jews and of course you understand that they translated our words in such a way that we were made to look much more unfavorable then we in reality were," according to Warlimont. This does not impede the fact that over the years I have seen Warlimont presented in numerous publications and encyclopedia as an objective, neutral expert concerning WWII *(see photos 38 and 39)*.

I had also wanted to make a documentary on Vietnam – especially about the "cruel bombing of the civilians of Hanoi" by the Americans. Because entry to Vietnam was very difficult for Western journalists, I proposed to do it in a Czechoslovak-Dutch co-production. It was 1966. The Czechoslovakian television agreed, and I would go with Jiří Sekerka. We presented the North-Vietnamese embassy in Prague with our plan and applied for visa. And never heard of it again, of course. Because they only allowed their own ideological friends to enter who would tell "the truth about Vietnam." They did not even trust the still totally communist television of Czechoslovakia.

CHAPTER 20

From kitchen to ministry

There have been opponents to the regimes in Eastern Europe as long as those regimes existed. They only have expressed themselves in the different countries in different ways or not at all and those expressions differed by country according to the tolerance or intolerance of the then-momentarily-elite-in-power. The greater the tolerance, the stronger the opposition. This sounds contradictory. But only a few stick their neck out when opposition gets you the death penalty. But you find more people who have the courage to open their mouth, if it only costs them their jobs. The bottom line was that those regimes rested on terror, regardless of whether it was the great terror of the death penalty or the small terror of losing your job. Fear of terror, great or small, was the only power base of the regime. Would that fear vanish, those regimes would be finished. They were not "giants on loam feet," as the Dutch expression goes, they were giants on air. As to me, this is not just retrospective reasoning, it has always been my conviction. A fourteen days general strike in Eastern Europe would have meant the end of those regimes. But just try to organize that. The great and small terror, of which the secret services in those countries were the executors, ensured that it would not come to that. I was sure that the system would collapse some day. Quite frequently I have disseminated the hypothesis, "I am a pessimist in the short run, but an optimist in the long run." As certain as I was that the system would collapse one day, I was equally certain that I would not live to see it. Fortunately I was mistaken. I saw the fear disappear before my eyes, because thanks to Gorbachev those regimes could not apply terror anymore. That's why in some of those countries it lasted not days but only hours to sweep them away; they rested on nothing but that air.

In those initial years of my journeys across Eastern Europe, only in private talks did you run into people who pointed out that the emperor had no clothes. Except for the outburst in East Berlin on June 17, 1953, spectacular opposition in the fifties and sixties came from people who still believed that the emperor was wearing clothes, but who were at the same time of the opinion that he should dress in a different suit: the so-called "reform communists." What those reform communists did not realize – and the "dogmatic" ones did only too well – was that at the end of the day their ideas would lead to a normally functioning democracy – and thus to the end of the one-party system. After the intervention of the Soviet Union in Czechoslovakia in 1968, it was clear to the last reform-communist optimist that the system of the "real exist-ing socialism" was not reformable and that the reform of the society was only possible if the system disappeared. Over the years, the notion of "dissidents" for all those kinds of opponents was created, literally, "deviationists." Actually, it's the wrong term. Those who deviated from the normal human pattern were the representatives of the party and the government in those countries. In fact *they* were the dissidents. But it's just like the notion of illegality during the German occupation in the Netherlands. Literally it means "unlawfulness." Factually the "illegals" did represent the highest form of lawfulness. That's why, to make things easy, I'll use the umbrella term "dissidents."

POLAND

The resistance against the regime was the strongest in Poland. For three rea-sons. In the first place, a tradition existed there of an age old struggle against oppressors and occupiers: Prussians, Russians. After the three Polish parti-tions in the last quarter of the eighteenth century, Poland had not been an independent state for 125 years. The end of the First World War meant the resurrection of Poland. In the second place you had the tremendous authority and influence of the Roman Catholic Church. It had represented the national Polish identity during those 125 years, again performed that national role dur-ing the Nazi occupation and had not committed any form of collaboration, in contrast with the Roman Catholic Churches in the other Eastern occupied countries. That's why that church had the moral authority to be the center of resistance in the communist time as well. In the third place, after 1956 in Poland it was a matter of "the small terror," not in the last place also as a result of those first two factors. Even most of the executive Polish communists were Poles in the first place and communists only in the second.

This does not mean that it did not take a lot of sacrifice to stand up for your opinion. Together with Karol Modzelewski, Jacek Kuroń got three years im-prisonment in 1965, because they had written a memorandum on the reform of the party, of which both of them were a member then. They had written it in 1964 and they would remain active oppositionists for 25 years. Thrown out of the university after a student protest in 1968, Jan(ek) Lityński would remain an active oppositionist for 21 years. (Kuroń and Lityński were each sentenced to 3½ years because of those students' actions). Another one of those: Janusz Onyszkiewicz. So I could mention dozens who kept fighting, indefatigably with an eternal optimism and in spite of everything with a great sense of per-spective. They went in and out of prison, had lousy jobs or no jobs at all, lived from day to day – but they were free people. I got to know them in their kitch-enettes, their small work rooms or in their overcrowded living rooms where ten, twelve, fifteen of them prepared leaflets, newspapers, books and political alternatives – but where they also had their frequent parties.

A law in the eighties made it possible to detain someone for 48 hours with-out accusation. You were picked up, they set you free after 48 hours – and then after some fifteen minutes you were locked up again. This could be repeated arbitrarily at their discretion. Jan Lityński was editor-in-chief of *Robotnik* ("The Worker") in 1980. You could not call it an illegal paper, because he made no secret of the fact that he was the producer. Some wrote under their own names in the paper, others under a pen name. It was in the turbulent days before the big strike in Gdańsk. I had visited him in the morning. In the afternoon he was taken away "for 48 hours." It was extended three times. He happened to be home just one hour when I visited him again. He knew what life in prison was about, because in worse times he had been sitting in there for 3½ years. But still. "You know, I absolutely cannot stand being locked up. Jacek [Kuroń] is different, he is able to take it. Not me." Nevertheless, that very afternoon he went on the move so that his *Robotnik* would appear on time. *Robotnik* (called after a prewar social-democratic daily) was the organ of *KOR*, the "Committee to Defend the Workers," established in 1976 after strikes in Radom. It was the first time that intellectuals and workers worked together, which would prove to be a decisive factor for the success of the strike in Gdańsk. But this is a sepa-rate chapter, too. The key figure of *KOR* was Jacek Kuroń. Quite often he was a moody grumbler with whom, moreover, you could not communicate directly, because he had no knowledge of any Western language. That's why he had always Ewa Kulik around, a student majoring in English at the University of Kraków who also worked full time for *KOR* and who because of her blond hair and pretty appearance was called "the Golden Angel of *KOR*."

Once, I had a difference of opinion with Kuroń. Paul Scheffer, then a journalist just starting out and nowadays a well-known columnist, scientist and profes-sor at the *Leiden* [Leyden] University in the Netherlands, was, in December 1980, for the first time in an Eastern European country and in those days kind of hanging around with me. The trade union *Solidarność* was legalized and he wanted to do an interview with Kuroń. We went to him to make an appoint-ment after a student's meeting, where he had been the speaker. He refused. That made me considerably mad. When *KOR* was still being persecuted, he very much liked you to interview him, but it apparently had become a favor now. I asked the intervention of Jan Lityński, also attending the meeting, and he returned with the message that we were welcome on the first of January,

Warszawa, 31.12.1980.

Dear Jacek!

Janek told me you would grant me an interview for a bottle of whiskey. Of course I give you with great pleasure a bottle of whisky – as you see!

But I never made and never will make interviews with representatives of democratic opposition groups or members of movements for human rights in Eastern Europe for my own sake of for the sake of my radio station (which is, by the way, a non profit public institution). I'm not that kind of a journalist.

I'm involved in reporting on Eastern Europe since 1958 and from the very beginning of all kind of critical movements in those countries I tried tot give those representatives the opportunity to express themselves, because they had no opportunity in their own country to do so. I paid attention to all those movements, including KOR, long before it became fashion to do so. My first and last consideration was and is: how can I help them. If they were not interested or had ather reasons not to speak out, I fully agreed – it was up to them to decide.

So if you think it is of no impotance now to confront Dutch listeners with your views, because you have opportunities enough in your own country – that is also up to you. You must not grant me an interview to do me a favour. That means: I don't accept your deal: a bottle of whisky in exchange for an interview. I would not react in this way, if I would not have noticed earlier, that KOR is much less approachable than before the strike. When I tried to phone KOR from Holland, I was very often rebuffed. I don't think this is in the interest of what we are both striving for: a more democratic society.

In spite of that you can of course always count on my support if things wil worsen in Poland, which I don't hope and don't expect.

I wish you, your collaborators of KOR and Poland as a whole a good 1981, in which the victories gained in 1980, will be consolidated!

With kind regards, also for your wife,

Dick Verkijk
NOS-radio,
Netherlands

Letter to Jacek Kuroń dated December 31, 1980, in which DV explains to him why he refuses to interview him in exchange for a bottle of whisky.

but only if we brought a bottle of whisky along. On New Year's Eve I went to Kuroń's home with a bottle of whisky, accompanied by a letter. I said in the letter that I had never interviewed him for my own sake but just to make his opinions more widely known. A bottle of whisky he could get – "of course I give you with great pleasure a bottle of whisky – as you see" – but as to the interview I'm not interested anymore, because I don't accept your deal: a bottle of whisky in exchange for an interview. Kuroń answered the door himself so I was able to hand him the bottle and the letter personally.

That evening, there would be a New Year's Eve party with dozens of figures of the opposition, for which a Norwegian journalist and I were invited as the only foreigners. Before that, I was at Lityński's. Kuroń called, furious about the letter, but Lityński fully agreed with me and even called it "a good lesson for Kuroń." The conversation revealed that Kuroń would also come to the party "so I will see him tonight." Halfway through the party, he arrived and came straight to me. With that bottle in his hand, which he wanted to give back to me. I refused but finally accepted it under the condition that it would be added to the general drink pot of that night. After some talking back and forth we made peace again and he invited me to come the next day for that interview – without alcoholic preconditions. So I went on the first of January, and I not only brought Paul Scheffer along, but, of course, also a bottle of whisky. I also had written in the letter that he could count on my support again if, Heaven forbid, things might go wrong in Poland – not realizing that within a year this remark would turn out to be not of a pure rhetorical nature *(see photo 16)*.

But Jacek Kuroń was a superman. He was the key figure of the opposition movement and he was the man who came forward with a new opposition strategy. Not fight anymore against the communist structure, but construct a second nonofficial society beside the official one and just ignore the communist structure. It did not stay with theory: between 1976 and 1980 independent newspapers, independent trade unions with their own complaints agencies, their own cultural organizations and their own publishing house *Nowa* were founded. It was so massive, that the authorities were powerless – because they did not want to apply more than just "the little terror." Sometimes very cowardly. A well-known oppositionist, Ewa Milewicz, was paralyzed, used a wheelchair and drove a specially adapted car. One evening, after a meeting with co-oppositionists, she gets to her car only to notice that all four of her tires are slashed.

Work of the anonymous heroes of the Polish security service.

CZECHOSLOVAKIA

January 1977. New Year's reception of Max van der Stoel, the Dutch minister for Foreign Affairs.[76] When it's my turn to shake hands, Van der Stoel says, "Do you feel like going to Prague with me?" You could have knocked me down with a feather, Van der Stoel to Prague? Just then, a manifest was published in Prague under the name *Charta-77*, signed by hundreds. Their main wish was, in short, the return of decency to Czechoslovakia, in particular to the administration. To indicate that it was about a civilian initiative of a broad composition here, three spokesmen were chosen from different segments of the society, who every three months would be replaced by three other spokesmen. The first three were Václav Havel, writer, Jan Patočka (ex) university professor, and Jiří Hájek, who had been minister of Foreign Affairs in the Dubček era.

The administration reacted all but decently. Rather: they were outraged. Havel was immediately arrested and the well-known Stalinist dung was spread over the whole movement. Not particularly a suitable moment for a Western minister of Foreign Affairs to pay a visit. However, an appointment between Prague and The Hague had already been made earlier and diplomatically it seems always pretty difficult to cancel something like that. But Van der Stoel made a virtue of the need. He lets them know that the visit could proceed under two conditions: 1. that every journalist who would like to travel with him would get a visa without exception and 2. that during the consultations no subject would be taboo. Already glad that a Western minister would come at all under these circumstances, they immediately granted his conditions.

It goes without saying that I responded to Van der Stoel's question at the New Year's reception in an affirmative way. We would leave on February 28. A few days before our departure, the Dutch Foreign Ministry handed to the Czechoslovakian embassy in The Hague the list of journalists who would be accompanying the minister. When they noticed over there that I was on it also, they immediately protested, but our ministry subtly pointed to the conditions under which Van der Stoel had stated he was willing to go to Prague. And without any doubt they recalled that Van der Stoel had canceled a visit to Kuwait shortly before, because a journalist of Jewish origin had been denied an entry visa. Such a disaster, the gentlemen in Prague were not willing to risk – and so I got a visa, too.

Shortly before we left, I did an interview with Van der Stoel for *NOS* radio and in the margin I asked him whether he was willing to speak with people of

---

[76] Max van der Stoel is the former High Commissioner on National Minorities of the Organization for Security and Cooperation in Europe, OSCE. In this capacity he also was the monitor on human rights in Saddam Hussein's Iraq.

Charta-77. "No," he said, "my advisers [of the Foreign Ministry] told me that it would be better for them if I don't do so. They are already considered agents of the West and if I would talk with them, those accusations would only be strengthened." I knew, however, that *Charta* would only applaud such a conversation and I told Van der Stoel that those accusations would be expressed anyway – not in the last place to prevent those kinds of contacts. I said that it would only strengthen their position when he would talk with them. But Van der Stoel maintained his point of view – on completely honest grounds, of course.

I then called Professor Maarten Brands, who at the time also devoted himself to the Czechoslovakian cause, and asked him to speak with Van der Stoel once again. He did indeed call him, used the same arguments as I did and appealed to him to do have a talk with *Charta*.

Right before our departure at Schiphol airport, Van der Stoel was interviewed by *NOS* TV. They put forth the question I had left out in my interview because no answer seemed better to me than a negative one, "Are you going to contact representatives of *Charta-77?*" You could conclude from his answer that he, seemingly slightly but in essence fundamentally, had changed his point of view, "I will not initiate it myself, but if they try to contact me, I will receive them."

I took this as a signal. Immediately after our arrival I looked up Jiří Hájek, also because Van der Stoel knew Hájek from former days.[77] It even had a political-piquant background. That meeting took place shortly after the war. Van der Stoel and Hájek both were members of the *IUSY*, the "International Union of Socialist Youth," a democratic-socialist organization. The issue in Czechoslovakia in those days was about whether the social-democratic party would merge with the communist party. Hájek as well as Van der Stoel were delegates at a congress of the *IUSY* and party member Hájek told party member Van der Stoel that he was an advocate of the merger of the social-democrats and the communists. Van der Stoel tried in vain to talk him out of it at the time. Hájek was left holding the baby only to find out later he was saddled with a miscarriage.

Hájek was living in a small street in a faraway suburb. In front of his house: a car of the StB. After I rang the bell of Hájeks wicket gate, two StB-ers got out and stopped me: it was not allowed to visit Hájek. Hájek, who had come out-

---

[77] After arrival at the airport in Prague, a small incident occurred. The spokesman of the Czechoslovakian Ministry of Foreign Affairs said at a short briefing about his minister Bohuslav Chňoupek, "His first language is Russian." Spontaneously I exclaimed, "Oh, I thought it would be Czech!"

side in the meantime, acted as an interpreter and through him I told them that I had traveled with the Dutch minister of Foreign Affairs as a journalist and that it was not against the law to visit someone. They went back into their car and mobilophonically consulted their superiors. They returned rather quickly and gestured that I could pass, after all. I took my tape recorder out of the cab (by which I had come), and wanted to go inside.

"What is that?" the StB-er asked.

"A tape recorder," I answered.

"That's impossible," they said.

"But if I am allowed to go inside, why can't my tape recorder?" I asked.

For a minute they consulted one another and then said, "It's alright, just go in." They did want to glance in my passport: they wrote down my name in their small note book.

Hájek could not go with me to Van der Stoel ("They won't let me pass"), but I did do an interview with him. After that, I wanted to leave, but the situation outside had changed. Now two cars are in front of the door. Two guys step out of car # 2, speaking only Czech. One of them does the talking. He waves an ID the size of a credit card in front of my eyes. I gesture to him to keep his hand still, because I want to have a good look at his card. Of course, you get nothing out of it, because his real name will not be mentioned and you can't even read his false name, because the letters are the size of the attachment of an insurance policy. But still you could see that he did not like it – and that was what is it was all about. He had a ball-head, a greased quiff and he wore a short, leather jacket: the prototype of a bouncer. If a director of a spy movie would have portrayed this type with this outfit as a secret service agent, you would have said that his characterization was too overdone-cliché-like. Hájek acted as an interpreter.

"He says you have to come with him."

"Tell him, that I refuse to come along. I had the permission of his service to visit you, I was allowed to bring along my tape recorder and so I have not done anything illegal." Hájek translates my words but Leathern Greaser repeats that I must come with him. Greaser-and-colleague are still on the other side of the wicket gate, we are on this side. I ask Hájek what would happen if I persist in my refusal. "I'm afraid they will drag you into their car," he says. And he apologizes that this is happening to me. And I apologize that he, because of me, has run into a situation which makes him have to apologize for something he does not need to apologize for at all. Both of us apparently have the tendency to put our norms of decency into top gear, since we are confronted with the height of indecency. Greaser stands right in front of me, with the gate still between us, but clearly indicating that there is no getting away from it. "Tell them that I will come along, but under protest." Hájek translates again, but Greaser is not impressed at all, of course. "Bartolomějská, I presume?" I ask. He nods in silence. In the car was a third StB-er. Stuck in the to me all-too-familiar way between two StB-ers on the rear seat we went to the to me well-known place.

The arrival of the second car was not that inexplicable. When the StB men after consultation had let me pass, they did not know who I was. After all, they only had written down my name. I assume that they passed it on to the "central" and that only there they discovered that I was the same guy from seven years ago – and that they did not want me to get off free.

Back home, after my previous interrogation on the Bartolomějská seven years earlier, I had thought things over at ease. As for the interrogation nothing had gone wrong, but it was just like a chess game: you are never sure which countermove follows on your move and I had decided: if it happens to me again, I simply don't answer at all. Then I don't need to think about any move whatsoever and thus any countermove is out of the question as well. But it did come as a surprise that I would have to apply that new method for the first time in that very same Bartolomějská.

Same entrance, same notice board – only Stalin and Gottwald had disappeared. A different interrogation room – one on the street side with a window. Interrogation by two men and a female interpreter. Name? Given. Why here? Explained.

"What were you doing at the enemy of the people Hájek?" In my eyes, this was already one question too many.

"Before I consider answering your questions, I want to know first which law I have violated on the basis of which you stopped me." They did not mind letting me know: article 40 section 10. Am I allowed to write it down? Yes, I was allowed to write it down. And what does article 40 section 10 say?

"The State Security Service has the right to interrogate anyone who finds himself on the territory of the *CSSR*."

"I see, but then only *after* he has violated the law. Which law did I violate?"

They had no answer for that, because I did not violate any law whatsoever. But they started nagging about Hájek again. Seven years ago I had been scared stiff, but now it was delightfully simple: every time I said I refused to answer their questions. From time to time, I demonstratively looked out of the window, where it started to get pretty dark. At a certain moment I "warned" them to hurry up "because our minister will hold a press briefing at nine o'clock and if I don't show up then, you get a diplomatic scandal, too." At last, it led to the following dialogue:

"Did you interview Hájek?"

"I refuse to answer your question."

"Will you hand over the tape?"

"Since I refused to answer your last question, this question is totally irrelevant."

Silence on the other side. One of the two gets up and walks out. After a few minutes he returns and says, "You can go." They did not dare to look in my bag and did not dare to confiscate my tape. It goes without saying, that the presence of Van der Stoel in Prague had determined their behavior a great deal, and without his presence they also would have confiscated the tape without any questions. But I'm convinced that, if I would have handed over the tape and later would have complained that they had confiscated it, they would have said, "Confiscated? He handed it over to us voluntarily."

So I saved my tape, but I had not achieved my main goal: to put a spokesman of Charta 77 in contact with Van der Stoel.

Hájek had told me that the seventy-year-old Professor Patočka was not constantly guarded and was still free to go as he pleased. The following day I rented a car and drove to Professor Patočka's house, arriving there at 11.00 a.m. Van der Stoel had an opening in his schedule between 12.00 and 01.00 and I asked Patočká whether he wanted to speak with our minister of Foreign Affairs. "If that is possible, that would be great," he answered, and he immediately went along to hotel Intercontinental, where we all were staying – and then that short but moving conversation unfolded between Patočka and Van der Stoel, to which all Dutch journalists listened breathlessly. Actually, it was not a conversation but a monologue from Patočka. His main theme was, "We are not against the law, we are simply in favor that our government sticks to the law." Photographer Vincent Mentzel took a picture of that meeting, in which it is clear to see that we all, Van der Stoel included, were profoundly impressed and moved – we are all looking somewhere else *(see photo 31)*.

Afterwards, I did not bring Patočka straight home, but first dropped in on Vladimír Škutina, the TV anchorman of 1968 who in June 1971 was sentenced to four years and two months, a punishment he had nearly completely served. There we talked it over a little bit. Patočká was beside himself with joy, "Imagine what this means," he emotionally said to Škutina, "we have spoken with the Dutch minister of Foreign Affairs. This is one of the finest moments of my life."

I then brought Patočka home, where in the meantime Ludvík Vaculík had arrived who in June 1968 had written the famous *Manifest of two thousand words* and who welcomed me with the words, *"Was, du alter Gauner, was machst du in Prag?* – What, you old rascal, what are you doing in Prague?" Vaculík got an enthusiastic report from Patočká on his meeting as well.

The Czechoslovakian hosts of Van der Stoel were not amused and drastically changed his program. Talks with Prime Minister Lubomír Štrougal and president Gustav Husák were canceled. The party daily *Rudé Právo* called his behavior an "interference in the internal affairs of Czechoslovakia without precedent"and an "insult to the people of Czechoslovakia who in tens of thousands of resolutions have said no to the drafters and signers of the anti-socialist pamphlet *Charta-77*." Patočka was called "a political adventurer"who did things outside the law. That's why "meetings of representatives of socialist countries during visits to a Western country with communist leaders was a different matter," because then one talked "with parties and representatives who were not outside the law," according to *Rudé Právo*. But in one blow Van der Stoel had become a legend among all the opposition movements in Eastern Europe.

Patočka was arrested after Van der Stoel's departure from Prague. He had a heart condition – which was unknown to me: nobody in his circle had told me. He did not survive the endless interrogations: he had a heart attack and died not two days after our departure. Immediately after his death the moral question arose, of course, as to whether that meeting had been a good thing. In view of the value Patočka himself attached to it, there is no doubt in my mind to answer that question with "yes." Neither Van der Stoel nor the undersigned is responsible for the death of Patočka, but the Czechoslovakian government, which knew about his health condition and wittingly subjected him to those lengthy interrogations.

Also in Czechoslovakia, dissidents were generally quiet, nice people with reasonable concepts. First of all, of course, Václav Havel. I met him for the first time in May 1969 for a *VPRO* TV-documentary "Stay or leave?" – at the time you still had that choice. Also then, he resolutely chose for staying, if need be, he would write for the "desk drawer" – but he stayed. In between his prison periods I quite often interviewed him by phone and only in 1983 I did see him again for the first time at such a typical dissident's party. Once again I had rounded up a visa and my stay happened to coincide with the birthday of Anna Šabatová. At the time, her husband Petr Uhl was sitting out a seven-year-sentence.[78] She had been in prison herself before, at the same time as her brother Jan Šabata and her father Jaroslav Šabata, who in the Dubček era had been secretary of the communist party in Brno.[79] I was invited to her birthday, exclusively attended by fellow dissidents, what, of course, was journalistically convenient. Other birthday guests there also present included Václav Havel

---

[78] Petr Uhl had already been in prison from 1971 to 1975 as a "Trotskyist"(which he was). In 1979 he was rearrested; he was released in 1984.

[79] Jaroslav Šabata was arrested in November 1971 and in 1972 sentenced to 6 ½ years. He was released early, but rearrested after his participation in 1978 at a meeting of *Charta-77* and representatives (Lytiński, Kuroń and Michnik) of the Polish *KOR* at the Czechoslovakian/Polish border and in January 1979 sentenced to nine months plus the eighteen months he still owed *(see photo 25)*.

and Jiří Dienstbier, ex-journalist-now-fireman. But it turned out badly with the interviews I did there.

The Czech dissidents had their own special way of dealing with the agents of the StB. When these agents in the landing tried to keep an eye on who was coming and leaving, the dissident sometimes hospitably offered them a chair, so that they could perform their duty sitting. It was kind of a habit to offer them a cup of coffee from time to time. Then those StB guys absolutely felt awkward and actually got embarrassed with their job. They also were fooled by the subtle Czech humor. When the Czechoslovakian government had to receive a high guest from a "brotherly country," the most prominent dissidents were put into prison for "reasons of security" for that period – as if the Patočkas and Havels were bomb throwers. Once, Brezhnev would pay a visit and dissident Rudolf Battěk, ex-sociologist-now-window-washer also understood that he once more would be put away for a couple of days.[80] When the door bell rang on a morning around six, he knew exactly, not surprisingly, that the StB was standing in front of the door. He went downstairs and whispered through the mail slot in the front door, "Who is there?" One of the StB guys, on the re-bound also whispering, answered, "State Security Service." Battěk, whispering again (and, of course, asking for the sake of asking), "What do you want?"

StB-er, as softly as before, "We've come to pick you up."

Battěk, "My mother-in-law is living in with us. She gets pretty quickly annoyed, even more so when she is woken up that early. Couldn't you come back at nine?"

StB-er, whispering very softly, "That's OK, we will return at nine."

And so it happened. To deal like this with the StB was also some self-protection, of course. To try, also for your own sake, to put even that service into perspective; to try also to laugh about it as a part of the strategy to survive. In essence, the secret service was a criminal organization – for which the Patočka case is only one of the proofs.

Of course all were there – if not imprisoned – at Patočka's funeral. But the speeches given were unintelligible. Just above the heads of the mourners helicopters loudly thundered.

Work of the heroes of the Czechoslovakian secret service.

---

[80] Dr. Rudolf Battěk was arrested for the first time in August 1969 and sentenced to thirteen months. Second arrest and trial in 1972: 3½ years received and served. June 1980 third arrest; in 1981 sentenced to 7½ years, on appeal reduced to 5½ years.

SOVIET UNION

Good friends in 1966, bad friends in 1970. After my expulsion from Czechoslovakia, the Soviet Union was forbidden territory for me as well. Yet I got a visa as an accompanying journalist when a delegation of the Dutch parliament went there for an official visit in August 1976. At the time, there was a small group of journalists who, in consultation with Amnesty International and supporting committees for dissidents, tried to establish contacts between politicians and dissidents. Parliamentarian and ministerial visits were, of course, extremely suited for that purpose. I would try to organize a meeting between the Dutch delegation under the leadership of the president of the "Second Chamber" (comparable with the House of Representatives in the United States) Anne Vondeling, and Andrej Sakharov, in those days the number one dissident in the Soviet Union. There was not much latitude, because the Soviet authorities had designed a program that almost completely took place outside Moscow; in my opinion on purpose, because they knew very well that a great value was attached in the Netherlands to the respect of human rights, the advocates of which lived mainly in Moscow. We would arrive on Thursday, August 12, our trip would start on Sunday or Monday, and bring us back to Moscow only the following Friday; we had to return to Holland right away the next day. A supporting group for Soviet dissidents had given me the address of someone in Moscow, who was not known as a dissident, not even by the Soviet authorities, but who had a good connection with Sakharov. The day after our arrival I took myself to that address. Not by cab, because you could hardly get any, but by a government's limo. You see, they are parked by the dozens, provided with sleepy drivers waiting for hours for their yes-or-no-political bosses. Quite often, they turn their empty hours to advantage by bringing people from pillar to post for a lot of rubles. With such a limo I reached the stated address. The residents did not react in the least suspiciously to my request and said that Sakharov was visiting his fellow dissident Tverdokhlebov who was in exile somewhere in Siberia. In the course of the coming week he would return, however, and they promised me they would warn him to stay home on Friday evening so that he could receive the Dutch delegation. We agreed that I would call them after our return to Moscow that Friday and from some inane statement I could then conclude whether Sakharov would be at home that evening or not.

I got that confirmation and immediately warned Vondeling and his company that we would be welcome in the evening. I did not want to make a media circus out of it, all the more because Russians are cramped for space and such conversations traditionally took place in tiny kitchens.

Sakharov lived on a wide boulevard, but his apartment was extremely small: a kind of hallway-room, a bedroom-living room combo, a teeny-weeny kitchen and all that connected by tiny corridors only one-and-a-half-man's width. That tiny kitchen was overcrowded with the Dutch delegation minus a communist member of parliament who wisely was not informed by Vondeling, Valentin Turchin, president of the Moscow branch of Amnesty International, and his wife Tanja, the parents of Tverdokhlebov, the writer Vladimir Kornilov, me and of course our host and hostess: Sakharov and his wife Jelena Bonner. Sakharov did not speak a Western language and Turchin, a Cybernetic who spoke English very well, acted as a translator.

It became an unforgettable evening. It was for me the first time I spoke with Russians who used simple human language. Up to then, I had to deal for all those years with cliché-producing *apparatchiks* or anxious hangers-on. The people we were speaking to, although having lived and worked nowhere else but in that rigid Soviet Union, observed a normal democratic way of thinking and this reinforced my conviction that the sense of freedom is ingrained in every human being.

Sakharov was very tired of his trip to Siberia, he had been obliged to walk the last fifteen miles (and back again), because there was no public transport and the KGB had forbidden the local cab drivers from taking him.

Just before our tour through the country I was able to bring two Dutch parliamentarians, Frans Andriessen (later Commissar at the European Community in Brussels) and Ad Ploeg to the mother of Vladimir Bukovski who was sentenced in 1971 to twelve years imprisonment for disclosing the abuse of psychiatric institutions to silence dissidents. He had protested against his conviction with repeated hunger strikes. They had forcibly fed him artificially (through his nose) and he was physically in bad shape. A worldwide campaign was already going on for him and after their return Andriessen and Ploeg also did what they could to get him free. A few months afterwards, on December 18, 1976, Bukovski was exchanged for the Chilean communist leader Luis Corvalan, who was sitting in Pinochet's prison.

But sometimes your attempts fail miserably. It happened to me between December 9 and 13, 1981, when I traveled to Moscow with the Foreign Affairs Commission of the Second Chamber. One of the delegates was Jan Nico Scholten whom I took along to Larisa Bogoraz to her teeny-weeny home on the Muscovite Lenin Prospekt. In August 1968, she had, together with others, protested against the invasion of Czechoslovakia in Red Square. It cost her two years in exile. She was still married then to Juli Daniel who in 1966 together with Andrej Sinyavski had been sentenced – as mentioned before – to five years because of his publications in Western magazines under a pen name.

Larisa's second husband Anatoli Marchenko was because of underground publications sentenced to fifteen years camp and was somewhere in Siberia in 1981.[81] Because of Scholten's visit, Leonid Charanski also showed up; he wanted to plea for his brother Anatoli, the most well-known Jewish activist then, sentenced in 1978 (after more than a year of custody) to three years imprisonment and ten years camp-"strict-regime" because of "espionage." Scholten listened to their stories, but said to my bewilderment that he could not do anything for them. He dragged in the detente between East and West, which could be in danger if the West would intervene in cases like these. Both of them were deeply disappointed and I later returned to Larisa Bogoraz to apologize for Scholten's attitude. And yet, he could perform so vigorously in the Dutch parliament if it was about infringements of human rights in South Africa. But that was likely more marketable. Marchenko died in that camp on December 8, 1986. That was just one dead person too many for Gorbachev. Eleven days later he lets Sakharov return to Moscow from his place of exile in Gorky. The beginning of the end had come.[82] Later on, Larisa Bogoraz cooperated quite a bit with Andrej Kovalyev (released in 1984 after his full term of three years imprisonment and seven years camp) and he bore no malice either, as I was able to observe after his release.

In 1966, I had tried in vain to get hold of my guide Slava Zjilin from 1958. In 1976 I gave it another try – again through *Inturist*. Sure enough, I got him on the line and we made an appointment. "I knew you were coming," he said laconically, when we drank a cup of coffee in a restaurant on Gorky Street, because he was promoted at *Inturist* and now managed the Benelux and Scandinavian countries. Things went well with him, he had gotten a son and he had received the pictures – finally, after eighteen years the confirmation that they were not lost. Ten years later, I tried it again at the *Inturist* service stand at the International Press Center of *Novosti*. "Do you know him well?" they asked me carefully, after I had asked for Slava. I explained how I got to know him. "He died four years ago from a heart attack," they said, "but his son is also working for *Inturist*, and he looks like his father like two peas in a pod." I was not able to check it out, because every effort I made to get in touch with him led nowhere.

By the way: that meeting at Sakharov's in 1976 had a tiresome consequence for the Dutch delegation. The official limos, with which they had themselves

---

[81] Anatoli Marchenko had been in a camp from 1968 until 1970 because of his public sympathy for the Prague Spring. He was sent into exile in Siberia from 1975 until 1979 and since 1980 had again been in a camp after his condemnation.

[82] See appendix page 379.

transported to Sakharov's address, appeared – against the protocol – not to have waited: the delegation had to go on foot.

Work of the heroes of the Soviet secret service.

HUNGARY

The book was difficult to read, it contained sentences which ran to over half a page, but the theme was interesting, the country from which it came still more interesting and the author the most interesting: György Konrád. The book was called, "The intelligentsia on its way to class power. "He had written it in a small country house together with the sociologist Iván Szelényi. The Hungarian authorities were after the manuscript, but the writers could have literally hidden that under the ground. Later on, they had it smuggled out of the country and a German translation would appear at the German publishing house Suhrkamp.

The communist culture popes had reached a typical Hungarian compromise. Nothing would happen to them if the book would be published in the West, they were even allowed to be present at the presentation of the book, but all of that under the condition that they would remain abroad for a while.

That's how I met Konrád for the first time: at the presentation of that book in Frankfurt in 1978. Subsequently, he lived for some time in Paris and after a few months just returned to Budapest. There, I visited him many a time; he never made a secret of his opinions and neither he nor I were ever faced with any problem. He hoped once to live "in a boring democracy" as he called it. His "opposition" showed similarities to that of *Charta-77*: return to normal, human forms of decency. It goes without saying that he was not allowed to publish, but his works appeared in the West, he got his money regularly and he could travel to the West as well. Because it must be said that the Hungary of party leader János Kádár was in a positive way a strange country in those days. In essence it was communist, but under the slogan "who is not against us, is for us," Kádár slackened the reins quite a bit. Non-communistic was possible as long it did not change over to anti-communism.

It was not like that in Kádár's initial years. When the Russians crushed the Hungarian uprising of October 1956, they were in need of a Hungarian communist who could justify that violence. János Kádár lent himself to that and he let down his political associates, fellow party member/Prime Minister Imre Nagy and fellow secretary general of the Central Committee of the party Ferenc Donáth on November 2, 1956, just before the Soviets dealt the final blow on November 4. This is not the place to give a whole discourse on that uprising, a sufficient number of books have appeared about it, but even now the whys of Kádár's treason – because treason it undoubtedly was – are still not clear. In the first years after his appearance Kádár had hundreds of participants in the uprising executed with as an inexcusable low point the trial against Nagy, Maléter, Donáth and six others in June 1958, which ended with the, also executed, death penalties for Nagy and Maléter among others. The trial was secret and an official statement was issued only after the execution of the sentence.

Donáth got twelve years, but in 1962 all those, convicted because of the uprising, were released. "We even got a statement which said that we had no record," Donáth told me when I was at his place in the year of his release. It was the first of a series of meetings with him which continued until his death in 1986. He spoke a laborious German and his wife, fluent in German, always helped him quickly if he once again looked helplessly in her direction because he could not find the right word.

Donáth was a prewar communist and had been in the resistance during the war together with Kádár. When after the war the rage of Stalinism broke out, which in Hungary under the leadership of Mátyás Rákosi raged fiercer than everywhere else in Eastern Europe, he was dismissed as a minister and shortly afterwards arrested as a "revisionist." Kádár, who was considered the leader of that revisionist group, met that fate at the same time. They staged a Kádár trial with Ferenc Donáth as the second main defendant. Both were sentenced to long imprisonments. During his interrogations, Kádár was severely maltreated by members of the secret service; his whole life he bore the scars of it. They were released after the de-Stalinization and belonged to the communists who strived for a "socialism with a human face" – even if it was not then called so. During the uprising, Nagy, Kádár and Donáth took over the leadership of the party and they were unanimously against military intervention by the Red Army. "On still the very same second of November, Kádár and I were talking," according to Donáth, "and then he said: 'When the Russians catch us, they will finish us.' After our conversation, we know now, he drove straight to the Soviet embassy." He remained without a trace until November 4, when he announced through a radio station in Szolnok that he had formed a new government which would put down the "counterrevolution" with the help of the Red Army. And that's why Donáth stood again in front of communist judges in 1958. And again he was the second man. This time not in the Kádár trial, but in the Nagy trial, set up by Kádár. Donáth acted rather laconically about his own conviction "but that he let Nagy to be hanged, that I will never forgive him for. Maybe he was forced [by the Russians] to pronounce the death penalty, but then he should have put his hat on and stepped down." During the trial Nagy behaved, according to Donáth, very bravely and did not give an inch.

In his new function at the ministry of Agriculture in the seventies, Donáth met Kádár on different occasions at receptions and he was treated kindly by him, as if nothing had happened. "No, I never came out right and asked him what he thought of the death of Nagy, but I did notice that it was kind of hard for him to cope with it," according to Donáth.

By the way, Kádár had not been the choice of the then Soviet party lead-er Khrushchev. During those turbulent days, Khrushchev had traveled to Yugoslavia to consult with the Yugoslavian leader Tito. Tito, who pretended to the outside world to side with the communist reformers, was in reality very much worried by the developments in Hungary. He agreed to a Russian intervention and also with the pushing aside of Nagy. But he was against Khrushchev's proposal to push forward Ferenc Münnich as the man for the countergovernment, because he was known as a harsh Stalinist. "Take Kádár," Tito proposed – and Khrushchev agreed. It was also agreed that the Yugoslavian government would offer political asylum to Nagy and his compa-ny at the Yugoslavian embassy in Budapest, not for humanitarian reasons, but to make them incapable to act so that Kádár and Khrushchev would have free play. Donáth was very bitter about that. "We fell into the trap, we never should have gone to the Yugoslavian embassy." Tito cheated Nagy, but Khrushchev for his part cheated Tito. He was promised that nothing would happen to Nagy and his company and, not surprisingly, the dismay in Belgrade was sincere when the verdicts were made public. Yes, but Tito could have known better, because that's how the traditions are in the Mafia.

A "good" communist has two consciences: his personal and his party con-science. If a conflict between those two arises, the party conscience has prior-ity. Of course, there were unscrupulous crooks within in the party also who did not have any conscience at all. In my opinion, Kádár had definitely a per-sonal conscience. As long as it was possible, he let it speak. If as a result the party suffered, he let that personal conscience down, being, after all, just a personal interest. This has to be sacrificed to the "higher," the party interest. A philosophy like this seems unthinkable now, but for the old communists "the party" was not just an organization, but a mythical unity of a religious na-ture. In 1979, I had a conversation about this way of thinking with the Czech Zdeněk Mlynář in Vienna. He had been a confirmed communist, had studied in Moscow, but lost his hardlinerishness when he had to sort out in the sixties what happened to the confiscated properties of those who were sentenced in the show trials of the fifties. He had converted to "reform communism" and as a secretary of the Central Committee had drawn up a new and democratic party program in April 1968 during the Prague Spring. He had been a lead-ing figure of *Charta-77* and was thrown out of the country at the end of 1977

– and had completely lost his faith. He characterized the communist world "as a sect, but the danger is that it is a sect which is in power."

Well then, Kádár has stuck his whole life to that sect-thinking. He always let that party conscience prevail at the sacrifice of his personal conscience. It must have been a tragedy for him that still during his lifetime, the party has recognized that the uprising had been a good cause and the death penalty for Nagy an injustice. So he had not made the sacrifices *in* the interest of the party but *against* the interest of the party. I think he did not watch the reburial of Nagy on television. To me, who always had an immense admiration for Nagy, it was an equally immense satisfaction that I could give a live commentary of that reburial for the Dutch television. With Donáth I say: Kádár should have stepped down and not have let that death sentence pass. But he was caught in that absurd sectarian higher-interest-net – and in this way he was a victim of the system as well.

The stupor after the blow of 1956 had kind of worn off in the beginning of the sixties. Moreover, Kádár slackened the reins somewhat and here also the law goes: the more tolerant the regime, the greater the opposition. Initially, the oppositionists were followers of György Lukács, the grey eminence of Marxism. During the short-lived communist government of Bela Kun in 1917, he had been a minister of Cultural Affairs. Afterwards, he played an influential role in the international communist philosophical circuit, but in the postwar Stalinist times he proved himself to be no hard-liner. He sided with Nagy and his company in 1956 and was part of the top group which sought asylum at the Yugoslavian embassy. He was released without conviction in 1958 and led a withdrawn life ever since. I visited him in his spacious Budapest apartment on the bank of the Danube in 1962/63, but he was as timid as a hare. He did not want to make any statement whatsoever and we just talked about this, that and the other. I had that same strange feeling as at Ernst Busch's – they had been militant their whole life as long as it went against "the enemy." No fear of arrest, not scared to be put in isolation by their surroundings. But whatever criticism, even fundamental criticism, they had on the state of affairs in the communist world, it remained "somehow" their own world from which they did not dare to step outside. He did, though, hold seminars at his house, in which he critically approached the system and so created a number of followers who crystallized out to the new opposition. Like the philosopher György Bence, they initially were Marxist-oriented, but over the years they threw their Marxist coats in the trash can and evolved themselves into regular nonideological democrats. They started to publish their own magazines and books. The punishments remained limited to high fines and from time to time a beating by members of the secret service. I was frequently in touch with the producer of one of those underground magazines: Gábor Demszki. He was end-editor of *A Hirmondo*. Like in Poland, the Hungarian oppositionists made no secret of who the producers were. The trick was to have the magazines printed somewhere else each time and to get rid of them before the secret service could confiscate them. Gábor Demszki always looked like the neatest boy of the neighborhood, neatly-cut hair, dressed conventionally and according to my memory always in the same blue-grey suit, mostly with a tie and his appearance did absolutely not square with the type of an "underground fighter." Still, many a time he was beaten up by one of those secret street-agents when they once again caught him with the whole edition of his magazine in his small car. He took this, however, with an admirable casualness; I never heard him say one resentful word and he continued his oppositionist work for years and remained imperturbable until the liberation.

Still, it seemed that the Hungarian government combated the opposition without enthusiasm as a kind of dire necessity in order not to drop out of the Eastern European customs. Behind the scenes they sometimes tried to talk them into coming around. The then "culture pope" of the party György Aszél liked to play the noble liberal. Once, he also tried to get Konrád on his side. He invited him to his office and Konrád went. Aszél played the jovial-approachable card and to show that Konrád and he "really" were on the same page, he said, "We do know don't we: the Russians *are* barbarians." Konrád did not need to be "pro," if he only stopped making statements against the system – then he would be allowed to publish again. Of course, Konrád let his advances pass.

But Kádár's Hungary was a paradise compared to that of the Stalinist Rákosi in the first ten years after the Second World War. I will never forget the horrifying story told to me by Julia Rajk. Her husband László Rajk, first minister of the Interior and later of Foreign Affairs, was arrested as a "Titoist" and in the first of the infamous show trials in Eastern Europe sentenced to death and hanged. He was rehabilitated in 1956. His corpse was exhumed and Julia had to be present for identification. Of course only a skeleton was left. Julia, "I took his skull in my hand, stroked it and felt the shape – and then I knew: this is my husband." And where had he been buried? Just alongside the road, at a milestone a half an hour ride from Budapest.

Work of the heroes of the Hungarian secret service.

ROMANIA

Nowhere else was I as scared as in Romania. With the exception of a short revival in 1968/'69, it went from my very first visit in 1962 up to the last one in

1988 from bad to worse. You were *always* followed as a foreign journalist. At the time that there was no opposition yet, it was just highly unpleasant to go to that country, but after fighters for human rights became active there also, it simply became risky to go there. Many a journalist has been beaten up on the street by the boxing team of the *Securitate*, the secret service. Remarkably, it was relatively easy to get a visa for Romania, but then you – and I am talking here about journalists of course – were essentially outlawed.

Once again, I had not behaved quite nicely in Romanian eyes and hence did not get an official visa at the Romanian embassy in The Hague. I asked for an interview about it and got an appointment with the Romanian ambassador Traian Pop. He stuck to his refusal and added threateningly, "And I don't advise you to go on your own. [He meant: as a tourist.] You know that in the evening in Amsterdam you run the risk to be beaten up. It is no different in Bucharest. If you go on your own, we can't guarantee that nothing will happen to you." And we both knew that he was talking about the boxing team of the *Securitate*.

In spite of that, I went several times "on my own," but the second-to-first I went to after my arrival in Bucharest was Florian Țuiu. He worked at the national state press agency *Agerpress* and was the liaison officer between foreign journalists and "the apparatus." There is no doubt whatsoever that he belonged to the higher echelons of the *Securitate*. Since the secret service knew you were there after a one night's sleep anyway, it appeared to me best to report myself right away to Țuiu. This worked out well – I have never been beaten up.

The first I reported to had convictions which were absolutely contrary to those of Țuiu. It was Emanuel Valeriu. I had gotten to know him in a remarkable way. *Radio Free Europe* not only made broadcasts to Eastern Europe, but at the time kept track of what was officially and nonofficially published over there. Sometimes people were derogatory about *Radio Free Europe*. Unjustified. People in Eastern Europe listened to it like we did to the *BBC* and *Radio Orange* during the war. The producers were professionals, themselves originating from those countries and they were incredibly well informed about the good and the suffering over there. They had a nice joke about it in Romania. There is a meeting with president and party leader Ceaușescu. The meeting takes hours and is super secret; so secret that nobody is allowed to go out for the bathroom. One minister had to go badly. He is not allowed to leave. He is hopping on his chair, but Ceaușescu is relentless. Finally, he had to let things run their natural course. When the meeting is over, the minister's wife is waiting outside the door with clean pants. The minister asks in amazement how she found out about the urinal incident. "*Radio Free Europe* reported that you wet your pants," the minister's wife answered.

Many leftishers in the West were not shy to proclaim that *Radio Free Europe* was a "propaganda station." But if you asked them from where they got that knowledge, it turned out that they had never heard a broadcast. It's true that initially the station was paid for by the *CIA*, to the great chagrin of the whole staff. And it was a great relief to them when the financing was taken over by the Congress. It did not change the program policy, because they also held on to the journalistic standards during the *CIA* times, but at least they lost now the stigma *"CIA."* The material they collected about Eastern Europe and the press reviews from the official publications over there were sent in weekly bulletins to interested persons. No one seriously dealing with Eastern Europe and the Soviet Union could do it without those bulletins.

Not surprisingly, nearly all of my trips to Eastern Europe went through Munich, the seat of *Radio Free Europe*, where I stayed for a couple of days to talk with the chiefs and their staff of the different sections about the latest developments in their region. At one of those occasions the chief of the Romanian section Noël Bernard said to me, "Just drop by Emanuel Valeriu's." That is what I did and it was the beginning of many, mostly one-time meetings.

Secret Services in the Eastern Bloc could only pinpoint your location after your first overnight stay: you check in with the hotel reception, your name is entered in the Big Book, the contents of which lies the very same evening on the desk of the guys who have to know it and the following morning you already have company. That did not matter for Poland or Hungary, because there you were left alone as a journalist, even if you went to dissidents. It was much stricter in countries like Czechoslovakia and Romania and that is why I always crossed the border as early as possible. As far as Valeriu was concerned: I drove straight to his neighborhood, parked my car somewhere and went on foot to his home. We could talk for the whole day and he was very well informed about the situation. He was not an active dissident, but as an ex-communist he was regularly in touch with other communists, who had fallen out of grace, or other ex-communists. He had been a sports reporter of the Romanian television, but he had been purged. Toward the evening, I left for my hotel with the agreement to revisit him only if I thought that I was not being followed. Over the years, I had acquired some tricks to get rid of the supervisors. Particularly, manipulative use of traffic lights produced good results. So different times I succeeded in seeing him a second or third time; often, though, I saw him on such a Romanian trip only once: on the very first day. He knew Noël Bernard personally from former days and he wrote for *Radio Free Europe*. Once in a while, I took along an article, simply in the chest pocket of my jeans jacket. But for fourteen years I had a trump card to fall back on. I had made an interview with Ceaușescu in 1975, a separate story, and official pictures were made of it. I had gotten one of them as a gift and always had it in an envelope in the top in my suitcase, which literally and metaphorically was most obvious during border checks. If one of those customs officers opened my suitcase I said, casually, that I "had something possibly interesting for them" and then I took the picture out of the envelope on which I was seen together with "the president." That worked like WD-40.

Sometimes, even the picture did not help. In February 1988, I went to the Romania of Mister Ceaușescu for the last time. The circumstances were really horrifying and did not differ much from our "hunger winter." No lights anymore in the streets, no heating in the houses, water and electricity for private persons was either not available at all or sporadic at best and worst of all, there was hardly any food. For some years I knew the dissident couple Professor Mihai Botez and Mariana Celac. In the end, he was expelled from the country, she lived downtown on Bulevardul Dacia. From time to time she was in prison and when she was free, sometimes she was guarded, sometimes you could enter her place just like that. On one of those unguarded moments, I visited her. She was an architect and collected quite a bit of material about the scandalous destructions Ceaușescu caused in Bucharest in order to build his dream palaces. She invited me for dinner the following day. I refused, mindful of the black joke which went around in Bucharest, based on two questions:
"What is second worst?"
Answer, "To invite someone for dinner."
Question, "What is the worst?"
Answer, "That someone accepts your invitation."
But she insisted, I absolutely had to come.
Her apartment is a part of a big building, located around kind of a yard, surrounded by a big fence. When I arrived at the gate of the fence, I was stopped by a plainclothesman. He did not identify himself but simply said that I was not allowed to pass. I said him that I was expected, and asked whether I could at least go to inform her. Not allowed. I was terribly embarrassed. She was sitting there with food scraped up from I don't know where and I simply don't show up? I said that I would not leave and wait in front of the gate. I approached people who lived there and went inside, and finally I ran into somebody speaking a foreign language. I asked him to go to such and such house number to inform that I could not come. He promised to do so but I saw him entering a door which did not lead to the staircase of my hostess. I carried my trump card. I showed the stopper the picture and it obviously confused him. He spoke only Romanian and I understood that he said something to the effect that he had gotten the unavoidable order not to let me pass. Leaning against a lamppost, I waited for half an hour. Then, a regular uniformed policeman came strolling by, very slowly, but he headed straight for me. He asked

for my passport and ordered me to move on. Obviously, he had been warned by the plainclothesman, but I had not the slightest clue how – he just stood to stand. Back in my hotel, I tried to call her – every time the conversation was interrupted after ten seconds. Later on, I complained to Ţuiu that I was not even allowed to visit a friend. "Why didn't you ask us, then we could have arranged it," said this merry little fibber, who defended the regime through thick and thin.

A year before, when it was already extremely bad in Romania also, he had taken me with him to Braşov for a weekend – not out of altruism, but to keep me away from other plans. On our way back we were overtaken by a blizzard between Ploeşti and Bucharest. That always meant in Romania: traffic jams. We spent the whole night in a jeep, running the engine from time to time to drive the worst cold out. I had already told him before that there was no heating and even no water in the rooms of hotel *Ambassador*, still an establishment of the better grade. He simply ignored this. In the jeep he repeatedly said, "When you are home, just put your feet nicely into the hot water, that will straighten you out." I had told him as often that there was no hot water available. Yet, when he dropped me off at the hotel totally numbed with cold after a ten-hour-ordeal in that jeep, he had the nerve to say, "And do take my advice and go to sit nicely with your feet in the hot water, " at which I angrily cried out to him that there was no water at all in *Ambassador*, let alone hot water.

One morning he came to pick me up to go somewhere, but first we would have breakfast together in the restaurant of that very same *Ambassador*. It was ice-cold there. We were both wearing our coats and fur caps. There were only some rock-hard, three-week-old dry rolls available. No butter, no filling. The waiter brought some kind of tea and apologized that it was not warm "because we have too little gas pressure." And what says Mr. Ţuiu? "When you come back here next year, you will see that the butter will run through the streets."

In that last terrible year 1988 my camper was parked in front of the headquarters of the Romanian state tourist agency *Carpaţi*. The cars of the *Securitate* were also parked on that lot. Not one or two, but at least half a dozen; waiting for foreigners leaving hotel *Ambassador* across the street. At half past nine in the evening, everything is still alright. When I come back less than half an hour later, the window on the driver's side has been smashed. Not much has been stolen: a bottle of wine. No Romanian would have dared to break into a car on that square, because everybody knows, that it is infested by *Securitate* people. That burglary is pestering by the *Securitate*. My desire to stay any longer diminishes considerably.

Officially, I got nobody to interview and the oppositionists were absolutely out of reach. The *Securitate*, not even standing in front of their house doors,

Romanian names and addresses (not the real ones, but mnemonics for DV to remember the real names and addresses) in micro-letters on micro-pieces of paper.

simply did not even let you pass the door of the apartment building. Ţuiu had promised me to arrange some official interviews, but nothing came of it. The following day my decision is final, when I had come to complain to Ţuiu that after a week's waiting nothing had been arranged yet. "What do you think? Everywhere they say: 'We don't want to have anything to do with that journalist who insulted our president.' You are persona non grata in Romania," he said. After that, I had only one wish: to leave the country as soon as possible. That insult surely referred to an article, in which I had indicated that I doubted the intellectual powers of Seigneur Ceauşescu. Right away the following morning I left, mistrusting every oncoming truck, because the *Securitate* was very skilled in staging car accidents. When I crossed the dam in the Danube at Turnu Severin and came back to my country of residence-home-away-from-home-Yugoslavia, I got papal inclinations to kiss the ground.

In March 1977 I had met the bearded dissident author Paul Goma, shortly after the meeting between Van der Stoel and Patočka. "That is what I call a minister of Foreign Affairs. He knows how it should be," he commented. Three months later I was in Bucharest again. No Goma. He had been arrested. They pulled out his beard – hair by hair.

Work of the heroes of the Romanian secret service.

YUGOSLAVIA

Milovan Djilas was one of the ex-communists who appealed the most to my imagination. He spent quite some time in prison in his prewar younger years because of his convictions. During the war, he was a key figure in the communist partisan resistance and the first man after Tito. He has even negotiated with the Germans in Zagreb on behalf of Tito about an exchange of prisoners, although the Germans did not know, of course, exactly whom they were dealing with. He was rock-hard during the wartime: in villages he let people be shot to death if they were not willing to join the partisans. After the war he became somewhat milder and still was the vice president of Yugoslavia when he wrote an article in the daily *Borba* in 1954, in which he made a plea for democratization. The story has it that he thought to act in line with Tito and was shocked to death when he found out that this wasn't true. But he stuck to his opinion, was expelled from the party and published his famous book *The New Class* in 1957. Famous not because of its content, because I have not found any spectacular point of view in it, but because of the fact that it was written by such an outstanding communist like Djilas. He was already imprisoned then; he had been sentenced to three years in November 1956. After his book had appeared in 1957, they added another five years to it in October of that year. He was released in January 1961 under the condition that he would not publish anything more. He did not comply with it: he finished his second book in November 1961: *Conversations with Stalin*, because he had not only negotiated with the Germans on behalf of Tito, but with Stalin as well. Only the announcement that it would appear was enough for his rearrest in April 1962 and he was sentenced in May to five years "for betraying state secrets" with on top of that the not-yet-served three years and eight months of his first verdict. On New Year's Eve 1966, he again was released early.

I met him for the first time nine months after his last release. I don't like descriptions of a person that much, but I have to make an exception for Djilas, because each time I was struck by his merry, twinkling eyes. His house on the Palmotičeva right behind the Parliament building in Belgrade had two front doors: one went to the living part and one to his work room. If you had an appointment with him, he always answered the work-room-door. And he was a precise man. One day, I was a little bit earlier than we had agreed on and he made a remark about it; not unkindly or reproachful, but nevertheless. In view of my principle: better fifteen minutes early than one minute late, it happened quite often that I sauntered up and down in front of his house for a few minutes or waited in front of his door before I rang the bell *(see photo 29)*.

The first time I was there I noticed a bust of Lenin on a sort of windowsill of his book case, but it appeared from our conversation that he has left communism in any sense whatsoever – as a matter of fact he had become a social-democrat. That's why I asked him why he still had that bust of Lenin standing there. "I got it on my 40th birthday as a gift from Tito, and I could not find it in my heart to do away with it," he said apologizing. But the following year the bust had disappeared. "Where has Lenin gone to," I asked him. He opened the little compartment below that windowsill and there stood Lenin's bust – pushed away in a corner. "I gave it a second thought and actually I thought as well that I could not continue to show it off there."

He could only sit for a short time. Then he continued his discourse pacing up and down, his hands on his lumbar region. "There never was heating in the prison and that's why I got a lot of trouble with my back. Because of that, I have to stand up from time to time," he once explained to me. I visited Yugoslavia very regularly, generally once a year, sometimes with one year in between, and to me a visit was not complete without a meeting with Djilas. I interviewed him for only a few times, but it simply was interesting to talk with him about the current events in the communist world. He was a walking history book. As a vice president, he had experienced the breach with the Soviet Union in 1948. Right after that breach the Bulgarian party leader George Dimitrov, famous because of his courageous behavior during the *Reichstag*-fire trial in 1933, had to go to, I think, Hungary. In those days, you still went by train via Belgrade. Formally, Bulgaria, Dimitrov included, had sentenced Tito and his company in the well-known Stalinist mudslinging terminology. But the protocol requires its own demands and Djilas as vice president had to greet Dimitrov at his transit trip at the Belgrade railway station. "When he got off the train, he was alone without his entourage for just a minute. He quickly came to me and said to me: 'Hang in there.' But as soon as members of his entourage were approaching he clammed up," according to Djilas. I have not read all Djilas' books, so I don't know whether he ever published this incident somewhere. It stuck in my mind as again one more example of those heroes-through-thick-and-thin, who downgrade to timid hares when "the party" is at stake.

He did not let himself be dragged into nationalistic emotions after the war broke out in Yugoslavia. He did not agree with Serbs who were of the opinion that Tito wanted to keep Serbia down "because Tito was a Croat, after all." They could not accuse Djilas of this, because he was a Montenegran and sometimes those are more Catholic than the Pope.

"We did not want [in 1945] any of the republics to become dominant. That's why we created in Serbia the autonomous regions Vojvodina and Kosovo, but for the very same reason we have put down Croatia and made an independent republic of Bosnia/Herzegovina which until then was a part of Croatia," according to Djilas.

He also completely rejected the Serbian propaganda which made it appear as if "the" Croats all would have been fascists during the Second World War – and who on top of that wanted to go ahead and do all over again what their grandpas and grandmas supposedly would have done half a century earlier. "The *Ustaši* were only a small minority among the Croats and besides, we had our own fascist government in Serbia under Nedić as well," according to Djilas. He had a mild opinion of Draže Mihajlović as well. Mihajlović created with his Royal Partisans the first resistance army against the Germans in April 1941. The communists went into resistance only a couple of months later when the German invasion of the Soviet Union brought the nonaggression pact be-

4 maj 1980, 19.15č

Vratio sam se iz šetnje, sa
Stankom.
Štefica mi saopšti: umro Tito.
Mada se to dugo očekivalo —
uzbudilo me, premda ne mogu
definisati svoja osećanja:
veliki deo moga života i naj-
značajnije moje aktivnosti
vezane su — na ovaj ili
onaj način — za njega.
Ne očekujem promenu svoje
sudbine, ali verujem da će
to u Jugoslaviji otvoriti kontra-
diktorne, tj. i slobodnije
procese.

Milovan Đilas

First reaction of Milovan Djilas immediately written down after he learned that Tito had died.

tween Hitler and Stalin to an end. Mihajlović and Tito not only fought against the Germans, but against each other as well – and this caused the vast majority of the fatalities. Local units of Mihajlović did make deals with the Italians and the Germans once in a while to have a free hand towards Tito. The Tito regime sentenced him to death after the war and he was executed. When during one of those conversations with Djilas the subject of Mihajlović was brought up, he said, "No, I don't consider Mihajlović a traitor" and he pointed to his own talks with the Germans to come to some kind of agreement one way or the other.

One time, I came in through the living-room-door. It was in 1980. Every time Tito threatened to die. I may have been four times between January and May in Belgrade "because it's only a matter of hours yet." I urgently had asked Djilas whether I could drop by immediately after Tito's death to lay down his first reaction about it. He did not like the idea, but he would think about it. After my fourth futile journey I had resolved not to go to Belgrade unless Tito was really dead. On May 4, the time had come. My first steps in Belgrade went in the direction of Palmotičeva. I rang the bell – and the door toward the living room was opened. Djilas let me in. "I've thought of you," he said, "I have immediately written down my first reaction" – and he handed me a small piece of paper with a five liner:

"May 4, 1980, 19.15 h. I returned from a short walk with Stanko [a nephew of Djilas. DV]. Stefica [Djilas' wife. DV] told me that Tito had died. It was expected for a long time – and a feeling of excitement came over me, although I was not able to define my feelings. A great part of my life and my most important activities are, in one way or the other, connected with him. I don't expect a change in my fate, but I do believe that it will open the way in Yugoslavia to controversial, i.e. liberating processes. Milovan Djilas."

I still had one issue on my agenda I wanted to talk about with him: his harshness during the war. During our initial conversations I did not know anything about it and only later I learned from the new generation of dissidents that they did not want to have anything to do with Djilas, precisely due to his behavior as a partisan leader during the war. It never came to that. After I started living in Belgrade in 1984, I visited him much less often than before, because I thought: there is still time tomorrow. Mid-1994 he had a heart attack and he could not receive visitors anymore. In October 1994, I had to leave the country with a six-day notice. I did call him to make an appointment, but he still was too sick to receive anybody. Unfortunately, it stayed with a good-bye by phone. He passed away six months after my departure.

CHILDREN OF THE REVOLUTION

The most infamous trials in the "satellite countries" in the Stalin times were the Rajk trial in Hungary and the Slánský trial in Czechoslovakia. Both of them were leading party functionaries, both were innocent, both confessed to have been traitors, members of Western secret services and accomplices of Tito. And both were hanged together with a whole group. The wives of the "traitors" were also arrested and their children disappeared into institutions and got different names. They were so little, that they forgot who they were. László Rajk Jr. wound up at a sister of his mother and when his real mother was released after the de-Stalinization she was at first introduced to him as his aunt and slowly they prepared him that this aunt was his real mother. Marta and Rudolf Slánský and their mother in Prague and the brothers Jan and Karel Šling, sons of the second man in the Slánský trial, Ota Šling, suffered a similar fate.

Without exception, they all became dissidents and dropped communism.

The mothers kept believing in it for quite a while and Mrs. Slánská has never quite left it behind her. Especially the children, but in a way also the spouses, have an ambivalent attitude toward their murdered relatives. The Slánský case is perhaps the best example to make things more clear. First, the party secretary of Brno, Ota Šling, was arrested. He was accused of the most terrible things, also by Rudolf Slánský Sr who was secretary general of the Czechoslovakian communist party. After a few months, Slánský himself was arrested and they hurled the same accusations at him and he ended up together with Šling in the same trial. Both of them had been hard-line Stalinists, who persecuted people or had them persecuted. At one moment you were executor of cruelties, the next you were the victim of it. The children realized this profoundly, I met them all and some of them even many times. I don't know Mrs. Slánská personally, but I do know the widow of Šling, British in origin. I do have to admit that I had the greatest difficulty to bring up this subject, but at the same time I thought I could not ignore it. Mrs. Šlingova, Marta and Rudolf Slánský and László Rajk (resembling his father like two peas in a pod) plainly showed that they recognized the truth, "but it still remains your father, your husband." As a matter of fact, Jan Šling could not accept the truth just because it concerned his father. But how different their mutual views might have been, they all stuck their neck out. Particularly Jan Šling was so active against the Husák regime, that they expelled him from the country, together with his then-wife Zuzana Blüh, daughter of one of the founders of the Slovakian communist party, who also was in the opposition. It was always open house for dissidents at Marta Slánská's apartment in the historical Nerudová street, which winds up from the Old City Square to the Castle. Her brother Rudolf, an economist, wrote reports for *Charta-77* – and the widows supported their children. Other than Jan Šling, they all had jobs and despite their opposition activities, they were not dismissed because in a way they were invulnerable due to their history of suffering.

There was harassment, though. László Rajk had founded a small bookshop in a house in downtown Budapest, where you could buy oppositionist books and magazines or books not available in Hungary. A few times some stuff was confiscated, but László indefatigably went on. He lived in with his mother and subsequently, the authorities requisitioned the bookshop, based on the rule that nobody is allowed to keep two homes.

In one respect, Rajk was a hopeless case: he never kept his appointments. He simply did not show up. Finally, I gave up and just waited to see whether I might meet him at other dissidents, because in Hungary also they liked to hold merry meetings with great regularity.

One day, a British TV team had entered Hungary under some kind of pretext, but in reality to make a TV documentary on the Hungarian uprising in which Rajk would fulfill a key role. On a certain day they would shoot exteriors with him, but he simply had not been in touch and remained unreachable until the following day. And a British team has more the size of the Czechoslovakian one, with which I experienced my first TV-adventures than the one-man-team of the Netherlands in the sixties. But your forgiveness toward figures like Rajk is always spaciously sized. And so it ought to be, I think.

In my view, many Western politicians have pursued an unfortunate policy toward the bosses in Eastern Europe and the Soviet Union. Willy Brandt is the greatest example.[83] He was not only then, but is to my amazement still now praised for his *Ostpolitik,* "East Policy," just like the his then-right- hand in this respect: Egon Bahr. That policy originated with the viewpoint: whether you like it or not, the communist parties happen to be in the leadership there, that might last until eternity and we have to put up with it. Dissidents were considered a marginal phenomenon which did not carry much political weight and whom you had to ignore in order not to offend the rulers. Not surprisingly, Brandt refused to talk to dissidents in Prague and to Wałęsa in Warsaw. Even artists who were expelled or fled from the *DDR* to West Germany were not received there with open arms. Ignore them and keep silent, was the motto, because the [West German] state institutions did not want to question their connections with the official institutions of the *DDR.*[84] That's precisely what the rulers over there wanted: to be taken seriously, to be respected. It goes without saying that you had to talk and confer with those leaders, but on the same level as with hostage takers: talk to them and prevent that it comes to shooting. But the starting-point must be: they temporarily have the power, I wish it to be temporarily and we must do everything to shorten that temporariness as much as possible and the people who are right are the hostages, the dissidents, the ordinary citizens. Our sympathy, in all candor, has to go out to them, and there should not remain a single shred of doubt about it toward the rulers. The policy of Brandt meant the confirmation of the system, not the denial of it. It was unprincipled but it seemed pragmatic. The broadsword Reagan came in between with his "evil empire," but his rock-hard policy, based more

[83] Willy Brandt was an outstanding member of the German Labor Party. In 1966 he became minister of Foreign Affairs and vice chancellor of the so-called "Great Coalition" of Social Democrats and Christian Democrats. He was chancellor of a coalition government of Social Democrats and Free Democrats from 1969 until 1974. After his resignation he remained president of the Labor Party until 1987.

[84] See *Eingegrenzt – ausgegrenzt. Bildende Kunst und Parteiherrschaft in der DDR 1961 – 1989* by Hannelore Offner and Klaus Schroeder, Berlin, 2000.

on his foxiness than on an excess of intelligence, made a deeper impression on Brezhnev and company than Brandt's policy, so it was easier for Gorbachev to press internally for reforms than if Brandt's *Ostpolitik* would have played the first fiddle. So Brandt's policy was not even pragmatic. In spite of that, I have a profound respect for Brandt, in particular because of his resistance against Nazi-Germany. But exactly his behavior in those days reinforced my amazement about that *Ostpolitik* – hard he had fought against the "pragmatic" politicians of the thirties who also took the eternity of the Third Reich for granted, or at least the thousand years duration of it. History has recognized that the dissidents were right, not thanks to but in spite of Brandt. In my eyes, his *Ostpolitik* was a complete misconception.

The same can be said about the Dutch hustling around the Pershing II and the cruise missiles. The peace movement nourished the basic assumption that armament was the cause of the East-West antithesis and not its consequence. That's why its leaders saw it as their main task to strive for arms limitation, because then the contrast would also decrease. It was based on a wrong analysis, it was an exchange of cause and effect.

Once, a quarter of a century ago, every staff member of *NOS* radio had to explain in a kind of statement of principles on which philosophy his program was based. I produced a bimonthly program "View on Eastern Europe" then. I pointed to that exchange in my paper and connected this reasoning to it: fundamental disarmament will only be possible if the East-West antithesis no longer exists; meaning that either we get a system of communism-à-la-Brezhnev or that they get a system based on the democratic rules of the game. So, every democratically thinking person – and that was the vast majority of the members of the peace movement – shall have to fight for the change of that other system if he really wants to go for fundamental disarmament.[85]

The big leader of the Dutch peace movement, also internationally known, was Mient Jan Faber. I strongly doubted about whether his intentions were honest. He organized one of the biggest demonstrations ever in the Netherlands in the fall of 1981. It was a demonstration against the Pershings and the cruise missiles. No fewer than 400,000 people showed up on the Museum Square in Amsterdam. But when Faber told these people-of-good-will at this impressive mass meeting, that *Charta-77* had given its support to the peace movement, I thought: he knows better, he is fooling them. Because it was precisely *Charta-77* that had repeatedly stated that the existence of democratic regimes in Eastern Europe was a prerequisite for peace. *Solidarność* had the same point of view, as shown by its reaction of protest against an anti-Pershing statement of the (communist) World Trade Union, "Real peace can only be achieved if

---

[85]   See appendix page 380.

fundamental human and trade union rights are being observed, if there is justice and freedom."[86]

The Dutch peace movement had such a strong influence on the opinions in the rest of the world that the press in the United States referred to it as "Hollanditis."

Later on, I met Mient Jan Faber at different times and had discussions with him, and fortunately: he really did not know better. Fortunately, because it meant that he remained open for arguments. In the long run, he implicitly recognized that he had mixed up cause and effect, not in the least due to his more intensive contacts with *Charta-77* and oppositionists in the GDR. Particularly the oppression and persecution of the Polish trade union *Solidarność* in December 1981, shortly after that mass meeting, was an eye opener, he once told me. Why, I wondered and also asked him, does everyone have to learn his own history lesson and not look a little further back. Hadn't there already been the Sailor's Uprising of Kronstadt against the dictatorship of Lenin in 1921, the workers uprising in Berlin in 1953, the uprisings of Poznań in 1956 and in Gdańsk in 1971 in Poland, the Hungarian uprising of 1956, the Prague Spring of 1968? Uprisings and movements, not of conservative reactionaries, but of workers and/or progressives, often communist intellectuals. All crushed by the "communist" establishment in practically identical ways with harsh force and terror over a period of seventy years.

Not paid attention during the lesson. Apparently, many are keen on their own Waterloo.

By the way: Mient Jan Faber was very much involved in relief operations in Bosnia and he changed his mind so much, that he favored very strongly international military intervention in Bosnia as well as in Kosovo – and even in Iraq.

Worse are the politicians who do know better. The Soviet Union launched (metaphorically, fortunately not literally) a new generation of medium-distance missiles, the SS-20, aimed at Western Europe. Practically all politicians, also in the Netherlands, saw this as a direct threat. I still see the headline in the paper with the statement of the leader of the Dutch Labor Party Joop den Uyl, "If the Russians continue with their SS-20, we must position something against it." NATO did so with a countermove which I still consider brilliant: the so-called double-decision with the zero option of December 1979. We still had nothing, we would produce counterarms, but it would take some years yet before they would be operational. If the Russians would have taken away

---

[86] News bulletin of the Coordinating Office Abroad of NSSZ Solidarność # 18 of February 29, 1984

their SS-20's toward that time, we would not deploy our new missiles. The ball was back in the Russian court. *They* could prevent deployment (thus fewer arms) if they would back down (even fewer arms). Now you would expect the peace movement to make every effort with the Russians to come to "even fewer arms." Wrong. They did not opt for "even fewer," but only for "fewer"; not the Russians were approached (who already had deployed their missiles) but the Western world (whose countermissiles existed only on paper). Yes, but then, Mient Jan Faber and his company did not know better yet. But Den Uyl? And the majority of the party leadership? Of course they knew better. But the massiveness of the "peace-movers" represented such a tremendous piece of electorate, that in the long run even Den Uyl himself started to believe that those Pershings and cruise missiles would bring us considerably closer to the Third World War. They did not want to believe that the SS-20 was a political challenge with military means and an attempt to blackmail, to which for political reasons you should keep a military answer in reserve to show that you can't be blackmailed. At the time, it was not popular at all in the Labor Party (where Brandt was a kind of apostle) to listen to the democratic oppositionists in Eastern Europe who were desperately wondering (I experienced it numerous times), "Have the Western social-democrats gone out of their minds?" And those were not war mongers who were waiting for us to liberate them by force, but quiet people like Havel.

Max van der Stoel was the minister of Foreign Affairs in the government Den Uyl in those turbulent days and the only top figure in the Labor Party who had the courage to run counter to the fashionable leftishers, in particular concerning the missile issue – and he had to pay for it: after his term was over he was put on the sidelines. But history was also in agreement with him.

Within the framework of "making friends" also fits the approaching gestures with regard to Mister Ceaucescu. About Romania existed the most persistent misconception for many years. When Khrushchev started his de-Stalinization in 1956 and particularly when he went ahead and did it all over again in 1962, the very Stalinist Romania, at the time still under Gheorghiu Dej, did not want to go along. It broke away from the Soviet policy a little bit (it could do so more easily since there were no Soviet forces on its territory) and oriented itself more toward the rigid China of Mao Zedong. Ceaucescu continued that policy and that firmed up the opinion that everything in Romania was going in the right direction. As if Romania turned away from the Soviet Union because of liberal views while the reason was exactly the opposite: the Romanians considered the Soviet Union too liberal. Already then, the human rights situation in Romania was worse than anywhere else in Eastern Europe – and over the years it only became worse. Still, it appeared impossible to clear up that persistent misunderstanding. Only a few journalists went to Romania and the stories they wrote about it were either not believed or put aside as not fitting in with the desired image. And it went so far that none other than the president of the Dutch Labor Party Max van den Berg was sent to a party congress of the Romanian communist party as the official representative of his party. In a corridor chat I tried to substantiate my amazement of that official fuss with some examples of the Romanian reality, but I did not get the feeling that he was impressed by it.

In hindsight, the Labor Party should publicly be ashamed of this kind of practice and apologize for its treatment toward Van der Stoel.

EPILOGUE 2

And where did they all end up, all those people from the teeny-weeny kitchens and teeny-weeny-back-rooms? Jacek Kuroń, Janusz Onyszkiewicz and Jan Lityński became, respectively, minister of Social Affairs, of Defense and under-minister of Social Affairs in the first government after the collapse of the communist system in Poland.[87] Václav Havel became the president, Jiří Dienstbier minister of Foreign Affairs and Petr Uhl director of the national press agency Četeka in Czechoslovakia. Rudolf Slánský became the Czechoslovakian ambassador in Moscow. Valentin Turchin became a professor in the United States and Sergej Korvalyev commissioner for Human Rights in Russia, a function he left in protest against the Russian action in Chechnya. György Bence became a professor in the United States and in Budapest and Gábor Demszki mayor of Greater Budapest.[87a] Emanuel Valeriu became director-general of the Romanian television. I met a great many of them also in their new functions. When I said to them, "I cannot believe that you now have that function," nearly all of them gave the same answer, "Neither do I." *(See photo 15)*

[87] Jacek Kuroń died after a long illnes in June, 2004.

[87a] György Bence died November 2006 at the age of 65.

CHAPTER 21

Fashionable leftishness strikes

In 1966, France stepped out of the military part of NATO. The European headquarters (of the Allied Forces Central Europe, AFCENT) would be moved from Fontainebleau to Brunssum in the Netherlands. That meant the commander-in-chief-Europe, Johann Adolf Graf von Kielmansegg, would come to the Netherlands as well. It caused a storm of protest from the public, in the media and in the parliament. Questions in the Second Chamber made it clear that Von Kielmansegg was considered to be unacceptable. I agreed. He had been a senior officer in Hitler's headquarters *Wolfsschanze* (Wolf's Lair) in Rastenburg in East Prussia and was apparently jointly responsible for the execution of hostages. Besides, he had made ugly anti-Semitic remarks in a book: *Panzer zwischen Warschau und Atlantik* ("Tanks between Warsaw and the Atlantic"), written after the invasion of Poland in which he had taken part in 1939. In short: he was a war criminal who had escaped conviction. I proposed to make a TV-documentary about the activities of Von Kielmansegg to give the protest a solid foundation. The management of the *VPRO*, of which I was a staff member, agreed and I started digging. The story had it that Von Kielmansegg would have been involved in the plot against Hitler in July 1944 – but this was said about almost every senior German officer. To be sure, I called the German Dr. Fabian von Schlabrendorff, who had participated in all plots that were hatched against Hitler – from Ludwig Beck in 1937 until Von Stauffenberg in 1944. I expected him to have the same disdainful judgment about Von Kielmansegg as he had about Heusinger. To my surprise the opposite turned out to be true. "I don't understand why there is such a strong action going on against him in Holland. Von Kielmansegg played a very positive role in 1944. I personally asked him at the time to participate and he agreed without any hesitation," according to Von Schlabrendorff. In spite of that, I was still not convinced and I consulted prof. Eugon Kogon, just like Von Schlabrendorff an undisputed anti-Nazi who was as a social democrat in the concentration camp Buchenwald from 1933 till 1945 and who was the author of the first standard work on Hitler-Germany: *Der SS-Staat* ("The SS state"). He confirmed that Von Kielmansegg had chosen the anti-Nazi side, risking his own life. Both said that he never committed war crimes and already since 1942 had been involved in attempts on Hitler's life, to whose headquarters in Rastenburg he was transferred shortly before. There I was. Of course, I could have just forgotten about the whole documentary, because it would produce the opposite effect of which I had in mind. This did not appear correct to me; then just a documentary with a different outcome. For that purpose I made interviews in Germany with Kogon and Von Schlabrendorff and in France with Von Kielmansegg himself and only one conclusion could be drawn: he was one of the "good Germans." That book remained a stain, I did not pussy foot around it in that documentary and its aftermath. Von Kielmansegg said in that broadcast that those anti-Semitic remarks had been added by Goebbels' Ministry of Propaganda – on this point you had to take his word for it – but that he was sorry, nevertheless, that he had written the book. After the failed plot in July of 1944 he had been arrested, but there was no evidence left of it. The investigation against him had come to nothing and after a few months he had been released. He had spent the rest of the war in the army in subordinate positions. The testimonies of Kogon and Von Schlabrendorff were iron clad. According to them, Von Kielmansegg would have helped to disrupt the communications between Rastenburg and Berlin after the killing of Hitler and from then on only follow the orders of Von Stauffenberg and his people.

Of course, I waited in anxious anticipation what impact the broadcast would have. The bias against Germans, even more so if they had worn a *Wehrmacht* uniform, was still very strong in those years – including my own. But everybody was dumbfounded by the broadcast on October 4, 1966. Public opinion turned around in one stroke. The *PSP*, a pacifist socialist party, withdrew a brochure they had written against Von Kielmansegg and the leader of the Labor Party caucus of the parliament, G.M. Nederhorst, asked the government reproachfully why he had to learn about this kind of information through television.

The case seemed closed. But *Vrij Nederland*, ("Free Netherlands"), a prominent weekly founded in 1940 as a resistance paper, repeated the accusation, now based on a document with a seemingly crystal clear order to hang, under certain conditions, (innocent) civilians, signed by Von Kielmansegg. It consisted of three parts: the introduction, the order for execution, and the signature. This could not jive with the facts, because Von Kielmansegg had no function that gave him the authority to issue orders. I measured the document with a ruler and discovered that in each of the three parts it showed that in the width of the same numbers of millimeters a different number of letters appeared. In other words: it was a forged document. The three parts had to have come from different places, after which they were put together by the forgers into one compromising document. After a lot of research I discovered the original document in the National Archives in Washington. What kind of document was it? In the German army structure you had the departments "Ic"

(*Einz-c,* "One-c"). They existed on every level: companies, battalions, divisions, right up to Hitler's headquarters. The duty of that department was administrative, namely to list the incoming front reports in the so-called *Nachrichtenblatt* (Report Paper) and to send it up to department "Ic" at the battalion level, from there it went to the division level, until it finally ended up at department "Ic" at the headquarters in Rastenburg – and the other way around.[88] The officer in charge composed from all those reports his own one and, like every Ic-officer at the lower level, provided it with his signature. Thus the signature meant that the writer was responsible for the *drafting* of the report but by definition not for the *activities* reported in it. When an *order* is given from on high, then it has to be given downward as an *order*. When a corps commander gives an order, then it is for the divisions under him only operative as a real order, when it goes by the official title: *Divisionsbefehl Nr...* ("Division Order #..."). The division in which Von Kielmansegg served at the time as an officer of department "Ic," came under the XXXXIe Tank Corps of the infamous Nazi-general Reinhardt. In July 1941 shortly after the German invasion of the Soviet Union he issued an order which actually contained the murder of innocent civilians. When this order came in at the division where Von Kielmansegg served, the division commander Landgraf had in fact to pass it on, but he did not like the idea at all. He consulted his assistant Von Kielmansegg and together they came to the conclusion, seeing that they could not wriggle out of it and had to at least do something with it, so they just hid it away in a survey report, the *Nachrichtenblatt* of the department "Ic," between other different subjects, which made it clear for the limited circle of readers (it only went to brigade- and regiment commanders) that it was precisely *not* about an order. If it would have been passed on as an order it would have been the responsibility of division commander Landgraf and in that case it must have carried *his* signature. The signature of Von Kielmansegg under the survey rapport meant, as a matter of fact, a sabotage of Reinhardt's order.

Just as I had assumed, the *Stasi* forgers had indeed extracted the order from the report, put the header and footer of it above and below the order – and it seemed like Von Kielmansegg was responsible for a criminal order. To show how easy it is to manipulate documents, I made a forgery in the same way from the same document, in which it seems that Von Kielmansegg identifies himself out of anti Nazi considerations with the Soviet army.[89]

---

[88] In the immediate front area the duty of "Ic" also was the interrogation of POW's.

[89] The same method was used in the Kurt Waldheim case. He also was an officer in the Intelligence and he also was made responsible for military activities which he did not commit or take part in, but had only signed *the reports* on it. But it does mean, that Waldheim was better informed

After the war, Von Kielmansegg had been a board member of the BVN (*Bund Verfolgten des Naziregimes* – "Union of Those Persecuted by the Nazi regime") and as such had been approached by the *Stasi* to see whether he was willing to work for them. He refused and already then, they told him that they would get even with him. In October 1996 Von Kielmansegg told me that in the late eighties a defected officer of the Military Historical Institute of the *DDR* visited him. He told Von Kielmansegg that he was there when *Stasi* guys were working on that forgery at his Institute.

In 1968 I was in the process of making a TV documentary on German resistance against the Nazi-regime, because I had noticed around the Kielmansegg case that there was only a measly knowledge of this in our country. Browsing around in the files of the Munich *Institut für Zeitgeschichte* – "Institute for Contemporary History"), my eye fell upon the *Tätigkeitsbericht des Chefs des Personalamts General der Infanterie Schmundt, begonnen 1.10.1942* (Activities Report of the chief of human resources department Infantry-General Schmundt, started on 10.01.1942), where it says on page 189, dated September 4, 1944, "In the pursuit of the arrests concerning 07.20 [meaning here the plot against Hitler on July 20,1944], based on the interrogation of *Oberstleutnant* Smend, up to now adjutant chief of the general staff of the army, have been arrested..", and then four names follow. The second one is *Oberst i.[m] G.[eneralstab] von Kielmannseck,* (spelled incorrectly in the original). The evidence of his arrest was found. Von Kielmansegg took leave as the AFCENT commander-in-chief shortly after this discovery. I handed him a photocopy of this document at his farewell reception in Brunssum. He was very pleased with it.

Von Kielmansegg was not a "hero of the resistance" – he did not see himself as such in the least, and it also was not the intention of the documentary to make him one.[90] The bottom line was this: did he commit war crimes, yes or no? The answer was no. Apparently, his accusers could not find a scrap of evidence, otherwise they would have come up with more than a forged document. Again, it was one of those set-up political campaigns by the *DDR* to discredit West-Germany. In those days, though, there were quite a few fellow travelers

about war crimes than most of his fellow soldiers. The difference between Von Kielmansegg and Waldheim is, that Von Kielmansegg, because of his knowledge, joined the resistance movement in 1942 and Waldheim did not.

[90] Being at Hitler's headquarters in Rastenburg, Von Kielmansegg has proposed in 1942, according to Kogon, to direct a full division to Rastenburg – in his function he could organize that – to capture Hitler and bring him to court. The anti-Nazi top had discussed this at length and finally rejected the idea as impossible to pull off. Von Kielmansegg never brought it up to me and even after I confronted him with what Kogon had said me about it, it took the greatest effort to get him talking about it.

Two forgeries in the Von Kielmansegg case. One by the "Stasi", labeled as "genuine" by "Vrij Nederland" (above) and the second - much better - forgery by DV (below), performed by the design department of the NOS, in which it looks as if Von Kielmansegg is on the Soviet side. It says: "Comrades, Red Guards, Commanders and political collaborators! I know and believe that you will accomplish your duty toward the Fatherland and the Soviet people. You will bravely defend our Fatherland and your splendid city of Leningrad. Behind you stands the City of Labor Leningrad, behind you stand our Soviet people! For our successes in combat! For our socialist fatherland! For our honor and freedom! For our tremendous Stalin! [...] Von Kielmansegg."

who attached more value to *Stasi* forgeries than to statements of firm anti Nazi's like Kogon, Von Schlabrendorff and the widow of Von Stauffenberg, who provided a testimony to me of Von Kielmansegg's anti-Nazi activities as well.

A new era set in, the era of, as I later on would call it, the "fashionable leftnish-ness"; New Lights who could not separate the left chaff from the left wheat. There were quite a few former orthodox Christians and -Catholics among them who had indeed lost their faith, but not their rigidity and just would tell the "old" socialists what socialism was; folks cherishing the philosophy that "the new society had to be built on the ruins of the old one." Not having any idea yet what the new society would have to look like, they were willing to ruin the old one in the meantime. It was also the era of the "nonconform-ists." Seldom have I seen such conformists as those nonconformists. Because seldom have points of views been so predictable as theirs. You just had to listen to what non-socialists or conservatives said, and you knew for sure what the nonconformists would say: namely exactly the opposite. And since politi-cal opponents did have intelligent standpoints from time to time, you could hear quite a few unintelligent things coming from the side of the noncon-formist. The nonconformists did not have their own opinion, they had the anti-opinion of what they considered to be the conformists; their opinion was decided by their political opponents. I think that you could attribute a great deal of the flirtation with the communist regimes of the fashionable leftish-ers to that. "Right" was "anti"-communist, thus as a leftisher you could not very well be "anti"-communist, too. No greater fear among the leftishers than to be taken for a rightist. I usurp the opinion that I was one of the few real nonconformists in those days. Just because I was a social democrat, I had an intense aversion to everything what smelled of dictatorship. And the system which called itself communism, not only smelled of dictatorship – it reeked of it. But the nonconformist "fashionable leftishers" suffered from a serious cold: they smelled nothing at all. And those who claimed to indeed smell something were in their view a "sterile anticommunist" who was actually already in the rotting, reactionary stage. It was in this category that I was classified by "left"-Netherlands. To my deep distress but I have not suffered under it. I just leaned on the self-sacrificing dissidents in Eastern Europe, of whom the vast majority really was left and who nursed standpoints parallel to mine.

At the time, Arie Kleijwegt was the manager/director of *VPRO-TV*, an old social democrat whose opinions did not differ that much from mine. In 1968 he did not resist, though, against a kind of internal *coup d'état* which suddenly brought the factual power at the *VPRO* into the hands of fashionable leftishers. The ideologist of the new school became the former orthodox Christian ruins-philosopher Jan Kassies; the most important executive became the writer and moviemaker Jan Blokker.

The first clash followed almost immediately – and again it was about my aversion to communist practices. From the very beginning, it was known at the Communist International, the Comintern, that direct propaganda for their cause was important, but that the indirect kind was much more effective. The inventor of those indirect tactics was the German Comintern agent Willy Münzenberg, a genius of his kind. Just create committees dealing with something, which can count on general sympathy, attract generally respected folks as a front, but leave the daily leadership to a communist. Under no circumstances can he be a well-known communist, but, on the contrary, he had to be a relatively anonymous one – yet one who fulfills the orders of the Comintern. For this the word "cloak organization" would be invented. Münzenberg was a master in his profession. One of the first and best known "cloak organizations" was the committee, which published "The Brownbook of the *Reichstag* Fire" [1933]. It went all over the whole world, but the text was from Willy Münzenberg. Inspired by an article from an Austrian journalist, he unleashed his fantasy and invented the existence of an underground corridor from Goering's office to the *Reichstag* in Berlin that would have been used by *SA*-men to set the *Reichstag* on fire. Because that was the bottom line of his story: the slightly retarded communist Marinus van der Lubbe had just been a tool in the hands of the Nazis, who had been the real culprits. His genius was that he made up a story, which the whole world wanted to be true. And with enormous success; not a few still believe in this legend. In the beginning of World War II, Willy Münzenberg broke with communism and in June 1940 he was murdered by Comintern agents in the not yet occupied part of France.[91] The Comintern was dissolved in 1943, but the leopard did not change its spots. In 1954, the International Auschwitz Committee was founded according to the very same well-tried method. It was not remotely about standing up for the interests of former Auschwitz prisoners, it was about pursuing communist policy under the cloak of the Auschwitz notion, which was, after all, invulnerable. The first secretary of the International Auschwitz Committee became the Austrian Hermann Langbein, a former Auschwitz prisoner himself, a member of the communist party and appointed as a secretary by the international communist movement. His duty was to set up local Auschwitz committees everywhere else in Europe, following the same pattern as that of the International

---

[91] Data taken from *Willy Münzenberg, eine politische Biographie, mit einem Vorwort von Arthur Koestler* (Willy Münzenberg, a political biography, with a foreword from Arthur Koestler) by (Münzenbergs life companion) Babette Gross, Stuttgart, 1967

Committee. In this way the Netherlands Auschwitz Committee was established in 1956. The majority of the Dutch executive was composed, according to that well-tried recipe, of maybe-or-maybe-not-unsuspecting noncommunists – the secretary was Eva Tas, a member of the Dutch communist party, *CPN*, the pivot around which things revolved. The Dutch Auschwitz Committee issued a monthly newsletter, totally written around two main themes: the non-materialization of a compensation law for Jewish war victims and the danger of West Germany where actually anti-Semitism and revanchism were the orders of the day. I already found it a crying shame that party politics were pursued under the protective disguise of Auschwitz. But I only got really indignant when in the papers of the Auschwitz Committee not one word was said about the anti-Semitic campaigns of the Polish communist authorities in 1967/68.

"The country is buzzing and vibrating by 'anti-Zionist' cleansing," the Polish/Dutch journalist Sasza Malko writes about this period in *Vrij Nederland* of March 15, 1997. "People are being chased out of the country, newspapers from those days still read like a *Stürmer* [the infamous anti-Semitic periodical of Julius Streicher in Nazi-Germany]. The *Kristallnacht* was in full swing." Not one word from the Auschwitz Committee about this extended Kristallnacht, perpetrated for years by the Polish government, but no expense was spared when some idiot in West Germany turned over a tombstone at a Jewish cemetery.[92] And to me it was the limit when in April 1967, at the unveiling of the Auschwitz monument, the Polish Prime Minister Cyrankiewicz had the nerve in his twenty-minute speech to not once use the word "Jew" (he pretended that the gas chambers and crematoria were mainly used for the annihilation of the Polish people) and the Dutch Auschwitz Committee in an equally great silence passed over it. This Dutch Auschwitz Committee fooled us Dutch in a disgusting way and I wanted to expose it. A committee like this had in my view no right to exist. In Holland, for this matter, I interviewed the director of the Netherlands Institute for War Documentation, Dr. L. de Jong and in Vienna Simon Wiesenthal, both of whom testified that the whole Auschwitz Committee had nothing to do with Auschwitz and everything with communist agitation. But the most important confirmation came from Hermann Langbein, who after the Hungarian insurrection had broken with communism and then immediately was fired as secretary of the International Auschwitz Committee;

---

[92] In a yet to be published study of Vera Ebels, scientific collaborator of the Eastern Europe Institute in Amsterdam, dealing with the position of Jews in former Czechoslovakia, it turns out that the communist security service of that country, the StB, organized the overturning of Jewish tombstones in order to stir up anti-German agitation out of it. We can only hope that the Dutch Auschwitz Committee had no knowledge of it.

the secretariat was moved from his home town of Vienna to the Polish capital Warsaw. After his criticism on the communist methods got stronger and stronger, in 1961 he was completely expelled from the committee.

We also went to Auschwitz for our documentary in January 1968 for the annual commemoration of the liberation of the camp and in my opening statement I pronounced my disgust that the name Auschwitz was abused for political ends. With all our necessary material taken care of and all knowledge of their own publications in my head, I called Eva Tas and said that we wanted to make a feature about her committee. She agreed and we went with our camera team to her home somewhere in Amsterdam. To be on the safe side, we had taken Arie Kleijwegt along. The camera stood ready, the conversation could start, but when during the pretalk it occurred to her that we wanted to approach the activities of the Auschwitz Committee in a critical way, Eva Tas refused to cooperate. She asked us to tell the viewers that they "did not find it necessary to take part in the discussion" and that Hermann Langbein "was thrown out of the International Auschwitz Committee because he was not able to work in a 'collective' [the communist jargon for working together in a group] and that because of that we have no intention of arguing with Langbein." We talked for hours, told her that she could refute everything but she stuck to her refusal. I asked her about how many people were involved concerning a compensation law for Jewish war victims. She did not know, they had never investigated it, she had to admit. It was clear: here, too, it was not about compensation but to keep a possibility for agitation open.

The broadcast was planned for February 9, 1968, if necessary then without a refutation from the Netherlands Auschwitz Committee. But they already anticipated the upcoming disaster. They tried with all their might to prevent the airing. And they found a willing ear with Jan Kassies.

It was far from being a habit at the *VPRO*, that the executive board interfered in the programs, but the democratization marched on with great strides, thus the independence of the program makers was reduced proportionately.

Kassies watches the documentary. Grumbles. And says disparagingly, upon hearing Langbein's statement, "Yeah, what do you want, he is a renegade." So the ruins-philosopher had already mastered quite a bit of the Stalinist jargon. When I pointed this out to him, he added apologetically, "Well, I'm a renegade myself, too" – referring to his apostasy from the Christian Reformed Orthodox Church. But he was not an advocate of airing. Not until the 1997 publishing of the book "Forty years [of the] Netherlands Auschwitz Committee" by Maarten Bijl, did I learn that Kassies had said to the in Holland well-known author Ed Hoornik (who had been successfully lobbied by the committee to intervene at the *VPRO* in order to prevent the broadcast) that "the cold war mentality shown in the documentary did not fit the *VPRO* as a progressive broadcasting station," but he took great care not to use this as an argument with me. To me, he said he "considered the broadcast damaging to the cause of the Jewish war victims." Well, I proposed, then let's do what the Auschwitz Committee stubbornly failed to do: to try to locate the people involved by appealing at the end of the broadcast for the Jewish war victims to report to the *VPRO*. We could pass the names on to the Ministry for Social Affairs, but at the same time create our own committee which could continue to exert pressure so that the case would not drag on for years. But this was strictly forbidden by Kassies. After a lot of talking back and forth he came up with a compromise: I had to do an interview with C. Egas, a member of parliament from the Labor Party and former Under Secretary of the Ministry for Social Affairs, under which fell war compensation affairs, and who was at the same time a member of the *VPRO* advisory council. With that interview, it was ordered, the documentary had to be closed. I did not have any problem with that – and for Jan Kassies it had an opposite effect. Because Egas said that as an Under Secretary he had never received "a reasonable answer" to his request "for concrete cases and concrete wishes," but that it had remained hanging in "giving vague slogans." Those are "communist activities, which are well-known in all kinds of matters to be suited for agitation; those are political aspects mixed with these human needs. I think that we should acknowledge this, but that we at the same time (but most likely you did this already in your program), we must be careful that the persons involved will not be the ones to suffer." Actually, Egas gave a summary of the documentary and therefore airing it was still not for sure. The documentary and his addition had to be submitted to a panel of experts. It existed of prof. Dr. L de Jong en Ben Sijes, director and deputy director of the Netherlands Institute for War Documentation, respectively. It was not Jan Kassies who was present on behalf of the *VPRO*. He left the dirty work to Karel Roessingh, a soft, weak and clumsy guy of the "old school" who as a front had been maintained as the president of the executive board. After the show, De Jong only said, "Excellent."

"But don't you think that the broadcast would harm the case of the Jewish war victims?" the poor Roessingh said timidly, repeating Kassies' argument.

"If you think so, why don't you appeal to the Jewish war victims at the end of the broadcast to report to the *VPRO*?" De Jong asked, and he got up and left with Sijes. Just before leaving, he put his head around the corner of the door like inspector Colombo *avant la lettre* and said, "Oh yes, if you prohibit the broadcast, I just have to inform Simon Wiesenthal." That closed the door. Roessingh had no other choice but to air the documentary, including, please note, the appeal now proposed by De Jong as well. This all occurred a few hours before the planned broadcast. But, contrary to the censorship attempts of the Soviet embassy two years earlier, it did not result in a belated broadcast.

The victims reported by the hundreds. In consultation with Arie Kleijwegt, I immediately threw together a committee, which, as it were, would accompany those letters. Among others, Egas and the first postwar Dutch Prime Minister Wim Schermerhorn were in it. The board reacted furiously and Jan Kassies called the committee members with the statement "that Verkijk had acted on his own and that it was not the duty of the *VPRO* to execute those kinds of activities," and he dissolved the committee on the spot. I have disputed that with Jan Kassies in what you may call a heated conversation. I found it irresponsible to appeal to people to report with their problems and then as a program maker lean back with folded arms and leave the solution to their problems completely to a third party. But Kassies was of the opinion that the letters had to be handed over to the parliamentarian commission of Social Affairs. Unfortunately, my objection that the matter could end up in a bureaucratic mill without a *VPRO*-pressure-committee, which would delay a ruling for years, proved to be true. Though there were some small in-between-solutions, it still took years before it resulted in a definite ruling. But its irrefutable – as also appears in the records of the parliament – that this TV broadcast was the fundamental boost for the realization of the rulings – in spite of Jan Kassies and the Dutch Auschwitz Committee.

Well over three years later, on September 11, 1971, the then-spokesman of the *VPRO*-new-style-à-la-Kassies, Ad Kooyman, wrote in an editorial in the *VPRO* weekly *Vrije Geluiden* ("Free Voices") about "whether it would not be the obligation of the *VPRO* – often so fiercely taking sides in all kinds of cultural and/or political phenomena – to support its viewpoints not only with words but also with deeds." Such an action, according to Kooyman, "can vary from the opening of a bank account to the formation of action groups under the leadership of the *VPRO*." After all, a program maker should not only report problems but "at the same time [take] responsibility for what happens to the persons who are directly or indirectly involved in the problem."

Apparently, I had been too early with my by Kassies-torpedoed committee proposal. That I would also be too early with "the obligation to open a bank account" was something I had yet to sorely experience.

My colleague Herman Wigbold accused Kassies of attempts to exercise censorship in a letter to the editor in *Vrij Nederland*. Kassies' answer in the same weekly on March 16, 1968, is so characteristic for the atmosphere in those days that it's worth quoting it quite extensively:

"Some weeks before the broadcast I had been informed as a member of the *VPRO* board that Verkijk was planning to dedicate a program to the "Auschwitz Committee." That plan had already come along quite a bit, Verkijk was in Poland at the time. I was afraid that the broadcast was going to become what it actually became, namely a new attempt by Verkijk to add fresh fuel to our distrust of communists. That fear was not unfounded. At the time I read what Verkijk wrote in this weekly about some Eastern-European countries. I have seen his *Barbarossa* and his plea for Von Kielmansegg. At first I put some small, then some big question marks. Consequently, I did not need the explanation in the *VPRO* papers that Verkijk would show that the "International Auschwitz Committee" was in the hands of international communism. I knew what awaited us.

What awaited us was a program from someone rooted in the cold war mind-set. Who confronts us with information which is not to the point and is mixed with sniffs of anti-communism. [...] As a member of the *VPRO* board, I am of the opinion that the *VPRO* should not be broadcasting those kinds of programs [...] It absolutely escapes me how you can speak of preventive censorship if you as a board member believe that a certain program does not belong within that broadcasting organization. I regret that the program leadership of the *VPRO* agreed to broadcast the program made by Verkijk. I regret that the top of the *VPRO* yielded to the pressure exercised by Dr. De Jong. It is clear who have made a political affair out of Auschwitz.

Amsterdam, Jan Kassies."

A message from a different world – McCarthy dressed in red.

Meanwhile, the broadcast was disastrous for the Dutch Auschwitz Committee. The incoming voluntary contributions of credulous Dutchmen dropped to close to zero, as the policymakers themselves made public. Bijl states, "The ties between the Dutch and the International Auschwitz Committees deteriorated at a rapid pace after Verkijk's documentary. In March [1968] the Auschwitz Committee protested to the Polish government in connection with the 'anti-Jewish campaign' in Poland. Shortly afterwards it cut off its ties with Warsaw where the secretariat of the International Auschwitz Committee was located, because 'it had not been able to give a satisfactory answer to the repeated protests of the Dutch Auschwitz Committee concerning the anti-Semitic action of the official authorities. As long as this has not turned around, neither the Auschwitz Committee nor its president will participate in the activities of the International Auschwitz Committee,'" Bijl quotes the Newsletter of the Committee. It's the implicit admission that the Dutch Auschwitz Committee first had tried by all means through Hoornik and Kassies to prevent the true character of its conduct from being revealed, and only after they failed to do so, renounced what they were blamed for in the documentary: pursuing communist policy by trampling on the victims of Auschwitz. A week after the broadcast, Eva Tas still had not learned her lesson. When a reporter from the social-democratic daily *Het Vrije Volk* asked her at a press briefing whether she was not afraid that the Committee would be harmed "by all that grease in the fire," Eva Tas replied, "Well, you know, if you have survived Auschwitz, you also survive the broadcast of Dick Verkijk" a "one liner" so writes Bijl triumphantly, "which reached many dailies and weeklies." I was at that press briefing and at the time, I did not want to react to it. But that statement should not go into history without a footnote: Eva Tas had not survived Auschwitz at all, she, fortunately, had never been there. Maarten Bijl knows it. He should have reacted to such a remark sadly rather than triumphantly. But the cold war legend is persistent.

Ten years after the Auschwitz documentary the *VPRO* airs a program about children of communists who had suffered under that Cold War because of the opinions of their parents; a documentary made by one of those children. And suddenly I see myself standing again in Auschwitz – the beginning of the documentary of 1968. And again I am put in the cliché-framework of the coarse anticommunist, who wanted to wipe the floor with well-intentioned idealists. I felt deeply hurt. I called the maker and talked for hours with him. In vain.

Again ten years later – communism has collapsed in the most dishonorable way. I visit my Polish/Dutch friend Sasza Malko. In comes another visitor. He is the maker of the documentary about the communist children. He looks at me, kind of helplessly shrugging his shoulders. He does not say one word, but the gesture is clear: sorry. I don't feel hurt anymore.

Before the *coup d'état* of 1968 it was a chaotic mess at the *VPRO*. Every week there was a program-staff meeting in which everybody participated, even the administrative personnel; only the phone operator had to remain at her post. Everybody could have their say, just like that. Of course, this had little in common with democracy. Structural democratization had to be done, which meant that those who did not think along the new philosophical lines were not invited to the meetings anymore. I belonged to the non-invited. The situation became more and more intolerable. From the very beginning, Jan Blokker had shown me that he did not agree with my view on Eastern Europe, although it never happened directly. For instance, he poked fun at my precautionary measures in Czechoslovakia and found it "boy-scout stuff" that I sent him agreed-upon innocent statements by phone from there from which he could conclude that another "bread-roll for the pilot" was on its way. He did not realize (or because of fashionable leftish reasons did not want to realize) that you had to try to minimize the danger for yourself or anybody else. Why take a ten percent chance, if you can reduce it to three or zero?

```
___ 31677-PRAHA CS 11561TB ASD NL ___        1909

  * 000040              HANS KRIJT JANACHKOVA
                        MABRESI 51 PRAHA
      Přijat/
                                                    Vyproven na


   Druh  Adresní        Hodina  Prepravní cesto · bezplatné a slueební údaje
      ZCZC 73 HILVERSUM 29356 32 8 1230
  ___ PLEASE INFORM DICK VERKIJK VPRO WANTS HIM BACK AS SOON AS
  _POSSIBLE ULTIMATELY AUGUST 14 PROGRAM NEEDS JUST ONE STATEMENT
  ON EVENTS DURING PAST YEAR           BLOKKER
```

Jan Blokker, who publicly stated that DV liked nothing better than to go into prison in Eastern Europe in order to make it to the front pages, was in this respect always willing to do him a favor. On the 8th of August 1969 he did a manful attempt for that, by sending the telegram to DV's Dutch friend Hans Krijt in Prague. not in Dutch but in English, which came in handy for the co-readers of the StB.

In August 1969, after a report on Nixon's visit to Romania, I would travel on to Czechoslovakia for the occasion of the first "anniversary" of the Warsaw Pact invasion. I had told Jan Blokker explicitly not to get in touch with me in Czechoslovakia and that I on my part would call only to tell him in the familiar way that material was on its way. What does Jan Blokker do? On August 8 he sends a telegram to my Prague friend Hans Krijt, whose address he knew from quieter times, with the text, "Please inform Dick Verkijk VPRO wants him back as soon as possible, ultimately August 14. Program needs just one statement on events during past year. Blokker." To make things easier for co-readers, he sent the telegram in English. Hans Krijt was livid and asked whether I was completely off my rocker to have these kinds of telegrams sent to his address. I was only with the greatest effort able to convince him that it was absolutely Blokker's own initiative against my explicit instructions. Jan Blokker belonged to the *Schreibtischhelden*, desk-heroes: endanger others provocatively, while they themselves conveniently stayed safe and sound at home.

I ignored the telegram, though, and stayed in Prague until after the 21st of August, one year after the invasion. Just before my cameraman Tuma and I were followed by the StB, I had been able to do an interview with Vladimír

Škutina, who had played a leading part in the Prague underground television during the invasion in 1968. It was intended to air around August 21 under the motto, "One year of occupation." Thanks to that accursed "code," I had been able to send it by KLM as a "bread-roll for the pilot." The interview was recorded under rather difficult circumstances, to put it mildly, and after my return to Holland I asked Blokker when it was aired. He had not aired it at all, because, according to his comment, "Who in the world knows Škutina?" It remained on the shelf until February 1971 when it still reached the screen due to a trial they then started against Škutina.

As could be expected, big demonstrations took place on that 21ˢᵗ of August – and I reported for *VARA*-radio and even for *VPRO*-radio, I believe. By crossing a small part of Austria on my way to Czechoslovakia through Hungary, I had sent my film material of Nixon's visit to Romania in a normal way with instructions for the "home front" in Hilversum on how to edit it. Ignoring the instructions, they succeeded in extracting a useless report out of it.

From 1968, I had interviewed the Czech chess Grandmaster Luděk Pachman with some regularity. He had been a hard-line communist, who still during the Prague Spring had written against the liberal advocates of *Literární listi*. But the Soviet invasion had been an eye-opener for him, "For every human being there comes a moment of repentance, also for a communist," as he formulated it in our first interview a few days after the Soviet occupation in 1968.

During that very same August 1969, I had talked with him in café Evropa (the StB had taken a picture of it, which they showed in that film of January 1971) and he told me that he had spent all his savings because of his many opposition activities and had to write a chess book pretty soon to be able to make ends meet again. I was still in Prague when he was arrested a week later. Back in Holland, I thought – and so did *VPRO* director Arie Kleijwegt – that we should do something about it. In consultation with the Royal Dutch Chess Union we decided to create a Pachman Fund in order to give a hand to Pachman's wife and other family members of arrested people who had run into difficulties. The Dutch Grandmaster Max Euwe was a member of the committee of recommendation and would also appear in a broadcast in which we would introduce the Pachman Fund, including an appeal to the viewers to put money into the fund's bank account. The show was ready-to-go. A few days before the broadcast, I was called in by Arie Kleijwegt. In his room: Jan Blokker as well. Arie Kleijwegt, "Jan thinks that we should not air that program on Pachman. He himself will explain why." Jan Blokker said he thought it was nonsense that the *VPRO* was going to broadcast a program "for the benefit of a personal little friend of yours." I explained that I had gotten to know Pachman in my capacity as a journalist, and consequently was not a personal friend of mine; that he was arrested partly because of the interviews with us; that, of course, we were not bearing the responsibility for his arrest, but that it was simply a matter of solidarity to support his wife since we knew that she was in financial trouble. But, I added, looking at Arie Kleijwegt, "it may be interesting to hear what Jan is saying, but what do you think, because you happened to agree with it, didn't you?" Arie hesitatingly admitted that he thought Jan was right. I stood up, stated that I had nothing more to say, went home and offered my resignation the very same evening by telegram to the umpteenth general manager of the *VPRO* S.J. Doorman. I thought, that was it, but it wasn't because Doorman wanted to know why and did not accept my resignation. He invited me for a conversation during which I told him some of the recent events, among others the way they blew my Nixon program.

"But after all those differences of opinion, how could you expect them to make a good program out of it?" after which I posed the counter-question, "How could I expect them to be so unprofessional as to fight out those differences by trampling on the viewers?" Doorman said to sort out how the program had come into being and if my version was the right one, it would still be aired. I pointed out to Doorman that I absolutely did not want to give the impression that I was forcing him to air the program by threatening my resignation and that I would leave whatever his decision would be. Doorman's conclusion one day later was: broadcast. We collected 18,000 Dutch guilders, quite a lot of money in those days, and we were able to support twenty persons regularly in a changing composition for two years. The money was only earmarked for those who stayed behind, not for activists. Who was entitled to it was established in consultation with oppositionists in Czechoslovakia itself. If Jan Blokker would have gotten his way, those people would not have received a dime. Just how much he was offended by it, is shown in the "minutes of the editorial meeting of September 8, 1969," where it says under point 11, "The editorial commission wishes to express its disappointment about the fact that it was kept in the dark about the apparently intended and subsequently also realized plans concerning the item on chess player Pachman, that was anchored by Dick Verkijk on Sunday night the 7th."

After the broadcast, Doorman still tried to keep me as "a stumbling block." But I only wanted to be a stumbling block if it was based on respect and not on rejection and my answer remained "no." That was the end of my television career. Doing television was my passion and my life but I don't regret for a minute that I made that decision at that time.

I gave an interview about it, simultaneously to Han Mulder (*Het Parool*) and Phillip van Tijn (*Nieuwe Rotterdamse Courant*). Two quite different but both correctly reflected stories about what I called then for the first time "fashionable leftishness." It was so badly received by the persons concerned, that friendly *VPRO*-colleagues advised me not to enter the *VPRO*-lots anymore in the interest of my own safety. But also without that, I felt that I had no business being there for the time being. Many canceled their membership. One of them was the best-known columnist of the Netherlands: Simon Carmiggelt.

EPILOGUE 3

The number of membership cancellations got alarmingly high and desperate attempts were made to turn the tide. Once, a good year after my departure, TV boss Arie Kleijwegt appeared personally, with his famous worried-disarming face, on the screen with an appeal to remain a member or to become one (anew). The TV critic with the initials A.F.L. quoted in the *Nieuwe Rotterdamse Courant* of November 6, 1970, Kleijwegt's statement that the *VPRO* "is and remains a quality broadcasting organization [...]. He substantiated with three entries to the *Prix d'Italia* within five years. Among his list was a documentary by Dick Verkijk *Operatie Barbarossa* [Operation Barbarossa] and this sounded a bit strange, because there was no room in the new-style *VPRO* for this very same Verkijk anymore." But by then, the leftish storm at the *VPRO* had subsided somewhat and the climate seemed to be reduced to a level where I could feel at home again. In December 1970 I contacted Doorman and Kleijwegt and both of them would be pleased to see me return. I stipulated as a condition that Jan Blokker would totally agree with my return so that collisions like in the past would not occur again. I talked with him, too, and he stated he had no objections either. Until then only the four of us knew of the consultations and the agreement was that it would remain so. For reasons unable to trace, however, immediately after Blokker's agreement, a signature petition was started at the *VPRO* offices to prevent my return. The new crop was against, the leftovers from before the *coup d'état* were in favor. The first were in the majority and there was apparently nothing else to do for Doorman and Kleijwegt but to cancel my return.

Yet, I did still make another big documentary for the *VPRO*, in my personal opinion the best one after "Operation Barbarossa." It happened in 1978/79, the prime time of Euro-communism – the trend especially in the Italian and Spanish communist party to break away from the "real-existing socialism" in the Soviet Union and the other Warsaw Pact countries. A revaluation took place of the Hungarian uprising of 1956 and the Prague Spring of 1968. It appeared to me an appropriate occasion to walk through the whole history of communism from 1917 to date (1979) and especially pay attention to the unremitting struggle, also from the very beginning, of democratic thinking communists against the dictatorial views and practices of the party elite. I presented it to Jan Blokker. Because I did not want to go wrong with it, my proposal was extremely detailed: whom I wanted to interview, what I had in mind and how long it would become: a serial of in total seven hours. He considered it an excellent idea and I went on the move. The last three months of 1978 I interviewed dozens of former and Euro-communists in Germany, Hungary, Yugoslavia, England, Austria, France, Italy and Spain; thrashed through archives, dug up interesting facts about the sailors uprising in 1921 in Kronstadt near Leningrad/St. Petersburg, brought down by Trotski under the motto, "We shall shoot them down like partridges"; about the backgrounds of the Hungarian uprising – all in all nearly a tragedy. That was also the form I had given it: a tragedy in four acts with a kind of non-singing chorus singer in the person of Wolfgang Leonhard connecting the scenes and acts. Leonhard was the writer of "The revolution lets her children go." Before the war, he had fled Nazi-Germany as a child with his parents to go to Moscow. There he attended a special school for foreign communist children and belonged to the first group of nine persons who under the leadership of Walter Ulbricht were sent to Berlin immediately after the German defeat to prepare what later would be called the *DDR*.

The first half of 1979 I was editing and in June the documentary of four acts with a total length of indeed seven hours was ready. My intention was to show for once and for all that what from 1917 on was executed in the Soviet Union in actual practice had nothing in common with socialism or communism; that from the very beginning real idealists had fought against it and that also from the very beginning every attempt by them was crushed by harsh terror – just to deprive everybody, who still flirted with the establishment in the Eastern Block or explained away the regimes over there, the alibi of I-did-not-know. Everything was recorded on film and in the studio we put the four acts with subtitles and all on videotape, ready-to-go for broadcasting a few weeks later.

But I had reckoned without my host. While editing, the host Jan Blokker left the *VPRO*, and the new host was Roelof Kiers, who was so leftish that he belonged to the first addressees of the documentary. He saw the final production and let me know that it's "way too long," that there was "way too much talking in it" and that it had to be shortened to at most two hours. That was absolutely against the agreements with Jan Blokker, but he had disappeared in the mean time and so I asked for the intervention of Arie Kleijwegt, still TV director and Roelof Kiers' boss. He also watched the program and told me "that it was not as dull as he had been told" and asked me to put some more "Leonhard" in the program, while I had just given him a less important part because Jan Blokker found him "too arrogant." But most remarkable was Kleijwegts' main objection, "After the broadcasting of the documentary there is nothing left to discuss."

"But that is exactly my intention," I objected to him but no compromise came up.

" No broadcast then," I said. And that was it. The videotape has been deleted, but the film version laid for years in the attic of the *VPRO* – from time to time I asked about its well-being. I learned in 1996 that it was not in the attic anymore and might have been moved to one of the Dutch archive institutes. Inquiries over there did not result into anything – until 2005, when it suddenly surfaced out of a forgotten stock of files.

And what was put on the spot where the first episode of the Euro-communism documentary should have aired? A documentary of three hours-on-end about the Spanish Civil War; in which three times as much was spoken in for the Dutch incomprehensible Spanish as in the documentary prohibited by Kiers. But yes, this was about fighting against authoritarian fascism and it was not a cold war documentary like mine against authoritarian communism. There is no doubt in my mind that Roelof Kiers and consequently the *VPRO* did not want to air the documentary for political reasons, because indeed after it "there was nothing left to discuss."

Once, in the afterpains of the Cultural Revolution, Kiers had made a very positive film about communist China. When I criticized him because of it he said, "I could not live there myself, but for the folks over there.... " The same argument was given to me by Jan van der Putten, at the time a very well-known correspondent in Latin America. It was in Caracas, Venezuela, in 1979 during a reception with the Dutch minister of Foreign Affairs Chris van der Klaauw, when Van der Putten and I were arguing about Fidel Castro's Cuba, which he admired intensely. These maybe-or-maybe-not-fashionable leftishers don't realize how much a contempt for people is hiding behind that seemingly casual remark. As if a second-rate human species exists for whom a free society is a luxury they don't need.

Many of those fashionable leftishers now have completely come around. They would not admit it for anything. It's amusing to see how they pretend not to have changed and that their revised opinions really are a continuation of their former ones.

A funny example is the case of Joris Ivens. This world famous movie maker was the idol of the fashionable left, the guy "who always took sides with the oppressed," the by the Dutch government "misunderstood genius." When I then made the rebuttal that no movie maker had taken sides with oppressing authorities as much as precisely Joris Ivens had, it equaled blasphemy. The fact he had made propaganda films in and for the *DDR* for years (to mention only one example), was irrelevant – you always had to "see it differently."

Everybody may make mistakes, make a wrong judgment, follow an idol.

What amazes me is that all those fashionable leftishers-of-then act as if they did not try to talk us into whole clothing warehouses to make us believe that the emperor really was walking around in festive costumes under the motto: why should you make programs in Prague about the ideas of Havel if you can also film fine façades there? In my eyes the fashionable leftishers have failed in fundamental matters at fundamental moments. It would be to the credit of some of those talked-about-cultures, if they would admit it for once[93].

---

[93] Joris Ivens lived from 1936 to 1945 in the United States. Recently, a Californian State University researcher discovered copies of two unknown documentaries shot in 1940, made by Ivens for the U.S. Department of Agriculture (*The Windmill*, March 8, 2004).

CHAPTER 22

My political "career"

Between 1970 and 1974 I wrote, as sort of sideline, a book about the Nazi broadcasting in the Netherlands during the German occupation: *Radio Hilversum 1940-1945*, but it was not my only sideline in those years. I was also a member of the first employees council of the *NOS* and a member of the city council of Haarlem for the Labor Party. But I was first "noticed" nationwide by something which had nothing to do with politics, but with my work as a television maker. That first big TV documentary *Operation Babarossa* suddenly made me "a well-known personality," whose name you could use if you were striving for a certain goal. That was the reason that not even a month after the airing in 1966, I was approached by Jan Nagel on behalf of some "concerned" members of the Labor Party. In their eyes the party was just a dead, rusted out bustle through which a fresh wind of change needed to blow. With *that* I agreed. The first meeting was convened – a dozen "concerned" people showed up, among them André van der Louw and, of course, Jan Nagel himself, still a member of the nationwide central board. Not even a few hours later I turned out to be one of the godfathers of *Nieuw Links* ("New Left") within the Labor Party. But let there be no mistake about it: with my full awareness. I saw, however, "New Left" as a stimulator and not as an opponent of the party leadership. After a few more meetings we agreed on ten main points and an editorial commission would write a booklet around it. That booklet turned out to be much more radical than what I had read in those ten points. Especially the passages about the *DDR* and the way the editors strived for the recognition of "the First Worker's and Peasant's state on German territory" were unacceptable to me. For practical reasons I was not against recognition of the *DDR* (on purpose I don't write, "was in favor of recognition of the *DDR*"), but since the *DDR*-leaders were enormously keen on such a recognition, they had in my view to pay a price for it. In what form was open for discussion, but I was opposed to giving away undeserved presents. More and more it appeared to me that the advocates of an unconditional recognition of the *DDR* used it in the first place for domestic-political reasons to frustrate the leadership of the Labor Party, which did not want to put a spoke in the wheel of the socialist leader Willy Brandt. And that was exactly the second reason for the pro-*DDR* folks of "New Left": True, Willy Brandt was a "party fellow" but in their eyes (at the time) too far to the right and on top of that an important politician in West Germany, and West Germany was out and his *Ostpolitik* still had to be born. André van der Louw and Jan Nagel manifested themselves as more friendly towards the *DDR* than they were when we were traveling around together over there six months earlier.

The life and soul of "New Left" only took note of my objections. Some "New Leftists" shared my objections, some had objections on other points which I in turn shared. But the editorial commission said it was pressed for time and considered it impossible to rewrite the paper in the short term. Consensus existed on the main points, clearly not on the interpretation thereof – which was explicitly laid down in the eventual publishing of the booklet. I did not attend the subsequent meetings. At the Labor Party congress of 1969 they finally succeeded in getting a proposal accepted for the unconditional recognition of the *DDR* and consequently it then became official policy of the party. But I still remained a "loyal party member." For years, I was on the list as a parliament candidate for the Labor Party. Many a time, I even got as far as number 28 or 29 out of 31 on the list for the local pre-elections, but I never ended up on the nationwide list. I scored better on the local level. I never ran for a safe seat in the city council, but was still so close that in 1971 I suddenly turned out to be a member after some unexpected vacancies occurred. My achievements there were thin. City councils are the heart of democracy. For the average citizen it's of the utmost importance whether the street light at the corner of the street really works. And this is not meant facetiously, but I was not cut out for it. If you want to be a good council member, you have to have oceans of time at your disposal, because your are flooded with files. You are lost when you don't study them well. Having all those other sidelines, I was not able to pay sufficient attention to it. I only caused a sensation with three vote motivations: two of a light and one of a serious nature.

In those days smoking was a widespread evil. Once every three weeks on Wednesday afternoon there was a council session. Every preceding Monday evening we had a caucus meeting. Our caucus met in the historical *Schepenkamer* ("Aldermen's Room") of the equally historical 16th century city hall of Haarlem. But the *Schepenkamer* was a tight fit and for a nonsmoker like me it is unbearable when nearly everyone is smoking nonstop from eight o'clock in the evening till one o'clock in the morning. Once in a while, I had asked for a prohibition or if need be a limitation on smoking – in vain. One of my fellow caucus members even called me intolerant by denying him that pleasure. After the meeting the tears in your eyes disappeared pretty quickly, but you could not say that of the smell in your clothes and your hair. The council hall was quite a bit bigger, but they were annoyingly smoking up a storm in there as well. Those were the days when two fads came into fashion: the environment and the inner city.[94] Those had to be safeguarded from dirty air and cars, respectively; goals to strive for and which had my full support. But everyone who has consciously experienced the seventies knows that it had its fashionable aspects. Politics run off with it, you could put on a show of friendliness with it to make yourself look good. Our caucus came up with the proposal to erect air pollution detectors around Haarlem, nicknamed *snuffelpalen* ("sniff poles") so that air pollution would immediately be recorded at a center.

Good idea, everything is peachy keen. During the council debate, I declared my self an advocate, but, I added, "I would like to propose that we erect the first sniff pole right here in the council hall." I did not get the impression that the with-complete-devotion-against-pollution-fighting smokers considered it a correct suggestion.

About the same time the mayor and aldermen proposed to give all the council members a free-of-charge parking card for the parking garage in the center of the inner city so that they wouldn't have to pay every time they had to come to the city hall in the inner city for caucus-, commission- or council meetings. On this proposal I was allowed to declare my vote motivation as well. "I thought we were in favor of a car-free inner city. Then it seems obvious to me that we ourselves set the example by coming by bicycle. I don't want that parking card." The shuffling of quite a few legs under the narrow desks of the council hall showed that I had touched a sore spot. Yet, another council member declined his parking card – he had no car. I kept on coming by bike – enviously peering at every car overtaking me.

This was just meant to burst the bubble playfully.

The third incident was anything but playful. The war in Vietnam was in full swing. Action groups made it appear as if the victory of North Vietnam and the Vietcong would bring the much desired democracy to the reactionary-ruled South Vietnam. In the long run the more sober minded people were also unable to abstain from the intoxication-of-the-day. Even the conservative Dutch party *VVD* (People's Party for Freedom and Democracy") was carried away, afraid of getting out of touch with society. In this atmosphere the Labor caucus, after consultation with the "Medical Committee Netherlands-North Vietnam," came forward with the proposal: Haarlem should adopt a city in North Vietnam "for humanitarian reasons," I think it was Danang. In pre-consultation the board of the Labor caucus had dropped in on all parties and every one of them had agreed. At the Monday caucus meeting I learned that

---

[94] Most centers of towns and cities in the Netherlands – and generally in most of Europe – date from the 16th to 18th century. The narrow and winding streets cannot accommodate modern traffic and more and more of those centers had and have to be changed into pedestrian-only areas.

it would be submitted as a proposal from the mayor and aldermen and would be dealt with as a formality. I said I was only in favor if we would at the same time adopt a city in South Vietnam – otherwise it would not be a humanitarian but a political decision. As a front, the Medical Committee Netherlands-North Vietnam had selected Piet Nak, the organizer of the famous strike in February 1941, which paralyzed the capital of Amsterdam and quite a few other cities in the Western part of Holland, as a protest against the first anti-Jewish measures imposed by the German occupiers. The actual leadership of that Medical Committee was in the hands of prof. J.H. de Haas, of whom everybody knew that he was a Mao-communist. Again it was such a classic example of an excellently orchestrated communist policy: take a sympathetic subject – medical assistance for a war-stricken country -, give it a political twist under the skin and foster political sympathy for the regime in that country. In this the committee had succeeded outstandingly.

I had taken along photocopies to the caucus meeting of the book of Babette Gross about her life companion Willi Münzenberg, explained how those kinds of organizations worked, and tagged onto it the following reasoning, "South Vietnam has a reactionary government, there are political prisoners there, that regime has to go, but there still is a parliament, there still is an opposition party. Somewhere deep under the ground is still a tiny root, out of which a democratic plant could possibly grow. If you allow the Vietcong and thus North Vietnam to win, it will cut off every possibility for democracy by definition, because then a one-party system will come. I do go along with a humanitarian choice: two sister cities, but not a political choice: one sister city." I was looking at it the wrong way, they said. The Vietcong wanted a democratic society. The Vietcong and North Vietnam were not identical. The discussion went on for hours. Finally they appealed to my solidarity as a member of the caucus, "Don't drop out now, just this afternoon we consulted with the VVD and they will also join in." I must admit that after a great deal of humming and hawing I finally said, "All right then, let's go." I had already planned, however, to do a radio program on that Medical Committee, analogous to that on the Auschwitz Committee – and had made for that purpose an appointment for the next day, Tuesday, with the real leader of that committee, the above-mentioned Prof. De Haas, a doctor but a die-hard. My view that the committee was more politically than medically intended was confirmed. One thing settled it for me. The Vietcong had just recently been shooting rockets at random at a South Vietnamese city. That was an indisputable fact. Many innocent civilians had been killed or wounded because of that.

"Don't you think, that your committee, if here we're talking exclusively about humanitarian principles, should help these people as well?" I asked.

"That's not our business, just let the South Vietnamese government take care of it."

"But you are a physician, how can you discriminate between wounded and wounded?"

But he remained rock hard: it was up to the South Vietnamese themselves to deal with it. My mind was made up: Wednesday I was going to vote against.

Wednesday morning, preceding the afternoon session, I called our caucus secretary Jan de Bruin to inform him of my decision. We hung on the phone for a couple of hours. I tried to convince him that my nearly coerced "yes," now, after my conversation with De Haas, could not be anything but "no" – and he tried to convince me to stick to my approval from Monday. I said that my "no" was irrevocable.

Wednesday afternoon. Mayor De Gou reads the sister city proposal and already raises his hammer, looking around whether somebody still wants to say something. I hold up my finger and get the floor for a vote motivation. I declare that I am going to vote against and explain why, using the arguments I had already expressed during the caucus meeting and to the caucus secretary that morning. The caucus president of my party Tinus van de Water looks at me in bewilderment (in retrospect it appeared that the secretary had not informed him about my intentions), and I go to sit down, so that De Gou can let his hammer fall. But now the miracle, about which I am bewildered. The president of another caucus, named *D66*, stands up and says that, since there is no longer a consensus and a political debate is arising because of it "we are not able to vote in favor of the proposal anymore." Then the caucus president of the Christian Democrats (*CDA*) takes the floor with the reasoning, "If *D66* does not vote in favor anymore, we also disassociate ourselves from the proposal." And the conservative party *VVD* of course rushes to declare the same. And De Gou does not want to look like a fool with the proposal being turned down and withdraws it: Haarlem does not adopt a North Vietnamese city.[95]

The next caucus meeting is not a meeting, but a party session. I am very seriously talked to. President Van de Water was an honest man of integrity, whom I admired greatly. Within the Labor Party he was one of the last real workers of the classical type who in a combination of self-study and idealism worked his way up to become a gifted politician who did not consider the job as much as the goal. He strongly criticizes my behavior, states that I had torpedoed a most important party proposal about which, please note, there existed a consensus, and concludes solemnly; "Dick, you have acted in defiance of the interests of the party."

I know only one answer, "History will prove that I acted in the interest of

---

[95] *D66* stands for *Democrats (19)66* and is comparable to liberal Democrats; *VVD* stands for *People's Party for Freedom and Democracy*, comparable to moderate Republicans.

the party and only you are the one in defiance."

Years later. Birthday party of an old-time important Labor party city alderman. Vietnamese boat refugees are drowning by the hundreds or wash ashore half dead on desolate beaches. I am one of the visitors and, of course, meet quite a few (in the meantime: former) fellow council members. Vietnam is not a topic. Only one female former fellow councilor brings it up. With exactly the same gesture as the documentary maker and son of communist parents, whom I met at Sasza Malko's: also without words. And once again: more satisfaction I don't need.

CHAPTER 23

Liberation – three

After my expulsion from Czechoslovakia in 1970, I was not allowed to enter Poland either. Nevertheless, at various times I got a visa, because of special circumstances – which are going to be addressed in the next chapter. One time it was in 1980. The principal promise dated back to the fall of 1979, but it took another six months of nagging at the highest level before the promise was turned into a permit. It was March of 1980. But I let the Polish embassy in The Hague know that I would not use the permit until June/July. I the meantime I had them put the visa in my passport (which I had to use within six months) and waited for better weather. In the beginning of June it started to rumble in Poland, strikes all over the place which each in itself did not last that long, but all together stretched out for a longer period.

At the *NOS* they thought that I should leave the politics alone for a change and focus on the "normal matters" in Poland. For instance, how foreigners spend their vacation in Poland and for which I should particularly interview Dutchmen in Polish vacation resorts. I said I found it a ridiculous proposal, especially with an eye on the rumblings in Poland, but in the editorial meeting it was accepted. Out of desperation I reconciled myself to it and would try to make a virtue of the need. It just had to become a kind of working vacation and I asked my son to come along for a ramble, from campground to campground across Poland, looking for Dutchmen.

We left at the end of July. Through the *DDR* to Gdańsk. The rumblings in Poland became louder and louder, but we pretended to be deaf and looked for a campground close to Sopot, a famous seaside resort, just West of Gdańsk. Whether there were any Dutchmen in the campground, we asked the manager. Not a one of them. And the Poles – they kept on striking. And erected here and there and everywhere in Poland "independent trade unions." Kind of sad, we drove on to Gdańsk where we stayed with friends whom I had known since 1958. Daughter Ewa, still a toddler in 1958, was married and had a son of her own now. In the meantime, she had joined the group of opposition trade union folks. When I learned from her, what all was going on and how the resistance against the regime became more massive day by day, my mind was made up: that visit to the first campground would at the same time be the last one. Forget about Dutchmen looking for vacation pleasures, I would switch over to Poles looking for a different order.

"You should talk to Andrzej Gwiazda," Ewa said. "He is a good friend of ours and representative of *KOR* ("Committee for the Defense of the Workers," erected in 1976 – as mentioned before – after the June strikes in Radom). He has created an independent trade union here."

I followed her advice and visited Gwiazda at his home on August 8, 1980. He talked about that independent trade union as a theoretical possibility in a distant future. Ewa also asked me whether I wanted to speak with another interesting worker – a certain Lech Wałęsa, father of half a dozen children. But I expected to hear from him approximately the same story as from Gwiazda and so I declined. I wanted to go to Warsaw to talk with the main organizers of all actions: Kuroń, Lityński, Onyszkiewicz. More and more strikes broke out – the party did not know what to do and the borders were closed to foreign journalists. So the ironic situation arose that I, who actually was not allowed to enter Poland, was at that very moment the only Dutch journalist in Poland, whereas my colleagues, who had not been on a black list at all, were not able to enter even though they were itching to be there.

I managed to have a talk in Warsaw with a in those days communist phenomenon: Mieczyslaw Rakowski. He was editor-in-chief of the party daily *Polityka* and a confidant of party leader Edward Gierek. He always seemed to be just one little step ahead of Gierek, but this was their mutual game. He was not willing to be interviewed, but a background conversation was alright. He was considered to belong to the most far-reaching liberals among the communists, an opinion I shared, absolutely wrongly as would turn out much later. We came to talk about the rotten economical situation in Poland, the cause of the strikes. Stating that a centralized economy is possible in a relative simple society, he admitted, however, that it is not possible in a more advanced and consequently more complicated economy. "Even the Hungarians (who had introduced far-reaching liberal economic reforms) have not yet found a solution," he said. "There is only one solution: capitalism." And after a deliberate moment of thought he added, "And that's what's not possible." With this, of course, he meant to say: that's not possible because we would not be a communist country anymore. So from the two impossibilities he preferred the first: living in an order of which the economic problems are by definition and by principle unsolvable.

After a few days in Warsaw I went on to Kraków, the Catholic stronghold where the communists always had been utmost unpopular – and then the strike of all strikes broke out: the one at the Lenin shipyard in Gdańsk. Strike leader: Lech Wałęsa whom I had spurned as a person to speak to. Second man: Andrzej Gwiazda. Poland had become a pandemonium and my work kept pace with it. Everybody was pulling at me and I was busy day in and day out from six in the morning till twelve at night – with the greatest pleasure. And with the eternal struggle to get phone communications with the Netherlands; most of the time it took hours. Some unworldly desk editors simply could not relate to it. Once, when I finally had a connection with *NOS* TV-news, a foreign-desk editor said, "I'm busy right now, can you call back in a quarter of an hour?" I think that I reacted to his proposal with a refusal in rather fierce words. Meanwhile, my visa, valid for three weeks, was going to expire. I asked for an extension at the local foreigners' registration office in Kraków and without any song and dance I got two weeks added to it. Back to Warsaw. Communication with Gdańsk did not exist anymore – on August 15, the government had closed off the telephone communication between Gdańsk and the outside world. A couple of oppositionists begged me to take them to Gdańsk: there it is happening, there history is in the making. I myself would be only too happy to do it, but what to do in Gdańsk if I was not able to communicate with Holland? Jacek Kuroń and his *KOR* had their own channels to Gdańsk and I had an excellent contact with them through the aforementioned English-speaking "blond angel of *KOR*" Ewa Kulik – I got the news of the Lenin shipyard as fast as it came in at *KOR*.

Initially, the government refused to negotiate with the strikers, but they were forced to abandon this standpoint due to solidarity strikes in the rest of the country. The first demand of the striking committee *MKS*[96] was: re-instatement of the telephone communications. This demand was accepted on Monday evening the 25th of August; the next morning at six I was on my way to Gdańsk, and in late morning I got my entry permit from the *MKS* at the gate of the Lenin shipyard, signed by Lech Wałęsa in person. It was an occupation-strike, which means that the strikers remained day and night within the fences of the yard.

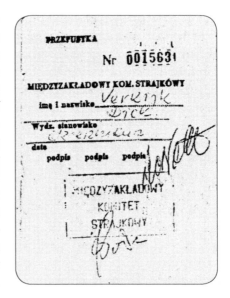

DV's entry permit for the "Lenin shipyard"-in-strike in Gdańsk, signed by Lech Wałęsa.

---

[96]   *MKS* was the abbreviation of *Miedzyzakladowy Komitet Strajkowy*, literally translated, "Inter-factorial Strike Committee." It consisted of 800 persons, representing 400 factories and enterprises from the whole region, with a presidium of 19 persons.

Nobody was allowed to enter unless he had an entry permit – and these were scantily issued, although all journalists were admitted. The strikers had imposed a ban on alcohol upon themselves – and that says a lot in Poland. In the whole region of Gdańsk nobody drank alcohol out of solidarity. When an unsuspecting foreign journalist ordered something alcoholic in a restaurant, the only reaction was an annihilating look from the waiter. Legendary is the story of the wife of a striker, who appeared at the gate of the shipyard with a bottle of vodka. She urgently requested the guard to bring it to her husband. "He is an alcoholic and can't do without his daily ration of vodka." The guard was prepared to pick up the husband. But he refused to come. "Just tell my wife that no alcohol is consumed here, not by me either." It was characteristic for the atmosphere at the shipyard. The workers knew: it's now or never. The organization was perfect, thrown together in no time. Not a bit of lengthy prepared, underground strategies. When I talked with Gwiazda on August 8, he did not know anything about it – six days later he was a strike-leader. Wałęsa was the charismatic leader number 1. The continuation of the strike and the occupation of the yard would probably not have succeeded without him. But the man who formulated the demands, the architect of the negotiations: that was Andrzej Gwiazda. There were 21 demands and the strikers were not remotely willing to give in on any point whatsoever. The delegation of the government was under de leadership of Vice Prime Minster Mieczyslaw Jagielski, whose courage I admired. Every time he entered the yard, he practically had to run the gauntlet through a hedgerow of workers who stood on both sides behind a rope which they held themselves. But the discipline was un-Polish. Not one indelicate word was spoken, no yelling, no calling names. In deep silence, Jagielski each time walked the 200 to 250 feet from the entrance of the yard to the negotiation room. This was a small side hall, only separated from the hallway by a glass wall. It looked a lot like an aquarium. The two delegations were seated opposite each other. You could not only see them debating, but you could hear them as well via speaker installations in the big hall on the other side of the hallway, where the strike committees of all the striking enterprises from far and wide were anxiously listening in. Dozens of students had volunteered to act as translators for the foreign journalists; they translated simultaneously. A big banner was hanging in the hall with the slogan: *Solidarność* – in freakish letter shapes with a small red-white Polish flag attached to the pole of the "n." It was a gift from the graphic artist J. Jaruszewski. Solidarity came from all sides. In the trade union delegation there were not only workers, but also university professors, historians, sociologists from Gdańsk and a few had especially come over from Warsaw. Artists from the surrounding area performed on the podium of the big hall, food (very scarce at the time in Poland) came from all sides. Volunteers were constantly busy preparing sandwiches with sausages; from time to time there was soup and we were allowed to join in and eat whatever was cooked.

Jagielski stood with his back against the wall. Once, when he appealed that they believe him on his word, Gwiazda gave it to him straight, "You have cheated us for more than thirty years. We don't believe in your word anymore." Now, after the collapse of the communist regimes, it does not sound that strange anymore, but then, it was 1980: the Soviet Union and the Eastern Block looked more stable than ever – and in such a situation it was breathtaking to hear somebody say anything like that against a representative of the communist establishment.

One who thinks that the western political leaders were watching the strikers in Gdańsk with admiration will be disappointed. Especially the West German government of Schmidt/Genscher, the social democrats up front, was extremely worried. Now it turned out, that the so-called *Ostpolitik* was not only based on the acceptance of an unavoidable evil with which you have to live one way or another, but even on the positive wish, that the "stability" there would be maintained in favor of the governing elite. And all of a sudden here were those stubborn, spontaneous, unpolished Poles, frivolously frustrating their political play, with their strikes upsetting their applecart. The West German government hurried to help Polish party leader Gierek with a credit of 1,2 billion German Mark, which outraged the democratic opposition in Poland. But even the Polish cardinal Wyszyński warned the workers in Gdańsk "not to go too far with their demands." Fortunately, the workers and intellectuals assembled in Gdańsk were wiser than the wise Brandts, Schmidts, Bahrs and Wyszyńskis and stuck to their guns. The strike could have been suppressed with violence, of course. The great merit of Gierek is, that he did not want it. He himself came into power in 1970, when the once so liberal party leader Gomułka had stifled in blood a strike in that same Gdańsk under the leadership of that same Wałęsa. During the negotiations it became clearer and clearer, that Gierek did not want to go down in history with that same odium as Gomułka. The disciplined determination of the strikers and the national solidarity surrounding them contributed a lot to Gierek's attitude of course. And of essential importance for the success of the strike was the unique cooperation between the workers and the intelligentsia. In 1968 the intelligentsia revolted against the regime, but the workers stayed out of it – they thought that the students and professors had privileged positions, anyway. In 1970, the workers struck in Northern Poland, but now the intelligentsia refused to take part "because, after all, the workers abandoned us in 1968." Both groups, but especially the intelligentsia, realized that this difference played directly into the hands of the communist government, which actually was their common opponent. That's why already during the big strikes in Radom in 1976 Kuroń and his companions immediately founded that *KOR*. Dismissed workers could get professional judicial and material help at *KOR* intervention offices all over Poland. Out of that, a cooperation and combined action of worker's groups and representatives of the intelligentsia came into being, creating a base of confidence as a result of which the mixed negotiation delegation at the ship-yard could act iron-strong and actually represent all of Poland. Consequently, a violent intervention would not have remained limited to a couple of dozen deaths, as in 1970, but would have resulted in hundreds if not thousands of victims.

Of the 21 demands, the first two were essential: recognition of "an inde-pendent, self-governing trade union" and "the right to strike." On these points, the government defended itself most stubbornly through Jagielski. Then they jumped over to other points, about which they did agree, but the strikers' del-egation refused to sign anything whatsoever unless those first two demands would be granted. Early Saturday afternoon of August 30, Jagielski buckled under, but he still had to ask the approval of the government (read: the party). The whole afternoon one needed to wait. And then, in the early evening the releasing message: the government had said "yes." Everybody hugs everybody: journalists, translators, strikers. The strike has been won.

That evening I had to comment on the strike for the Dutch television and I begged them, whatever they would eliminate from my text, to maintain under all circumstances that one sentence, "From today onward Poland has become a different country" *(see photo 23)*.

But the agreement was still burdened with a minor flaw. In the beginning of the strike a number of *KOR*-members had been arrested in Warsaw, among them was again Jan Lityński. And they were still imprisoned. To my surprise, it was never brought up during the negotiations. On Sunday morning I ad-dressed Gwiazda about it, saying that they also had to demand the release of the *KOR*-prisoners. He was kind of shocked that they had overseen this in the hectic goings-on and he promised to do something about it. I did not give it much thought anymore, but nearly a year later, Lityński wrote in an article in the Dutch weekly *Haagse Post* that I had "in August 1980 contributed to [his] release." By the way, according to Lityński it required a great deal of effort for Gwiazda to persuade Wałęsa to include their release as a condition for signing the agreement, caused by Wałęsa's "distrust towards his associates" and his "excessive fear of everything that could undermine his position."[97]

In the afternoon they agreed on all points: the agreement was solemnly

[97] Article by Jan Lityński in the *Haagse Post* of July 25, 1981.

signed. That very same Sunday the *KOR*-members were released. Even without Gwiazda's intervention it would have happened anyway, but it might have been only on Monday or Tuesday. And every day in prison counts.

The very same evening, we set up a party in honor of the different Poland in my hotel room with our "steady" translator Anna Maksimiuk, a few oppositionists and some Dutch colleagues who still had dropped in during the latter days.

The trade union, still referred to with the abbreviation *MKS*, had not gotten a real name yet. It did get a building, though: at the *Grunwaldzka* – not more than some 60 feet from the house in Gdańsk-Wrzeszcz where I used to stay. I went there on Monday morning. In one of the rooms stood a bunch of people around Gwiazda and Wałęsa. What should the trade union be named? We all participated: journalists, accidental passers-by, (ex) strikers. I belonged to the group which said: name it *MKS*, that name has become famous. Until somebody said: why not *Solidarność*, like that slogan of Jaruszewski, which was hanging in the hall. Yes, everybody kind of liked this idea. And so not only the trade union but also its name was born. With its freakish letters.

CHAPTER 24

Visa tricks

Because I was convinced that I would not live to see the collapse of the communist regimes, I was just as sure never to be able to disclose the tricks I had to invent to enter countries where I was not allowed to enter in the first place.

Preceding this goes the general, moral question: was it allowed to cheat those governments over there? Without any doubt my answer is: yes. For the sake of a good cause you were allowed to cheat the German occupiers, the fascist Franco regime in Spain, the authoritarian half- and whole-fascist regimes in South America – and therefore the totalitarian regimes in Eastern Europe as well. My basic assumption was: the communist regimes have the appearance of legality, but are in essence illegal. So everything you undertake against them has the appearance of illegality, but is in essence legal. But, whereas doing this, I avoided unnecessary risks – I tried to keep my tricks as much as possible within the appearance of their legality.

The simplest was the transit-trick. It only worked if you were not on the black list of at least one of the communist countries. Until my expulsion from Czechoslovakia in 1970, I never had any problem with Poland. After my first Eastern European trip in 1958 I not only got, as mentioned before, an entry ban from the Soviet Union, but from Czechoslovakia which used to stay firmly in line with the Soviet Union as well. Apparently, the Poles did not care about that Soviet ban: I could keep on coming. When I was in Poland the second time in April 1960, I applied for a transit visa, as mentioned before, at the Czechoslovakian embassy in Warsaw, pretending that I had to go to Austria. By then, I had already committed my first "little lie." At the time, your profession was entered in your passport. All communist authorities were allergic to the word journalist. Based on international agreements, they were more or less obliged to give you a transit visa, but if "journalist" was mentioned in your passport, the consulates had even for that to ask permission in their capitals. So I already had pretty speedily changed my profession into "employee." I always filled out my applications in German, because the German word for "employee" is *Angestellter* – which quite generally means that you are employed – and everybody is employed somewhere, so it could not be more neutral. Not surprisingly, with my employee status I got my Czechoslovakian transit visa without any problem.

A transit visa was always valid for 48 hours, but it did not go by the hour but by the day. If you entered on day 1, you were allowed to leave on day 3. If you only took care to cross the border very early on day 1 and to make it late on day 3, you actually could stay in that country for three days. That's what I did the first time and also in the eyes of the Czechoslovakian authorities there was nothing illegal about it. That's why I immediately reported to the Foreign Ministry in Prague with the question of why I could not get a normal visa for their country. I don't know whether it was due to this intervention, but three years later I got a "normal" visa. And those three days in 1960 I could easily use to do some news reports.

After the invasion of Czechoslovakia in 1968, it became more and more dif-ficult. For a while, the Czechoslovakian embassy in The Hague was still "good," but after Husák came to power in April 1969 I was back on the black list in The Hague again. Apparently, it had not been (then) transferred to their other em-bassies yet, because I did obtain a visa in Vienna. But for that, I had to invent some additional tricks. Because you not only had to report your profession on the application forms, but your employer as well. Of course, I could invent something at random, but upon a possible arrest I did not want to be caught having reported a false or nonexistent employer. *Angestellter* – employee, that I could more or less prove, but reporting a shoe factory as an employer while working for the broadcasting system – that I had to try to avoid. (Mis)using their own bureaucracy against them, I had thought of something that would be waterproof in the short term, but unstoppable in the long term. I just had to speculate that I only needed it for the short term.

Every application form had to be filled out in triplicate. Part 1 remained at the embassy, part 2 was taken at the border. Part 3 you carried with you dur-ing your stay and was taken when leaving the country. I always filled out the three forms separately, so I did not use the carbon which was even appreciated because this worked out so bad that the third copy was hardly legible. When I worked at *VPRO*-TV (in Dutch written as Vpro-tv), I wrote down as employer: *Spoor*, the Dutch word for "Railway (company)." I made a flamboyant letter of the S, the first "o" was almost a stripe and I left a small space between the sec-ond "o" and the "r." Once having crossed the border, I extended the flamboyant S and made a flamboyant V out of it, the stripe-like "o" got a little strip to it, so that it became a "r," between the second "o" and the real "r" I put a dash, the pole of the "r" was a little bit extended that made it into a "t," behind which I then put a "v." Now, I no longer worked at *Spoor*, but at *Vpro-tv*.

When I was arrested in 1970, I worked for the *NOS*-radio. That was much simpler. On the original forms I filled out as employer, "N.S." (I apparently had something with the railways, because it is the abbreviation of *Nederlandse Spoorwegen*, "Dutch Railways." After having crossed the border, on the third copy I put an O between the N and the S, placed a dash behind the S and then wrote behind it, "radio."

N. S.

N.O.S.-radio

In cold sweat and with my heart in my boots, I pointed out to Pichrt during my interrogation that I had obtained my visa as the man of "NOS-radio." Back then, telefax did not exist yet and I assumed that it would take oceans of time before they had gathered those three forms in Prague to compare the one with the other. That worked. They did not find out in the week I was locked up. It took them at least a couple of months, because only in the documentary of January 1971 the commentator says mysteriously "and why did Verkijk write N.S. on his form in Vienna and changed it later into N.O.S.?"

The visa policy of those countries was often unfathomable, most likely also due to their own chaotic bureaucratic system in which the left hand does not know what the right hand is doing. In December 1980 I was denied a visa for Poland – I'll come back to it later – but for the party congress in the spring of 1981 I did get it again. At the time, I was already on record at all Eastern European embassies as an undesirable person. Despite that I gambled and applied at the Czechoslovakian embassy in Warsaw for the famous transit visa to Austria. Unintentionally, I came close to closing time – so they were in a hurry. That could be the reason they did not look into the big book. The other could be the assumption that nothing could be wrong with a person who got a visa for Poland. As the case may be: within five minutes I had my visa. I had asked for 48 hours, but got only 24 hours. So two days. An early border crossing, and eleven in the morning I was already in Praque. Immediately, I parked my car in the underground garage of hotel Alcron, telling the guard that I already had a room. After going around to different addresses in vain (nobody was at home during the day), I found Professor Ladislav Hejdánek at home, former spokesman of *Charta-77*, but still a member of the spokesmen collective. He lived on Slovenská street # 19, two houses from the former apartment of the Sekerka's where I had stayed in the sixties – sometimes you have the idea that all the events in your life link together. He called Václav Malý, then one of the three spokesmen of *Charta*, who came immediately. Inside, at Hejdánek's house, he did not want to talk because of the danger of eavesdropping and so we walked around some blocks. In front of the door of Hejdánek he pointed at a delivery van with a viewing window ("There is the StB"). After a few streets we were stopped by an ordinary street-policeman (without any doubt sent by the StB) who checked our ID's. I could only hope to be outside Czechoslovakia before the bureaucratic mill would realize that I was who I was. I made a nice, nostalgic day out of it, visited old friends and old spots and only late in the evening reported to the hotel for lodging. "You are not allowed to spend the night," the receptionist said, after viewing my visa.

"But I got 24 hours, so I don't have to leave the country until tomorrow, right?" I asked.

"No, 24 hours means you must drive straight through, and you are not allowed to stay over."

That upset all my calculations. I tried at hotel Yalta: the same answer. "Just try at hotel Adria, there they don't check as strictly as we do," said the receptionist. But also there I was met with a refusal. On a chair in front of the reception desk a man was sitting who said, "Go with me, I have an acquaintance who works at hotel Lido, you can possibly sleep there." Off we went to Lido, but there an unrelenting "no," as well. Never mind, you can stay with me, the man said. I accepted. He lived in an apartment in a very decent neighborhood pretty close to Lido. We went up by elevator, he opened his door and behind it a chaos was hiding like I had never seen before. It was one big mess, it was stinking, a broom had not been remotely run over it for months if not for years, chairs were piled on top of each other, there was no space to move – but what could I do? I considered that I might as well spend the night sitting. I just went to the bathroom for a minute which completely fulfilled the expectations aroused by the living room. When I re-entered the living room, a neighbor appeared to be visiting. He had noticed that my host had brought someone along and, knowing his neighbor, he came to size up the situation. When he learned that I had "spending-the night-problems" (of course, I didn't tell him why) he said, "Just come and stay with me, that's somewhat better than here." He had an abundance of space, he said, because his wife and children were at their weekend house somewhere in the mountains. Six feet down the hall I landed from hell into heaven. I got a splendid bed and an ample breakfast the next morning. Finally, he gave me his business card and said I was always welcome. Immediately after I left, I tore it up and threw it away, because you never knew what possibly could happen to you. His name was something like Berger or Bergman, fourteen years later I tried to find him again through phone directories and by wandering through the neighborhood where I thought he used to live – in vain.

Meanwhile, I was in a funk, because I should have already left the country the previous day. What kind of excuse would I invent at the border? Fortunately, I had gotten a little trouble with my glasses: a small screw had gotten lost because of which one of my lenses did not stay in the frame anymore. An optician repaired it and I still had the receipt. At the border I would say that I had a one-day-delay due to that repair. But the border guards took my visa form with a routine gesture; they did not say or check anything, so my tapes with the interviews reached Austria intact as well.

In June 1983 the communist World Peace Council organized an international congress in Prague to which the noncommunist peace movements also had been invited. The organization was being conducted by the secretariat in Geneva, Switzerland, which was run by members of the British communist party. I applied for a visa at the Czechoslovakian embassy in The Hague which was denied, of course. The British in Geneva did not understand this at all and they said they would take care of it. After a few days they told me that everything was OK and that I could pick up my visa in The Hague. But there they claimed not to know anything about it – they stuck to their refusal. Once more a call to Geneva, once more amazement over there, once more intervention in Prague – and indeed: I got the visa, issued to me by a gnashing Czechoslovakian consular civil official in The Hague. In those days, I had a big motor home in which I spent the night on the parking lot of Park Hotel in Prague where I formally was registered. I was told by others that StB guys, sometimes four or five simultaneously, showed a great interest in my motor home when I was not present. So I did not know what was the safest: to keep the tapes with the interviews I had made at Anna Šabatová's birthday with me or leave them in the motor home. I decided on the former. There was among Western participants as well as the members of *Charta-77* a great need for mutual contact, and some of their leaders like Václav Havel and Jiří Hájek, asked interested persons to come on such and such a day at such and such a time to such and such a park to exchange views. It was an absurd situation. Dozens of congress participants talked with dozens of dissidents outside in the open, surrounded by dozens of StB-agents. Initially, they only watched, they intervened, however, when interviews were being filmed. I stood there and watched, because I had already done my interviews. Suddenly, one of those agents came up to me and ordered me to open my bag. "I have not filmed anything," I said, but still I had to open my bag. When they saw my sound tapes, I had to go with them to a car where they took the tapes out of my bag, and threw them into the trunk. On top of that, we had to leave the park. "They confiscated the tapes with the interviews I did with you," I said to Havel to which he reproachfully reacted with, "Why then were you carrying them with you?"

Fortunately, the man who always stood up for the rights of the oppressed was a congress participant as well: Wim Klinkenberg, vice president of the *Nederlandse Vereniging van Journalisten* (Dutch Union of Journalists), who had acquired the nickname "the last Stalinist of the Netherlands." I asked him to intervene with the congress leadership and to protest against the confiscation. He refused, "because I am here as a private person and not as a representative of the *NVJ*" which did not prevent him one month later from writing an article on that Prague congress in *The Democratic Journalist*, the organ of the (communist) *International Organization of Journalists*, with under his name the explicit mention, "vice president of the Dutch Union of Journalists."[98] So then I just submitted my protest on my own and sure enough: I was received by the president of the Czechoslovakian Peace Council, "professor" Tomáš Trávníček who lived on the Nerudová street in an historical house, restored at the expense of the state. He promised to do his best and verily: one morning I pass by the reception of the Park hotel and there sits the man who had conducted the StB operations in the park. "I have been waiting for you here for several hours already," he said. "I've come to give you back your tapes. But you will understand that we did delete them." By the way, these recordings and those diary fragments of 1970 are the only materials I lost in 31 years-Eastern-Europe.

November 1989. I'm back in Prague. Now absolutely legal. The communist system still exists, but already "gorbachevized." One month before, I had applied for a permanent accreditation at the Czechoslovakian embassy in Belgrade where I lived. The answer was positive. I get my press ID-card at the Foreign Ministry in Prague on November 23 – one day later the regime is wiped out. In all kinds of respects, I am the last one to get his accreditation from the communists.

Even without black lists, Hungary was a difficult country to enter after the

---

[98] By reason of that article in *The Democratic Journalist*, I asked for clarification at the Dutch Union of Journalists, the nationwide and only union of journalists in the Netherlands, because, apparently, he was present as the vice president of the *NVJ* yet. Answering me on April 17, 1984, President M.M. de Bok wrote that Klinkenberg "in agreement with a decision of the executive was present in a personal capacity. Consequently, he does not take the responsibility for the mentioning of his function in the *IOJ* organ. It may be unpleasant for a Dutch journalist, at the same time a *NVJ* member, that he did not get on the spot some help from the vice president of his organization, but it still seems to the executive that Wim Klinkenberg was in his right to act formally." The wording of the letter and the attitude of the *Nederlandse Vereniging van Journalisten*, having one of the hardest of hard-line communists as a vice president, is typical of the atmosphere in the seventies and the eighties in "independent" thinking circles in the Netherlands and in Western Europe generally.

insurrection of 1956. In 1961 I covered the first Montreux TV festival in Switzerland and I happened to sit next to the director of the Hungarian television Ferenc Kulcsár at a dinner offered to us by the city. The animated conversation resulted in an invitation to visit Hungary some day. In 1962 I contacted him, told him when I intended to come and what I would like to see and whether he was able to organize something for me. He agreed. But visas are not the responsibility of those kinds of people; that, you have to organize yourself. At the time the Hungarians had the same system as the Soviets: you apply for hotel accommodation through a travel agency. If the agency gets the confirmation, you go with this confirmation to the embassy concerned, which gives you the visa without delay. It goes without saying that the confirmation from the motherland only comes if the applicant passes the screening of the local security service. If this does not work out all right, then the hotel system over there lets you know "that there is no hotel accommodation available." This way, there was no hotel accommodation to be found for me in Moscow for dozens of years. The authorities there sidestepped the problem of a visa refusal this way, it simply was a matter of hotel accommodation.

The Dutch travel agency did indeed receive confirmation from Budapest. But still before I had picked up the telex message, the agency called to say that they had received a second telex from Budapest stating that the first telex was based on a misunderstanding and that the hotel reservation had been canceled. I asked the agency to join in the game and give me only the first telex so that I could try to get hold of a visa at the Hungarian embassy, anyway. The trick succeeded. Stupidly enough the Budapest guys had not sent a copy of that refusal to their embassy.

In Budapest I went to hotel Astoria where initially a room had been reserved for me, but the receptionist did not know anything about a reservation. He checked this and that, and cried, "Oh, there you are, it had been reserved but it was canceled." I pretended to be completely bewildered and he said that it must be due to a misunderstanding, but there was no problem, because they had plenty of rooms. The next morning I called the woman from the television with whom I had regularly been in touch for preliminary consultations, and cheerfully said, "Here I am."

In disbelief she asked, "How do you get here?"

"By car," I answered, and I told her that I wanted to drop by for further arrangements. And now the funny thing comes in: once I was there, for whatever the reason (politeness, fear of causing a scandal by expelling me) – they did not dare let me down. They kept their promises punctually, took me around the country along the route mapped out by me, left me alone when I wanted them to, and I was able to leave the country without any problem whatsoever. I did not get a normal visa for a considerable time, but initially I did get a transit visa when I had to go to Romania. Traveling through Hungary to Romania had an extra advantage: you also had to cross it on your way back. That's why I always requested a "double transit": that meant six days Hungary.

In 1966 I wanted to make a TV documentary "Ten years after the insurrection" (of October/November 1956). A second documentary would deal with the Dutch influence in Debrecen in Eastern Hungary close to the Romanian border. One of the greatest "national heroes" in Dutch history is admiral Michiel de Ruyter who once liberated a dozen Hungarian Protestant ministers who were degraded into galley slaves by Spanish Catholic villains. To commemorate this, a statue of De Ruyter was erected in Debrecen. Ever since, the ties between the Netherlands and Hungary have remained and since the 17th century Hungarians get scholarships to study theology at the University of Utrecht. For that, Hungarians have to master the Dutch language and for centuries Dutch was and still is taught at the University of Debrecen, really a Protestant "bulwark" within Catholic Hungary.

For some reason our staff cameramen were not available and I was going to shoot with the excellent cameraman André Gunn, a free lancer. On the way going, I would go alone and in that first Hungarian period prepare the programs. When I would be finished with the preparations for the programs in Romania (which are irrelevant for this story), André would come to Bucharest by plane, in order, after finishing our work in Romania, to make our documentaries during the second three-day-Hungarian period.

I had asked André to apply at the Hungarian embassy in The Hague for a transit visa only after my departure, thus without me, and I impressed on him not to say one word about our film plans. However, free lancers are scared to death that something may happen to their equipment – rightfully so, by the way, because it represents tons of investments and their whole existence depends on it – and by further consideration he felt uneasy about just going and chancing it. That's why he preferred to ask at the embassy as a precaution whether he needed permission to film. The consul asked what the subject could possibly be. "Ten years after the insurrection," André said honestly and innocently. So no visa. That is: the consul promised to ask for permission in Budapest. Where could a possible positive answer be sent? "To your embassy in Bucharest," replied André, still being equally honest and innocent. So, the Hungarians sent a warning to their consulate in Bucharest that, if a certain André Gunn would report there, they were not allowed to grant him a visa under any circumstances. Although I realized that it would make no sense, we still dropped by the Hungarian consul in Bucharest. The answer was of course: no. "And don't try to get a visa at the border, because you won't manage to get it." But we had no choice. So tried anyway. At the border I went with André's passport without, and my passport with a visa to the visa office and said casually that I already had a transit visa, but that we didn't have time in Bucharest to pick up a visa for my fellow traveler. No problem, said the border official – and within three minutes André's passport had a visa. Not until 300 feet beyond the border, we jubilantly stuck up our fist.

In Debrecen I had set up all appointments via Prof. Pakozdy, the university teacher in Dutch language there. In one day everything was done; the very same day we drove straight to Budapest. The problem was that we for sure were registered in the police records there in the evening due to our reporting at the hotel desk. Quickly, we shot my opening statement the next morning at the statue of the Polish general Joseph Bem like, "Here started ten years ago.... " and so on, but I actually found it too risky. If you don't ask anything and you are stopped, you can always say that you can film everywhere in the world without permission so why not in Hungary. But André had asked for permission and had in fact received no for an answer. In this case filming means that you knowingly were in breach of the law – and there you are with your equipment worth a couple of tons. After the first recordings, we went to the press officer of the Foreign Ministry to still formally ask for a permit – a matter of a few steps because the statue of Bem stands on the square in front of the ministry. I knew the press officer from earlier occasions – and he me, too. A permit was out of the question, "but as private persons you could stay, of course." I hastened to say that we did not have time for that, that we had to go to Czechoslovakia and would cross the border at Komárom. We were not going to Czechoslovakia at all, but simply to Austria via Hegyeshálom. But you never knew whether or not he was going to have the border guards warned to search our car extra carefully. In that case he would alert the wrong border guards. I did not consider the likelihood he would do so too great, but I held on to my principle of limiting the risk (in this case that our stuff would be confiscated) to the extreme minimum. On the film reels we had written, "Romania 1, 2" and so on. At the border the check was thorough but routinely, the film reels were in the rear for all to see and we told them that we had made documentaries in Romania. We were allowed to drive on without any problem. It never came to the documentary "Ten years after the insurrection," but "The Netherlands and Debrecen" we literally and metaphorically succeeded in dragging out of there.

It was obvious that the authorities in those countries noticed that I used their transit facilities and also realized that only the concerned embassies in the Netherlands were informed about me. And from 1970 on – after my expulsion from Czechoslovakia – I was registered at every embassy of every communist country and at all border crossing points. Every time I was abroad, whether it was in Helsinki or Paris, I always tried to obtain a visa at one or more of the Eastern European embassies – it hardly ever worked. On my way to Romania I tried two, three Hungarian border points – in vain. From now on I had to go all the way down through Yugoslavia to get to Romania. What remained was traveling along with official delegations, using international conferences and leaks in the bureaucracy.

In 1974 the city council of Haarlem decided to enter into a sister-city relationship with the Polish city of Kielce, halfway between Warsaw and Kraków. A council delegation would visit Kielce. We applied for visas for four men: Mayor De Gou and three councilors – one of them was me. The Polish embassy made objections that I was on the list, but De Gou let them know that they could forget about the sister-city relationship if I would not get a visa. They changed their minds. We would go for ten days, we got a visa for ten days. As usual, I wanted to maximize the use of that visa. We agreed that I would go to Warsaw by car a week ahead of time to do what has to be done there. The rest of the delegation would go by train and I would pick them up in Warsaw, from where we would drive on to Kielce. But because of that, my visa expired three days after our arrival in Kielce so it had to be extended. It was denied. Mayor De Gou said that he would leave Kielce immediately if I did not get an extension. So I got an extension. After the end of the consultations we returned to Warsaw, where I brought the delegation to the railway station. It was on a weekend, my visa had actually expired, but on Sunday I could not apply for a second extension. So I did on Monday – and they added another week. Why? I would not know.

In 1979, Chris van der Klaauw, the successor of Max van der Stoel as the minister of Foreign Affairs, went for an official visit to Poland. Ten to fifteen journalists would travel with him – I would be one of them. They denied my visa. Van der Klaauw promised to bring it up with his counterpart in Warsaw. My colleagues showed a lot of solidarity and repeatedly asked Van der Klaauw whether he had already talked about my visa problems and if so, what had been the answer. Finally, Van der Klaauw could state that his Polish colleague had told him that the refusal was "due to a misunderstanding" and that I "always" would be welcome in Poland. It goes without saying that I immediately applied for a visa: no answer. This, our ministry could not let pass by, because, as they told me, this was about "a promise by a minister to a minister." There was a squabbling back and forth all the winter and finally in March 1980, as mentioned in the preceding chapter, the promise was turned into a permit. Thanks to that tremendous delay (and my own postponement because March did not suit me very well) I was in Poland exactly when the strike in Gdańsk broke out. My compassion for my excluded colleagues (after all, the borders were closed) was extra great, because they of all people had made so many efforts to get that entry ban lifted against me. But, as the Polish consul had told me while handing over my visa, it's a one-time-thing, based on the agreement between the two ministers: one time and nothing more. That's why I was not really surprised when they once more denied me a visa in December 1980. In Gdańsk, a monument would be inaugurated in commemoration of the workers who had been killed during the strike of December 1970. I absolutely wanted to be there.

I had learned that you could easily get a visa on the boat from Copenhagen, Denmark to Swinoujšce (Swinemünde), a few miles from Gdańsk. After the refusal in The Hague I tried it this way. The travel agency in Copenhagen, which sold the tickets for that trip, told me that just a couple of days before that system had been abolished, but I was still allowed to buy a ticket. In Swinousjšce I said to the border guard-in-charge that I was on my way to a friend in Gdańsk, that they could check it there (this time it was about Alois Trendl, painter and a professor at the Academy of Arts in Gdańsk) and I asked whether I could get a visa. The Polish guard was very kind and asked me to wait for a minute. After ten minutes he returned very angrily, grabbed me by the collar and brought me straight back to the ship. A few hours later I was back in Copenhagen. But there is also a boat going from Karslkruna, Sweden straight to Gdańsk. I called Alois Trendl and said with which ship I expected to arrive and asked him to pick me up. Off I went by train from Copenhagen to Karlskruna. Actually, the shipping company was not allowed to sell me a ticket, not having a visa. "I'll get it over there," I said optimistically – and they gave me the ticket. The voyage took nine hours, in a violent storm, the water even glanced off the windows of the upper deck. But to me these were all side events – my eye was focused on Gdańsk. Right before midnight, on Saturday, December 13, we arrived. At not even a hundred feet, my friend was waiting on the other side of a rope. The border guard asked me what I had come for. "I'm on transit to Hungary. Tomorrow I fly from Gdańsk to Warsaw and then from Warsaw to Budapest," I lied.

"But you don't even have a visa for Hungary," he said.

"That's not necessary, because I'll get it at the airport in Budapest."

Well, then I did have to fill out a form. I went with him to a small office and he himself would fill the form out for me. The conversation went in English which he spoke very moderately.

"What is your profession?" he asked.

"Budgeteer," I blurted out. Of course, he did not know what this nonexistent profession involved, but he thought it was due to his bad English and found it embarrassing to ask for specification[99].

---

[99] A word "budgeteer" does exist in English speaking countries but is used for for instance parliamentarians who audit government's budgets.

"Where do you work?"

"Radio factory." After all, I made budgets (for my own programs) at a radio enterprise.

"How long do you want to have?"

"Twenty-four hours," I answered generously, "because I will continue my journey right away tomorrow."

When the papers were filled out, he asked me to wait outside for a minute. I considered this a bad omen, because now he was going to look in the big book, of course. I waved to Alois and made a gesture of "wait and see." After five minutes the guard came out of his booth. "It's OK, you got 24 hours" and seconds later Alois and I greeted each other extensively the Polish way. The most important stage was won. But it was only the first one.

The stamp carried just the date of the new day: Sunday. So I had till Monday evening. The commemoration would take place on Tuesday. Sunday, I called good friends in Warsaw, asking them whether they were willing to go with me to the visa office in Warsaw where we would make up the following story, "I was on my way to Hungary, but my friends in Warsaw asked me whether I would like to spend Christmas and New Year with them and whether I could get a visa for fourteen days." On Sunday evening I went by night train to Warsaw. My friend Jacek Damięcki (whom I had known since 1958, too) picked me up from the station and at ten o'clock in the morning we were at the visa office. "But why did you not directly apply for a visa in the Netherlands?" they asked, after having listened to my story.

"Because at that time I did not know that my friends would invite me for Christmas."

"OK, well, go ahead and start exchanging money and submit your forms, then you will hear Wednesday if it's all right."

Wednesday! That was one day after the commemoration-Tuesday. It already sounded good that I had to exchange money. In those days it was mandatory to change fifteen dollars for every day you intended to stay in advance. Applying for a visa for fourteen days meant exchanging 14 x $ 15.- at the official rate (to prevent you from exchanging all your money on the black market). That proof was the basis for granting a visa.

Now, cab driver Jerzy Sekreta had to get involved. He often drove for western journalists. I called him and for 200 German marks he would bring me that very same Monday to Gdańsk and return me to Warsaw on Wednesday morning.

The commemoration and the unveiling on Tuesday were impressive events which brought a million people out. It was clear: it was not possible to smash *Solidarność* anymore.

On Wednesday morning departure at six; at half past nine we had covered the 200 miles to Warsaw and I was back with the guys from the visa office as if I had not left Warsaw.

"What's your name?" the official-in-charge asked.

After I had mentioned it, he rummaged through a pile of passports, produced mine and said, "Fourteen days, good-bye." As if it was the most natural thing in the world.

I spent Christmas in Gdańsk with Ewa and her family. At the time, the food situation in Poland was still disastrous and you had for instance to stand in line for hours for a small piece of meat. "I find it below human dignity to do so, then rather no meat," Ewa had told me once. But during the Christmas dinner on Christmas Eve she had sausages on the table.

"I stood in line for eight hours to get it," she said.

"Then I don't dare to eat one bit of it," I reacted startled, but her answer was of an irrefutable logic, "Please do eat it, otherwise I stood in line for nothing."

According to tradition, the table was set for one person too many "for an unexpected guest." Present indeed were Andrzej Gwiazda and his wife, and Ana Walentynowicz, the crane operator whose dismissal had been the reason for the strike at the Lenin shipyard.

By then, my admiration for Wałęsa had already gone down quite a bit, because he had used all sorts of undemocratic methods to frustrate both, fearing that they could be competitors in his strife for power. Related to this, I wrote a letter to Wałęsa, translated in Polish by Ewa, in which I told him that the strike was started to restore democracy in the first place, and that it was inappropriate for him to use undemocratic methods himself. It was not very helpful: in the longer run he disposed of both of them completely. Years later, I happened to be able to visit Gwiazda once more: he had grown into a lonely, embittered and disillusioned man. Ana Walentynowicz took it more even-tempered.

I had never applied for a visa for the Soviet Union anymore except for traveling along with parliamentary delegations in 1976 and 1981. After Gorbachev had come to power in March 1985, I regained hope and I gave it a try once again for the party congress in February 1986. And I got my visa. And immediately after that, all those other communist countries were open to me again, too. It was as clear as day that the KGB had entered my name on the black list for all communist countries in 1970. But it was also as clear as day, that the same mechanism that did me end up on that list in 1970, had taken care to take me off in 1986 as well. The fact that those in Moscow had said to their brother-countries: you can take these and these guys off the black list, was one of the indications to me that something fundamental was changing in the Soviet Union.

Between that absolute entry ban in 1970 and the lifting of it in 1986, I still have been in those areas twenty one times by the above-mentioned methods: four times in Poland (1974, two times in 1980, 1981), three times in Czechoslovakia (1977, 1981, 1983), two times in the Soviet Union (1976, 1981), three times in Bulgaria (1975, 1977, 1979) and one time in Cuba (1979). I was not successful in Hungary until 1975, when that country lifted the ban on its own. After that I have been there six times, of which two times in 1981. They re-imposed the ban in December of the same year. In the fall of 1985, a Cultural Forum was convened in Budapest within the framework of the CSCE, but by assigning Budapest as the convention city, the Hungarians had to promise that nobody would be denied a visa, so they had to give me one, too. From the journalistic point of view, the preparatory meeting, one month before the real one, did not amount to anything and not surprisingly, the press center had hardly anything to do, because only two journalists had shown up: Ronald Eggleton of Radio Free Europe and me, both blacklisted. Rightfully, there was a great interest in the real Forum: in Budapest fled or expelled Czechoslovakian dissidents met dissident colleagues from Prague who had come to Budapest as well, using the rather easy intra-Eastern-European travel opportunities. In the margin of the official conference, a number of (packed) living-room-meetings were held. The Hungarian security service did show to be highly interested in those meetings, but they could take place uninterrupted *(see photo 17)*

The *DDR* never attracted me that much, besides, important events always occurred in *Berlin – Hauptstadt der DDR*, as the GDR capital East Berlin always was called in the *DDR* jargon. Due to the special status of the city, you could always easily obtain a one-day visa to go from West- to East Berlin, so those visits never produced visa troubles. Romania never participated in that 1970-ban, but there, exactly after 1985, it became more and more difficult. As an ordinary tourist, you could easily obtain a visa at the border crossings. That's what I did most of the time and then, as already has been said, I reported to mister Țuiu of Agerpress immediately after my arrival.

It was not all that funny, but rather nerve-racking. And I always literally breathed a sigh of relief, when I again crossed unharmed a border to a western country.

CHAPTER 25

Interviews with "statesmen"

What moves people, who with great personal sacrifices out of idealism had sided with the oppressed, to later become oppressors themselves, in some cases even merciless? How much humanity is still hiding behind the *apparatchik* masks of the communist leaders in Eastern Europe? And how "liberal" are the liberals among them? I always have been very curious about it and all those years – in the periods I was not completely *persona non grata* – I applied for interviews with the party leaders. Especially figures like Khrushchev, the Pole Gomułka and his successor Gierek, the Yugoslav Tito, the Hungarian Kádár and the Romanian Ceauçescu intrigued me. But they were all Olympic gods, inaccessible to ordinary mortals, especially when you came from such a small country like the Netherlands.

Just a few I met by accident. On that tour around the *DDR* in July 1960, my Indian colleague Dilip Malakar and I, plus our companion Eugen Betzer, were dining in the famous hotel *Elephant* in Weimar, when all of a sudden a bunch of *SED* functionaries walked by, headed by none other than party leader Walter Ulbricht who went for a bite in a specially reserved room. Our otherwise so bullyish companion now timidly mumbled, "*Guten Abend, Genosse Ulbricht* – Good evening, comrade Ulbricht." Quickly, we wrote a note with the request for an interview (under great protest from Betzer, "You cannot bother somebody of his stature just like that"), and through the waiter it landed on his table. After a few minutes, a functionary nicely told us, that a thing like that was impossible unfortunately.

At party congresses, leaders were kept far away from the masses, except in Hungary. It looked like an ordinary European party congress. During the intermissions, politicians, congress participants and journalists were mingling. So in 1980 I suddenly found my self opposite János Kádár of whom I knew that he spoke some German. Could I do an interview? Smiling very friendly, he put one hand on my shoulder and made with the other one a rejecting gesture: no dice. Of Gomułka, who came to power in 1956 on the wings of the Polish "springtime in October," the *Październik*, after the Stalinist regime was wiped out by a semi-revolution, I have not seen more than his simple row house in the Warsaw district Praga, close to the bridge across the *Wisła*, Vistula. Through Ţuiu, I had also submitted numerous requests for an interview with Ceauçescu. Routinely, I did it again in 1975 – and to my amazement he reacted more or less positive. What was going on? The Dutch queen Juliana would pay a state visit to Romania and *NOS* television had in connection with this applied for an interview with the Romanian president and party leader. On occasions like this, the highest authorities are always willing to perform for each other's media. If the interview was granted, *NOS* television (back then, I worked only for *NOS* radio) agreed that I would do the interview. After quite a bit of humming and hawing, the permission came through, but the exact date was still unknown. Whether I would be so kind as to submit the questions to the ministry of Foreign Affairs to begin with. I was invited by some functionary or other to talk about the questions and I had to fight for every comma and period. I already could foresee that it would not be an interview at all, but a skit for two gentlemen in which I would serve as the stooge.

"Am I allowed to ask an in-between-question if there is something that I don't understand? Because if there is something I don't understand, the Dutch viewer will not understand it either."

"Of course," he answered.

"But then a good interpreter should be present during the interview," I remarked.

"That goes without saying," the protocol said.

After this, I gave up my fight for commas and periods – my real questions would be the in-between-questions.

The interview was certainly on, so they assured me, but the date was still unknown. Meanwhile, I had already been in Romania for more than three weeks and had finished all my other (radio) work. The *NOS* television had sent a producer, Gert Corba, and together we kind of hung around in Bucharest. At a certain moment they let us know that we had to be in our hotel room every morning between ten and eleven to be informed of the exact point in time. That lasted a week. Then the ukase came that we had to stay in our rooms all day, because the interview could take place any moment. After five days of house arrest we said loudly to each other, being sure we were bugged, "If the interview does not come within two days, we are leaving." And sure enough – the next day a call: in a quarter of an hour you will be picked up. We drove to the building of the Central Committee with rooms as big as palace halls. We had to wait in one of the halls. Ţuiu was there – and a few other functionaries. Two cameras with Romanian personnel were ready to shoot.

"Where is the interpreter?" I asked.

"He isn't here," the protocol said.

"But there would be an interpreter, so that I could put in-between-questions if the president is saying something I don't understand."

"Our president always gives such clear answers, that further explanation is not needed," was the protocol's response. "Then I have to talk to you for a minute," I said, and we went to a side hall. "In Holland I do not have the reputation for doing flat interviews. When this is aired, it will not be announced as an interview *with* the president but as a statement *of* the president."

"Just do what you like most," the protocol said.

True, Ţuiu was fluent in English, but officially he was not an interpreter for the president, so he did not qualify. We sat and waited in the building for at least another half an hour. With the moment of truth approaching, we had to draw up in a certain battle-array and were told where we had to stand, accurate to the inch. Ceauşescu would enter from his working room through a communicating door on the right. Gert stood on my right side. Suddenly slight panics from the protocol: I was the reporter, Gert and I had to change places, because it would be against the etiquette if "the most important person" (in their eyes I was, because I was the interviewer) would shake hands with the president later than the producer, who apparently was put lower on the scale. We stood there for minutes – and at last he came, accompanied by his then-second man: Cornel Burtica.

The interview itself did not amount to anything, of course. I read my questions in English and he responded in Romanian. I was able to understand quite a bit because a: Romanian is a Latin language very akin to French, b: it was not my first trip to Romania, c: I had been sitting in this country for six straight weeks already and d: the party-vocabulary was so limited-cliché-wise that the answers were nearly predictable. Of course, I did not know when Ceauşescu had said his say and that's why there were long gaps between his last words and my next question. But in a to them spectacular way it would be shown, that this was not the end of it *(see photo 10)*.

For that, we have first to go back to the Yugoslavian capital Belgrade in the year 1968. On a terrace of the Square of the Republic I got into a conversation with a Romanian-on-vacation, Radu Botez. He is the son of a well-known writer (which explains his permission to go on vacation in Yugoslavia), but it's obvious that he does not want to have much to do with communism – neither does his father, so he hints. He invites me to look him up when I would be in Romania again. That's a year later when Nixon visits Romania and during the period it seemed like Ceauşescu would turn in a more liberal direction.

I call Radu in advance, tell him that I want to speak with some students, and ask whether he could organize this. The first thing he does after my arrival is to take me for a car ride – he has to get rid of something. He tells me that our phone conversation had been bugged; that they (with "they" the representatives of the secret services, in this case the *Securitate,* is always meant) will give me "a student" who is anything but a student, and that they had asked him to report everything about my actions.

"I plan to leave the country on a tourist visa and won't come back. If I don't cooperate, I don't get that visa, of course. Is it OK if I inform them about you?" he asked.

It goes without saying that I had no objections whatsoever. In the spring of 1970, he got his visa, went to Switzerland and got political asylum there. His mother, sickly, missed her son badly and had already applied numerous times for a visa to visit him – in vain of course. When it looked like I was going to do an interview with Ceaușescu, I told his mother that I was willing to hand a petition from her to Ceaușescu in which she could explain her problem. "Consult your family, because it can turn out badly. It seems unlikely to me, because if something happens to you, Ceaușescu knows that I know that he is personally responsible for it. There remains a risk, though," was how I summarized my view. An intense family consultation took place and the result was: she would write the petition.

In order not to forget my mission, I had put the envelope with the petition on top of my cassette recorder, with which I also recorded the interview myself. After it, the hand-shaking-routine had to be done again. I had the letter in my hand, called Țuiu over and said to Ceaușescu that I had a petition from one of his citizens and that I would like to hand it to him – and I gave him the letter. His face set, he took the letter by its extreme tip as if a goat's pellet was pressed into his hand and he immediately passed it on to a bewildered Burtica. Ceaușescu, Burtica and some other functionaries left literally by the back door and a great consternation developed among those staying behind, Țuiu in the first place. In the meantime, Burtica returned indignantly (apparently due to protocol, he had to bring Ceaușescu back to his adjoining study) and asked me through Țuiu how I did get it into my head to hand a petition to the president.

"An acquaintance of mine left Romania. I don't want to judge whether that was legal or illegal. But his mother is ill and dearly wants to visit her son – and up to now she has not gotten an exit visa. And what can a citizen do in such a case better than to address his president? That's why I agreed for humanitarian reasons to hand that petition," I explained to them. But it was obvious that the whole group thought it unheard of that I had taken "undue advantage" of the situation.

The result of that intervention was absolutely zero. The mother did not get a visa, but no problems either. Not once the *Securitate* addressed her. In 1977 I was once more in Romania on a tour through Eastern European countries in connection with the first Helsinki-follow-up conference, which was going to take place in Belgrade in the fall. I had a conversation at the Romanian Foreign Ministry about human rights and the official I was speaking to said that Romania strictly observed the agreements concerning family reunification. "That's not true," I responded – and I told him the story of that petition which had not amounted to anything.

"But why didn't you come to us with that case at the time?" he asked.

And I repeated what I also had said to Burtica two years before, "To whom can you better turn than to the president?" He asked me whom it concerned. Since name and surname were known at the highest level, anyway, I provided him with all the details. Two months later, the mother got her visa. And the matter did not end with that one visit: not once was she denied subsequent applications. Țuiu brought the incident up every time I came back in Romania. "What grief you caused me, back then. The interview came about under my responsibility and they gave me hell, because I was supposed to prevent you from handing over that petition."

But I had no compassion for that Ceaușescu-zealot.

In my whole career, I interviewed just one other "statesman": the communist-turned-nationalist Franjo Tudjman – even twice. He was president-elect of Croatia in May of 1990. A few days before his installation, I interviewed him for the *EO*, another Dutch public TV channel, in the then headquarters of the *HDZ* (Croatian abbreviation for "Croatian Democratic Community") in a big villa on the outskirts of Zagreb. In front blew the party flag: red-white-blue with the very controversial red and white checkered chess board in the white field. Tudjman was just not yet quite a statesman, but he had already assumed the air of it – not until after two hours of the agreed time he was able to receive us. From the very beginning, it was a gruff interview, because he considered critical questions inappropriate and he responded with irritation to them. At a certain moment I asked him, "Do you think that the flag hanging outside there will also be the state flag?"

"Of course," he replied – but he got extremely angry when I remarked, "So once again a party flag becoming a state flag." His mood did not really improve when I spoke critically about the notion of nationalism.

"But are you, for instance, not proud of your army in the Netherlands?" he asked.

"We Dutchmen are not nationalistic, at the very most chauvinistic." I meant it ironically and wanted to add that I was mostly thinking of soccer. But he interrupted me, saying, "Chauvinistic? That's even worse." And here his communist past came out of the closet, because in the communist mind-set chauvinism was about equal to committing a crime. Subsequently, I asked him quasi-ignorantly, "It's not quite clear to me what your party program actually involves. I have the feeling that's based exclusively on nationalism."

That was the limit for him.

"It's quite obvious that you know absolutely nothing at all about us and it's better we finish this interview now."

I told him that this was his democratic right – end of interview; pack and clear off.

Not yet a year later I was sitting across from Tudjman again. Gert Corba, who had moved to another PBS station in the meantime, had asked me to interview the Croatian president. Actually, I was the second choice because initially they had asked Theo Engelen, Dutch correspondent in the Slovenian capital Ljubljana, but he was ill (a few years later he would die due to this illness) and so they ended up with me. But Corba had already notified the Tudjman cabinet of Theo's name. When Corba learned that I had already had a run-in with Tudjman, they would rather not pass on to them that I, and not Theo, was the interviewer. As a matter of fact, it was more a kind of private press conference, because teams from the Australian and Russian television were present also. This time he did not keep us waiting that long and when he entered I saw him peering at me with a look of, "I know him from somewhere," but I think he was not able to place me. It goes without saying that the Serb/Croat relations were brought up and Tudjman said that the Serbs in Croatia could get all rights. "Except their own territory," I remarked, more or less casually and intended as the establishing of a fact. But Tudjman, not the most intelligent of the leaders in Yugoslavia, thought that I thought that the Serbs had a right to it. He was so mad at me that he gave his answer not in my direction, but looked instead at the Australian reporter, saying, "In Australia, you have a big *Croatian* minority, but you would not give them their own state, would you?"

After the interview somebody from Tudjman's cabinet came to me and asked "who I actually was." I gave him my name and added that I was based in Belgrade.

"Yes, that we noticed, that you live in Serbia. You are an excellent defender of the Serbian cause."

I tried to explain to him that a possible critical question from a journalist does not mean that the journalist represents the point of view which seems to lie hidden behind that question. But it was like pouring water into a sieve. The Croatian government folks, Tudjman in the first place, absolutely did not know the first thing about what a free press means and how journalism works. A few years later the "excellent defender of the Serbian cause" is expelled from (Small) Yugoslavia because he was "an enemy of the Serbian people." Marxism may have died out, but dialectic still plays its distressing little games.

That little devil also cropped up during the TV interview I had in 1993 with the fierce-nationalistic Serbian Vojislav Šešelj of the Serbian Radical Party.

Šešelj was sentenced in 1984 to eight years as a dissident by the Bosnian/ Herzegovinian court in Sarajevo (sometimes it seems to be forgotten that in the post-Tito era the most die-hard communists were in power there) which after an appeal to the Federal Court was reduced to 1½ years. He had already served that time and he took to his heels to Belgrade, where the climate was much milder indeed in those days than in Bosnia/Herzegovina. Back then, I belonged to the great many journalists who stood up for him and defended him because his conviction and treatment in prison were in defiance of human rights.

When I approached him for that interview, he demanded six hundred German marks, otherwise he would refuse to do it. The *KRO* (a Catholic PBS channel which had borrowed me for this occasion) was willing to go for it, but it frustrated me. That's why I did not start the interview with a question, but with the remark, "When you were in prison I defended you and now I have to pay six hundred marks for an interview with you. I must tell you I feel uneasy about it." Šešelj, always sure to find more than one hole to crawl out of, replied, "When you end up in prison, I will defend you, too. But you represent a country which is anti-Serbian – and then you have to pay. But I don't put that money in my own pocket or into the party cash, but we buy a Kalashnikov with it, for our struggle in Bosnia."

I urged the *KRO* to leave this statement in, but they found it too embarrassing apparently, and deleted it.[100]

Regularly, also pseudo-statesmen came to have their say at the International Press Center in Belgrade. One of them was the gang leader of the Bosnian Serbs in Pale, Radovan Karadžić. He was extremely unpopular among the correspondents' corps – and with this I put it mildly. Even most of our Soviet colleagues did not like him. You could cut the atmosphere with a knife at his press conferences. Once his lies were so cynical that almost simultaneously four or five colleagues stood up and walked out on him out of protest – this, I had never experienced during my whole career. Another time he came sailing in with a complete body guard, armed with machine guns. Two of them were posted behind him in the corners of the press room. After this event, I went to the director of the press center telling her that the presence of armed soldiers in the press center was unacceptable and that Karadžić would do better to hold his press conferences somewhere else, if he felt unsafe in our center. She promised me that it would never happen again.

[100] Šešelj is now in prison in The Hague, awaiting his trial as a war criminal at the *International Criminal Tribune for the former Yugoslavia.*

Before it was Karadžić's turn once again, that other statesman held a press conference as well: the successor of Milan Babić and then-"president" of the Krajina (the Croatian territory that was occupied by Serbs with the help of the *JNA*) Goran Hadžić who also had two of those armed guys standing straddle-legged behind him. Before he started, I asked the floor and repeated that military presence was unacceptable. Hadžić apologized and ordered his body guards to disappear immediately. And until my expulsion, I have never seen them again in the press center. In the meantime, all these cronies of Milošević have fallen into disgrace with the big chief and except Karadžić, they all have disappeared into the great nothing or ended up at the International Criminal Tribunal for the former Yugoslavia in The Hague.

CHAPTER 26

Collisions with secret services

The secret services of the Eastern Bloc countries were always especially interested in journalists. In the first place because they could reveal the real reality of the "real-existing socialism," and secondly because they thought that most journalists were collaborators of western secret services. In their own world this was very common. Quite a few eastern "colleagues" became a foreign correspondent only if they were willing to cooperate with the secret services of their home countries and more than a few, sent out as a "journalist," were a member of those services. In Belgrade as many as twenty correspondents of the Soviet Union were working: from the *Pravda*, the *Komsomolskaya Pravda*, the press agency *Novosti,* the press agency *Tass*, the Soviet television – just to mention a few. On top of that, each medium was quite often represented by two or three men. Ideologically, communist Yugoslavia was (in the mid-eighties) with its philosophy of workers' self-management a bad apple in the eyes of the Soviet Union. Not surprisingly, hardly anything on Yugoslavia appeared in the Soviet media and it certainly did not justify its twenty-some representatives. The journalist-secret service entanglement was so natural in the communist way of thinking that those regimes assumed it was the same story with us.

As the opposition in the Eastern Bloc increased, so increased the interest of the secret services in us. And the other way around: without that opposition it was not so relevant to us whether they kept an eye on us or not. The necessity for us western journalists to pay attention to this increased, as the opposition got more widespread. It also depended in which country you were, because they pursued different policies. In some of them, they only kept an eye on you, but no measures were taken against you: you were neither stopped from visiting oppositionists nor arrested afterwards. As already said before, this counted for Poland and Hungary and to a certain extent even for the Soviet Union. In Czechoslovakia, Bulgaria and Romania they tried to prevent meetings and, if unsuccessful, to catch you afterwards. In that situation, you had to try to get rid of them, at least when you wanted to come home with your material. But regardless of whether you were in "easy" or in "difficult" countries: you knew that they were *always* trying to keep an eye on you and therefore you were *always* in suspense. In this indirect sense you had constant collisions with the secret services, which sometimes had severe consequences, as we have seen in earlier chapters, but which most often blew over.

During the aforementioned trip across Eastern Europe as a prelude to the first "Helsinki-follow-up-conference" in Belgrade, I also went to Bulgaria where in its capital Sophia an international writers' conference was being held in connection with that Belgrade conference. I still was on the KGB-list and the Bulgarian embassy in The Hague had, as usual, denied me a visa. Nevertheless, I gave it a try at the Romanian-Bulgarian border. Successfully. It might have been settled by my statement that I was on my way to that international writers' conference. I don't know. It was not my usual practice to ask the generous givers in amazement, *why* they were so generous, since they actually were not allowed to give it to me. In Sophia, I reported to the press desk and got my accreditation for the conference without any problem. One day later, I was summoned by "somebody" who asked me how I acquired my visa. Apparently, he was as amazed about it as I was, but of course I acted as if I was amazed about his question. And now it went the same as at the time in Hungary: they did not dare to kick up a fuss. Initially, they were not willing to put studio space at my disposal for my transmissions and for editing my reports on the conference. But finally they gave in, because they did not want to say why they were not willing to help me and so at the end of the day they had no reason to persist in their refusal anymore.

The next collision with the Bulgarian secret service was of a more serious nature. In January 1988, the congress of the Bulgarian communist party was going to take place, and I had gotten my visa to cover it – it was after 1986! – without any problem. In those days, they were executing a rigorous Bulgarization of the Turkish minority. All Turks had to change their Turkish names into Bulgarian ones, they no longer were allowed to speak Turkish and tens of thousands had taken refuge in Turkey. There was a lot of local opposition, though, and regions where the Turks had a majority, mainly in the eastern and northeastern part of Bulgaria, were informally forbidden territory for foreigners. Formally, nothing was the matter and I had asked the press officers from the ministry of Foreign Affairs on purpose whether my visa was valid for all of Bulgaria. Officially, they did not dare to say no, so they said yes.

So covered, I went to Romania through Popovo, a nearly total Turkish town which was situated in those informally forbidden territories. A detour, that's true, but not a big one and after all, my visa was valid for all of Bulgaria. I had learned that there would be roadblocks to prevent foreigners from entering "Turkish" territories. But I drove into the small town just like that; I had not seen any roadblock. There was one (bad) hotel. I arrived in the evening toward dinner time and I decided to have a bite. The restaurant was full and I ended up sitting at a table with two girls, who were feasting on the to me well-known lemonade, the ingredients of which seem to be pure chemical poison. Over the rock-hard music of the restaurant orchestra, ever-present in Eastern Europe, I tried to enter into a conversation with the girls: they spoke Bulgarian, I Serbo-Croatian – but those languages are pretty much cognates, so you can easily manage back and forth. At a relevant question, they claimed to be Bulgarian, but they paid the bill so hastily that it was clear that they were two frightened Turks, not willing to talk to a foreigner. Absolutely legitimate, I always completely accepted those kinds of reactions. For a while, I was sitting alone at the table. I put my tape recorder on it and recorded some music "for the local color." A young man asked me whether the chair opposite me was vacant and sat down after my affirmative answer.

"Are you Bulgarian or Turkish?" I asked, after we had silently stared in front of us for a few minutes.

"Bulgarian," he answered.

"Do you speak Turkish?"

Yes, he spoke Turkish.

"Does this mean you belong to the Turkish minority?"

Yes, actually he was a Turk. We talked a little bit and carefully he let on that he was not too happy with that Bulgarization campaign. The waiter came and told him that there was a phone call for him. "That was my father," he said when he returned after a few minutes, "I have to go home." Again I sat alone. I recorded some more music (the conversation with the Bulgarian-Turk was also on the tape) and then went to my room. After about ten minutes somebody from the hotel personnel came with the request to go with him to the office of the hotel manager for just a minute. In that small office: not only the sniggering manager, but also two "gentlemen," one of them behaving absolutely rudely. Coarse, and treating me like dirt, he asks me what I am doing here. And then develops one of those absurd dancing-around-conversations. They don't want to say that there is a problem with the Turks in this town and I don't want to say that this is exactly the reason why I am there. And each side knows that the other knows it. I tell them to have been at the party congress and that I am on my way to Romania.

"Then you are making a detour."

"It seemed interesting to me to pass by this little town," I say.

"But you are not allowed to come here at all."

"I don't know anything about that, at the ministry they told me, that my visa is valid for all of Bulgaria. Just call them. Why should I not be allowed to come here?"

"Certain territories in Bulgaria are forbidden for foreigners," he yells.

When I deal with these kinds of rude characters, I always get angry on purpose. We went at it with each other, he in Bulgarian, I in Serbo-Croatian. After a while the second man, who until then had listened in silence to our loud dialogue, stepped in and said, "We are not accusing you of anything, maybe it is a misunderstanding, but we have heard that you were making interviews."

It was clear that the "father" of my table partner was, in fact, the couple which was interrogating me.

"I only recorded the music of the hotel orchestra," I say.

"May we just listen to it?" asks the rude one.

After my affirmative answer they asked me to get my cassette recorder from my room. The hotel manager accompanied me silently. When we had returned to the office, the rude one put the recorder in front of him and pushed the re-wind button, and I could only hope that he would not reel back to the part on which you could hear the Bulgarian/Turk. He stops, pushes the play button: gay music of the hotel orchestra. They are reassured. But I have to leave the town immediately for Romania. I tell them I find it irresponsible to drive that late in the evening on snowy roads. They are willing to compromise: I can stay overnight until it is light, but I must return to my room immediately and not leave it until my departure tomorrow morning: actually, I am grounded.

When I want to drive off the next morning, both my wipers turned out to be broken into three pieces. Wipers were beloved items in Eastern Europe – to steal, but never to wreck. I am sure that the couple or their friends had done it. They knew that in doing so they would handicap me heavily, because wipers were a non-available product in Eastern Europe in those years. I succeeded in remodeling the right one a little bit and by placing it to the left I got kind of a look-through-hole when it snowed. But I had a much bigger concern: could they have done something to my brakes? The first time I tried them out, I was scared to death: they did not grip. But I just happened to be driving on a piece of black ice, so there was nothing the matter. And my tape with the table con-versation was saved – and that was the most important thing.

In March 1979, the then-Dutch minister of Foreign Affairs Chris van der Klaauw paid an official visit to Romania and Bulgaria – I was part of the journalistic entourage. I had informed his spokesman Jan Willem Bertens in advance that I wanted to visit two dissidents: Pavel Nicolescu, who had set himself up as an advocate for freedom of religion, and Gheorghe Brașoveanu who had founded an independent trade union. Both of them had already been imprisoned several times.

Those official visits have the disadvantage of lasting only a day-and-a-half but the advantage that you are free during the official meetings until the fa-mous "briefings" afterwards. On the first morning, I went to Nicolescu. His parents immediately came outside when they noticed me at the gate and quickly told me that their son had already been arrested fourteen days ago. Almost immediately "somebody" rushed up, asking me for my passport and then ordering me to get into the car, which had meanwhile arrived. They interrogated me briefly at the police station and I told them exactly why I had gone to that address, that there was nothing illegal about it, and that it was in compliance with the Helsinki Agreement, also signed by Romania. An agreement, so I went on, which was one of the subjects of the conversations between their Minister of Foreign Affairs and ours who was in Bucharest right now and with whom I had traveled along. They brought me to a small room, where a soldier searched through my stuff (when he picked up the case with my *Sennheiser*-microphone, I joked, "Take care, a hand grenade" – not a very clever remark, I thought later, but now and then I could not help myself from showing my deepest disdain for those guys of the secret services). Subsequently, I had to sit down on a straight chair; the soldier went to sit on a chair at the door, his rifle between his legs. That lasted a couple of hours, in complete, total silence on both sides. Finally, I was summoned back by the mister-interrogator. "We apologize for having arrested you. But on that street there are quite often a few drug dealers operating and that's why our police are patrolling there. They thought you might be involved in dealing."

"Your service on this street is to prevent people from making contact with Nicolescu and his relatives. That's the reason you arrested me and this is absolutely in defiance of the law," I said, taking courage from the fact that he was forced onto the defensive. He did not respond and I was allowed to go.

In the afternoon I wanted to visit Braşoveanu but I thought it would not be bad if we would have a good picture of him in the West. That's why I asked Vincent Mentzel, photographer of the Dutch quality paper *Nieuwe Rotterdamse Courant* who also had made that famous picture of Patočka, whether he would like to go with me. But, rightfully, he did not think it loyal to set out professionally without his own editor Raymond van de Boogaard, also present in Bucharest. Generally, traveling with such a team, I went to oppositionists on my own because you can't drop in on them with two dozen journalists. I was also rather uncommunicative because quite a few colleagues were acting rather giggly about my interest in dissidents. I have never quite understood that, because the situation for those oppositionists was anything but humorous. Besides, I have not understood it from a professional point of view either, because even if you don't feel emotionally involved with their cause, it's still journalistically interesting to speak in a dictatorial state with the few, brave enough to dare to resist it.

But I respected Vincent's viewpoint and so the three of us proceeded to Braşoveanu. His wife answered the door and let us in, and then it turned out: Braşoveanu had also been arrested fourteen days before. It was characteristic for the situation in Romania that neither any *Helsinki Watch Group*,

Amnesty International branch nor any other human rights organization, nor any Western embassy, were aware of it, in spite of the fact that the twosome had top priority in the actions of those organizations and embassies.

We were with her for about one hour and then stumbled down the stairs. To be sure, I had put a new tape in, started the recorder and put it into my bag, with the hidden microphone stuck right between the zipper and the side of the bag. When we got outside, two men were waiting for us: we had to go in the well-known "stand-by" car with them. It was a small Dacia, the French Renault-10 built under license. They wanted to snatch away Vincent's camera, but Vincent refused to let them have it. An argument developed because Vincent gives as good as he gets, and they let him keep his camera. The three of us were squeezed on the narrow rear seat and off we went. Apparently, they were agents from outside Bucharest because they had the greatest difficulty in finding their way. A few times, we passed by the same street and only after 45 minutes we turned into a gate. I saw the driver make a too tight turn and it was, not surprisingly, with the greatest pleasure that I heard the Dacia hit the right side of the wall. Just when we climbed the stairs of the police station, I heard a click coming from the bag: my tape was used up. Inside, we were not left alone one second and unfortunately, I did not see any chance to turn the tape and restart it. Those forty five minutes, though, the arrest, our mutual conversation, our attempts to talk with the two companions and the collision with the wall, were taped crystal-clear – later on I was able to make a nice documentary out of it. Because this tape also survived the arrest.

It went just like that morning: a brief interrogation, our explanation why we were here, departure of the chief, waiting under surveillance. The guard started talking to me in Romanian in a surly tone of voice. I told him in Dutch that I did not understand him. He continued in Romanian. The conversation became heated. In Dutch I said everything bad you could imagine about the existing system in Romania and he answered me in Romanian. What you call a dialogue between two people just talking to a wall, an image of a surrealistic movie. After a while we had nothing more to argue and then, to kill the time and calm our nerves, Raymond, Vincent and I performed a kind of "role-playing" game in which Raymond played the manager of a bank to whom Vincent and I came to borrow money. The Romanian must have watched and listened in bewilderment, because Raymond showed himself to be an excellent manager who was not willing to loan money to anyone just like that, so quite some discussion was involved before we had reached that point.

To Raymond, the arrest was pretty embarrassing because it was his first trip to an East-European country and now this happened to him; and his father already had him so emphatically warned "not to associate with that Verkijk because there is always something going on with him."

Here also, we waited for hours. Finally, the local chief returned. And believe it or not: he came up with exactly the same drug story as his colleague that morning and also he apologized. I took the liberty of repeating my reply from that morning as well. He still asked whether we were willing to sign a statement that we were treated well or something to that effect, but I stated on behalf of all three of us that we categorically refused to sign any statement whatsoever. They behaved very timidly and said, "OK, you can go then."

"But how do we get to our hotel? (which was located on the outskirts of the city)," I asked. "You brought us here by car, so I think you should also bring us to our hotel with your car." Apparently, they shared this opinion, because they saw us off nicely, and had not dared to look in our bags. This explains the saving of my tape.

The very same evening, I was able to report on our current affairs radio program *Met het oog op morgen* ("With the eye on tomorrow") the arrest of the two dissidents and the next day, Raymond van de Boogaard had the story in his paper. Subsequently, five members of the Dutch parliament wrote a letter to the then president of the Romanian parliament with the request to grant Nicolescu and Brašoveanu permission to emigrate.[101] This all was of the utmost importance to them. It has been proven that by making arrests public and the subsequent actions of human rights groups, parliamentarians and government representatives, have always had a protective effect. It was not for nothing that the Romanian authorities had tried to keep those arrests secret. Many political prisoners have stated (the Soviet dissident Vladimir Bukovski personally told me so, too) that they noticed by the (positive) changed attitude of the prison guards that in some way or other, attention had been given to their case in the West.

In Bulgaria, where we arrived the next day, we got a Dutch speaking interpreter assigned to us. I had never met her, but still she was an old acquaintance: Elena Atanassova. In 1963, sixteen years before, I had visited the Atanassovs in Sofia. She was Dutch and her husband, whom she had already married before the Second World War, was a Bulgarian. He was a professor at the university but dismissed and arrested in the Stalin time. He had even been exposed to a mock execution. Well, the Dutch interpreter was their daughter, who had not been home at the time, but who did know me by name. Immediately after our arrival she took me aside for a moment and said, "Be careful. They have asked me to especially watch you, and other people will keep an eye on you

[101] Letter of June 26, 1979, of F. Bolkestein, M.P.A. van Dam, M.B. Engwirda, C.F. Kleisterlee and J.A. Mommersteeg to the "president of the Great National Assembly, Mr. Nicolae Giosan."

as well." I don't know what kind of reports circulated about me among those secret services, but I did enjoy, of course, that they overestimated my role in world events so heavily.

Once in a while, I went to Eastern Europe for fun. Acquaintances of mine in Budapest had invited me to spend Christmas with them. The visa was already in my passport. It was 1981 and the first half of December I first went with the Dutch parliamentary delegation to the Soviet Union. This meant that you have to deliver your passport at the Soviet embassy way ahead of time and you only got it back at the last minute; either with the visa stamped in it, or on a separate sheet of paper. On Sunday, December 13, we flew back from Moscow to Amsterdam. We had just learned that morning that in Poland martial law was proclaimed by Jaruzelski and his ilk which meant the end of "aboveground" *Solidarność*.

A week later I boarded the plane to Budapest. Passport check at the Budapest airport. They looked at it, looked into the big book and asked me to wait for a while. After a few minutes, some uniformed chief came up to me and stated, "Your visa is invalid, you have to return to Amsterdam." I claimed not to understand it at all (and this time my astonishment was not feigned), and that man did not know anything about it, of course, but the fact that I was a *persona non grata* did not increase his kindness toward me. The first plane would not leave until the next morning, so I still had some time to undertake some steps. In the course of the years I had built up a reasonable relationship with the Hungarian establishment and even had the private phone number of Ervin Palosi from the press department of the Hungarian Foreign Ministry. I called him and asked him to intervene, because there had to be a misunderstanding somewhere. That's what he thought as well, and he promised to call me back. He did not do so. After a few hours, I called him again and already at that point noticed from his guarded-declining phrasing that it was not about a misunderstanding but that there was really something going on here. There was no getting away from it: I had to return. I asked for permission to spend the night in the hotel at the airport, but this would mean to cross a border and that was not allowed. So I spent the night on a small bench "on this side of the border" and was back home the next day.

In 1987 for the first time I again got an "ordinary" visa on the occasion of a party event and in the Journalist's Press Club I ran into Ervin Palosi, who told me, "Don't worry, from now on you can come whenever you want."

"What was going on, anyway?" I asked.

"Don't ask. Be happy that it is behind you," he responded.

I myself have two possible solutions for this riddle. Officially, I was still on the black (KGB)-list in 1981. At the time, the Soviet Union granted me a visa because I was traveling with that parliamentary delegation, but this did not mean that the ban had been lifted. They went through my passport and saw the Hungarian visa in it. Subsequently, they let the Hungarian secret service know that they had given me a visa against instructions, and that service, in turn, ordered all border crossing points that, if Mr. So-and-so should show up there, he had to be send back immediately.

The second possible solution is connected with the proclaiming of martial law in Poland. During the time *Solidarność* was legalized, in the summer of 1981, I had exchanged telexes via the International Press Center in Budapest with Janusz Onyskiewicz, then the official spokesman of the new trade union and of Wałęsa personally. It goes without saying that this had not passed unnoticed, but there was no harm done here, because there was nothing illegal about it at all. But after December 13, *Solidarność* was all of a sudden the enemy of the state again, and Onyskiewicz had changed from top-trade-unionist into top-prisoner. And just like in Czechoslovakia at the time: my status changed right along with his. And this also could be – and then an internal-Hungarian – reason to put me back on the Hungarian black list. Personally, I think the first reason speaks more for itself than the second, but it is not that relevant, because the result was the same: another entry ban.

CHAPTER 27

Liberation – four

"The Russians are coming." That was the widely-heard opinion in December 1980, shortly after the foundation of *Solidarność*. I did not share that opinion. In 1968, the Russians knew that the Czechoslovakian army would not resist an invasion. That was precisely the reason they took the plunge. In 1980, they knew that, in contrast, the Polish army would resist. That's why they would not venture to try this time, so I reasoned. Of course, the Poles would lose that war, but even if they would be able to carry on for only one week, it would be unpredictable what the Czechoslovakian soldiers would do. Wouldn't they refuse to cooperate and if they were forced to do so, wouldn't they go over to the Poles to take on the common enemy: the Soviet Union? Without any doubt, the East-German army would take sides with the Soviet Union. But where was a conflict like that going to end? So many uncertain factors were involved and so many risks linked up with an invasion that in my opinion the Russians wouldn't take that on.[102] On top of that, to eliminate *Solidarność* and the whole movement around it, they would have to arrest thousands of people – and this I considered out of the question as well.

The Polish government had admitted the editor-in-chief of *Polityka* Rakowski as a minister and appointed him the negotiator with *Solidarność* concerning the elaboration and application of the agreements made in Gdańsk in 1980. These negotiations were not proceeding smoothly and more and more the government blamed *Solidarność* that they placed too many demands. Initially, Wałęsa negotiated on behalf of *Solidarność* on his own, but after he had made some strange concessions, he got his hand slapped by other leaders and more or less kept tabs. Gwiazda, pushed aside by Wałęsa, was designated as a co-negotiator and no decision would be taken without consulting a group of advisers just like it happened during the strike in Gdańsk. Although the top leadership of *Solidarność* did not believe in an invasion by the Soviet Union either, they

---

[102] Only recently, documents from Moscow archives reveal that Jaruzelski, then president of Poland, asked the Soviet leadership different times for intervention of the Red Army, just because he did not trust his own Polish army. The Soviets refused categorically. Finally, a desperate Jaruzelski phoned with Politburo member and party ideologue, Michail Suslov, again asking for intervention. Suslov gave a "no way"-answer – just take care yourself with it, he commented.

(Stated in a letter to the editor of the Swiss paper *Neue Zürcher Zeitung* dated June 25/26, 2005, by Cornelia I. Gerstenmaier, during the Soviet period a well-known German human rights activist.)

did let me know in the course of the summer that they seriously taking a kind of "martial law" into account, but by fall it seemed that this threat had passed.

In the meantime, the popularity of Solidarity in Eastern Europe rose at a fast pace. In the summer of 1981, I visited the Economical Institute of the Hungarian Academy of Sciences in Budapest which was working out proposals for economic reforms in Hungary. There, I spoke with the then-government's adviser Tamász Bauer: he was wearing a *Solidarność*-badge on his lapel. On the wall of his office room hung posters of Solidarity and the page of the Polish daily *Zycie Warszawy* on which the famous 21 demands of the strikers of Gdańsk were printed.

On Saturday, December 12, 1981, a party was held somewhere in Warsaw, where also minister Rakowski was present. Toward midnight, he left the cozy get-together with the excuse "that he still had something to do." A few hours later, it became clear what this was: he belonged to the group under the leadership of Jaruzelski which in the night of Saturday 12th to Sunday 13th of December proclaimed martial law. And what I thought the Russians incapable of, the Poles now did themselves: they arrested thousands of "activists" of Solidarity that very same night, among them some from the party which Rakowski left prematurely. He remained loyal to his opinion that the only solution for the Polish problems was impossible. The strikers in Gdańsk, who had not shared my positive opinion of Rakowski ("We workers hate him," they even told me), turned out to have been right.

After the "coup d'état," the government thought it was smart. They speculated on the lust for power of Wałęsa. They did arrest him, but he was lodged at a very luxurious estate where he was treated with the highest respects and provided with such a rich diet that he came out of the "prison" heavier than when he went in. Once more, Rakowski was his partner to speak to. He had come to know best the weaknesses of Wałęsa and according to me he was convinced that he could come to an agreement with him, since he was untied from the uncompromising Gwiazda and his competent advisers; an agreement in which Wałęsa would formally remain the president of a rubber-stamped Solidarity. It would legitimize the coup d'état retroactively. I feared with the greatest fear that Wałęsa would yield to the temptation, but all of a sudden he showed the unbending Wałęsa of the strike of Gdańsk again and refused to negotiate without his advisers. And he persisted in his refusal. It's my feeling that in doing so, he torpedoed the whole set up and strategy of the coup d'état: Jaruzelski and his ilk were left empty handed and completely isolated from society.

Those thousands remained "interned." Also Kuroń, Lityński and Onyszkiewicz were caught, only a few got off scot-free. One of them was Zbyczek Bujak, the president of the Warsaw branch, who would be the legendary underground leader of Solidarity for five years. Ewa Kulik happened not to be at home either when "they" came and she became Bujak's courier and direct collaborator. One time they got hold of him, but he was able to literally tear himself away, leaving his coat behind. Finally, on May 31, 1986, they were caught simultaneously but at different addresses. Ewa was surprised in the middle of the night, lying completely nude in bed with her friend Konrad Bieliński (of the underground publishing house *Nowa*). The security agents said she had to go with them, upon which she informed them she was totally naked and therefore politely asked permission to dress without their presence – a permission which was granted. In September 1982, five members of *KOR*, Kuroń, Lityński, Henryk Wujec, Adam Michnik and Jan Jozef Lipski, were indicted "for attempts to overthrow the government by force." Four of them were "promoted" from internees to prisoners; the fifth, Jan Jozef Lipski, was in London then for medical treatment, but he let them know that he would return to Warsaw – which he really did. On December 23, seven other already-interned leaders of Solidarity suffered the same fate: among them Gwiazda and Modzelewski. The next day all the other thousands of internees were released. The trials against the twelve-some were long in coming, but it seemed to get serious: they were all given their indictment in their cells and if found guilty, even the death penalty could be given.

During this period something happened that can only happen in Poland. Every Friday evening I called Lityński's wife, Krystyna, to inquire how her husband was doing. On one of those Friday evenings, June 3, 1983, a male voice answered. I heard a lot of noise in the background. For a minute, I thought that the secret police had busted in and were in the process of searching the house. So I carefully asked for Krystyna. "One moment please, there is a party going on here," the voice said in English. A party? Under these circumstances? A second later: again a male voice, who said, "Janek speaking." Lityński was at home! What happened? Lityński had a daughter from his first marriage, Barbara. That little girl, who suffered from Down's syndrome, would be baptized as a Roman Catholic. Somewhat peculiar because Janek, as well as his first wife, are of Jewish origin, but you are not a Pole, Janek explained to me some time later, if you are not baptized as a Catholic. Lityński's father who had already passed away a long time ago, had been an important figure in the communist party, and his now very active oppositionist mother still knew a number of functionaries "from former days," of course.[103] One of them was

---

[103] There still exists a film newsreel sequence in which you see Janek as a little boy presenting a bunch of flowers to the then notorious-Stalinist party secretary Bierut. During Lityński's oppositionist time, it was used a few times as propaganda against him.

Czeslaw Kiszczak, the Polish minister of the Interior in the Jaruzelski regime, the big boss of the secret service and directly responsible for all arrests and trials. She called Kiszczak, told him about Barbara's baptism and asked whether Janek could be released for a while in order to be present at the baptism. And indeed: Kiszczak said "yes": Janek got "time off" from Friday till Monday. At noon sharp he had to report back at the prison. So a *communist* minister gives a few days off to a defendant, against whom a trial is proceeding on the charge of high treason which carries the death penalty, so that he – the *Jewish* Pole – can attend the baptism of his daughter in a *Catholic* church.

That Monday morning after the Sunday's baptism, I tried at different times to call Janek at home just to say goodbye and wish him all the best. The telephone rang, no answer. At the time, Janek lived right across the street from the prison where he had to report and I continued my attempts until a quarter to twelve. Still, no answer. That very same afternoon I had to leave for Paris to cover a meeting of the council of ministers of *NATO* and in the evening visited a common friend (Mietik Grudziński, also a Pole who had been active in *Solidarność,* but who after his release in December 1982 had gotten a permission to emigrate to France) and there I learned the why of that answer-less phone ringing: Lityński had not reported at the prison at all but had made a run for it. He had gone upstairs, went over the roof to the house of the neighbors and left from there through a back exit, where a car waited which brought him to his hiding place – everything prepared by his friends of the underground-*Solidarność*. The agents of the security service, who all the time had tried to keep an eye on him, of course, had not been aware of that back exit. They never caught him again. More than that: they also never noticed that after that Krystyna and Janek went several times on vacation together. Seldom has the solidarity in Poland been so great as in the time that *Solidarność* was prohibited.

And then came Gorbachev. In Poland times changed as well. In September 1986, all prisoners were released, the trials against the fourteen (Kulik and Bujak had been added to the list after their arrest) were canceled, the people-in-hiding got amnesty.

And then came the Pope – for his second visit to his fatherland. The first time I was denied a visa, the second time, in 1987, fell in the period when also for me the tide had turned. Once more, it was such a half-half situation in Poland. Solidarity was still prohibited but actually existed and the "underground" press worked at full speed. On the eve of the Pope's departure from Warsaw to Gdańsk, the rumor went around that the most important leaders of *Solidarność* would be picked up to prevent them from going to *Solidarność*-stronghold Gdańsk – the authorities feared big anti-government demonstrations over there. That's why a lot of them did not sleep at home at night. I had another motor home at the time and Lityński spent the night with me in that motor home in front of the lion's den: the international (state) press center *Interpress* at the Plac Zwycięstwa. The next morning we picked up some other people who had spent the night elsewhere, among them Bujak and Bieliński, plus some Dutch colleagues.

Gdańsk was completely cloaked in papal yellow and white and the all-overwhelming, shimmering feeling of like-mindedness made it clear that the regime was nothing more than a formal skeleton, actually no longer recognized by any Pole. The "uncompromisingness" in 1980/81 of the Solidarity leaders in their negotiations with the communist authorities must also be viewed within this frame work. According to me, their attitude was determined by the notion that the communists had forfeited their right to place demands – apart from the question whether they were ever entitled to have that right in the first place.

How many people did the Pope attract in Gdańsk? One million? Two million? It was not about an "anti"-demonstration that would have meant too much honor for the regime. It was "pro" something else and everybody joined in, Catholic or non-Catholic.

In the evening, we continued the feast of the peaceful revolution in a smaller circle at Adam Michnik's, the Warsaw "philosopher" of Solidarity, who has a *pied-à-terre* in Sopot, a holiday resort near Gdańsk. Some of us spent what remained of the night on the floor at Michnik's and some in my motor home. The liberation was in sight *(see photo 13)*.

The break through came in 1989, when the Jaruzelski government realized that it could not go on like this. It had no other choice but to reopen the dialogue with the tough maintainers of Solidarity. And there they were sitting together at "the round table," in front of the TV-cameras. Ex-enemies, but all of them still Poles in the first place. Like Bujak and the man who chased him for years: the minister of the Interior Kiszczak. Kiszczak came smiling up to him and said, "I think I still owe you a coat." That's what I have always appreciated – that the Poles (at least the ones I have been in contact with) under all circumstances preserved their sense of humor. They agreed that after a session the main negotiators would each get exactly the same TV-time to give their comments. One evening, Kiszczak had commented, after which it was Adam Michnik's turn, a notorious stutterer. When the TV people wanted to interrupt him because his time was up, he said, "Might be, but I st-st-stutter, I need much more t-t-t-time t-t-t-to say what I want th-th-than the mi-min-minister." The Roundtable-conference resulted in a for those days far reaching compromise from the communist side: free elections would be forthcoming, but for the ordinary parliament, the *Sejm*, at least half of the seats were guaranteed to go to the communist party. For the Senate, though, everything would run according to the normal rules of a parliamentarian democracy. In those elections, held shortly afterwards, the communists got in the *Sejm* not more than the guaranteed minimum. In the Senate, a reflection of the reality, the communists did not get any of the one hundred seats available; the party was completely wiped out. The liberation of Poland was a fact. After the elections, Bieliński, Lityński and I kind of reflected a little bit and I asked them, referring to my own "feeling of emptiness" of May 5, 1945, how they felt since they had achieved what they for a quarter of a century had fought for. And, with a nod of approval from Bieliński, Lityński said with still a kind of nostalgia in his voice, "I don't want to say, that we are longing back for that time, but we do miss it."

The Poles forced and pressed open the door for the liberation of Eastern Europe; the Hungarians threw it wide open. When the Hungarian minister of Foreign Affairs Gyula Horn refused to stop the East Germans anymore at the Hungarian-Austrian border who wanted to go via Hungary and Austria to West Germany, he actually put a period behind the regime of the *DDR*. It still fought back, introducing a mandatory visa for East Germans, wanting to go to Hungary. But then the Czechs had to absorb thousands of East Germans which caused chaotic conditions at the West German embassy in Prague. An absurd compromise was reached: East Germans in Czechoslovakia were allowed to travel from Prague to West Germany through the *DDR* in locked up trains. That meant an even greater flow of East Germans into Czechoslovakia. Should the border with Czechoslovakia also be closed?

Berlin, Thursday, the ninth of November 1989. Günter Schabowski, spokesman for the *SED Politburo*, would give his daily briefing at seven o'clock in the evening. I have never been a go-and-sit-in-the-front type, but this time, for a reason I still don't know, I wanted to sit near the podium. That's why I had come extra early so I could secure the first chair to the right of the aisle in the first row.

Schabowski enters and takes a seat behind the table at the podium; to the left and right next to him a few other functionaries. He finishes off a few points and says then kind of casually, "Oh yes, the *Politburo* has just decided that from now on GDR citizens, who want to leave for the Federal Republic [of Germany] can do so, because we don't want to inconvenience our neighbors [meaning Czechoslovakia and Hungary] any longer." An exit visa is not necessary. Only those, who want to leave the GDR temporarily for a visit to a relative, have to apply for a visa, but this will be granted immediately. "Does this also apply to going from East to West Berlin?" asks a colleague on my left. Schabowski does not know the answer right away and consults his colleagues on the left and right of him for a moment. And then, as if it is the most natural thing in the world, he answers, "Yes, it applies to Berlin as well."

After 28 years The Wall is abolished in one subordinate clause. We are flabbergasted, nobody believes his ears. As quick as a wink I go to my friends in East Berlin where I am staying. The press conference was broadcasted live, but they had not been watching. They think that I misunderstood it. They turn on the radio and listen to the West Berlin radio station *RIAS*.[104] There, interviews can meanwhile be heard with East Berliners who had already made the step cross the wall. They get into the highest level of excitement and decide to go immediately with their East German *Barkas* to the checkpoint at the Oberbaum Brücke. There: oceans of people. But the passage is narrow and everybody has to show his identity papers. My friends do pass, but I am sent back, because this checkpoint is only for Germans. For foreigners there is only one: Checkpoint Charley. I go back, interview some East Berliners who for the first time in their life are going to have a peek at West Berlin. I hear cheering, shouting. And then, all at once, at a quarter to twelve the miracle happens: the enormous entry gate beside the narrow passage swings open and thousands pour into West Berlin without any checking whatsoever. I go with the stream, with a lump in my throat, microphone wide open into which an about fifty year old East Berliner shouts:*"Das verdanken wir dem Gorbatsjov* – we owe this to Gorbachev." On the West Berlin side we are welcomed by cheering West Berliners, who are greeting us as if we are returning from a barren expedition back into civilization – and for many East Berliners it really is a little bit like that.

A 35-year-old woman is already standing on the West Berlin side. She is from East Berlin and was seven years old, so she says, when the wall was built. "When I learned that you could go through the wall, I said to my husband: 'I 'm going there, it's such an historic event, I want to be there.'"She did not have the money to go any further than one meter into West Berlin territory.

"Would you like to see Kurfürstendamm [the most important entertainment center in West Berlin]?" I asked. Yes, please, she said. We went there by cab. On the Kurfürstendamm: one big people's festival. In the restaurants and snack bars the East Germans could eat and drink free of charge, the authorities gave 100 German marks to each of them, the bustle did not end. There was no day and no night, just celebration. For hours we were hanging around together, looking around everywhere, the East *Berlinerin* in continuous bewilderment. Early in the morning I brought her back, but at the checkpoint – which was literally and metaphorically again more or less under control – was still the same border guard who had sent me back earlier in the evening. "I already told you: this checkpoint is not for foreigners." The East Berlin woman went on, I

---

[104] *RIAS* is the abbreviation of *Rundfunk im Amerikanischen Sektor* – an American station, created immediately after occupation of Germany.

back. I never knew her name, I never saw her again. But I know for sure that she – in all decency – had gotten the night of her life.

With a detour via Checkpoint Charley, I finally ended up in the home of my friends. Fortunately, I had a key because they still had not returned home. It was only after three days that they surfaced, all the time they had roamed around, greedily soaking up close to choking everything what *da drüben,* over there, had to offer. The liberation of East Germany was a fact.

A few weeks later, with three liberated countries around them, even the laconic and flexible Czechoslovakians did not put up with it any longer. They take to the streets by the hundreds of thousands. That means: going to Prague's Václavské náměstí, which is packed from left to right and from up to down. On a balcony, above the building of *Svobodne Slovo,* in front of which the Soviet tanks stood in 1968 with their barrels pointed threateningly at hotel Evropa, stand this time the men and women of Charta 77. Václav Havel takes the floor and announces that Alexander Dubček, symbol of the Prague spring, is about to arrive in Prague from his hometown Bratislava. Pressed away by the crowd, I stand stuck between others in the revolving-door-opening of that very same hotel Evropa. Again after twenty years, the singer Marta Kubišová sings that moving song, which in 1968 and 1969 was the national resistance song against the invasion. For twenty years she was silenced, but her voice has not changed a bit in all those years and no tremble reveals the emotion which is no doubt present in every fibre of her body.

And then again a voice, which had been silenced for twenty years: Dubček. I saw him for the last time in November 1968, already after the invasion, cheered by thousands, when he went on foot to the National Theater in Národní street, where the 50th anniversary of the independence of Czechoslovakia was going to be celebrated. Also now, cheering people, even more than then. And also Dubček must have thought that he would never live to see this day.

That very same evening. Press conference of the Civil Forum [the name of the opposition movement] under the leadership of Havel. Next to him Dubček. In the middle of a speech by Havel somebody enters the podium and whispers something into Havel's ear. Havel interrupts his story, stands up and says, "Just now a report has come in, that the whole *Politburo* has resigned." Freely translated it means: the communists give up their rule. Gone is the objectivity of the assembled journalists. Everybody jumps up cheering, Havel and Dubček throw their arms around each other. Czechoslovakia is liberated. In the hallway I meet Jiří Hájek. Twelve years before we apologized to each other because of the inconvenience we thought we caused one another when I was picked up by the StB in front of his home. Now we congratulate each other that we had lived to see the end of the regime.

During the Jan Palach commemoration in January 1990 I would meet two other old acquaintances: the Sekerka's, back in Prague after twenty years. The three of us drink a cup of coffee – looking at the square where Jiří and I had filmed the demonstrations against the invasion in 1968. The liberation was complete.

December 1989. I am in the Netherlands for Christmas. The revolution in Romania breaks out. After the Christmas dinner, I drive straight through to Arad in Western Romania and the next day to Bucharest where the shooting is just over. The Committee for National Salvation, a kind of provisional government, gives a press conference. And who stands there as a genuine journalist, making notes? Florian Țuiu. Well, that absolutely did not go down very well with me at all. To me for years he had been the personification of the regime. Maybe it was not nice of me, but since he had the nerve to show up here, I decided to give him a good dressing down in public.

Immediately after the conference I went to him and said pretty loudly, so that everybody would understand that an incident was developing, "How dare you come here? You have defended the system through thick and thin. You don't belong here at all."

Because most of the colleagues fell within the category of "fire reporters" and therefore had no clue what it was all about, I just explained who and what Țuiu was. A whole circle gathered around us and to my utmost pleasure television cameras started running: he deserved that his humiliation would be increased to the maximum.

"I don't understand, I have saved his life," he defended himself, with a kind of helpless look at the gathered colleagues – and he referred to that trip when we had to spend the night in a jeep during a blizzard. As if I owed him the running engine which kept us kind of warm.

"What about saving my life! You told me that I was *persona non grata* in Romania, because I was said to have insulted Ceaușescu."

"How could I have acted otherwise? The microphones were fixed under my table."

"You very well could have acted differently. Nobody forced you to become a journalist. That was an absolutely voluntary decision. You knew by doing so you had to defend the regime. You took advantages of the regime and you definitely don't belong here. You better disappear." And off he slunk, with his tail between his legs, stared after by the TV cameras. Off, forever, I thought. Wrong. He not only remained in his position, he was even promoted at the legal successor of *Agerpress*. There are no two ways about it that he was not only an informer but a high-ranking member of the *Securitate*. It makes me feel skeptical about the whole process of renewal in Romania, that such a seasoned Ceauşescu-zealot could come through the change of power more than unharmed, even more so because the Țuiu case was not unique. Romania is liberated also, but still a little bit between quotation marks.

A few days later we are permitted to look around in Ceauşescu's residence in Bucharest. It's a chaos there: books all over the floor, newspapers here and there. On a table stands a set of books, neatly bound according to year. It contains all the interviews ever given by Ceauşescu. Quickly I grasp the part which reads: 1975. I leaf through it and darned, there it is, on page so-and-so: interview with (my name follows) of NOS-radio and television. I put it back neatly. Looking back I regret I did not take it along as a souvenir, because those books ended up in the trash can for sure – "on the rubbish heap of history," like the communists so nicely used to express it, when they wanted to indicate the place where, according to them, party members belonged who had broken with communism.

CHAPTER 28

The Soviet Union of Gorbachev

I have used my re-issued permission to enter the Soviet Union with great greediness: I went there in 1986, 1987 (two times), 1988 and 1989, in the beginning by plane, later with my motor home. It was a wonderful, confusing period. The old Soviet-secrecy was still freewheeling, the new openness fell as a shadow cast over it. From the very first moment Gorbachev took office, I had the feeling: something new was coming up. Just like in January/February of 1968, when the signals from Prague were hardly picked up, so it seemed to now go the same way with Gorbachev. My first attempts to break through that barrier sometimes surprised my home editorial staff.[105] "You were always such an anticommunist, and now, all of a sudden, you are a fellow traveler," one of my bosses told me once, and I could not convince him that *they* not *I* had changed.

My acquaintances and friends in Moscow did not share my opinion either. Sakharov was still in exile and dissidents were still persecuted – one of the most evil "freewheeling phenomena." Sakharov had a wide circle of followers who were like-minded although they did not say so openly. The ideas of the dissidents were generally accepted within that circle of scientists, at universities and among students, and they agreed that the Soviet system had gotten completely stuck. During the party congress of 1986, a friend of Valentin Turchin, who in the meantime had been expelled, asked me to give my thoughts about the developments in the Soviet Union. Another ten or twelve people were present, all scientists and friends of Turchin and Sakharov. They found it very peculiar that a journalist came all the way from abroad for a congress of the communist party – which was ignored by them. I tried to convince them that Gorbachev really wanted something different. But they contradicted me, "It's the same old story. Every new party leader starts with announcing reforms, but when he has established his power, he reverts to the old patterns." My argument that this time it really would make a difference was met with great skepticism. One of the participants of the discussion formulated in a monumental way his skepticism and at the same time his hope, "I will only believe in Gorbachev when the only reason I can't travel abroad is, that I do not have the money to do so."

---

[105] See appendix page 378.

Yet, the signals were unmistakable. In the winter of 1987 I was in Vilnius, the capital of "The Soviet Republic of Lithuania" – one of the Baltic states which had been previously hardly accessible. I was allowed to use the studio of Radio Lithuania for a live broadcast for the *NOS*. "You are the first Western journalist who got permission to broadcast through us," said the extremely delighted local editor assisting me – it was for him a sign, too, that something new was in the making. He openly declared himself in favor of the independence of Lithuania. I still traveled by plane then, but in 1988 I got permission to travel with my motor home from Moscow via Leningrad to Estonia and Latvia – and back. A Russian couple with whom I had become friends, coming from the circle of the Sakharov-minded, traveled with me ("Two years ago, this would have been impossible," they said) and everywhere we camped for free: in downtown Leningrad on a side street of Newski Prospekt, in the Estonian capital Tallinn just outside the town on a parking lot; in the Latvian capital Riga somewhere in the middle of the town.

"The police don't know what to do with us," explained my Russian friends, "formerly everything was forbidden which was not explicitly allowed; now Gorbachev has said that everything is allowed which is not explicitly forbidden. And nothing is mentioned about camping – so they let us stay."

In Tallinn, on the 18th of June 1988, I have experienced the first big demonstration of 150,000 people for independence in a big stadium, where communists and noncommunist alike pleaded for that independence. For the first time, dozens of, then still actually strict forbidden Estonian flags, were waved – God knows from where these suddenly cropped up, but they were not improvised, home made flags which first had to be cooked in paint. I smelled the Prague Spring in Tallinn *(see photo 27)*. In Riga: the same atmosphere. At their radio station I was received like an old friend although I did not know anybody there. A co-worker took us to his home, some fifty miles east of Riga, in the direction of Moscow, but not via the main road. Nobody cared that I was not allowed to go there at all – neither did the policeman at a checkpoint on our way. It just had been "Midsummer night" which is exuberantly celebrated over there with a lot of drinks and food around a big campfire. Actually, that celebration falls on the 21st, but because the son of the house – the colleague of the Latvian radio station – only came home on the weekends, they postponed it to Friday evening the 24th. We spent the night in my motor home in front of the house and through all kinds of side roads we ended up again on the Riga-Moscow "free way" the next day. On our way I took a side road for a while to have a look at the town of Velikiye Luki – a name engraved in my memory because it was there that Marshall Timoshenko dealt the first blows to the Germans in 1941.

My Russian friends said they were ashamed of what the Russians had brought about in the Baltic states as occupiers and they actually did not want to speak Russian in order not to irritate the people. It's just like with the good Germans, it's mostly the wrong ones who are ashamed.

Only sixty more miles to Moscow. There would be the start of the real four-lane freeway, which would bring us to Moscow in one and a half hour. We were not yet driving 100 yards on it, when we were pulled over and subsequently stopped by a police car. The officers said that this freeway was prohibited for foreigners and that we had to do an about-turn, and take the old road to Moscow. Ten miles down the street: a permanent police check point. Here the new *glasnost*, openness, was again superseded by freewheeling tomfoolery, because we were not allowed to go on. We were on a forbidden road. I thought they were referring to the road ahead of us, but this turned out to be based on my western logic. The road we *came* from was forbidden.

"But I have permission to go to Leningrad, Tallinn and Riga by car, just look at my visa," I let the officer know through my Russian friend.

He looked and said, "There it says you are allowed to go to Leningrad, Tallinn and Riga, but in your visa is no mention of Moscow."

"But you can see that I got that visa in Moscow and how for Pete's sake can I go by car to all those cities without using the roads to and from Moscow?" I defended myself. But this logic was lost on him. His solution was even more il-logical. I had to go back and then in Velikiye Luki (this was already 150 miles) turn in a northeasterly direction until I would hit the Leningrad-Moscow road, and from there I could return to Moscow: all in all some 300 miles. Because I had driven on a, in his eyes, strictly forbidden road, I had to drive 150 miles back on the very same strictly forbidden road. Maps were not available in the Soviet Union in those days but I had bought some good ones in the Dutch equivalent of a triple-A shop. When the officer was alone with my Russian friend for a moment, he whispered, "How can he have taken this road, because it's even not on the map" – meaning, of course, their own, by the way unavail-able, map. But returning was no option. I just had enough diesel to reach Moscow, but not to make a detour of another 300 miles – and diesel and gas were only available on coupons through an utmost complicated system that I could not make an appeal for at a distance of 50 miles from Moscow. That's why I announced to the officer that I would stay camping on the spot until they would let me pass. And then, the new openness broke through a little.

"If the KGB in Moscow agrees that you may pass, then it is OK with me, too," said the officer. But we had to take care of that ourselves and he would wait until he was called by the KGB about it. And he not only gave us the num-ber of his station, but of the appropriate department of the KGB in Moscow as well. From a technical-telephony point of view, we were already in the Moscow district and the post office was opposite the police checkpoint. But the window-woman was not willing to help us, she was only there for long distance calls; local calls should be made via the phone booth outside in front of the door. But, as was to be expected, it turned out to be out of order. Back to the post office. Of course, she knew that the booth was not working (it had been already like that for months) but the bureaucratic rules were complied with and now she was willing to help us. Although it was Saturday afternoon, I was able to reach somebody from the Dutch embassy who would try to call the KGB. We had to call him back a couple of times, because he had not yet found the right person at the appropriate department of the KGB. And every time the lady from the post office said that we had to use the phone booth and every time we told her patiently that it was out of order. Finally, the situation-saving statement of the embassy man: the *KGB* would call the officer and tell him to let us through. He only took note of our message; he had not heard anything yet. But after about a half hour: yes indeed, the phone call had come in, we were allowed to drive on. We raced and arrived just in time there on the 25th of June to watch the final of the European soccer championship between the Soviet Union and the Netherlands. Given their political views, my friends were in favor of the Netherlands. "We" won with 2-0 – and after the game there were three delighted viewers in that Moscow living room.

By a miraculous coincidence, in the spring of 1987 I met Tatyana Velikanova – she was the mother-in-law of one of my best friends. Velikanova was a close collaborator of Sakharov and had been co-producer of the at the time very respectable quality underground publication "Chronicle of Current Affairs." Because of this, she had been arrested in 1979 and sentenced to four years concentration camp and five years in exile. Formally, exiles were entitled to a leave if one of their closest relatives was seriously ill, but in practice it had never been allowed. As a matter of routine, she had applied for a leave because her sister had cancer and was in the terminal phase. To her amazement, she did get it; already here also the change was noticeable in the early stages of Gorbachev's administration. Exactly during that period of leave I was in Moscow, too, and I talked with her about the new man in Moscow. She was very positive about him. "The Soviet Union is lacking in awareness of justice. With the arrival of Gorbachev our people are offered the last chance to make themselves familiar with that awareness of justice."

"So you do believe that Gorbachev is an honest man?" I asked, which was more intended as a remark than as a question.

"Of course not, if he would have been an honest man, he never would have become the secretary general of the party." And in a certain sense she was right. If he ever would have shown openly what he wanted to change in the

Soviet Union and how far he wanted to go with this, they never would have elected him. So he had to hide his opinions – and in this sense he had not been honest.

Once, I had called this the Šik-method.

Ota Šik was the minister of Economic Affairs in Czechoslovakia in the Dubček era and a far-going reformer. Immediately after the invasion of 1968, he went into exile in Switzerland where he told me a year later that he already had in essence broken with the old form of communism back in 1952.

"I was convinced at the time that the trials against Slánský, Šling and the others were show trials and that the defendants were innocent. So I had two options: either leave the party – then I would have been put on the sidelines. I opted for the second: to remain a party member, but not openly show my doubts. Carefully, very carefully, I could trace some allies. We contacted the writers and asked them to become more critical to which we in turn could connect.[106] We pleaded in the first place for economic reforms, as if we were striving to improve the system, but we knew – and that was our real goal – that it would also lead to political reforms. And we reached that goal in 1968."

That was one of those perverse, dialectical sides of the so-called communism: you had to lie to let the truth triumph. According to me, Gorbachev applied the Šik-method. Personally, I considered the process irreversible when Gorbachev permitted Sakharov to return from exile. Shortly before, Anatoli Marchenko had died, who despite persistent campaigns by international human rights movements had not been released. I never had the opportunity to ask him this, but I believe that this tragedy was the breaking point for Gorbachev and also gave him the tool to put an end to the persecution of people thinking otherwise. Immediately after I had heard the news on the radio that the exile had been lifted, I wrote spontaneously in the daily *Het Vrije Volk* that in the Soviet Union from now on two dates would be considered historic: November 7, 1917 – October Revolution, and December 19, 1986 – Sakharov back to Moscow – not realizing that *both* dates would vanish from the Russian history books.[107]

---

[106] German was the official language in Czechoslovakia during the hundreds of years (from the 16th century until 1918) when it was a part of the Hapsburg Empire. Czech and Slovak were not prohibited and the writers published their books in their own language. In this way, a piece of national self-esteem was preserved. Besides, they often dealt with themes directed against the supremacy of the Hapsburger by which writers ended up in prison and at the same time a great solidarity between writers and readers developed. So, writers playing a political role had a long-lasting tradition in Czechoslovakia which continued also in the communist era.

[107] See appendix page 379.

Outside Moscow, traveling by car was still a thrilling adventure because you never knew whether you would make it to the next gas station – and whether they would accept your coupons there because it was not possible to pay in cash. Tourists could buy coupons at the state travel agency *Inturist*. Theoretically. When I wanted to buy them in Moscow, a female worker said laconically, "We have already sold out our allocation for this month." The plan was accomplished, they did not get more coupons. Via-via I learned that a gas station 15 miles outside Moscow sold coupons. There I bought enough of them for the trip to the Baltic states. On the back of the coupons there were at least five or six stamps; for the layman, even for a Russian-speaking one, an incomprehensible crisscross of announcements. At some stations, coupons were refused because there was something wrong on the back. Others did accept them, though. On the last stretch from Moscow to the Hungarian border I had just enough coupons to make it to Hungary. When I wanted to fill up, my coupons were weighed and found wanting. With the last gallons I made it to the next station. I handed over my coupons and was about to fill up at the pump, when I was angrily summoned to return immediately to the small station office. Apparently, according to him, I had the wrong stamps and I was sent away as if I had attempted fraud. But something of the new spirit had started to blow among the ordinary people as well (in the meantime long blown away again). A truck driver asked me what my problem was and I explained it to him.

"You will get some from us (they were with a whole convoy)," he said, but not here – it had to be out of sight of the gas-station-boss because otherwise he would catch the driver red-handed stealing state property, and me receiving it. "Just follow us, we'll stop somewhere down the road and then we'll siphon some over. A few miles onwards, the whole convoy stops along the narrow road, blocking half of it. They suck up the diesel with a small hose and siphon it over into my two 3-gallon-cans which in turn I can empty into my tank: I am saved. They don't want anything in return, but I give them a tin with ham I still have somewhere in my car. Not much indeed, but I don't have anything else.

I arrive at the border. The Russian border guard, one mass of kindness, takes my passport inside to stamp it. After a few minutes, he returns and says, "Happy belated birthday" – he had noticed in my passport that it had been my birthday the day before. The *perestrojka* had now also struck at the human level.

CHAPTER 29

Serbian hassles

With regard to journalism, around the turn of the year 1989/1990, a kind of sluggish satisfaction descended over me. Contrary to some other colleagues, I had no feelings of regret whatsoever that my "work territory" had been lost, but only feelings of joy that the communist regimes had collapsed. I kept on going to those countries at different times to cover the first free elections, and despite all problems and obstacles the freedom had returned there or had been established. Fundamentally, there was not too much difference with the democratic countries anymore, but it did exist in the translation of the new freedom into practice. Journalistically, this was interesting of course, but I still was kind of surprised about the flow of foreign correspondents, specifically in Prague, *after* the revolutions over there. During the communist period when, in my eyes, it was much more important to ferret out the real news, hardly anybody was there – now that it was less necessary, they were flooded with correspondents. "Why don't you become a correspondent in Bern?" I sometimes teasingly asked such a new Eastern-Europe-rookie.

In 1984 I had opted for Belgrade as a base to get easier access to Eastern Europe. Yugoslavia itself played a minor role in my reporting. But under the influence of the collapse of all those communist regimes, the Yugoslav communists started to reflect as well on: how to go on? On Belgrade television there were interesting debates to watch and to listen to, in which there was much criticism going on, and I had the idea that Yugoslavia also was shifting in the direction of "democratization." It seemed fascinating to me, to now concentrate somewhat more on the developments in my country of residence and to leave Eastern Europe Eastern Europe. It seemed to me a quiet conclusion of my journalistic career. Little could I know that the most turbulent years of my career were still ahead of me. Despite threatening words, I never expected the Yugoslavs to go at each other. Since 1955, I had visited Yugoslavia very frequently, had already lived there for five years and had the impression that the vast majority felt like a "Yugoslav." There were some mutual feelings of rivalry, especially between Croats and Serbs, but I always thought it was still in the spirit of a football game. Besides, the various republics had a great deal of independence. Formally, Yugoslavia was called a federation, actually it was a confederation, and there was no objective reason to be at each others' throats.

It started going wrong in 1987 when the local Belgrade party functionary Slobodan Milošević in a coup d'état-like way put the moderate then-party leader of Serbia Ivan Stambolić on the sidelines. Milošević seized upon the "problem" of Kosovo to get rid of him. Stambolić acted "much too weak" against the Albanians who constituted 90% of the population and "mistreated," "chased away" and "raped" the Serbs there. It's true, it was not that easy for the Serbs over there and their position was indeed capable of improvement, but after Milošević's take over, the anti-Albanian propaganda machinery cranked up to full speed – a taste for what was in store for us in the nineties. Already then, Milošević was beating the nationalistic drum. Somewhat peculiar for a communist party, especially for the one in Yugoslavia. For dozens of years the slightest utterance of "nationalism" carried the heaviest punishment and the seasoned communist Milošević had maintained this policy. But for Milošević only two things mattered: 1. How do I *come* to power and 2. How do I *remain* in power. He was an utmost sly politician with an unfailing intuition for how and when to create circumstances in which those two conditions can be fulfilled. He succeeded in doing this for as many as thirteen years until even he made his fatal error to commit election fraud too obviously, which brought him down in the fall of 2000.

In my opinion he did not give a hoot for the Serbians in Kosovo and his fight for their cause was only a means in his strife for power. It was clear that he who wanted to exercise power in Yugoslavia could not come forward with communist slogans any longer – they were out of date. Milošević looked for and found the way to power in nationalism. He knew that he, by doing so, could build up a new kind of ideology, on which his power could rest. A good friend of mine, an absolute opponent of communism, told me at the time, "We are in an identity crisis now since communism has ceased. Even for me, an opponent of that system, it still was the frame of reference within which I was functioning. Now nothing is left at all." Milošević has skillfully taken advantage of that feeling of emptiness. There was one event which made my strong objections against this person as a political leader turn into absolute rejection. In the spring of 1989 a big protest meeting was held in Belgrade of at least a million Serbians against the "mistreatment" of their fellow nationals and against the "separatists" in Kosovo. The party leader there was Azem Vllasi, an Albanian, a loyal communist, and in no way an advocate of a secession of Kosovo from Yugoslavia. Shortly before, there had been a miners' strike of Albanians in Kosovo against the dissolution of the legally elected parliament of Kosovo. Vllasi was under "suspicion" of having organized the strike. Firstly, he had not done it and secondly, even in the times of Tito-Yugoslavia this had not been a crime. But Vllasi was an Albanian and a scapegoat had to be found. At the time, Milošević was only the party leader of Serbia, he had no government's or judicial function whatsoever. Milošević took the floor. He referred to the numerous rapes in Kosovo (in fact, the rate of rapes in Kosovo was below the average for all of Yugoslavia according to the official statistics) and in this context had the nerve to promise "that the Serbian children would be able to go to school unharmed again" – suggesting that "the" Albanians were child-rapists. After this scandalous suggestion, something inaudible was yelled from the audience. Also Milošević acted like he had heard only part of it, because he said, "I did not hear exactly what you said, but if you are referring to the leaders of the strike, I guarantee you that they will be arrested – so it is and no other way." A party leader, guaranteeing arrests. Nobody had really gone to town on this since Stalin. And he had the power to keep his word: a week later Vllasi was arrested. The show trial against him, which started in November 1989, did not lead anywhere; even for Milošević it was a bridge too far. Under great international pressure, the judges had no other choice but to let only the facts count: in April 1990 Vllasi was acquitted. By then, he had already been innocently in custody for a year and put on the sidelines as a politician.

Another crisis was caused by the totally different views between the leaders of Slovenia and Serbia. The Slovenians were democratizing in step with the developments in the rest of Eastern Europe; the Serbians under the leadership of Milošević held on to the old, authoritarian patterns. When the Slovenians saw how Milošević "solved" the Kosovo problem, namely with the help of federal institutions (e.g. the Yugoslavian People's Army), they were getting worried about the possibility that Milošević would solve the "Slovenia problem" by the same means – and they hastily passed laws in which it was laid down that federal institutions were not allowed to interfere in the internal affairs of the republic (Slovenia). And Milošević in turn considered this to be in defiance with the federal constitution – and therefore illegal. Verbally, the gloves were taken off, but I still did not see it resulting in armed conflicts. The "home front" asked me regularly during broadcasts, "Will the army take over power in Yugoslavia?" And every time I responded, "Things here are never as bad as they look." I was badly mistaken about this: things would get tremendously worse.

The story is well-known (and in this book already partly referred to): *de facto*, the *JNA* – that means: the central government in Belgrade – took sides with the "rebellious" Serbs in Croatia in 1991. But it sometimes seems to be forgotten that this war was not popular at all. Desertion (among the Serbian conscripts) was enormous and many Serbians of conscription age went into hiding or at least took care not to be home during the night; they warned each other openly when rumors flew around anew that the military police were going on a raid.

All of a sudden I was bombarded from a contemplative correspondent into a war reporter. I did not look for the war, the war looked for me. Because I thought it kind of childish, since I was a correspondent in Belgrade, to stay at home and quietly ignore the essential events in that country: the war-acts.

I always received excellent logistical and moral support from my direct radio-colleagues in the Netherlands. I was at the time a staff member of *NOS*-radio, but the managerial twosome, the big bosses of the station, were not hyperactive in keeping in touch with me. After having already been in situations at different times which would have been more pleasant, had I been the owner of a bulletproof vest, I asked one of the managers, Henk van Hoorn, by phone during a short stay in Holland in December of 1990, to provide me with a something like that. He hesitated and said he would think about it. That thinking resulted the next day in his reasoning, "You don't get a bulletproof vest, because we absolutely don't want you, ever, to go into situations in which such a vest is necessary." My objection that he was liberally late with this announcement, because I already had repeatedly been in situations like that, which he apparently had failed to notice, did not make any impression: I did not get a vest. Subsequently, I phoned somebody in the management of *NOS*-television, and they took care that a vest was delivered the very same day.

It's not completely true that I never heard anything from the *NOS* supreme beings: I have to make one exception. That had to do with my expense claim. It was agreed, because the mail connections between Yugoslavia and Holland were not functioning optimally, especially in a war time, that I would personally carry my expense claims with bills, receipts etc. each time I would come to Holland to prevent the danger of getting things lost. Due to the demanding activities, I did not return until August 1991, so I carried eight months of expense claims with me – a shoe box full. It looked very complicated because due to the galloping inflation of the dinar, I had not been able to do one dinar-to-guilder calculation. At the end of September, I had experienced the execution of the four Croats in Tovarnik. After that, I had immediately left for my apartment in Montenegro, because six miles from my home, the Yugoslavian People's Army had started its offensive toward Dubrovnik, where I very soon after ended up in a shooting party during a cease fire. One day, when I returned home from such a trip to the war theater, I found a big parcel, sent by the *NOS*. It was the shoe box with my claims and an angry letter from Van Hoorn asking whether I had no respect for the colleagues of the accounting department by giving them a whole shoe box full of my claims. On top of that, I had done something wrong with the "green form" (on which you had to fill out the total amount of your claims). Whether I would be so kind to correct it. Of course, I was extremely delighted with this letter, because it proved that my highest bosses in Holland had not forgotten about me. Unfortunately, it would remain the only oral or written sign of life from them in all those four war years I spent in Yugoslavia. But better something than nothing.

A few times, I ran into serious collisions with the Serb *soldateska*. In March/April 1993, *NOS*-TV asked me to accompany their team under the leadership of Gerri Eickhof for a report on *Republika Srpska*, the part of Bosnia which was in Serb hands *(see photo 19)*. We properly had all our permits, we had done interviews at the Serb headquarters in Pale and had everything arranged quite officially. On our way back, we were stopped at the routine checkpoint in Sokolac (one of the military headquarters of the Serbs). We were not allowed to drive on right away. After half an hour, a second controller showed up. Also he checked all our documents and also he said we had to wait a little while yet. Subsequently, a car of the military police popped up and the crew ordered us to follow them. They brought us to a military post and we were left behind there under surveillance without any explanation. When after a while I had to go to the bathroom, I did not get permission. After some urging, our guard went for somebody else and under his supervision I was allowed to do what I urgently needed to do. After a while, some commander showed up, starting to ask me questions. He assumed that I was the leader of the team, because I was the only one speaking Serbian. I drew his attention to the fact that Gerri was the boss – and he seemed surprised by it.

"Are you telling me that this black one is Dutch?" he asked.

"Have you ever heard of Gullit?" I asked.

He nodded in the affirmative.

"And of Rijkaard?"

Again, he nodded.

"They are Dutch, aren't they?"

For the third time he had to say "yes."

"Well – so he is Dutch as well," I said, pointing at Gerri.[108]

We were there for about three hours without any interrogation or explanation whatsoever. Then, a man in plain clothes and a few soldiers entered who said they wanted to check the car. The cameraman, anxious about his stuff, did not like the idea at all. As tactical as possible, I tried to explain his refusal, but

---

[108] Gerri has a white mother and a black father and because of this his skin is slightly darker than that of a Caucasian. Gullit and Rijkaard (I pronounced their names with a Serbian accent) were in those days internationally famous players on the Dutch national soccer team and household names in Yugoslavia as well. Both of them are Dutch but of Surinam origin and much blacker than Gerri is. Serbo-Croatian for "black" is *crni* (adjective) or *crnac* (noun) and it's very often pronounced with a disparaging undertone. It is also often used in a disdainful way to refer to a Roma: *ovaj crnac* – that black one. Our guard also said it with this disparaging undertone.

they thought that I was unwilling. They grabbed me by the collar, kicked my behind and my ankle and took me along to the TV-jeep.

"I have no key," I shouted, "because it's not my car at all." I was transported back in the same stern way. Meanwhile, a translator had arrived, and now the cameraman had to go with the Serbs, including the female civilian translator as a reassuring companion. After a while, we were also summoned to come to the car to open up our personal luggage.

"Hey Dick (he did not say "*gospodin* Dick," "Mister Dick," and his way of addressing was by Yugoslavian standards extremely impolite), open up your suitcase," said the soldier who had kicked me.

"How did you find out my name?" I asked.

"I have known your name since January," he answered. And then a bell rang. In January that *KRO*-tv show had been repeated by Belgrade television, I was apparently in the *Republika Srpska* pointed out as an "enemy" and that was the reason we were stopped and detained. Consultations with Pale had apparently resulted in letting us go after checking.[109] Meanwhile, it had gotten dark and we were only a quarter of the way from Pale to Zvornik, the border with (Small)Yugoslavia. It was too risky to drive on and there was nothing else left to do but to return to Pale. The Head of the Department for Information of the rulers in Pale was Sonja Karadžić, the daughter of Radovan. She always looks extravagant: long bangs into her eyes, a big black, wide-rimmed hat on the back of her head and she is, to put it mildly, a little on the sturdy side – I had baptized her Miss Piggy, but I must admit I never approached her as such. Often, she was impossible, occupying the only phone which had a good connection with the outside world for dozens of minutes for long-winded private conversations, while journalists, bursting with impatience, were waiting to get unloading their news. But for some reason or other, she liked me (maybe because I once had given her an effective Dutch pain killer when she suffered a headache, or maybe because I was a generation older than most of my colleagues), so from time to time I got something out of her. That's why I asked her why we had been detained. She said it had been a misunderstanding and that I could return whenever I wanted. And sure enough, after that I was never refused a permit, but just to be sure, I never went to Serb-Bosnia alone anymore.

After my return to Belgrade I told the story to what I considered a good-natured-well disposed-toward-me though very nationalistic Serb, who used to work as an interpreter for foreign teams. She had pretty good connections in

[109] Unlike English, most languages differentiate between the "polite" form of "you" and the familiar form, used between friends, which turns "impolite" when you don't know each other. So it is in Serbo-Croatian; respectively *vi* and *ti*. The soldier used the "impolite" form *ti* toward me, I stubbornly continued to use *vi* towards him.

nationalistic circles and warned me the next day by phone that it would be "life-threatening" for me to go to Serb-Bosnia or to the Serb part of Croatia, because I was blacklisted. I did not see it that black myself and I told the Dutch TV-team (which also wanted to go to that Serb part of Croatia) that I personally did not see any problem in going with them, but at the same time would find it unpleasant for them if they would run into troubles because of me. The TV team thought it better to take a different translator – an absolutely legitimate decision.

Yet, a few months later I went with a *KRO*-TV-team to that part of Croatia. We entered in the North near Erdut, because a group of Dutch "blue-helmets" was stationed there. In spite of a ban by the Serb militia, the cameraman had taken some shots on the bridge over the border river Danube – and they had noticed it. We were stopped and brought to their headquarters, in Erdut as well. At the inner court they were busy with a paint sprayer to conjure a green army tank into a blue police tank: an agreement had just been signed in which the whole region would be demilitarized; only a small police force was permitted – that explained the spraying. A farce, as the whole agreement would be a farce because the Serbs did not give a dime for agreements – and for which they paid in 1995 dearly: lose it all. In the headquarters were five or six men. One of them asked what our nationality was.

"Dutch," I answered.

"Half of the Dutch are fascists," he sneered.

Well, this is something you should never say to me. Then I'm not playing angry but really angry. I made it extremely clear to him that I did not accept his accusation and I demanded his apology, because I don't allow anybody to call me a fascist. Of course he refused, despite my repeated demands. I gave up after I noticed that the *KRO* colleagues were getting worried about the furiousness of our dialogue. An officer asked the cameraman to hand in the videotape, but he had managed to change the used tape for a cleaning-tape. Fortunately, they had no video recorder on hand to check it. We were ordered to leave their territory immediately (about which they formally had no say whatsoever, because the supervision over it had been taken over by the United Nations). What's interesting is that the militiamen accompanied us beyond the bridge into (Small)Yugoslavian territory and there they stopped us anew, asking where we were heading for. I told him that this was absolutely none of his business and that I was allowed in Yugoslavia ("It's a free country here," I said optimistically) to go wherever I wanted to go. He got angry and said I should not dare to come into their territory again (meaning the part of Croatia which was in their hands), because then I would be arrested.

We drove back to Belgrade, got a new permit for the Serb/Croatian territory from the Federal Ministry of Defense (which, by the way, illustrates nicely how the real situation was in those days) and we re-entered the territory from the south – via Tovarnik where I always gasp for breath when I pass by the spot where that frightened tiny bird summarily executed the four Croats.

In Vukovar we asked and got company from the United Nations *(see photo 26)*. A Canadian UN-jeep drove ahead of us to Erdut, exactly past the check-point where a day earlier we experienced that incident. The Serb militiamen did recognize us immediately but did not dare take any action against us since we were heading for a UN-post under UN-escort.

Sarajevo, June 1992. We drive from downtown to the airport. The road leading to it is under UN supervision. Next to me sits a Sarajevo-er, a Moslem, who kind of familiarizes us with the town. On the rear seat Veronique Pasquiers of the Swiss paper *24 Heures*. Then halfway down, horror: in defiance of all agreements, at the to-be-abandoned former Serb check point stands an armed Serb nonetheless. He stops us. We are not allowed to proceed to the airport, but have to pick up a permit at the Serb commander in Ilidža. Ilidža is a district of Sarajevo, which is in Serb hands. Well, now this spot is really life threatening for our Moslem friend. I tell the Serb that we are not interested anymore in going to the airport and that we will go back. He does not allow us to do so and asks for our documents. What can you do in such a case? Make a U-turn and drive off? Before I have a chance to turn my nearly 20 feet-long Chevy-truck on the narrow road, he would have at least shot out my tires. So we showed our papers, the Moslem his. The militia man looks at it without expression and sends us on the way to Ilidža. Five to six other cars with journalists are parked in front of the police station. A militiaman tells us to wait. It turns out that our Moslem guide is carrying his ID of the Territorial Forces, the Bosnian army, as to the Serbs the hostile army. We put it in Veronique's handbag. Our guide looks deathly pale. I guarantee him, two, three times with strong emphasis that I absolutely will not leave without him, no matter what happens. We agree that, in case our passenger is detained, Veronique will return to warn the UN-authorities. The waiting lasts forever, papers are not requested. After one-and-a-half-hours a militia man walks by all the cars and hands over an already signed permit. "Just fill in the license plate number of your car," he says kindly, "and glue it to your windshield." That is the whole permit. We leave the Serb territory. When we have returned on safe soil, our friend sighs, "I'm born for the second time."

Spring 1994. Anew, I opted for Montenegro as a domicile. In the context of an agreement between (Small)Yugoslavia and Croatia under the auspices of the UN, the Yugoslavs have withdrawn from Southern Croatia and restored it to Croatia with the exception of a narrow peninsula (Prevlaka that remained under UN supervision). The agreement even included limited border traffic between both territories. It would be getting too far off the subject to explain the complications to obtain that permit – but I got it. So I was able, like in the older days, to drive from my home to Dubrovnik, a distance of 50 miles. Upon crossing the border, the Montenegran border guards asked me when I was planning to return.

"I guess Wednesday, but it might be one day later." In Dubrovnik I learned that just then the road to Mostar was released after the cease fire agreement between the Croats and the Moslems over there – and I drove off to it. The UN headquarters was just before Mostar. From there you could be brought to the Moslem part of Mostar by a small UN armored car (a so-called APC). The world is small: one of my co-passengers was Mient Jan Faber, the famous leader of the Peace Movement of the seventies and eighties. The devastation of Mostar was tremendous and has already been sufficiently described elsewhere. I knew the city very well from former days and was back for the first time since the war. What the Croats have been up to there is a war crime as well. They know, for instance, exactly which barbarians shot the world-famous bridge to pieces. Once, they ought to account of it.

The trip to Mostar did mean that I indeed was not back at the border until Thursday. The Croats did let me pass, I stood before the barrier of (Small)Yugoslavia. Still, a good quarter of an hour and I would be home. The border guard returns with my passport and says, "You have to go back and enter Yugoslavia via Hungary."

"I got permission from your commander," I said, "just call him" (It had been an oral permission, I had nothing on paper). That's what he did. He came back and said, "You are one day late, you should have crossed the border here yesterday." I was flabbergasted. I put my arm around his shoulder and pointed a peninsula out to him, not even six miles away as the crow flies.

"There, on that peninsula, is my home. It is just pure madness to have me drive back via Hungary."

He did not want to deny that, but still could not do anything about it.

"Nobody told me that there was a time limit connected to that permit," I continued, "and I refuse to go back and I will stay here at the border just as long as it takes for you to let me through."

After an hour, some other upper-boss showed up (not the commander who had given me the oral permission), drunk and angry, summoning me from the other side of the barrier to disappear. I stayed where I was and spent the night in my truck. But the next day, the Croats also came to tell me that I could not stay in no man's land. I returned to Dubrovnik, where I had been in touch with a radio amateur who in turn got in touch with a friend of mine in Herceg Novi in Montenegro, a radio amateur as well (the phone connections had already been severed for years). Via-via I asked him to get in touch with the commander and via-via I heard back that the commander had confirmed that I was one day late and that on top of that I was writing very bad things about the Serbs. It was clear that stopping me was just harassment – a preview of what was still in store for me that year. There was nothing left to do but to take that detour. I still was able to shorten it quite a bit by means of a by-telefax-granted permit from the Croatian authorities in Zagreb to use part of the Zagreb-Belgrade freeway, possibly avoiding Hungary. But another part of the freeway was for a change in hands of the Serbs and they did not let me pass either. Via a parallel-running back road, pointed out to me by the Jordanian commander of a UN battalion on the site, I was able to sidestep the Serb part, and return to the Croatian part until the Yugoslavian border. My (in the meantime expired) press accreditation still worked magic: they let me in, with the kind remark, though, that I just had to extend my accreditation. Via Belgrade I went all the way back to my apartment in Montenegro. A detour of 1100 miles....

CHAPTER 30

Croatian hassles

Lieutenant-colonel Milutinović was very close friends with alcohol. He was the spokesman and press officer of the Serb army in Banja Luka, the stronghold of the Serbs in North-Western Bosnia, and the story went around that he did everything for a bottle of whiskey. I myself have never tried it, because he was always a big help to me also without such a bottle. It was from him that I got permission in the fall of 1993 to go to Jajce, 50 miles south of Banja Luka which as a matter of fact was closed territory. And on my way back I was even allowed to use the crossing at Bosanska Gradiška, which would put me on the Zagreb-Belgrade freeway at Okučani, 50 miles North of Banja Luka. This way I could avoid taking the long, winding and bad road via the Brčko corridor to Belgrade.

The freeway was in fact partly under supervision of the Serbs, partly of the Croats, but formally under that of the UN. With our UN accreditation we were allowed to use that freeway and travel from one territory to the other and from one republic to the other.

The trip went smoothly, no chicanery at the checkpoints and once on the freeway, you could get on very nicely, because, except a sporadic UN vehicle, not a soul drove there.

Lipovac. The border between Croatia and Yugoslavia. Only another 60 miles to Belgrade. I show my UN press card to the Croatian border guard who was housed in a kind of mobile home, because only a short time ago the dividing line was still invisible. Now, it looks like, driving from Washington to Baltimore, you have to cross a country border halfway. The border guard checks my luggage and notices my spare cans with diesel fuel; I have seven of them, five of which are meanwhile empty now. I am not allowed to take the other ten gallons along due to the boycott against Yugoslavia. I propose to empty them right there, but he first has to make a phone call. Due to the diesel, I thought. He returns and says, "Without a special permission, you are not allowed to cross this border." I point at my UN accreditation and the fact, that I have crossed this border at different times before. But for two weeks now there are new rules, so he explains: I also need a special permission from Zagreb now – and these are only provided to journalists who are accredited at the Croatian government. This I am not, but they do know me at the Department of Information of the Ministry of Foreign Affairs in Zagreb and I give him some names of functionaries, with whom they can check on me. He goes to call again and returns with the message, "It depends on the military commander in Zagreb and he just left for a moment. I will be called back any time" I wait, ask, wait – for hours. A UN-jeep passes by, an officer with a driver. I ask his help. He can't do anything, he says. Yesterday a UN convoy with relief goods, although provided with all the required documents, was also sent back because according to a border guard a certain paper was missing. The whole convoy had to return to Zagreb – 180 miles.

At last, after four hours the message arrives: it's not allowed. How else do they expect me to get to Belgrade? Via Hungary, they answer. Whether I liked it or not – they did not let me through. Thirty miles back, then behind the Serb-occupied part of Croatia north via Osijek to Hungary, then east to the Yugoslav border near Subotica and subsequently along the familiar road via Novi Sad to Belgrade – a detour of 300 minus 60 = 240 miles. Actually, I should be happy, because it's only one-fifth of the detour described in the previous chapter, which was waiting for me the next year. An advantage with all this chicanery was that I had mastered Serbo-Croatian more or less. That means: since the war it was not longer called Serbo-Croatian – it was either Serbian or Croatian. The differences are minimal: the most important is that the Croats pronounce a "y" in front of the e-sounds. One example: in Serbian for "always" you say *uvek*, in Croatian *uvyek*. If a distinction has to be made anyway: I speak Serbian, not Croatian.

One day, en route from the by Serbs occupied part of Croatia to Croatia proper, the, by the way very kind, Croatian border guards had a chat with me. One of them came from Dalj, six miles back into the now Serb territory and he was curious what things looked like over there. After a while, he said, "You speak Croatian very well." That meant two things: a). that also to him there was absolutely no difference between Serbian and Croatian and b). that he had become so nationalistic that he could not bring himself to say the word "Serbian." It was also that kind of childish behavior I ran into in a less pleasant way, when I again left Croatia at the Slovenian "border." A Croatian border guard checked my passport and then walked around the car. Then he returned and said harshly, "You have a sticker with 'YU' on the back of your car. That has to come off, because Yugoslavia does not exist anymore." I explained to him that every car crossing a border has to have a sticker of the country where it is registered.

"But Yugoslavia does not exist anymore, so that sticker has to come off," he persisted.

"But what kind of country sticker am I supposed to put on then?" I asked.

"Croatia," he answered – and my objection that my car was not registered in Croatia at all, did not make any impression on him. He ordered me to get out and pull the sticker off. I started to try to pry it off with my forefinger, but, as is well-known, those stickers are unyieldingly stuck on your auto body. And there were dozens of cars waiting behind me. "Just drive on a little bit and put your car further on," the border guard said. But "further on" was already Slovenia – and the sticker stayed on for many years to come.

CHAPTER 31

Yugoslavian inconveniences – *one* example

Damn it, the red warning light of the fuel filter lit up again. If we only could make it to Knin. We were on our way from Pula on the northern coast of Croatia to Knin, the capital of the republic *Krajina*, as the Serbs had baptized the territory they had conquered from the Croats in Croatia west of Bosnia. The trip was preceded, of course, by the usual fuss to get permits, this time from the Croats, which actually did not seem to be valid at the checkpoints but became so yet again after some calling back and forth. We were with two cars. The couple Runa Hellinga and Henk Hirs in theirs, the other colleague Karin Veraart and I in mine.

Even before the war, diesel and gas were difficult to get, after the UN boy-cott the gas stations closed completely. Nevertheless, you could buy plenty of gas and diesel (which I needed): on the black market for about $ 5 ½ to $ 7 ½ a gallon. If it only were diesel. Because to earn a little extra, the sellers added at least 20% water to it. No matter how carefully you tried to avoid it – inevitably some water came along with the diesel as you filled up your tank with your cans. The lighting up of your warning signal told you that sooner or later your fuel filter was filled up with water and urgently had to be changed, as long as you wanted to get home. It was still 60 miles to Knin. Changing the filter was in itself not a big deal, but restarting the car was mostly quite an effort. In Knin we would have the opportunity to go to a UN headquarters – and where there is a UN headquarters there are car mechanics, too.

We made it to Knin. The mechanic of the UN fleet of cars was a nice Scot who was willing to take care of changing the filter (I always had at least one in reserve). But the engine refused to start. He diagnosed a corroded fuel pump (due to all that water). It was a closed type, so it could not be opened up, but he would nevertheless try to repair it. It did not work – another fuel pump was needed. I carried a lot of spare parts, however not a fuel pump. There was no other solution left than to leave my truck behind and see to it that a pump in one way or another would make it to Knin. We went along with the Hirs couple to the *Krajina*-Croatian border north of Banja Luka, from where they drove through to their base-Budapest. In Knin I had succeeded in getting in touch by phone with a good friend-cab driver-former dissident in Belgrade, called Cvetko, who came to pick us up in that border town (200 miles coming and 200 miles going).

Now, how to get the pump to Knin? Luck was with me. I learned that Jan ter Laak, leader of the Catholic peace movement *Pax Christi*, would go to Zagreb shortly. The Dutch dealer of my truck delivered to him a pump at high speed, which Ter Laak gave to a Dutchman working at the UN headquarters in Zagreb. He in turn had promised me to have the pump brought to Knin by a UN convoy. The kind Scot had no phone in his workshop and I had to try to get in touch with him via the UN switchboard, fortunately manned by Dutch operators. His workshop was too far away to get him to come to the switchboard; the best they could do was to pass a message to him asking whether he would call me back. And this never happened. The phone connections with Knin, as well as with the UN headquarters, were extremely bad and most of the day the small town was not reachable. It was two weeks later when I learned that the Scot was on vacation. After four weeks I finally got him personally on the line: they had sent the wrong pump, it was much too strong for my fuel system.

There was still a regular bus going from Belgrade via *Republika Srpska* to Knin in the *Krajina*, a distance of 400 miles and a fifteen-hour's drive along freakish front lines. There was no other way than to bring the pump to Knin myself by that bus. Ordered another pump, now through the *ANWB*, the Dutch equivalent of triple-A. However, there were no air connections between Belgrade and the rest of the world, also due to the boycott, so the pump had to be sent to the airport of Budapest. This was no problem. Inventive bus and minibus enterprises drove with great regularity back and forth between Belgrade and the Budapest airport – 250 miles up and 250 miles back. In the morning at six with the first bus up, pick up the pump (unexpected, long-lasting custom formalities included), back with the afternoon bus.

Meanwhile, though, it was nearly two months later and the winter had closed in. From Bosanska Petrovac via Jajce and Banja Luka to Belgrade it was reasonably flat, but the first 50 miles from Knin to Petrovac went along windy, narrow mountain roads. The snow chains from my former camper were too small and I did not want to drive on those mountain roads without snow chains for all the tea in China, all the more so because I had an automatic transmission which is a disaster on slippery roads. I had a good acquaintance who was working at a van line company. Yes, he was willing to go with me to Knin (it did not seem wise to me to go all by myself) and yes, he also had snow chains at his disposal. Applied for permits for both of us at the "embassies" of the *Republika Srpska* and the *Krajina* in Belgrade. And granted. On the eve of our departure it was impossible to get in touch with my acquaintance. Not until midnight (the bus would leave at seven the next morning) did I get him on the line. He did not have the snow chains yet. He had loaned them out to a friend who had not returned them in time. Postponed the trip by a week.

Applied for new permits at the "embassies" because they were dated for a specific date. A week later: on the eve of departure the acquaintance calls to tell me that his little daughter has fallen ill and consequently he cannot go with me, but he had found a friend who was willing to go with me, and who is, on top of it, a car mechanic. And yes – he had the snow chains. Other dates, other persons – so for the third time asked for and was granted permits.

Finally, on a cold Saturday morning, I stand and wait for the bus. I am still not yugoslavized enough to arrive at the last moment or to be late. Actually, late is never that bad because public transportation is always late, too. I don't know my fellow traveler and ask from time to time the wrong person whether he is the one. On the stroke of seven he comes sailing up: at last something adds up.

For about 120 miles towards Knin no flake of snow is to be seen on the road but close to Brčko the first snow edges on the road turn up.

"How happy I am we took the snow chains along," I say to my fellow traveler.

"I don't have them with me," he answers laconically.

I don't believe my ears.

"No," he explains, "I heard you have a truck, and that means you can manage without snow chains."

"If I had known that, I wouldn't have gone," I remarked, but there was no way back and I look worried at the increasing thickness of the snow cover, because you can forget about road cleaning in this time of war, as the front is only a few miles away.

Due to the snow, the bus was already hours late. Between Prijedor, a Moslem town from which all Moslems are chased away and where you can still see on the remnants how crosses neatly indicated which house had to be set on fire (those without a cross are still standing, because there Serbs are living), and Sanski Most, we have to stop on a heavy-snow-covered hill because a big truck got stuck there despite its snow chains. On the left is still some room to pass, but the snow is very high there. In turn, passengers clean that part alongside the truck with shovels – and we are able to go on. In pitch-darkness we drive the last 50 miles across the mountains to Knin. Argus-eyed, I measure every hill, the bus driver lets his bus slowly come down in the first gear. At three o'clock in the morning we enter Knin – four hours late. I had ordered rooms – and a dinner! – with an acquaintance of Cvetko with whom I had also stayed some time before. He had already written us off, but his wife was willing to prepare the promised dinner in the middle of the night.

In the morning, still Sunday, we went with the pump under our arms to the UN headquarters. There was no sign of my car anywhere. Neither was our Scot whom I had notified through the "Dutch" switchboard that we would arrive this day. Fortunately, a Czech UN officer had a list with private phone numbers of the most important co-workers. Of our Scot as well. No answer. Vaguely I remembered the name of his (Serb) assistant. Glancing through the list, I recognized his correct name. Called him. He did appear to be at home and promised to come immediately which he indeed did. My car turned out to have been towed to a private workshop which used to do some work for the UN from time to time. And there it was, my lame draught-horse. Now just install the new pump under it. New setback. The wrong pump had blown up my brand-new fuel filter and irreparable destroyed it. Nobody had told me that. Fortunately, in the truck bed was still a watery specimen what we nicely blew dry. Without it, we still would not have been able to drive one inch. The acquaintance of my acquaintance had the pump installed in fifteen minutes, as usual the starting up was very difficult but then all of a sudden: the engine runs; it is as if I hear the "Ninth of Beethoven."

Back to the UN headquarters, where they would try to find some snow chains that we could borrow. No, unfortunately not. But we had more than one string on our bow. Our host, working at Radio Knin, had said, in case the UN was not able to help us, he would supply us that Sunday with chains which we could convert to snow chains ourselves. He would be home all day. Called. No answer. Went to his house. His wife had arrived in the meantime. She knew where her husband was hanging out. Called. No, today it would not work anymore, most likely tomorrow. I was fed up with all those promises. The acquaintance of the acquaintance and I looked at each other and said: we have no choice, let's have a go at it. Meanwhile, it was two o'clock in the afternoon. That was partly our luck. Especially the first part shows quite some hairpin curves but they were perfectly exposed to the afternoon sun which had melted down the snow a little bit. But the higher we climbed, the thicker the snow cover on the road. We made all the hills and got stuck only once on a flat part of the road in part because we had to make way for an oncoming truck. After three and a half hours of wrestling we had the 50 miles behind us. The remaining 350 miles were relatively peanuts. At seven in the morning we arrived in Belgrade and we just did not get worked up when sixty miles before Belgrade the warning light of the fuel filter turned red again.

CHAPTER 32

Disappointments

From 1968 until the soft end of communism in 1989, Petr Uhl was in the Czechoslovakian oppositionist movement (and spent, due to that fact, and at different periods, altogether about nine years in prison). It was always very difficult to determine whom you could trust and whom not. Looking back, it turns out that he always cooperated with the right persons. A friend of his fared a lot worse. It started with Milan Daniel who lived in the town of Chrudim and who was active in the opposition there. One day, he is arrested by the StB who gave him the choice: either go to prison for ten years or work as an informer for the StB, especially concerning Petr Uhl. He planned to say "yes" but to inform his friends simultaneously, so that the opposition could play a game with the StB instead of the other way around. He presented this plan to Petr Uhl who advised him to play that double game indeed, but to tell the StB only things approved by Uhl. He also consulted another member of the opposition movement, Jaroslav Suk, with whom he cooperated very closely, and he also said: do it. Suk in turn told a fellow member of Charta 77, his best friend Egon Čierny, about the double game. For years they were able to play this game and the StB was not aware of anything. The liberation comes in 1989, the StB files open. And what comes out? This very best friend and close cooperator Čierny was on the payroll of the StB who due to this, had been aware in great detail of all his doings. In one blow he discovered that all his activities, all his efforts to lead the StB up the garden path so they would not notice that he played a double game, and this for years – that all this had been in vain and that they had monumentally made a fool of him. That he had not fooled the StB but the StB him – all via the man whom he had considered his very best friend.

"He has known it now already for years, but he still is not over it – and he will never get over it," Uhl told me in 1994. "As to my work for the opposition, I fortunately only had to deal with him indirectly, so it did not harm us here in Prague."

I haven't been spared such disappointments either. In August 1969, after he had driven as a madman across Prague to get rid of the pursuers of the StB, I visited my cameraman Vladimír Tuma one time at home. He showed me pictures of Jan Palach, made in the hospital where he was admitted after he set himself on fire, as mentioned before, on Václavske náměstí. Palach did not only do so to protest against the invasion, but also against the compromises the then Czechoslovakian leadership, Dubček included, had reached with the Soviet Union. Palach survived his act for a few days.

"When you come next time, I'll give you some prints of the pictures," he said. How he had gotten hold of them, he did not tell, but I got the impression that he had made them himself. My next trip to Czechoslovakia was exactly a year later, but for all sorts of reasons it did not seem wise to me to get in touch with him. In January 1990, in Prague for the Palach commemoration, I called him to make an appointment. He immediately came to my hotel. The greeting was like old comrades who had not seen each other for years. Almost the first thing he told me was that he could lay his hands on a sound tape of a conversation between a doctor and the dying Palach. It was in the possession of the (female) doctor but she was willing to give me a copy for 500 German marks, then about $200.-. Nobody else knew of the existence of the tape, let alone that it would already have been published.

The *NOS* agreed that I buy the tape from him. After some pressure I exerted via Tuma, the doctor was also willing to give an interview. She was Dr. Zdenka Kmuničková and it turned out that she had not been the doctor in attendance, but sent from the outside. The real doctors in attendance, Drs. Jaroslavá Mozerová and Zdenka Koničková, whom I have interviewed as well, had always been amazed about that outsider. It's true, you can hear on the tape that the questioning doctor talks friendly and forthcoming with Palach, but that it is her main reason to find out whether others would also set themselves on fire (which was announced by Palach in a letter left behind), and who those people might be. The sound quality of the tape was excellent and it was clear that it was very professionally recorded with two microphones; it was certainly not just a tape which just an amateur had thrown together. I remembered the pictures which Tuma had promised me at the time (he claimed to no longer have them), recalled also his qualities as a sound technician (which was part of his profession) and I was convinced that *he* had recorded the tape at the time. He denied it – but I did not give much credit to that. If the doctor as well as Tuma had been sent to still worm some information out of Palach in his last minutes – then, who could have sent them? Obviously: the StB. Nevertheless, it was a dramatic recording (the *NOS* had the scoop, but the Czechoslovakian radio and others took it over, free of charge of course); dramatic not as much to the content as to the heartbreaking softness of the voice of Palach who, haltingly and stumbling, gasping for breath, answers the questions of the doctor.

As yet, I have no confirmation that Tuma worked for the StB. I have my doubts. Looking back, I wonder sometimes whether that whole pursuit of August 1969 might have been a sham (as I mentioned before, I had not seen any pursuer) to provide himself by order of the StB with an alibi not to have to shoot with me anymore. When I confronted him in 2000 with my suspicions, he vehemently denied ever having had anything to do with the StB, but on the contrary had experienced a lot of problems due to me – and as a piece of evidence he showed me a copy of his interrogation by the StB.

Just before that pursuit I had interviewed Vladimír Škutina, also with Tuma as a cameraman. In April Dubček was removed (he had served his purpose) and replaced by Husák. The interview took place close to the vacation home of Škutina on top of a hill in the Giant's Mountains. In 1968, Škutina had been the symbol of the underground television. Immediately after the invasion, the Russians had occupied the television studios, but they could not find any Czech willing to run the broadcasts. So they aired a kind of test image with in the background anonymous, in badly-phrased Czech, pro-Soviet propaganda slogans. With great inventiveness, the Prague TV people had set up an illegal TV station in a suburb of Prague, covering all of Prague. In the first broadcast, the camera pointed at a presenter keeping a mask in front of his face. The voice behind the mask said, "There is a TV station here in Prague which imageless sounds the voice of an anonymous speaker. That's not the way we are. I am Vladimír Škutina – and with this sentence he took the mask off his face. Subsequently, the camera panned to a cameraman, "And this is our cameraman." Pan to the director's room, "And this is our director" – and he mentioned all their names. The Russians searched like mad for this station – but they never found it. It needed to last for only a couple of days, because after the "agreement" in Moscow between Dubček and company and Brezhnev and his underlings, a week after the invasion, the Russians withdrew from Prague and the studios were returned to the legitimate owners. The leadership of the Prague TV remained "good" for a little while and decided to assign Škutina for security reasons as a correspondent in Belgrade. When the general-director Jiří Pelikán had to resign after the invasion, Dubček and company appointed him for the same reason as cultural attaché at the Czechoslovakian embassy in Rome. When Husák came to power, Pelikán quit and stayed in Rome (he would become a key figure in the Czechoslovakian opposition movement-in-exile). After Husák's take over, Škutiná was called back and he did return "because I am an obedient man, so if they order me to return, then I return," so he ironically explained to me at the time. This was very courageous because he knew he was one of the people most hated by the Russians and their pals. Not surprisingly, he was already arrested in August 1969 but three months later released without a trial. Because he did not stop to raise his voice (not through the *VPRO* due to Jan Blokker's "who in the world knows Škutiná?"), he was arrested anew in February 1971 and in June sentenced to four years and two months imprisonment. He was very seriously ill a couple of times while in the prison (he suffered a stomach ulcer) and was released a couple of months before his term was over. Also his family suffered due to his opposition activities. His daughter was a top tennis player, but was not allowed to appear on the courts anymore – and I know that it struck him as terrible. I saw him back again for the first time in 1977 when I dropped in at his place with Prof. Patočka. He looked reasonably well then. In 1974 I had written a book on the Dutch radio during the German occupation which I had dedicated to him and via-via I had tried to have it handed to him. Successfully: it was in his bookcase. In 1978 he was allowed to emigrate; he left for Switzerland. Shortly thereafter he presented the new magazine on human rights *Artikel 19* ("Article 19") at the national press club in The Hague. On that occasion we also talked about Tuma and about the question of whether or not he had cooperated voluntarily on the film against me in 1971. Tuma said in it that he had shot that interview with Škutina "because I already knew Verkijk from the time he cooperated with Telexport, I thought he was here officially" and that he therefore had not been aware he had done things "which were harmful to our socialist state." I still assumed that they simply had forced him to make this statement, but Škutina was of the opinion that he already then was connected to the StB.

After the velvet revolution, Škutina returned to Prague and became leader at the first free elections of the People's Socialist Party (the party of Beneš, the last democratic president of Czechoslovakia whose party was forbidden by the Nazis and communists alike). In the nineties rumors surfaced about Škutina: he would have been working for the StB. I could hardly believe it. But in 1994 I got the confirmation from an unimpeachable authority: his friends Petr Uhl and his spouse Ana Šabatová and his other best friend: Jaroslav Hutka, the protest singer who after his expulsion ended up in the Netherlands in 1978. It turned out that Škutina had remained "good" almost up to the end of his imprisonment time. He was not able to stand it anymore and bought his early release with the promise to henceforth provide information about his relations with his old friends in the opposition. "He told them for instance exactly who were present at my farewell party before my departure to Holland and what all was said there," Hutka told me. So in 1977 I visited together with Patočka the "wrong" Škutina and it also put a peculiar light onto his opinion of Tuma. It is certain that he cut off all contacts with the StB after his emigration and did not pass on anything about the oppositionist activities of Pelikán and his people. I don't know what was greater: my disappointment or my sadness that even a man like Škutina could be a turncoat. The choice to go and help the other side must have filled him personally with dread. That's why I feel in the first place compassion, not anger. And I don't regret for one second that I have offered him to have his say through *VPRO*-TV and *NOS* radio, because he was still the "good" Škutina then. It has always been my view that one of the worst things of those so-called communist regimes was, that they could force even the best men to commit bad deeds – a crime against humanity, which the Nazis committed as well. Unfortunately, I never had the opportunity to talk it over with Škutina himself. He died in 1996, late but still, of the complications of his stomach ulcer.

I continue to commemorate him as the man who took off his mask in 1968.

Also, in a general sense I experienced disappointments. My hope was that the peoples in Eastern Europe would tighten their belts after all those liberations and all together would go hard at it in order to lug their country out of the mud. This did not happen. To most of them the motto read: wait until it gets better. It was so customary to them that everything was arranged from above, that the better life has to come as a present from above also. I had some good acquaintances in the Romanian capital Bucharest; no active oppositionists, but rank-and-file Romanians who not only disliked Ceaușescu but hated him. They lived in an apartment in the main street Bulevardul Magheru. One of the few streets where in winter the snow was cleared away, because it was one of the routes used with some regularity by mister president. In that last hunger-winter I visited them. The mother, meanwhile very old and sickly, and her daughter had rubbed themselves against a small electrical heater of which the use was strictly forbidden. Now and then there was electricity, the city central heating system had not been operating for months already.

"This week Ceaușescu passed by here with his expensive car. The ordinary people trudged across the snow on the sidewalk. Nobody even looked up. Why is nobody shooting him to death," the daughter said bitingly. I did not say so but thought, "Why does somebody else have to do it? You don't do it yourself either."

One year after the liberation I am back there again – in the very same room. The very old mother did not survive Ceaușescu, the daughter did. Again, she is biting, "There is nothing for sale, and if it is, it is terrible expensive. It is even worse than under Caușescu." Then I was not able to keep my mouth shut, "You must not say that. There is no secret police anymore who can send you to prison, you are allowed to say what you want – in this respect the present situation cannot be compared with the one under Ceaușescu. But to improve the economic situation, you must not wait to see whether it will get better, but take the initiative yourself."

A Hungarian acquaintance-interpreter, never much of a friend of the regime either, came up with more or less the same story. "But please understand," I told him kind of desperately, "you first have to go through an even deeper valley before you can climb up. That might take a generation."

"What good will it do me? During the communist regime we had it bad, and now we are supposed to get it even worse in order to get it better. That's after my time and I'm living now," he said indignantly – and that is also true, of course.

Many inhabitants of the communist countries considered the West to be paradise. Also in those times I have pointed out in numerous conversations that in the West they worked hard for it, much harder than they were used to under the communist regimes. But it was very difficult to talk them out of the idea that our prosperity was a kind of gift from the gods. And where is the gift now, now they finally had gotten rid of the communist regimes? No, tough tackling was not an option.

I am also disappointed in the citizens of the country I visited very regularly for forty years and where I lived for ten years: the Yugoslavs. In the first years, 1955, 1956, I had gotten to know them as decent workers like in the stories on the social-democratic movement in the thirties.

On Saturday evening they strolled neatly washed and decently shaven with their open collars on the main street of Belgrade Terazije, in those days absolutely car-free. They took pride in their new factories, their new country, in their leader Tito. I think that Yugoslavia was then the only communist country where the party leader also in completely free elections would haven been elected president by a vast majority. They did not make much, money to buy a car they did not have, but they were honest through and through. When you accidentally had left your bag at the railway station, you could quietly pick it up half an hour later: it was still in the same spot. They were hospitable, you could camp at every farm but not before you first had participated in the greeting ceremony: the consumption of a homemade sugar-confected piece of fruit to be washed away with a glass of water. Of course Yugoslavia went along with the tendency also touching our western world: less honesty, more greed, more swindle. But until the Miloševićes took over power it was a nice place to stay in a country with by and large nice people. But to my surprise and deep disappointment those cynical, only in their own power interested leaders were able in a massive way to force the best men to act badly – and to even manipulate them so far that they let themselves be forced voluntarily. In 1985, 1986, the television started to democratize and it became clear to the Yugoslavs that in the years before they really had been cheated by that medium. But when in 1987 the television started to anew make propaganda in the very same way, but now for the nationalistic cause, they fell, to my great disappointment, in large numbers without criticism, right back into that pitfall again. That Yugoslavs would ever stop calling each other fellow citizens; that they would ever exterminate each other like animals; that a Yugoslav would ever kick me; that a Yugoslav would ever call me a fascist; that Yugoslavs would ever threaten to kill me; that Yugoslavs would ever throw me out of their country – that never crossed my mind and that is also part of my disappointments.

When you came over to visit families, you often noticed that specifically the little boys were allowed to do whatever they pleased. One day, I visited one of my acquaintances and there the four-year-old son was busy driving a nail into a chair with a hammer. In a routine he was being told not to do so, but he just continued – and nobody cared. It is a characteristic example. Little boys are permitted everything, they always get their way and they are spoiled through and through. Of course, this has its consequences at a later age: you must take whatever you want or think you have the right to. It might be a kind of third-rate philosophy, but from time to time I thought, when I saw how they carried on against each other in the war: this is a nation of spoiled children. But I don't want to generalize: quite a few Serbs, Serbians and Croats are ashamed about what was done in the name of the Serbian or Croatian people. Yet – as already mentioned before – many more Yugoslavs than I thought could be possible, supported the extreme nationalistic leaders.

I am also disappointed in the leaders of the western world. For years, they strived for the downfall of the communist systems. Nobody expected that downfall in such a short time. But you would think that, just as military games have been played on how to react in case a war would break out, they would also have thought of games for what to do in case a peace would break out. But there was no concept whatsoever, no idea of how that breakthrough in world history would have to be met. No grand Marshall-plan-like set up. Now, in those former communist countries, the knot is cut with often hard capitalist methods of the thirties. It should have been *the* task of the international social-democratic movement to draw up a sort of Marshall-plan for Eastern Europe, but how can you expect something like this to come about, if the socialist movement in each single country is more a socialist standstill, which considers a glance at tomorrow afternoon already too far and limits itself at best to a preview of tomorrow morning. Of course, the people in the Eastern-European countries have in the first place to fix it themselves. But the mismanagement and the devastation of the personal and public morale is not their fault – and we should have met the consequences of that moral and material devastation in a more structured way and with more solidarity – I hardly dare to use this word because it seems to be out.

I am also deeply disappointed in the political leaders of the western world concerning Yugoslavia. After the Gulf war I thought a new period in world history had come: aggression will not be accepted anymore and punished un-relentingly. Again I was profoundly mistaken. With increasing despair we, correspondents in Yugoslavia, have experienced the absolute unwillingness of the international world to end that merciless war in Yugoslavia. How many ultimatums were not given to the Serbs by the international world and how many were let off unpunished. Day-in and day-out we have hammered it in, that you better give no ultimatum *at all*, than one you don't carry out. It just provokes the other party to go even further, to try out whether you can make your opponent look even more like a fool. After the first shot in Sarajevo, in April 1992, I shouted in a broadcast – and I believe I really *shouted* , "Go there immediately with combat helicopters and with highly trained commando units and knock out the guns and tanks of the Serbs. Then they will think twice before repeating it or carrying out their terror somewhere else." Nothing, nothing, nothing we did. And we saw a country being shot to shreds by a bunch of irresponsible crooks like Milošević and Karadžić (later on joined by the gentleman Tudjman, when he tacitly consented to the war against the Moslems in Mostar), stirred up racists to whom a "black" can't be a Dutchman and to whom a Moslem is "a Turk" – to them another word for *Untermensch.* I do recall how during a crisis around Goražde, when the western world let itself, day after day, be fooled by general Mladić and his gang, even our *BBC* colleagues were getting desperate. Everybody knows that a *BBC* reporter is not allowed under any circumstance to show the slightest emotion. But in their reports around that Goražde case for the World Service you could loudly hear their restrained rage about the indecisiveness of the United Nations. And also Martin Bell, who has for years been a correspondent for the *BBC* television in Sarajevo, left all so-called "objectivity" behind him and finally showed in no uncertain terms, that the western world let crimes pass unpunished.

Our being right came in 1995 *after* the murder in Srebrenica (where after the capitulation of the Dutch UN-unit 8000 Moslem men were murdered by Serb forces). Finally an ultimatum which was carried out. The Serbs backed down in three days. After *four* years of muddling, 97.279 people killed, millions who are chased away, hundreds of flattened towns and a destroyed city.

If I would have belonged to the responsible ones in the Western world – I would not have one quiet night.

CHAPTER 33

Dreams

Night dreams

It's 1942, 1943. I dream that I am in a thickly wooded forest. From the right upper corner in my dream-picture soldiers come running up. They are "the English." Running, they pass in front of me – from the right upper corner to the left lower corner. I am liberated! Then I wake with a shock of disappointment. I am not liberated at all, the Krauts are still there.

Almost 25 years later I watch war newsreels in Moscow for the documentary "Operation Barbarossa." All of a sudden: shots of Russian partisans, running in a thickly wooded forest from the right upper corner to the left lower corner. The camera stands on the spot where I stood in my dream of 1942, 1943. I put it in the documentary: a dream becomes reality.

Fifty years later, I am shot to death twice, in two dreams. The details of one dream are erased and I only know the sad end result. In the second I am chased by a man in uniform with a machine gun. I make a run for it and flee into a wide-open barn where I hide myself in the left back corner. I see the soldier in the light of the barn opening, coming from behind a house on the left. He crosses diagonally to the right side of the barn entrance and leans against the side doorpost, some sixty feet away from me. I think he does not see me in that dark barn, but I'm mistaken. He aims his gun at me – and kills me. Then I wake up with a shock of relief: I'm still alive.

After my expulsion, 1994. I dream that Karadžić stays at the Geerlings family, the social-democrat card-playing friends of my parents on that Saturday evening in 1943, when I insisted on distributing flowers to the neighbors to congratulate them with the capitulation of Italy – and whose daughter had experienced the execution of eight resistance fighters at the Jan Gijzen Bridge in Haarlem. Karadžić is in hiding there, which nobody knows: only our family does (the dream plays in the time I was still a teenager and living conventionally at home). I impress on my mother's mind not to talk to anybody about our knowledge, because we have to try to put Karadžić into the hands of the International Yugoslav Tribunal in The Hague. The Geerlings, apparently not knowing who is staying in their house, live across the street on the Junoplantsoen. The house is a hundred yards away and we look out upon it (these geographical details agree with the reality of 1942, 1943). An underground tunnel is running (now the dream again) from our home to theirs. I crawl toward it through the tunnel. Karadžić sits on the upper floor on a kind of balcony like you sometimes see them in a church. Below him is a small hall. He does recognize me (this also possibly agrees with the reality) but he does not react suspiciously. I crawl back to devise a plan to induce him to come through the tunnel to our home so we can turn him in. On my return it appears that my mother in all innocence has nevertheless talked with the neighbors about the whereabouts of Karadžić – and I grumble at her about it. But the dream fizzles out. No turning in, so neither a disappointed waking up. Apparently, Karadžić goes scot-free – just like in reality as well.

Daydreams

In the summer of 1940 I sit, together with Joop Jonkman, in his two-person sail-canoe named after a famous prewar Dutch submarine "O-16," on the *Spaarne* river in Haarlem. What if we would go to England with it? Not crossing right away, but first along the coast to France and from there cross the narrowest part of the sea. The boat is solid enough, I reason. But it remains just a daydream.

But what if I would become a member of the *Jeugdstorm* (the Nazi youth movement "Youth Storm")? Just pretend that I am a convinced national-socialist. And then see to it that I was a part of a group of Youth Stormers to be received by Hitler. Then I can kill him with.... yes, here the daydream stopped: how to do away with him? As is known, not surprisingly, it never came about.

They should not execute Hitler after the war. They should lock him up in a cage and display him on markets and squares all over the world. Everybody would be allowed to call him names, to spit on him, to humiliate him. He should be put on hunger rations and like this be dragged around until the end of his life.

EPILOGUE 4

A black coif of hair shifted by at the lower edge of the window of my rented home, being at a one-and-a-half-floor level. "There is Ljiljana," I said to my wife – black-haired Ljiljana is a good acquaintance of mine. The gate had probably not been locked. I already went to the hallway to greet her, when I heard the front door being opened – which appeared not to be locked either. I open the door to the hallway and two men, completely unknown to me, immediately enter the living room. One waves an ID the size of a credit card in front of my eyes and asks whether I am Verkijk. My confirmation produces the compelling invitation for both of us to go with them to the police station.

The expulsion from Yugoslavia in 1994 was coupled with an entry ban for five years. But in the meantime the sanctions against (Small)Yugoslavia had been lifted, the Dayton peace agreement had been signed, so I thought, "Different times, different possibilities, let's try and see whether I can obtain a visa again." And since I had become a US resident in the meantime, I sent the application forms and the passports of my wife and myself to the Yugoslavian embassy in Washington. Within a week they returned the passports, complete with a very real visa, valid for three weeks and, at our request, taking effect on October 1, 1996. On the second of October we were at the Hungarian-Yugoslavian border and within a minute we were allowed to pass. And so after two years I was back again in my old rented home in Belgrade which I had kept on as all of my stuff and part of my archives were still there. An acquaintance of mine had lived there for the time being so that it would not be occupied by squatters. At the time I had to leave in such a great haste that I had no chance to take more than an outfit for a vacation trip.

We were unsure about the situation to say the least. We decided to stay in Belgrade as short as possible and to go first to my own apartment in Radovići in Montenegro. There was the lion's share of my archives plus a great many very personal belongings like paintings, wall decorations, books, photos. Way too much to load into our small Mazda and so friend Cvetko lent us his mini-bus with which we drove straight through to Radovići one day after our arrival. Good neighbors over there hugged me as if the lost son had returned. Less pleasant was that Jokšimović who, feigned-or-not, had been after my blood, dropped by for a while for a chat when I was loading the car. Everything was all right with my apartment. There also, friends keep an eye on it. It appeared to us that it was better to return to Belgrade as soon as possible – via the well-known 390-mile windy road. We had arrived only just the day before, when the black coif shifted by the lower edge of my window.

The same route to the same police station as in October 1994. I was interrogated by a very kind, extremely reasonable plain-clothes police functionary, from the secret service I assume, who acknowledged that I was legally and officially in Yugoslavia but also pointed out to me that I, nevertheless, was not allowed to be here because the entry ban had not been lifted. I told him the goal of my trip: to gather my stuff which I had not been able to take along. How much time did I think I needed for that? Three, at most four days, I replied. With this, the conversation was finished. But in the meantime they had drummed up a summary judge and we got ourselves a virtual trial.

"You have committed the worst misdemeanor a foreigner can ever commit in Yugoslavia, namely to come here while it was out of bounds for you."

I referred to the official visa, to the lifting of the sanctions, to Dayton, but he was not impressed by this. "Unfortunately, I can do nothing else but send you to jail," he said.

"No problem, just send me to jail, but you can be sure that it is going to be a big scandal," I responded. Was I planning to create a scandal, he asked, to which I replied that it wouldn't be *me* making a scandal, but that it would become a scandal – period.

Then he mumbled something to the effect of, "Well, I don't like to send people to jail" – and he asked me how much money I was carrying. Subsequently, I was convicted to pay a fine of 450 German marks; fifty less than I pretended to be carrying.

After the conviction we were brought back to the police offices, where they meanwhile had typewritten out a new expulsion order – identical to the one of 1994. Again with an entry ban of five years, but taking effect the day of the new expulsion order; so actually they added two years to it. And I had to leave the country in.... three days, exactly the time I needed to organize the transportation of my stuff to the Netherlands.

And which date did the expulsion order carry? October (month *ten*, 2 x 5) 10 (2 x 5). That was almost exactly two years after my forced departure from Yugoslavia in 1994. Almost – with a difference of *five* days.

EPILOGUE 4 (CONTINUATION)

November 2000. Milošević finally made his fatal error – and is chased away. I am back in a free country in a free Belgrade. No worries about entry bans anymore. In the International Press Club I meet my friends and colleagues, who have returned to the jobs the regime had taken away from them. Anew a sense of liberation descends over me. I even lived to see the last "left" dictatorship die in disgrace. What else can I wish for?

APPENDIX

*Commentary for **Vara**-radio on September 11, 1963 (recorded in the studio of the Slovakian radio)*

Here in Bratislava is the stronghold of the Slovakian writers and journalists who with a remarkable stubbornness fight against every form of Stalinism. I had some conversations here with a number of those writers and journalists, conversations which were nearly breathtaking because of the fundamental criticism expressed in them.

"You can safely say that here in Slovakia we are working hard to eradicate Stalinism by root and branch," according to a Slovakian colleague. He meant: in contrast with the Czechs who would go only halfway about it.

There is a great sense of solidarity among the writing intellectuals here in Slovakia and a convinced party communist even told me somewhat melodramatically, "Finally, after nineteen years we are reborn as a nation again."[110] Because most striking with this whole strife of the Slovaks for a complete de-Stalinization is that the nationalistic feelings play such an important role.

In the journalist's clubs lively speculations are going on about what would be the consequences of Slovakian publications which have already aroused the rage of the Prague daily *Rudé Právo,* organ of the central Czechoslovakian communist party. A few days ago the *Rudé Právo* said about *Kulturni Život,* the organ of the Slovakian Writers Union, that it does not write "in the spirit of communism." They are worried here about these kinds of remarks, but they don't let themselves be put off the way they have taken. Stubborn rumors have it that Prime Minister Široký, whom they hold responsible for a great many of the wrong steps in the Stalinist era, will not resign before long. It goes without saying that it's impossible to check a rumor like that in a country like Czechoslovakia, but it speaks volumes that one is almost openly talking about this possibility.[111] There are, by the way, many more far-reaching wishes, by which the name of president Novotný does not remain unmentioned. There's a lot going on here and the criticism on all kinds of abuses in the past and in

---

[110] That meant he recognized the fascist Slovak state (1938-1944) under Monseigneur Tiso as a legitimate state, a remarkable point of view for a communist.

[111] Fourteen days later Široký really resigned.

the present is uncommonly sharp. In a parody-play I saw here, the criticism was just plain deadly and the reaction of the audience clear. It's clear as well, that the point of no return has been reached in Slovakia and consequently in Czechoslovakia, too.

(Below the original text, which I saved, I have handwritten, "Studio absolutely not soundproof – cars, voices from the technician's room" – an evil many studios in Eastern Europe were suffering under).

Fragments of an article in **Vrij Nederland** *of November 6, 1965*

In Prague I had an extensive conversation with the writer Ivan Klíma[112]. "Since the writers' congress in the fall of 1963," Klíma says, "no resistance exists anymore against new trends in the arts. Everything is possible, from concrete poetry to absurd theater. 'Socialist-realism' is not used anymore as a word, but even the form practically does not exist anymore. Maybe here and there in literature, but certainly not in the arts of painting and sculpture anymore. [...] We are of the new generation and want to be involved in the process of democratization of our country. We want to participate in the forming of a society in which Stalinism cannot occur anymore, but we are no politicians. Our basic thinking is to create an atmosphere in which the exchange of opinions and tolerance will be possible." Does this also include freedom of speech? "That goes without saying." [....] Klíma believes that the revival of the interest in Franz Kafka results from the feeling of the people that the society is a big, unreachable, unmanageable apparatus, exactly like Kafka sensed it. [*The halfway de-Stalinization, the article concludes, goes against the grain with the younger generation in Eastern Europe, it makes them*] write, debate, polemicize. I (*D.V.*) am afraid that around here [in Holland] we don't have a sufficient eye for this development behind the visible development. The time is ripe for an intensive contact between socialists from the west and communists from the east. Prominent democratic socialists (not so much direct politicians as people from the political-cultural level) should start talking informally with this new generation of communists. These searching, tolerant, terror-cursing communists will co-determine the policy of tomorrow and maybe even execute it. It is not devoid of importance that they determine their current position also because of exchanges of ideas with democratic socialists.

---

[112] At the time, Klíma was a staunch member of the Czechoslovakian communist party.

Fragments from an article in **Het Vrije Volk**, *written on September 23, 1985, half a year after the appointment of Gorbachev as secretary general of the communist party of the Soviet Union.*

Breathtaking. That is the speed with which Gorbachev makes a clean sweep of the Soviet Union. Thirty to forty percent of the middle management of the party has been dismissed or retired. [...] Even if they are of the smallest proportions and even if they are limited to the economy, reform plans in the leaden eastern bureaucracy are always met with great resistance from the middle management: the local party functionaries who see in any reform an infringement of their position of power. He, who wants to change something in those societies, has to replace those middle management executives. It is remarkable that he also replaced numerous guys in the army top brass. Why? We don't know. But it's clear that also in this area he wants to execute a different policy, otherwise not so many military functionaries would have been and are being replaced. The big dilemma with the Soviet-style bureaucratic systems which have to be reformed is: how far can you go with decentralization (economically necessary) without harming the central (political) power? Gorbachev remains vague on this. Many consider this a bad omen and are of the opinion that Gorbachev does not want anything but to improve the central planning. I view Gorbachev's vagueness as only positive. In this stage, already having to conquer so much resistance, he cannot speak his true mind. How does Gorbachev see the relations between the Soviet Union and the other East-European countries? Also on this tricky subject, he refrains from direct statements, at least publicly. In different Eastern-European countries there is optimism about his policy in this respect. At the conference on human rights, which took place in the Canadian capital of Ottawa in May/June of this year, I had a lengthy talk with the leader of the Hungarian delegation, Imre Uranovicz.

"I am convinced," he told me on that occasion, "that Gorbachev will bring about the greatest changes in the Soviet Union since the Second World War."

Gorbachev is, after Khrushchev, the first Soviet party leader of whom I will not exclude that he has much further-reaching plans than he is willing to admit now. [...] My general thesis about the Soviet Union has always been that it is impossible to estimate *when* fundamental changes would take place, but *if* it would happen one day, it would go very fast. It so happens that this is the advantage of the disadvantage of an authoritarian regime: everything can be imposed from above, including liberalization. [...] The problem for Gorbachev is that he has to make decisions on all fronts, including foreign policy. The Geneva summit [with president Reagan] will perhaps put the intentions of the Soviet leader in a different light. At the end of [an] interview with *Time* [Gorbachev] says, "I don't recall who, but somebody once said that foreign policy is a continuation of domestic policy. If this is true, I ask you to consider one thing: if we inside the Soviet Union are engaged in such monumental plans, then what external conditions are indispensable to be able to realize our national plans? I leave the answer to this question up to you." We have to hold Gorbachev to his words. He will understand then that with his domestic policy he indeed can win as well as lose confidence as far as his foreign counterparts are concerned. And if he really thinks that domestic and foreign policy are so closely connected, it also shouldn't be too hard for him to understand that the West occupies itself with the human rights policy of the Soviet Union. On this point, Gorbachev has not given any indication yet that a more humane policy is in the making. The punishments for the differently-thinking are hard as nails and the camps murderously severe. However, also on this subject my Hungarian conversation companion in Ottawa was optimistic. When in June everything (concerning human rights) was completely bogged down, he said, "Wait until the end of 1986 (when a new follow-up conference will take place in Vienna within the framework of the Helsinki agreement), then everything will turn out all right." Let us hope so. One thing is for sure: there is movement in the policy of the Soviet top brass. Surprises are not excluded. In February 1986, the five-yearly congress of the party will be held, exactly thirty years after the famous 20th party congress at which Khrushchev made his startling disclosures about Stalin. Without any doubt, the 26th congress will be the most interesting in thirty years.

Fragments of an article for **Het Vrije Volk** *on the return from exile of Sakharov, written December 19, 1986, immediately after the radio report on this and yet before it was known that Gorbachev personally had called Sakharov.*

"Sakharov is allowed to return from Gorky to Moscow and resume his work there as a member of the Soviet Academy of Sciences." I have never seen any sentence in which a revolution was described so compactly and so laconically. Because a revolution it is. [...] The authorities – read: Gorbachev in person – have opted for the most difficult road. It would have been much simpler to let Sakharov go to the West [for which he had finally asked after all the chicanery]. The whole Western world would have praised the Soviet Union and the Soviets themselves would have been released of a domestic problem. But no: they let him return to Moscow as a free man, accepting him as he is in full merits and dignity. Sakharov will not change his opinion. That's what they know. Sakharov will remain the symbol of the opposition against the dictatorial system. That's what they know. Sakharov will be interviewed by dozens of journalists. That's what they know. Sakharov will continue to devote himself to the cause of the political prisoners in the Soviet Union. That's what they know. Then send Sakharov into exile once more? Or even arrest him? They can't sell this – and this they know, too. It's all calculated into the equation. It's a challenge by Gorbachev to the dogmatists. It is a challenge to Sakharov as well. Maybe the Soviet Union will offer him the chance to leave for the United States, anyway. I don't know whether we can require it from Sakharov, but I do hope with all my heart that he stays in the Soviet Union for the time being. To be honest, I expect him to do so. He must realize that his position is stronger now than ever before. Maybe he also should give Gorbachev the chance to show that he also wants to change things concerning human rights. [...] I hazard the prophesy that Sakharov, if he stays in the Soviet Union, will support Gorbachev's strife for more democracy in the Soviet Union in a subtle way without renouncing his principles. [Gorbachev's decision is not a total surprise.] Around the beginning of the follow-up conference last month in Vienna, it appeared at press conferences that representatives of the Soviet Union went quite far with promises concerning human rights. According to me, they were not tactical maneuvers and my optimism then that we could very soon expect spectacular changes in this area, now turn out to be justified. At the death of Marchenko, eleven days before, I have written that his death was not in the interest of the Soviet Union, because it was harmful to the new image they had just built up in Vienna. Something had to be done to restore the damage and therefore, you cannot isolate the complete rehabilitation of Sakharov from the death of Marchenko. It goes without saying that the West should not be thrown off its guard because one spectacular case has been solved. However, there is a well-founded hope that the solution of the Sakharov case is not the elegant end of some tactical maneuvers but the breakthrough to a new beginning and that the history books on the Soviet Union will state: November 7, 1917: October Revolution. December 19, 1986: Sakharov back to Moscow.

Fragments of a memorandum for NOS-radio of April 23, 1982.

Three or four years ago I wrote a kind of program-philosophy once at the request of [the chief of the Current Affairs department]. As a result of the [recent] proposal of colleague Anne Boermans, I exactly reproduce this philosophy here:

It's customary in international politics to differentiate between two "main antitheses": the East-West and the North-South antithesis. North-South is a political-economical problem, East-West a political-ideological one. In principle, the North-South problem can already be solved now, because for this primarily material resources are needed. These resources are not sufficiently on hand with the expenses of armaments as the biggest inhibiting factor. This armament is caused by the East-West antithesis which in principle can *not* be solved now. We are going round and round in circles here, because the key to the solution of the North-South problem lies precisely in the solution of the East-West problem. This political-ideological contradiction is unbridgeable, as long as the bureaucratic-communist system in the Soviet Union continues to exist. Detente and disarmament are consequently still based more on tactical considerations: how can I gain the maximum advantage, than on principle-ethical considerations. This contradiction will only be bridgeable if either "the West" gets a similar bureaucratic system à la the Soviet Union or "the East" democratizes at least to a socialism à la Dubček (or a Poland à la "Solidarity" I would like to add now). In both cases, a condition is created for disarmament and for a real way to deal with the North-South problem. It seems to me that for a democratic institution like the *NOS*, functioning in an open society, it is necessary to choose not only subjectively but objectively as well, for democratization processes in the international field and not for a bureaucratic system *à la* the Soviet Union. Therefore, the developments within the Soviet Union are not only of the utmost importance for the peoples in those countries themselves, but also for the rest of the world because those developments are decisive for almost all other important world problems: disarmament, development of the third world, humanization of the international society. Based on the above analysis, I would like to pursue the policy of the foreign desk of the *NOS*; judge events from it; show connections and fundamental causes of problems. It also fits in the framework of the *NOS*: to strive for a pluralistic society, to give opportunities for expression to minorities who otherwise don't get a chance, and to give insight into and anticipate changes in the (international) society. Such is my story of some years ago, which I am still backing completely.

By the same author, all in Dutch

Operatie Barbarossa, Operation Barbarossa (1966)

Radio Hilversum 1940-1945 (1974)

Schuld en boete, Crime and Punishment (Co-author Martin van den Heuvel, 1998)

Die slappe Nederlanders - of viel het toch wel mee in 1940-1945?, Those spineless Dutch - or was it not that bad in 1940-1945? (2001)

De Sinterklaasrazzia van 1944, The Santa Claus raid of 1944 (2004)

Harry Mulisch, "fel ant-nazi" - vanaf wanneer?, Harry Mulisch, "ardent anti-Nazi"- since when? (2006)

NAME REGISTER